Modern Economics and the Ancient World

Were the Ancients Rational Actors?

Selected Papers from the Online Conference, 29–31 July 2021

Edited by Sven Günther

Muziris

Historische Papyrologie, Epigraphik und verwandte Gebiete der antiken Kulturen

Historical papyrology, epigraphy and neighbouring fields in ancient cultures

Band 2

Modern Economics and the Ancient World

Were the Ancients Rational Actors?

Selected Papers from the Online Conference, 29–31 July 2021

Edited by Sven Günther

Zaphon
Münster
2023

Muziris-Logo: Ägyptisches Seehandelsschiff (15. Jh. v. Chr.); Ort der Abbildung: Totentempel der Hatschepsut, Deir el-Bahari; Umzeichnung: Stefan Baumann, nach E. Naville, The Temple of Deir el Bahari, Part III: End of Northern Half and Southern Half of the Middle Platform, London 1898 (Egypt Exploration Fund 16), Tf. 74.

Cover-Illustration: Line drawing of the reverse of a New Style AR Tetradrachm, Athens, 124–123 BC. Coin from the IHACOINS collection of The Institute for the History of Ancient Civilizations (IHAC), Northeast Normal University, Changchun, China; line drawing by Dr. Elisabeth Günther, Univ. Heidelberg.

Modern Economics and the Ancient World: Were the Ancients Rational Actors?
Selected Papers from the Online Conference, 29–31 July 2021

Edited by Sven Günther

= Muziris 2

Printed in Germany. Printed on acid-free paper.

ISBN 978-3-96327-256-1 (Buch)
ISBN 978-3-96327-257-8 (E-Book)

ISSN 2941-6752

Contents

Acknowledgements VII

Contributors IX

Introduction: Were the Ancients Rational Actors?
A View from a Graeco-Roman Historian
Sven Günther 1

Trouble Brewing in Old Babylonian Mesopotamia
Kathryn Kelley 13

A Rational God? Rationality and Religion in the Ebabbar of Sippar,
an Old Babylonian Temple
Thibaud Nicolas 61

Rational Actors and the Ancient Israelite Jubilee Legislation
Christian Canu Højgaard 91

A City Fit for Business: The Justice of Moneymaking
in the *Republic*'s Healthy City
Daniel Silvermintz 111

Adam Smith, Plato, and the Stoics.
The Birth of Modern Economic Rationality and the Classical Heritage
Lothar Willms 137

Hoarding and Rationality in the Ancient Economy
Michael Leese 177

Old Ideals and Adaptations to a New Reality. Columella's *De Re Rustica*,
a Survival Handbook for an Elite?
José Remesal Rodríguez 213

"The gold-possessing market where flags of the old town cast a shadow".
Some Remarks on Maritime Trade, Markets, and Money
in the Early Cēra Panegyrics
Roland Ferenczi 231

Are the Moderns Rational? The View from Qin
Jason Hagler 263

Land and Credit in the History of Economic Thought.
Traditional China and Premodern Europe: *Dian* and "*pactum antichriseos*"
Bertram Schefold 317

Index of Sources 337

Acknowledgments

It is not just rational but indeed a great pleasure to thank all those who have contributed to the realization of both the Rational Actors conference which took place from 29–31 July 2021 and the proceedings that are now in the hand of you, the readers. First of all, I have to thank my conference co-organiser Dr Roland Oetjen for his support and remarks prior, during, and after the conference. Greatest thanks are more than due to all speakers and participants who made the conference not feel like a remote, i.e., online event (which it was) but like a real meeting in presence, with all the deep and fruitful discussions we have finally regained in post-pandemic times.

The stimuli arising from the conference fortunately made the way to the final publication rather comfortable, at least for the present editor. The authors submitted their papers (or revised versions at various stages) nearly always at the deadlines assigned; the internal feedback and external peer-reviews by internationally recognized referees who kindly accepted this task on top of their heavy workload arrived on time and, more importantly, deeply engaged with the argument of the respective paper; and for those papers finally approved and to be designed by the present editor Dr Kai Metzler from the Zaphon publishing company was constantly providing his personal support and help. Finally, I have to thank my colleagues of the Muziris series for accepting the proceedings for publication.

Changchun, Id. Iun. MMXXIII The editor

Contributors

Roland Ferenczi PhD (b. 1989) is an indologist-historian currently working as a librarian in the Oriental Collection of the Library and Information Centre of the Hungarian Academy of Sciences (LHAS). He is also a visiting lecturer at the Indology Department of Eötvös Loránd University (ELTE), where he teaches courses on Tamil history and language. His research interests primarily focus on Old Tamil Caṅkam literature, the political geography of the early Cēras, the pre-modern trading system of the Indian Ocean, and the legitimacy and mechanism of the ancient Tamil kingdoms.

Sven Günther is Full Professor of Classics and Ancient History at the Institute for the History of Ancient Civilizations, Northeast Normal University, Changchun, China. Among others, he works on Graeco-Roman economies, particularly on the frames and framing processes in ancient sources touching on socio-economic questions. He is executive editor-in-chief of the double-blind peer-reviewed *Journal of Ancient Civilizations* (JAC) and one of the executive editors of the *Marburger Beiträge zur Antiken Handels-, Wirtschafts- und Sozialgeschichte* (MBAH).

Christian Canu Højgaard is Assistant Professor of Old Testament at Fjellhaug International University College in Copenhagen, Denmark. One of his research interests is the application of social network theory on biblical legal texts for assessing social capital and ethical values. He is assistant editor of Hiphil Novum, a double-blind peer-reviewed journal on the intersection between biblical studies, translation, and technology.

Jason Hagler is a PhD candidate in East Asian Studies at the University of Pennsylvania under the guidance of Dr Paul Goldin, focusing on the intricate processes of state formation and social change through the lens of social networks and peer-to-peer interactions. He earned his MA at the University of Georgia under Baruch Halpern, employing work on texts and their composition and transmission processes alongside archaeology to better understand the ancient world. His forthcoming dissertation examines the role of elite networks in the working and cohesion of the Western Zhou polity through a combination of text-based work and digital archaeology. He also employs comparative data from the Ancient Near East to gain a richer insight into the ancient world and its socio-political dynamics as well as the theories people use to understand it.

Kathryn Kelley is a Research Fellow at the University of Bologna and member of the project "INSCRIBE: the Invention of Scripts and their Beginnings". She is a specialist in early Near Eastern writing and society, and works on technology transfer to the study of the ancient Near East, including imaging techniques and machine learning methods. Research for the current contribution was supported by a Canadian Social Sciences and Humanities Research Council fellowship at the University of Toronto.

Michael Leese is Associate Professor of History at the University of New Hampshire. His research focuses on ancient economic behavior and family law in the ancient Greek and Roman world. He has published articles on individual economic strategies as well as dowry, marital alliances, inheritance, and is currently working on a book project investigating long-term capital accumulation patterns and their effects on economic performance and decisions. He is the author of *Making Money in Ancient Athens* (2021).

Thibaud Nicolas holds a PhD in ancient history from the School of Advanced Studies in the Social Sciences (EHESS) in Paris. He is currently a part-time lecturer in Ancient Greek History at the Université Paris-Cité and in Classics at the Université de la Sorbonne. He is also an associate member of the research centre "AnHiMA" (UMR 8210 of the CNRS), where he works mainly on the economy of the Ancient Near East, with a particular focus on the cuneiform documentation from the Old-Babylonian period (2004–1595 BCE). His doctoral research led him to study the socio-economic role of the major organisations of the period, in particular the temples. He aims to explore these questions in greater depth by combining historical, economic, anthropological, and sociological approaches.

José Remesal Rodríguez is Emeritus Professor of Ancient History at the University of Barcelona. He is a full member of the Real Academia de la Historia; director of CEIPAC (Centro para el Estudio de la Interdependencia Interprovincial en la Antigüedad Clasica); director of the archaeological excavations at Monte Testaccio (Rome). His main line of research is the study of food production and trade in the Greco-Roman world and the social, political, and administrative repercussions this entailed.

Bertram Schefold *1943, Basel. Son of Karl Schefold, Archaeologist, and of Marianne Schefold, née von den Steinen. Humanistisches Gymnasium, Basel. Diploma in math., phys. and philosophy, Basel 1967. Doctoral studies: Cambridge (GB). Basel:

PhD in economics 1971. Res. Assoc., Harvard. Full Prof.: Frankfurt, 1974. Theodor Heuss-Professor at the New School for Social Research, New York 1984, and numerous other visiting appointments. Senior Professor since 2012. Hon. Prof. Peking University 2019. More than 40 books and 300 articles on economic theory and its history, energy policy. Dr. h.c.: Tübingen and Macerata. Th. Guggenheim Prize. Two Festschriften. Hon. Pres., European Society for the History of Economic Thought (2004); President Stefan-George-Gesellschaft 1995–2009. Main areas of research: capital theory and history of economic thought.

Daniel Silvermintz, PhD, is Professor of Philosophy and Humanities at the University of Houston-Clear Lake. He has held research positions as a Visiting Scholar at the Critical Theory Institute, University of California-Irvine and at the Institute of Classical Studies, University of London. His research focuses on ancient Greek political thought and has appeared in *Classical World*, *Polis*, *Omnibus*, *Metaphilosophy*, *Ancient World*, *History of Political Economy*, *Electra*, *Yale Economic Review*, and *Scientific American*. His book, *Protagoras: Ancients in Action*, was published by Bloomsbury Academic in 2016.

Lothar Willms is a Heisenberg fellow at Humboldt University, Berlin. Among others, he works on Ancient Drama, Historical Linguistics of Latin and Greek, and Ancient Philosophy. He holds a PhD in Classics (2004: University of Trier) and earned his postdoctoral qualification (*Habilitation*) at the University of Heidelberg in 2011. 2017–2019 he was a research fellow, sponsored by the Alexander von Humboldt-Foundation, at Brown University (Providence, RI). Main publications: Epictetus' Diatribe *On Freedom* (4.1) – Introduction, Translation, and Commentary (2011/12), Transgression, the Tragic, and Metatheater: A New Reading of Ancient Drama (2014).

Introduction: Were the Ancients Rational Actors?

A View from a Graeco-Roman Historian

Sven Günther

Abstract: In this paper, I shall show the applicability of bounded rationality approaches – in particular New Institutional Economics (NIE) – to (Ancient) History. For this sake, I link basic pillars of these modern (economic) approaches to the principles of History as outlined by Johann Gustav Droysen in his seminal *Grundriss der Geschichte* and to frames and framing methodology as essential tool for a 'communicative turn' in historical studies, in order to link 'etic' and 'emic' perspectives on historical source material. With a short case-study on Xenophon's carefully phrased proposal of an investment fund for financially re-establishing Athens after the devastating Social War (357–355 BC), I shall show the degree to which such a comprehensive study is necessary in order to fully grasp the communicative dynamics about (not only) economic affairs in antiquity.

Keywords: Bounded Rationality – Rational Actors – New Institutional Economics – Droysen – Principles of History – Frames & Framing – Xenophon

Johann Gustav Droysen's *Grundriss der Historik* (*Outline of the Principles of History*)[1] is probably not the first source in which one expects to find anything on the guiding question of our conference and subsequent publication of selected, double-blind peer-reviewed papers, namely, whether the ancients were rational (economic) actors. Even though Droysen reflects on the foundational principles of History becoming an independent and autonomous academic discipline within universities in terms of methodology, heuristics, critical analysis, and interpretation;[2] and despite the doctrine of History as a system and its systematic presentation seeming to be chronologically far away from modern rational choice and actor theories, one nevertheless finds a noteworthy thought in his *Grundriss*:

---

1 First published in 1868 (a slightly modified second edition published in 1875 and a fully revised third edition published in 1882). The *Grundriss der Historik* was written based on Droysen's 17-times given lecture series on the topic and the lecture manual firstly printed in 1858 and again in 1862.

2 Cf. Günther 2022a.

> Der Mensch wird, was er seiner Anlage nach ist, Totalität in sich, erst in dem Verstehen Anderer, in dem Verstandenwerden von Anderen, in den sittlichen Gemeinsamkeiten (Familie, Volk, Staat, Religion u.s.w.).
> Der Einzelne wird nur relativ Totalität: verstehend und verstanden ist er nur wie ein Beispiel und Ausdruck der Gemeinsamkeiten, deren Glied er ist und an deren Wesen und Werden er Theil hat, – er seihst nur wie Ein Ausdruck dieses Wesens und Werdens.
> Die Gesammtheit der Zeiten, Völker, Staaten, Religionen u.s.w. ist nur wie Ein Ausdruck der absoluten Totalität, die wir ahnen und glauben, die sich uns ergiebt aus dem *cogito ergo sum*, der Gewissheit unseres Ichseins, der uns gewissesten Thatsache.[3]
> The human being is, in essential nature, a totality in himself, but realizes this character only in understanding others and being understood by them, in the moral partnerships of family, people, state, religion, etc.
> The individual is only relatively a totality. He understands and is understood only as a specimen and expression of the partnerships whose member he is and in whose essence and development he has part, himself being but an expression of this essence and development.
> The combined influence of times, peoples, states, religions, etc., is only a sort of an expression of the absolute totality, whose reality we instinctively surmise and believe in because it comes before us in our '*Cogito ergo sum*,' that is, as the certainty of our own personal being, and as the most indubitable fact which we can know.[4]

In his attempt to establish 'understanding' as the basic principle of History based on a specific "historische Frage" ("historical interrogation"),[5] the highlighted relationship between the individual and the collective is reflective of the relationship between the extant sources, with their specific viewpoints on the historical events or developments, and the actual historical events or developments. As the extant sources testify to the "Willensacte" ("acts of will"), which conversely shaped them,[6] only a comprehensive study based on the critical analysis of all these factors and their interrelations can result in a comprehensive interpretation where, like in a body movement; the mechanisms (pragmatics), contextual conditions, individual

3 Droysen 1882, 11, § 12.

4 English translation taken (here and in the following) from Droysen 1897, 14–15, § 12.

5 Droysen 1882, 13, § 20 = Droysen 1897, 18, § 20.

6 Droysen 1882, 16–17, § 29 = Droysen 1897, 22, § 29.

psychological acts of will, and ideological frameworks dynamically interacting with the individuals' acts of will, are combined.[7]

However, this is, in essence, a basic description of the state in which the art of (bounded) rationality theories in economic studies (and beyond) have for some time existed. Based on specific aspects of these theories, New Institutional Economics (NIE) and other similar approaches could build upon their own models wherein it would be possible to examine how deeply intertwined the motivations of individuals are with their own interests, capacities, resources, choices and decisions, the available (limited) information, the institutional (e.g., legal, normative, or moral) frameworks, and the potential organisations which form collective action. As such, the dynamic relationship between the individual and the "sittliche Mächte" ("moral potencies"), as Droysen calls them,[8] are in the focus. However, they are, as ever, highly 'relative', that is to say, that the bounded character of any individual's act(s of will), when sharing only in a limited amount of their own 'little world' of "sittliche Gemeinsamkeiten" ("moral partnerships"), may simply be the manifestations of their moral potencies.[9]

Moreover, Droysen's historiological considerations perfectly describe the chances and challenges one faces when applying (bounded) rational choice & actor approaches to ancient studies. On the one hand, one has only a select number of sources, that is to say possible data, available which bear witness to the "acts of will" by which they are formed. On the other hand, however, this formation took place during the dynamic interactions between individuals and collective "moral potencies" being facilitated by the different "moral partnerships" to which the individual was linked. Therefore, any conclusion drawn by a modern historical researcher – who too is equally thinking and acting within their own such frameworks – is limited, being, to some degree, also bounded to rational logic.

However, this notion regarding our own limitations and those of the historical sources should not discourage us, quite the contrary. Although our awareness of all these frameworks limits our ability to discover "the 'eigentliche historische Thatsache'"[10] ("'the exact historical fact'"), as Droysen puts it,[11] it remains possible for us to examine the complexity of the "acts of will" which are preserved in the different

7 Droysen 1882, 19–24, §§ 37–44 = Droysen 1897, 26–32, §§ 37–44.

8 Droysen 1882, 23, § 42 = Droysen 1897, 30–31, § 42.

9 Cf. Droysen 1882, 25–26, §§ 45–49 = Droysen 1897, 32–34, §§ 45–49.

10 Droysen here phrases his critique of Historism in the form of a pun to Leopold von Ranke's famous dictum "wie es eigentlich gewesen" ("as it has actually occurred").

11 Droysen 1882, 16, § 28 = Droysen 1897, 21–22, § 28. Cf. Droysen 1882, 19, § 36 = Droysen 1897, 25–26, § 36.

extant source materials. In doing so, we are able to clarify not only their relationships and connections to but also their entanglements within the other sources (testifying to other "acts of will") which we still have before us.[12] In my view, this is the integral point of contact between the rather 'etic' rational actor theories (such as NIE) and the 'emic' approach of understanding the frames and framings in ancient sources which I, together with my wife, have advocated for in recent years.[13]

To give just one example of how fruitful such encounters may be in terms of economic research into antiquity, I shall focus on how the Greek polymath Xenophon in his *Poroi* (Lat. *Vectigalia*) frames his proposal for setting up an investment fund in order to revive the Athenian revenues through stimulating economic activities after the devastating Social War (357–355 BC). After having proposed some allegedly inexpensive measures, namely, honoring economically important foreign merchants and shipowners so that they would like to come and trade (more) with and within the city (cf. Xen. *Vect.* 3.3–6), Xenophon turns his attention to further possible economic stimuli which, being based on financial engagement and investment by the polis, would require a "start-up capital" or "capital fund" (*aphormē*), as David Whitehead has put it.[14] About this capital-stock-to-be-built he writes:

> (6) Εἰς μὲν οὖν τὰς τοιαύτας αὐξήσεις τῶν προσόδων οὐδὲ προδαπανῆσαι δεῖ οὐδὲν ἀλλ' ἢ ψηφίσματά τε φιλάνθρωπα καὶ ἐπιμελείας. ὅσαι δ' ἂν ἄλλαι δοκοῦσί μοι πρόσοδοι γίγνεσθαι, γιγνώσκω ὅτι ἀφορμῆς δεήσει εἰς αὐτάς. (7) οὐ μέντοι δύσελπίς εἰμι τὸ μὴ οὐχὶ προθύμως ἂν τοὺς πολίτας εἰς τὰ τοιαῦτα εἰσφέρειν, ἐνθυμούμενος ὡς πολλὰ μὲν εἰσήνεγκεν ἡ πόλις, ὅτε Ἀρκάσιν ἐβοήθει ἐπὶ Λυσιστράτου ἡγουμένου, πολλὰ δὲ ἐπὶ Ἡγησίλεω. (8) ἐπίσταμαι δὲ καὶ τριήρεις πολλάκις ἐκπεμπομένας σὺν πολλῇ δαπάνῃ, καὶ †ταύτας γενομένας†, τούτου μὲν ἀδήλου ὄντος εἴτε βέλτιον εἴτε κάκιον ἔσται, ἐκείνου δὲ δήλου ὅτι οὐδέποτε ἀπολήψονται ἃ ἂν εἰσενέγκωσιν οὐδὲ μεθέξουσιν ὧν ἂν †εἰσενέγκωσι†. (9) κτῆσιν δὲ ἀπ' οὐδενὸς ἂν οὕτω καλὴν κτήσαιντο ὥσπερ ἀφ' οὗ ἂν προτελέσωσιν εἰς τὴν ἀφορμήν·ᾧ μὲν γὰρ ἂν δέκα μναῖ εἰσφορὰ γένηται, ὥσπερ ναυτικόν, σχεδὸν ἐπίπεμπτον αὐτῷ γίγνεται, τριώβολον τῆς ἡμέρας λαμβάνοντι·ᾧ δέ γ' ἂν πέντε μναῖ, πλέον ἢ ἐπίτριτον. (10) οἱ δέ γε πλεῖστοι Ἀθηναίων πλείονα λήψονται κατ' ἐνιαυτὸν ἢ ὅσα ἂν εἰσενέγκωσιν. οἱ γὰρ μνᾶν προτελέσαντες ἐγγὺς δυοῖν μναῖν πρόσοδον ἕξουσι, καὶ ταῦτα ἐν πόλει, ὃ δοκεῖ τῶν ἀνθρωπίνων ἀσφαλέστατόν τε καὶ πολυχρονιώτατον εἶναι. (11) οἶμαι δὲ ἔγωγε, εἰ μέλλοιεν

12 Cf. n. 6 above.

13 See esp. the volumes E. Günther / S. Günther 2022 and 2023.

14 Whitehead 2019, 148–149.

> ἀναγραφήσεσθαι εὐεργέται εἰς τὸν ἅπαντα χρόνον, καὶ ξένους ἂν πολλοὺς εἰσενεγκεῖν, ἔστι δ' ἃς ἂν καὶ πόλεις τῆς ἀναγραφῆς ὀρεγομένας. ἐλπίζω δὲ καὶ βασιλέας ἄν τινας καὶ τυράννους καὶ σατράπας ἐπιθυμῆσαι μετασχεῖν ταύτης τῆς χάριτος.
>
> Now such additions to our revenues as these need cost us nothing whatever beyond benevolent legislation and measures of control. Other methods of raising revenue that I have in mind will require capital, no doubt. (7) Nevertheless, I venture to hope that the citizens would contribute eagerly towards such objects, when I recall the large sums contributed by the state when Lysistratus was in command and troops were sent to aid the Arcadians. (8) I am also aware that large expenditure is frequently incurred to send warships abroad, though none can tell whether the venture will be for better or worse, and the only thing certain is that the subscribers will never see their money back nor even enjoy any part of what they contribute. (9) But no investment can yield them so fine a return as the money advanced by them to form the capital fund. For every subscriber of ten *minae*, drawing three obols a day, gets nearly twenty per cent – as much as he would get on bottomry; and every subscriber of five *minae* gets more than a third of his capital back in interest. (10) But most of the Athenians will get over a hundred per cent, in a year, for those who advance one *mina* will draw an income of nearly two *minae*, guaranteed by the state, which is to all appearances the safest and most durable of human institutions. (11) I think, too, that if their names were to be recorded in the roll of benefactors for all time, many foreigners also would subscribe, and a certain number of states would be attracted by the prospect of enrolment. I believe that even kings and despots and oriental governors would desire to share in this reward.[15]

Past research discussions have very much focused on the character of the *aphormē* with regard to the concrete meaning of the frequently used semantic field εἰσφορά/εἰσφορεῖν in this passage.[16] Apart from discussing these 'facts', namely, whether these contributions were considered (by Xenophon or his readers) as forced 'taxes',[17] this passage is remarkable in its attempt of a semantic (re-)framing. For

15 Xen. *Vect.* 3.6–11, trans. by Marchant in Marchant / Bowersock 1984.

16 For the sake of brevity, just cf. the discussion in Whitehead 2019, 149, 153–154, and 160–162 and add the recent proposal of a public financial instrument by Gabrielsen 2019. Cf. the critical remarks in the review of the conference proceedings Gabrielsen's paper was published in by Günther 2022b, 253.

17 That is to say, whether this proposed εἰσφορά had the character of a non-compulsory giving, thus being an ἐπίδοσις, or whether it must be regarded as one specific type of

Xenophon here aims to turn the negative labelling of past εἰσφορεῖν-calls for wars which had no return for the ones taxed (Xen. *Vect.* 3.7–8) (especially in the then current situation of Athens' desolate state after the Social War!), into something positive positing that this newly proposed εἰσφορά would provide a return for everyone (Xen. *Vect.* 3.9–10). This re-framing is supported by 1) immediately jumping into the discourse about the financial returns before talking only later about the investment details[18] and 2) by comparing the first (= wealthiest) group's nearly 20 %-return with the (usually a bit higher) interest rates of a maritime loan (Xen. *Vect.* 3.9: ὥσπερ ναυτικόν / "as much as he would get on bottomry"). Notably, however, this comparison only becomes fully established in the following paragraph when Xenophon links the detailed return-scheme[19] to the aspects of security and durability which an investment in the polis of Athens could offer (Xen. *Vect.* 10: καὶ ταῦτα ἐν πόλει, ὃ δοκεῖ τῶν ἀνθρωπίνων ἀσφαλέστατόν τε καὶ πολυχρονιώτατον εἶναι / "guaranteed by the state, which is to all appearances the safest and most durable of human institutions").[20] Additionally, Xenophon sees in this situation an opportunity to attract foreign, non-resident contributors – inclusive of individuals as well as other (Greek) *poleis* and likely even non-Greek political entities[21] – whom he addresses as "benefactors" (εὐεργέται).

Therefore, not only can we identify a basic rational economic idea, namely, that infrastructural investments which are based on the financial engagements of citizens hoping for and with a public guarantee of return will result in economic stimuli and eventually in higher public revenues.[22] But, we can also see how Xenophon relates his proposal to some principle institutions (in the sense of NIE) which earmarked Athenian (and supposedly Greek) political, social, and economic discourses at that time, in our case, the payment of εἰσφορά (by citizens) and the honouring of

---

public financial secured instruments to improve the economic infrastructure for the sake of economic prosperity followed by higher revenues. On the different interpretations, see the previous note.

18 Whitehead 2019, 152–153.

19 For the reasonable numbers of this scheme, see ibid., 153–155.

20 On the meaning of καὶ ταῦτα ἐν πόλει, cf. ibid., 155.

21 On the different groups addressed, see the discussion in ibid., 155–160. The socio-political gradation scheme (Athenian citizens, [Greek, and non-Greek?] foreigners, Greek political entities, non-Greeks political entities) we can notice also in other instances in this work, e.g., in respect of market actors: see Günther 2022c, 317–321. It fits Xenophon's model of uniting eventually all under Athenian hegemony in one 'perfect' and ever-optimizing and -expanding system that benefits all: ibid., 324.

22 On the different interpretations research has offered so far and the respective framework of the particular interpretations, see Günther 2022a, 54–55.

(foreign) εὐεργέται. In so organising his rational argument, Xenophon too was bound to the discourse practices which one might call two very specific "moral partnerships" of Athenian communication and, probably, life. However, by comparing his specific application of these two key-concepts to his fundraising-scheme with the general notion of them, we can see how Xenophon modifies the frame. Thus, here, εἰσφορά is no longer an ad-hoc financial burden and dead-end 'call for war' tax demanded by the state from its subjects, offering no return, but becomes a profitable, secure, and long-term investment in the future of the polis which is based on its citizens' engagement, for the eventual benefit of all. Being a foreign, non-resident contributor to this capital fund becomes an euergetic act, similar to being a benefactor of the polis of Athens in other affairs such as conducting trade, which is also rewarded with specific distinctions and honours (cf. Xen. *Vect.* 3.4).[23]

While for the latter the financial gain (κέρδος) behind the façade is stated directly (see n. 23), for the foreign, non-resident, contributors to the proposed scheme the gain is not presented as having a direct benefit except for the granting of inscriptions, most likely in the form of honorific decrees.[24] We can, of course, suppose that there were a variety of political and / or economic interests which would incentivise active participation in the scheme and the subsequent new prosperity of the Athenian system, however, this is not the point Xenophon is keen to discuss at this particular juncture. Instead he is more interested in mirroring the basic principle of a prosperous system in this funding scheme with the overall work: every particular group (or resource) mentioned is assigned a specific function within the system, emphasising that progress can only be made in the case that all groups (resources) are contributing within the full range of their capacities and potentials to do so. In which case the system (of Athens), as a whole, will be successful and become a leading hegemonic power, not by relying on destructive warfare which leaves the polis ill-reputed (cf. Xen. *Vect.* 1.1) but through economic sustainability and the promise of prosperity to all those who participate therein (of course again benefitting according to their rank in the hierarchical-meritocratic system) (cf. Xen.

---

23 Honoring these merchants and ship-owners, however, is put in another institutional frame, namely, φιλία. Anyway, that this is just the public frame of reference and communication is directly pointed out by Xenophon: ταῦτα γὰρ τιμώμενοι οὐ μόνον τοῦ κέρδους ἀλλὰ καὶ τῆς τιμῆς ἕνεκεν ὡς πρὸς φίλους ἐπισπεύδοιεν ἄν. / "With the prospect of these honours before them they would look on us as friends and hasten to visit us to win the honour as well as the profit."

24 See the discussion in Whitehead 2019, 155–156 and 159–160.

Vect. 5.1–13).[25] This totality of collective governing and framing the particular[26] is key to our understanding of the degree to which Xenophon needed to modify and align the institutions he found in Athenian discourse for his own purpose. Therefore, the question we must ask is not 'how can we link his proposal to Athenian 'realities' (and whether they were actually implemented)?',[27] but is instead, 'how does Xenophon construct his socio-economic (as well as political and cultural) model in order to convey it to, and convince, his intended target audience?', given that this audience was most likely those who were well versed in such discourses.

Furthermore, one may also ask, what does this mean for the guiding question of both our conference and proceedings? Firstly, we can be assured that (bounded) rationality approaches are suitable for, but not limited to, meaningful research into ancient economies. Although the ancient concept(ion)s of state, society, law, economy, culture, religion etc. may not always be equal to similar such concept(ion)s in modernity, we do find institutions, in the sense of NIE framing actors, which are being constantly (re)negotiated by them. The analysis and interpretation of this dynamic interaction between the individual and the collective is at the core of historical investigation. As such it can be deeply enriched and refined by employing the methodological toolset of NIE and other such theoretical approaches; for instance, principal-agent-models, information asymmetries, transaction cost theory, and property & enforcement rights, to name but a few. Secondly, this does not only allow for the study of long-term developments and transformations[28] but, as the example from Xenophon has hopefully shown, also enables us to see rational (economic) thoughts, actions, and performances working on the micro-level, illuminating all of their limitations as well as frames and framings. Thirdly, and most importantly, this is not just a path for understanding the cultural, that is to say, institutional, shaping of ancient economies,[29], but is also a path which encourages research into how ancient economies (as well as economic thinking) shaped societies and their respective institutions. This search for mutual interactions, interdependencies, and entanglements is particularly useful as it helps us to avoid falling

---

25 On the *hegemonia*-aim, see esp. Farrell 2016. On the economic model and social system designed and imagined by Xenophon, see Günther 2022d; cf. Schorn 2011 (= 2012 in English) on the philosophical-ethical concepts innate in Xenophon's *Poroi*.

26 On this and the totalitarian stance blurring the lines between ancient aristocratic and democratic thoughts, see Günther 2018.

27 See esp. the summary of the discussion in Whitehead 2019, 21–30 (with comprehensive overview of evidence and secondary literature).

28 Cf. Terpstra 2018.

29 Cf. the papers in Droß-Krüpe / Föllinger / Ruffing 2016.

into the trap of limited source evidence and circular arguments. For instance, we find the Roman imperial 'state' (including the emperor with his *patrimonium*) regulating and therewith framing the economy of the Empire through its institutions (foremost through Roman law but also through, for example, taxation); however, specific imperial administrative units appear to be equally as engaged in economic affairs as certain organisations (e.g., in respect to grain trade; monopolies; imperial estates). We should also keep in mind that at least some imperial elites such as senators and *equites* were equally, or at least partly, involved in state administration while simultaneously being potential economic actors. In any such case, the fact that we see the imperial state being involved in the economy in such ways does not mean that every private economic activity became aligned to the imperial state economy or even ceased to exist.[30] In this respect the uneven source evidence which – except for Egypt with its papyri evidence of daily life and a few other places – often focuses on the emperor and the imperial elite (in Rome) (as in literary sources), administrative actions and legal regulations (as in inscriptions and legal texts), or representations of achievements of and for the emperor and the imperial state (e.g., buildings with its inscriptions; coins) should not lead us to form generalised, simplified, and shortsighted conclusions.

Knowing that we must go beyond any such framing boundaries which are found either in our source evidence or in past scholarship, I very much welcome the advent of papers in this volume which address the overall question from different angles and disciplines, making the formation and later interpretations of the Graeco-Roman economies which I am used to studying appear within a more global context. Instead of summarising the individual papers, whose respective scope can be easily understood through the abstracts preceding each, I would like to point out two aspects that were, and are, particularly striking for me and will definitely promote future research in the field. The first is the role of temples and religion in economic processes, a role which is often underestimated but widely present in our extant sources and is addressed by several papers in this volume. The economic roles of religious institutions and organisations were not confined to the typical economic activities which we have ascribed to them (such as the storage of valuable offerings or making use of their landholdings and the fruits thereof) but encompass further economic stimuli through, for instance: lending activities, organisation of festivals (with market fairs), and generally in providing persons and interest groups with specific settings and platforms for communication, exchange, and the building of

---

30 On these 'big' questions that can only be shortly touched upon here, see, e.g., the contributions in Wilson / Bowman 2018. Cf. Lo Cascio 2017, who explicitly views the Roman imperial state mainly as setting the 'rules of the game' for private business.

(trust)-networks which were the basis for business (and other) activities. This important function as a 'Middle Ground', to use Richard White's concept,[31] which affords (economic) space to others from different backgrounds but also participates in and benefits from this created space, is definitely worth further focus in the future.

The second notable aspect is that (state) institutions are not everything. Of course, both our extant source material and our use of (new) institutional approaches very much brings these aspects into the foreground whence it seems that the collective actually framed the individual quite substantially. However, several papers in this volume show that individual economic decisions and actions were possible and different from others': for example, whether to go into men's sphere as a businesswomen, or to decide on different money investment, and/or storage options, or to even (economically) act within an empire which demanded a consideration of the institutional frameworks but nevertheless offered different options and choices. In turn, the individual decisions taken thereupon were not just continuing (and thus stabilising) ever-repeating cycles within a closed system,[32] but could enforce thoughts about and actual modifications to and changes of institutions and whole systems, in terms of transformation or radical breaks. This consequently brings to question the degree of longevity of economically relevant institutions and different paths that have been taken (including the respective path-dependence).

Nevertheless, it has hopefully become clear that 'bounded rationality' is an integral part of historical research, both on the side of sources and researchers. Also illuminated throughout is that it is possible to effectively study ancient economies

---

31 White 1991.

32 Hence history (and History) is different from organic nature and Natural Sciences. Cf. Droysen 1882, 19–20, § 37 = Droysen 1897, 26, § 37: "... Die historische Forschung will nicht erklären, d.h. aus dem Früheren das Spätere, aus Gesetzen die Erscheinungen als nothwendig, als blosse Wirkungen und Entwickelungen ableiten. Läge die logische Notwendigkeit des Späteren in dem Früheren, so wäre statt der sittlichen Welt ein Analogen der ewigen Materie und des Stoffwechsels. Wäre das geschichtliche Leben nur Wiedererzeugung des immer Gleichen, so wäre es ohne Freiheit und Verantwortlichkeit, ohne sittlichen Gehalt, nur organischer Natur." / "... Yet historical investigation does not propose to explain, in the sense of deriving, as mere effects and developments, the latter from the earlier, or phenomena from laws. If the logical necessity of the later lay in the earlier, then, instead of the moral world, there would be something analogous to eternal matter and the changes of matter. Were the life of History only a reproduction of what is permanently identical with itself, it would be void of freedom and responsibility, without moral content and only of an organic nature."

within this framework and that satisfactory answers depend upon the degree to which we widen the limits: *propagemus igitur hos terminos hoc volumine!*

Bibliography

Droß-Krüpe, Kerstin / Föllinger, Sabine / Ruffing, Kai (eds.), Antike Wirtschaft und ihre kulturelle Prägung / The Cultural Shaping of the Ancient Economy, Wiesbaden (Philippika 98).

Droysen, Johann Gustav ([3]1882): Grundriss der Historik, Leipzig.

Droysen, Johann Gustav (1897): Outline of the Principles of History (Grundriss der Historik). With a Biographical Sketch of the Author. Trans. by E. Benjamin Andrews, Boston.

Farrell, Christopher A. (2016): Xenophon *Poroi* 5. Securing a 'More Just' Athenian Hegemony, in: Polis 33, 331–355.

Gabrielsen, Vincent (2019): "Mankind's Most Secure and Durable Institution": State, Credit, Trade and Capital Accumulation in the Classical–Early Hellenistic Aegean, in: Woytek, Bernhard (ed.), Infrastructure and Distribution in Ancient Economies. Proceedings of a Conference Held at the Austrian Academy of Sciences, 28–31 October 2014, Vienna (Denkschriften der philosophisch-historischen Klasse 506), 25–43.

Günther, Elisabeth / Günther, Sven (eds.) (2022): Frames and Framing in Antiquity I. Selected Papers from the First Frames and Framing in Antiquity Conference, 16–18 October 2020, Changchun (Supplements to the Journal of Ancient Civilizations 9).

Günther, Elisabeth / Günther, Sven (eds.) (2023): Frames and Framing in Antiquity II. Selected Papers from the Second Frames and Framing in Antiquity Conference, 15–17 October 2021, Changchun (Supplements to the Journal of Ancient Civilizations 10).

Günther, Sven (2018): (K)ein lupenreiner Demokrat? Überlegungen zur Erziehung des ‚guten Bürgers' in Xenophons Kyrupädie, in: Jordović, Ivan / Walter, Uwe (eds.), Feindbild und Vorbild. Die athenische Demokratie und ihre intellektuellen Gegner, Berlin / Boston (Historische Zeitschrift-Beihefte 74), 229–248.

Günther, Sven (2022a): Frames and Framing Theory *avant la lettre*? Johann Gustav Droysen's *Grundriss der Historik* and the Future of Ancient Studies, in: Elisabeth Günther / Sven Günther (eds.), Frames and Framing in Antiquity I. Selected Papers from the First Frames and Framing in Antiquity Conference, 16–18 October 2020, Changchun (Supplements to the Journal of Ancient Civilizations 9), 45–63.

Günther, Sven (2022b): Review of "Woytek, Bernhard (ed.), Infrastructure and Distribution in Ancient Economies. Proceedings of a Conference Held at the

Austrian Academy of Sciences, 28–31 October 2014, Vienna (Denkschriften der philosophisch-historischen Klasse 506)", in: Marburger Beiträge zur Antiken Handels-, Wirtschafts- und Sozialgeschichte 40, 251–255.

Günther, Sven (2022c): Xenophon's *Poroi*, in: Droß-Krüpe, Kerstin / Ruffing, Kai (eds.), Markt, Märkte und Marktgebäude in der antiken Welt, Wiesbaden (Philippika 100), 315–326.

Günther, Sven (2022d): Framing Capital: Xenophon's Economic Model and Social System, in: Koedijk, Max / Morley, Neville (eds.), Capital in Classical Antiquity, Cham (Palgrave Studies in Ancient Economies), 103–125.

Lo Cascio, Elio (2017): Die neue Wirtschaftsgeschichte des Römischen Reiches. Paradigmen und Ansätze, Bonn (Beiträge zur Wirtschaftsarchäologie 1).

Marchant, Edgar C. / Bowersock, Glen W. (trans.) (1984): Xenophon in Seven Volumes. Vol. II: Scripta Minora / Pseudo-Xenophon, Constitution of the Athenians, Cambridge, MA / London (Loeb Classical Library 183).

Schorn, Stefan (2011 = Engl. 2012): Xenophons *Poroi* als philosophische Schrift, in: Historia 60/1, 65–93 (= The Philosophical Background of Xenophon's *Poroi*, in: Hobden, Fiona / Tuplin, Christopher [eds.], Xenophon: Ethical Principles and Historical Enquiry, Leiden / Boston [Mnemosyne Supplements 348], 689–723).

Terpstra, Taco (2018): Neo-Institutionalism in Ancient Economic History: The Road ahead, in: Ménard, Claude / Shirley, Mary E. (eds.), A Research Agenda for New Institutional Economics, Northampton, MA, 233–240.

White, Richard (1991): The Middle Ground: Indians, Empires, and Republics in the Great Lakes Region (1650–1815), Cambridge.

Whitehead, David (trans./comm.) (2019): Xenophon, *Poroi* / Revenue-Sources. Translated with Introduction and Commentary, Oxford.

Wilson, Andrew / Bowman, Alan (eds.) (2018): Trade, Commerce, and the State in the Roman World, Oxford (Oxford Studies on the Roman Economy).

Trouble Brewing in Old Babylonian Mesopotamia[1]

Kathryn Kelley

Abstract: Law 108 from the collection of the Old Babylonian king Hammurabi of Babylon (1792–1750 BC) portrays a woman beer merchant (*sābītum*) as an egoistic rational actor with a strong profit motivation, contravening established exchange conventions and cheating her customers, for which she is condemned to death. To an extent, the merchant's actions and the development of the legal tradition may both be analysed using rational actor theory as drawn from modern western economic tradition. However, the law touches on issues that have been at the heart of debates regarding the applicability of modern economic theories to ancient societies, including the nature of markets, growth, and profit motivations in the context of ancient modes of production and exchange. This study seeks to understand the formulation of Law 108 from multiple perspectives by tracing the history of the female beer merchant in light of Babylonian legal, literary, and economic traditions. The cuneiform record reveals a scribal establishment alongside temple and palace institutions interested in the concept of profit and at the same time actively seeking to define its appropriate limits in relation to other social values. In the development of Hammurabi's law collection and other cuneiform traditions, different sectors of society face different choices and are weighed unequally in benefit calculations including access to wealth. Old Babylonian female entrepreneurs may have suffered disproportionately from institutional anxieties regarding shifting relationships between temple and palace industry and private mercantile activity, while the *sābītum* on occasion served as a symbol for inappropriate pursuit of profit.

Keywords: Old Babylonian Period – Women and Rationality – *Sābītum* (Female Beer Merchant) – Laws of Hammurabi – Subversive Contractarianism – Weighing of Silver – Beer – Redistributive Economy

1 I would like to thank Jana Matuszak, Martin Worthington, the anonymous reviewers, and the volume editors for their comments on earlier versions of this paper. All shortcomings remain my own.

1. Introduction

Clause 108 of the Old Babylonian king Hammurabi's law collection (LH 108) concerns a female merchant who is transgressing customs in order to maximize her profit:

> If a woman beer merchant (*sābītum*) does not accept grain for the price of beer, (if) she accepts silver by the large weight-stone, and/or she diminishes the amount of beer received in the exchange in relation to the amount of grain (according to the accepted rate), they shall convict that *sābītum* and cast her into the water.

Notably, the woman beer merchant (not the man) is singled-out in the law, and her punishment is more severe than that for most exchange-related crimes in the collection. *Sābītum* was a professional title for a merchant that flourished for several hundred years but disappeared in the later second millennium, to be replaced in the textual sources at least with male brewers.[2] How might this law fit into the overall historical arc of the woman beer merchant? This article explores what this portrayal of a greedy female merchant may tell us about attitudes towards profit-seeking behaviours in Babylonian society, and places this within the wider debates regarding the application of modern economic models. We will first introduce rational actor theory and review economic theory in relation to the study of ancient Mesopotamia and Babylonia in particular; then, we survey the relevant cultural and historical background for understanding LH 108. Finally, we return to a detailed discussion of LH 108 itself.

2. Rational actor theory

In rational actor theory, macro-level phenomena can be explained by micro-level behaviours, that is the choices of individual rational actors, and thus represents "methodological individualism". The "rationality" in this theory is that of modern western classical economics, which is only a small slice of the larger western concept of rationality and is defined by a simple preference – all other things being equal – for maximizing financial gain. Traditionally, financial gain is seen as the end in itself, a never-ceasing goal. Rational actor theory has also been applied to the development of institutions (such as legal institutions), on the assumption that institutions seek to maximise benefit. Identifying the suitable boundaries for the application of the rational actor theory to modern agents and modern phenomena is a topic of discussion, particularly in recent years in light of developments in

2 And in the 1st millennium on occasion, small-scale female slave-operated enterprises: Stol 2016, 363.

behavioural psychology, behavioural economics, and other fields.[3] With respect to the application of rational actor theory to pre-modern societies there is, furthermore, a disciplinary tension: the classical economic approach drawing on the Sciences aims for quantifiable and scalable explanation relying on few variables, whereas the Humanities generally prefer to richly describe the particularities of a given situation. Adopting a middle road between these approaches, or a "thick" version of rational actor analysis that incorporates more complex sets of preferences and constraints may risk the loss of verifiable explanatory power.[4]

In addition, a long pedigree of thinkers of various schools, including Max Weber and Karl Bücher have questioned the nature and significance of differences between the economic structures of past societies and of modern capitalist ones. Within these debates, the study of ancient Near Eastern economies is an especially daring adventure. The economic structures of the ancient Near East broadly speaking have been contrasted both with the ancient western Mediterranean[5] and with modern capitalist societies. There are differences of opinion regarding the ways in which concepts and models from modern economics are applicable to ancient Near Eastern societies, in particular those Mesopotamian societies whose economies are partially documented in cuneiform sources from the late 4th millennium BC through the first centuries AD.

3. A sketch of Old Babylonian economy

Before outlining the relevant theoretical debates regarding Babylonian economies, it is necessary to offer a very basic sketch of the Old Babylonian "economy" as it is generally understood. A central concept in the study of Mesopotamian economies is that of the household (Sumerian e_2; Akkadian *bītum*) as a socio-economic unit. Smaller households existed alongside larger ones, the largest being temple and palace households (both often referred to as "institutions")[6] dominating the textual record throughout most periods of history. One way in which ancient Near Eastern economic structures have been set apart is through a shifting and difficult to quantify balance between three "modes of exchange"[7] within and among members of

---

3 Steinbacher et al. 2021; Rutar 2019; Tibor 2019; Verboven 2015; Manzo 2013; Wittek 2013.

4 Ankarloo 2002.

5 Manning 2018 provides a history of the relevant scholarship and an appeal to reconsider this division.

6 In Assyriological publications this term is often used in a parallel way to how "organization" is used in sociology and other fields. "Institutions" in the sense of legal norms, etc., is less often found in Mesopotamian studies but is employed here.

7 A concept taken from Karl Polanyi and his colleagues and expressed in several works,

these households – reciprocity, redistribution, and market-exchange – which all co-existed to some degree throughout the region's history. In particular, redistribution was a hallmark feature of societies across Mesopotamian history, and is typically held to be especially dominant in the Early Bronze Age of the 3rd through early 2nd millennia BC, that is, the end of the Old Babylonian period we are concerned with here.

In 3rd millennium BC Babylonia, textual sources indicate that urban societies were partly organized along the lines of kin-based households, but were dominated by powerful temple and palace households; these great households were in turn "integrated into the patrimonial household of the ruler"[8] and were altogether engaged in wide-reaching redistributive behaviour, supplying members with much of their subsistence. The Old Babylonian period of the following early 2nd millennium BC Mesopotamia is typically described as a time of shift away from these earlier forms of economic organization, with palace-dominated economies that employed what Assyriologists call *Palastgeschäft*[9] – a system of outsourcing risk to certain entrepreneurs, sometimes described as "state agents".

While (semi-)private entrepreneurial activity can be observed already in the 3rd millennium,[10] the cuneiform documentation evidencing such behaviour increases in the early second millennium. As the management of agricultural production was transferred to smaller groups and various responsibilities related to provisioning and trade were outsourced, the era witnessed a weakening prominence of large household-organized redistributive behaviour, even if such behaviour did remain important to a certain extent.[11] For example, a strategy of outsourcing can be shown to have been increasingly employed in the southern Mesopotamian city of Ur in the temple storehouse the Ganunmah and an associated storehouse, which held durable and perishable goods from the 20th century BC, but by the 17th century BC had largely delegated management of some of the goods.[12] The *sābûm* and the *sābītum*, or male and female beer merchants respectively, were among the small-scale entrepreneurs whose positions developed around this time. These figures were integrated into the palace and temple economies as agents, although as purveyors of finished goods rather than traders in raw commodities. At this time, some products may have been increasingly acquired through exchange, although redistribution of certain essen-

including *Trade and Markets in the Early Empires* (Polanyi 1957).

8 Renger 2005, 210.

9 Földi 2014 provides an overview of this term as used in Assyriology.

10 Foster 1977; Wilcke 2007; Garfinkle 2012.

11 Renger 1984.

12 Van de Mieroop 1992; De Graef 2020, 59–60.

tial goods to some of the population tied to the palace or temples remained a significance feature of urban society.[13]

Many questions remain with respect to the relative prominence of redistributive, reciprocity-based, and private or market exchange and the provisioning of the urban population across early 2nd millennium Babylonia, how this shifted through various times and differed among places, and among what section of the population and for what types of products private exchange regularly occurred.[14] Substantial sectors of exchange and provisioning are unavailable to us in the textual record.

A system of credit in part associated with the outsourcing described above encouraged default and the transfer of property into creditor's hands, and the periodic issuance of debt-remission edicts demonstrate the seriousness of this problem during the Old Babylonian period. Like the reforms of Urukagina centuries before, the edicts express the establishment of justice and economic order as a matter of returning to the former state of things. The edicts distinguish between sales made under duress of debt, which were annulled, versus those not made under such pressure, which remained legitimate. Lawsuits were brought in order for judges to assess the circumstances.[15] Although we would describe the sale of private property as part of a "private" sector, the state promoted a view of a just society in which taking advantage of the financial misfortune of one's neighbor was not only discouraged but potentially reversible by law.

In a similar vein, a line from the Sumerian-language *Counsels of Wisdom*, a product of Old Babylonian scribal schools, advises:

> Don't cause financial ruin[16] to someone who owes you money; (because then) he will have even less (with which to pay you back).[17]

Alster's interpretation of this proverb is consistent with a rational actor perspective at the individual level, that is, an appeal on the part of the scribal establishment to the rationality of members of society. One should not extract ruinous indebtedness from others for the economically rational reason that this would not be in one's own financial best interest. At the institutional level as well, a major rational objective of the edicts may have been to curtail the disenfranchisement of significant portions of the population so that they did not disrupt the social and economic order.

---

13 Lamberg-Karlovsky 2009; Van de Mieroop 1999.

14 Renger 1984; Lamberg-Karlovsky 2009.

15 De Graef 2020, 68; Charpin 1980.

16 ur_5-tuku-zu-šè nam̩-ba-silig-ge "to one indebted to you don't 'finish'(?) ..."

17 Alster 2005, 252.

4. "Embeddedness"

On the whole, Assyriologists contend with poorly developed theoretical frameworks for studying ancient Mesopotamian economies.[18] Many scholars questioning the extent to which the tools of classical economic analysis are or can be sufficiently calibrated to provide insights on ancient Mesopotamia build on positions that adapt Polanyi's "substantivist" model, in which past societies' economic behaviour and institutions are "embedded" in other aspects of culture.[19]

In simple terms, one implication of this is that the maximization of profits may not be considered desirable when it interferes with other social aims – but more broadly, also that Babylonians were not necessarily thinking of profit in the same ways that we do. The manner and extent to which this alleged ancient "embeddedness" marks an unbridgeable contrast with modern capitalist economic behaviour is debatable.[20] The implications these differences have for the classical economic tool of rational actor modelling are not thoroughly elaborated, but clearly represent a challenge to analysis that aims at reducing variables so as to support abstraction and mathematical formula. By contrast, the "formalist" strand within Mesopotamian studies (often an unstated position) tends to apply modern economic analysis unproblematically.

"Embeddedness" means different things to different scholars,[21] but the basic idea is that purely "economic" phenomena (institutions, behaviours) as we understand them can rarely be shown to exist, and that a mismatch between our own conceptual categories and those employed by past societies impact upon the results of our economic analysis. Certain uses of "embeddedness" may thus be criticized on the grounds set out by Nongbri with respect to the related term "embedded religion" which can "produce the false impression that religion is a descriptive concept rather than a redescriptive concept for ancient cultures (i.e., that there really is something 'out there' in antiquity called 'Roman religion' or 'Mesopotamian religion,' which scholars are simply describing rather than creating)" by "allowing this slippage between descriptive and redescriptive uses".[22] The same problem may be said to apply to "the economy",[23] and there has thus been a long tradition of breaking discussion of the economic into smaller (re-)descriptive elements. Thus, Polanyi stressed the need to de-couple trade, markets, and money in the analysis of ancient

18 Jursa 2010, 17; van de Mieroop 2004, 54.
19 Polanyi 1957; Dale 2013; Renger 2005.
20 Jursa 2010, 17; Driscoll 2018; Garfinkle 2012, 8–15.
21 Dale 2011.
22 Nongbri 2008, 440.
23 Glendell / Larson 1982, 198.

economic behaviour,[24] and this trend has continued in much ancient Near Eastern scholarship up through the present.[25]

5. Theory and profit in Babylonia

In the 3rd millennium BC, Mesopotamian states promoted an image in which wealth was acquired from foreign lands, and accumulation was the prerogative of the state.[26] As tributary systems, the Old Babylonian states of the 2nd millennium were also invested in the image of inward-flowing wealth and just redistribution. Among the merchant classes, profit (*nēmelum*) was clearly sought by merchants, both on behalf of the state and for themselves, and capital for business ventures could be provided both by institutions and private persons.[27] While royal inscriptions present an image in which the wealth and prosperity of the whole land was represented (and ensured) by that of the king's palace household, both archaeological and textual evidence reveal that significant wealth and land ownership was in the hands of important families in Babylonia[28] and in some regions town collective ownership is attested.[29]

However, tensions regarding provisioning of urban households clearly existed at some points. Richardson has highlighted some aspects of state rhetoric on food security during the Old Babylonian period,[30] as a part of what he terms the "presumptive state",[31] suggesting that claims to the state's ability or willingness to ensure food security may often have been spurious. Letters attest to individuals who complain that they have not been adequately provisioned by state agents or by their own household relatives. In one letter, a woman called Tarīš-Mātum makes a request of one Kubbutum to send her silver through the intermediary of a woman beer merchant:

> I am living in a city of hunger ... you know, and there is no single quart of barley in the ... Do something that pleases [the god] Pabilsag and give one shekel of silver to Šāt-Šamas ("she of Shamash"), the barkeeper [wr. *sa*$_3$-*bi-tim*], so that she can bring (it) to me.[32]

---

24 Dale 2013, 160.

25 Monroe 2020, 147.

26 Lamberg-Karlovsky 2009.

27 Koliński 2010.

28 Family ownership was a greater reality than individual ownership.

29 Charpin 2008.

30 Richardson 2016.

31 Richardson 2012, 4 and *passim*.

32 AbB 9, 240, Stol 1981, 149. See also AbB 6, 178 (trans. Démare-Lafont 2016, n. 41): "I am

As distributors of a diet staple, the beer merchant would have been important intermediaries between the state and domestic household which had been historically linked through redistributive systems associated with both palace and temple institutions.

It is largely the importance of the redistributive behaviour that has led some scholars to express skepticism regarding the relative significance of individual profit motivations in Babylonia. According to Renger's "substantivist" interpretation of the Old Babylonian period, incentives might have been restricted due to the nature of markets (or "market substitutes", i.e., weakly integrated markets):

> The market, even in the restricted form of market substitutes and their subsystems ... was never more than an accessory complementing the economic processes essentially governed by the principles of redistribution and reciprocity on their respective societal levels. Another factor ... [is that] A socio-economic system based on mere subsistence farming (true for the majority of the populace) and self-sufficient agricultural households (*oikoi*)[33] (true for the upper segments of the society) leaves practically no room for a self-regulating market or market system. It even poses severe impediments and restrictions on the system of market substitutes and their subsystems. These limitations effect quantity as well as variety of goods available.[34]

Powell describes Renger's position as a minority one within the field, and offers an overview of the debate, in which by his assessment, many more Assyriologists accept the importance of profit motives.[35] This is especially so for those within the field of Old Assyrian studies, and indeed the entire Old Assyrian way of life as attested by the documents of Assyrian merchants present mainly in ancient Kanesh is structured around the search for profit.[36] However, this essay focuses rather on the evidence from neighbouring southern Mesopotamia (Babylonia).[37]

---

sending a woman innkeeper [*sābītum*] to you, give her my silver or one shekel of my silver. They will bring me some barley, because I don't want to starve."

33 For a differing opinion on the self-sufficiency of Mesopotamian households, see Garfinkle 2012, 15.

34 Renger 1984, 114.

35 Powell 1999.

36 E.g., Michel 2008.

37 Further study of northern and southern socio-economic structures in comparison may consider whether there are any considerable differences, and whether it may be appropriate to consider the concept of schismogenesis (e.g., Graeber / Wengrow 2021, 181–209).

From the perspective of the late 3rd millennium Ur III state of southern Mesopotamia that preceded the Old Babylonian period by several centuries, Garfinkle expresses the central problem of applying a rational actor theory as one of degree of difference with the modern economies for which the theory has been developed.[38] How much did the marked prominence of the redistributive traditions in southern Mesopotamia impact upon private financial accumulation potentialities and incentives? This should influence the way we build profit motivations into any analytical narrative.

Zagarell reflects on the situation across early Mesopotamia (3rd through 2nd millennia BC), stressing the weakness of models relying on one or a few explanatory factors:

> ... it is inappropriate to single out any one factor in attempting to delineate the motive and transformative forces of a social formation, especially given our tendency to "discover" in history the same motive forces, the same "psychology of man" [Lamberg-Karlovsky 1975] that we "know" from our own times. Exchange is not simply an economic act even in modern capitalist societies; politics plays a major role in setting the rules, the conditions, and the profitability of exchanges (Poulantzas 1980: 17). Early Mesopotamian exchange should be approached as part of the changing complex of social relations of production, affecting and being affected by the various cultures of production, consumption, and distribution that characterized Mesopotamian society.[39]

The problem of confidence in the explanatory potential of a single-factor for complex and large-scale patterns of behaviour is compounded by the challenging nature of the sources available for studying Mesopotamian economic activity[40] and for validating any explanatory hypothesis. Cuneiform sources represent particular traditions of literacy and select sectors of society; they are often terse, fragmentary, and decontextualized, and are irregular in their coverage of economic phenomena over the millennia. At the same time, they offer examples of micro-level behaviour for the would-be economic historian and present some tantalizing cultural continuities over long periods of time.

In "Structure, agency and commerce in the ancient Near East" Lamberg-Karlovsky outlined his views on 3rd millennium Mesopotamian economies, stressing the "diversity of co-occurring structures" that were "characteristic of the ancient

38 Garfinkle 2012.

39 Zagarell 1986, 415–416.

40 Van de Mieroop 1999; 2004.

economy", and took a traditional humanities-based position with respect to rational actor approaches:

> Profit and value, as countless other attributes, are perceived and acted upon by individual agents in a completely different manner, dependent upon the distinctive cultural context ... Interaction, whether it be between states or individuals simply cannot be treated as mere structural phenomenon confirming a universal or essentialist model. Interaction is a continuing process at times co-operative, often violent, almost always unpredictable ...[41]

Of course, the case should not be over-stated. LH 108 confirms that the rational actor, with reference particularly to profit, was conceptually familiar to Old Babylonian scribes. It implies that this merchant's incentives were seen to be strong enough to encourage engaging in illicit exchange practices. Countless other sources attest to profit motives as well. The existence of profit-seeking behaviour across the ancient Near East is not controversial, yet it arguably remains difficult to establish whether the priorities and constraints of Old Babylonian merchants render their behaviour conducive to explanations built on a traditional or "narrow"[42] economic rational actor analysis, and *which* macro-level phenomena might be successfully explained primarily by recourse to micro-level profit motivations.

In the *Logics of History*, Sewell uses a case study of the French Revolution to support the position that in undertaking historical analysis, "rational calculation of advantage needs to be joined to arguments about semiotic structures and their transformation", with "semiotic structures" acting to define which decisions are or are not perceived as open to actors within a given cultural context.[43] Thus, a semiotic approach may be seen to overlap with the notion of "thick" or "bounded" forms of rationality.

Sewell's focus on semiotics may be another way to frame the debates about Babylonian economies described above. Redistributive systems operate on principles of resource distribution that are pre-determined in a top-down manner and based upon idealized notions of the social order. In the simplest form, as demonstrated by various third millennium administrative archives, this is reflected in "ration" sizes tied to age, gender, and occupation.[44] "Overseers" get larger rations, reflecting that social hierarchy, too, was built into these systems otherwise rooted in basic physical

41 Lamberg-Karlovsky 2009, 82.

42 Wittek 2013.

43 Sewell 2005.

44 Gelb 1965.

differences. This redistributive framework may be seen to contrast with market-based trading contexts in which individual ingenuity and action should, at least theoretically, play a role in determining wealth distribution in an organic, bottom-up process. Therefore, we may question whether a certain semiotic tension existed between (clearly present) individual profit-seeking agents on the one hand, and the palace and temple redistributive households on the other, the latter which provided structure to urban society. Perhaps such a tension is illustrated in the Old Babylonian Sumerian-language literary composition the *Marriage of Martu*,[45] where we can observe a hierarchy of priorities that places silver-profit in particular below the institution of marriage. The protagonist is the god Martu, and the myth reflects a historical reality involving the incorporation of Amorite populations into settled city life of Babylonia. This is understood to have been ongoing from around the mid-3rd millennium BC and continued through the beginning of the 2nd millennium. Hammurabi himself was of Amorite origin and bore an Amorite name.

In the *Marriage of Martu*, the rations (niĝ$_2$-ba) were established for men according to their family positions. Since Martu is allotted a double portion, but remains unmarried, he decides to enter the city to take a wife. Having been successful in wrestling competitions at the festival, Martu is offered silver and jewels as a reward for his success, but he refuses, saying:

> Where does your silver lead? Where do your jewels lead? I, Martu, would rather marry your daughter.

The story thus champions the redistributive principles that were strongest in the preceding era but that also remained important to the Old Babylonian states. It associates this redistributive system with the proper integration of people into the social order, and particularly focuses on marriage. Earning silver is represented as a less worthy goal with uncertain ultimate benefit. Interestingly, the lessons of the *Marriage of Martu* are reminiscent of the family-promoting speech of the nameless *sābītum* in an *Old Babylonian Gilgamesh* episode, where it is a search for immortality rather than profit which is portrayed as pointless ambition for infinite advantage, contradicting the individual's appropriate (and limited) position in society. The opening words of the beer merchant's address to Gilgamesh repeat verbatim a phrase used earlier in the text by the god Shamash:

> Oh Gilgamesh, where are you wandering, you cannot find the life you seek.[46]

45 Electronic Text Corpus of Sumerian Literature, URL: https://etcsl.orinst.ox.ac.uk/section1/tr171.htm, last accessed: 01.05.2023.

46 George 2003, 279.

Her speech then continues, encouraging Gilgamesh to cease his hunt for immortality as it is not a suitable goal for mortal man, and instead to enjoy life by eating well and making merry. It culminates with the exhortation to marry and have children – a curious reference for the Assyriologist to whom the *sābītum*'s family position is not well understood (see below).

The motif of private wealth (Sumerian níg tuku[-tuku], "possessing things", níg-gur_{11} "accumulation, piling up") is touched on in a collection of Sumerian proverbs[47] known from Old Babylonian scribal schools. Proverb collections were used for training Akkadian-speaking scribes in the Sumerian language, and address concerns of the urban individual, particularly the scribal class, that is, typically small householders whose diverse clientele included temple and palace officials. Alster observed that, on the whole, "Proverbs are extremely conservative; they promulgate the *status quo.* They do not question the validity of the existing social order. Those at the bottom of the scale are told to stay there."[48] Klein reinforces Alster's observations, showing that among the proverbs the poor are fated to remain poor, and individuals remain within the wealth-class into which they were born.[49] Wealth accumulation was for some and not for others. However, among those accumulating wealth (presumably free skilled craftsmen, merchants, and urban elites) there is some skepticism expressed regarding its pursuit:

> 1.15: nig_2 tuku-tuku al-su_3-ud nam-uku_2-ra al-ku-nu
> Wealth is far away, poverty is near
>
> 1.16: nig_2 am_3-da-tuku-tuku igi am_3-da-uru_3-e
> He who possesses many things is constantly on guard ...
>
> 1.18: nig_2-gur_{11} $buru_5^{mušen}$ dal-dal | ki-dur_2 nu-pa_3-de_3-dam
> Wealth (like) migratory birds[50] never finds a place to settle ...
>
> 1.23: nig_2-tuku al-di $šer_3$-re nig_2-gig-ga-am_3
> To have and insist on more is abominable[51]

These proverbs offer the opinion that contentment with one's own financial position may be unattainable and some forms of wealth may be out of reach or not wholly desirable, and 1.23 chastises ambition as inappropriate greed. Complaint

---

47 Text and translation below after Alster 1997.

48 Ibid., xxiv.

49 Klein 2017.

50 Or: "like birds in flight".

51 gig "(to be) sick; (to be) troublesome", URL: http://oracc.museum.upenn.edu/epsd2/sux, last accessed: 01.05.2023.

regarding silver-wealth greed also appears, for example, in an Old Assyrian letter from two women to a male relative (Michel 2008), although as stated above the Old Assyrian way of life was structured around a highly significant private family profit motivation.

6. The law collection of Hammurabi

We can now turn to the specific background of Hammurabi law LH 108 to better assess its significance in discussions regarding Babylonian profit incentives and traditional rational actor-based historical analyses. The law collection of Hammurabi is a Babylonian language literary-legal composition that consists of a prologue and epilogue framing over 280 idealized legal rulings. In modern terms, the law collection is simultaneously literary, religious, and legal in nature, presenting exemplar cases that, to a certain extent, reflected and were influential upon actual practice. While the distance between provisions in the collection and known legal documents of practice has sometimes been stressed, remarkably, as demonstrated by the letters exchanged between king Hammurabi and his officials, some of the rulings may genuinely be those passed by Hammurabi himself.[52]

Roth succinctly summarizes some of the forces at work in the composition of the law collection: "In any one collection, there is a complex interplay of literary and compositional principles, of legal requirements, and of unusual cases and common circumstances. Associative principles draw law provisions together into larger blocks, and certain cases in the provisions serve as bridges linking together such blocks." In short, the composition's contents are significantly influenced by what we would consider literary principles, though which were in the Babylonian perspective likely to have been perceived as an essential part of the divine truth presented in the text.[53]

52 Charpin 2010, 73.

53 Roth 1997, 3–4. The laws are composed in the format of protasis and adoposis ("if – then") which parallels the divinatory sciences (Charpin 2010, 76–77), both of which were representatives of the "truth" (*kittum*) – a term also meaning "justice", "reality", and "stability" – upon which Babylonian scholarly rationality was based. Mesopotamian scholarly rationality was a hermeneutical practice heavily dependent upon observation that featured analogical and associative reasoning in which aspects of language and writing, including puns and literary form, were among the many types of clues from the gods that should guide decision-making (Rochburg 2016, 131–163). In this tradition, "rationality ... depended on informed reading. Reality had to be read and interpreted as if it were a text" (Van de Mieroop 2016, 10) and "The hermeneutic practices used to establish the connections between protases and apodoses were the same as those used to understand the universe" (ibid., 140). Thus if we are to take the closest approximation that

The most complete and most famous copy is a stele probably originally erected in the Babylonian city of Sippar, home of the e_2-babbar, the temple to the sun god and god of justice, Shamash.[54] Hammurabi names his intention "so that the strong do not oppress the weak" and describes the overall rationale of the composition:

> I am Hammurabi, king of justice, to whom the god Shamash has granted (insight into) the truth. My pronouncements are choice, and my achievements are unrivalled; they are meaningless only to the fool, but to the wise they are praiseworthy.[55]

Upholding Shamash's justice was a part of the state-building project. In the 18th century BC, Hammurabi of Babylon experienced a lengthy if tumultuous reign, which Goddeeris views in terms of modern economically rational calculation: "his innovations were characterized by a strong centralization and a maximization of the profits gained from the conquered territories."[56]

Within the laws, punishments for transgressions frequently reflect the relative social standing of the participants:

> 209: If an *awīlum* strikes a woman of the *awīlum*-class and thereby causes her to miscarry her fetus, he shall weigh and deliver 10 shekels of silver for her fetus.
>
> 211: If he should cause a woman of the commoner-class to miscarry her fetus by the blow, he shall weigh and deliver 5 shekels of silver.

The social order is value-indexed to wealth – a feature that is related to the redistributive practices of large households that had flourished since the 3rd millennium BC in which resource distribution was planned in accordance with the roles of individuals within a household.

7. The woman beer merchant (*sābītum*)

As a rare example of a female entrepreneur known through both literary texts and documents of practice, the *sābītum* has attracted attention within Assyriology,

---

we have to a scholarly Babylonian assessment of "rationality", the actions of the *sābītum* in LH 108 are in Babylonian terms explicitly *irrational* as they were unjust. This notion of rationality of course has little to do with Old Babylonian ideas about the existence and significance of profit-seeking behaviour (excepting where it aligns with the gods' plan of justice), as discussed elsewhere in this paper.

54 Cf. the paper by Nicolas in this volume.

55 Roth 1997, 135–136.

56 Goddeeris 2002, 7.

although we are only given small insights into her area of economic activity in the cuneiform record. While both male (*sābûm*) and female beer merchants are known from administrative, legal, and epistolary texts, with minor exception[57] it is the female who appears in literary and literary-legal texts in the Old Babylonian period.

The professional title can be written either wholly logographically (male LU_2.(KAŠ).DIN.NA; female MUNUS.LU_2.(KAŠ).DIN.NA),[58] or syllabically (male LU_2 *sa-bi-im*, *sa$_3$-bi-im* etc.; female *sa$_3$-bi-tum*, *sa-bi-tam*, *sa$_2$-bi$_4$-tum* [once, Hattusa] etc.). Although an updated survey of the cuneiform evidence is due, for the present study we can note that the *Chicago Assyrian Dictionary* cites fewer than ten references to the *sābītum* in administrative texts, as compared to nearly sixty for the *sābûm*. However, one Old Babylonian letter (BM 16970 = CT 43, 39) refers to a person with the clearly feminine name *Bēletum*, as a LU_2.DIN.NA – that is, logographically written without the expected feminine determinative MUNUS, warning us that not all references to LU_2.(KAŠ).DIN.NA are necessarily to male professionals.

In administrative texts, the *Chicago Assyrian Dictionary* identifies the female title only from the Old Babylonian period, with cited texts coming from Kish, Sippar, and unknown Babylonian sites, as well as (once each) Mari on the Middle Euphrates and perhaps Hattusa in Anatolia. To this we can certainly add more Babylonian references (such as AbB 9, 240 mentioned above), as well as references from other regions, including an uncertain one at Tell Bi'a (ancient Tuttul) in northern Mesopotamia[59] and another in an Old Assyrian Kültepe letter referring to a payment *a-na sa$_3$-bi-tim*.[60]

The male title is similarly known in largest numbers from Babylonian sites in the Old Babylonian period, as well as at Mari and Terqa on the Middle Euphrates, at Alalakh, and (perhaps once) at Susa in Western Iran. Beyond the *Chicago Assyrian Dictionary*, updated references to the *sābûm* include his presence in the Old Assyrian letters from Kültepe (ancient Kanesh) in Anatolia.[61] Although early 2nd millennium

57 The Sumerian *Debate between Summer and Winter* refers to the presumably male Sumerian beer merchant of equivalent title, lu$_2$.kurun, in this poem playing the role of "the beer peddler selling beer to the harvesters" (Renger 1984, 83, n. 180).

58 These writings are related to the Sumerian equivalent (munus) lu$_2$ kurun$_{(2)}$-na "man / woman of *kurun*-ale".

59 Krebernik 2001, 249 reads sa$_2^{!?}$-bi$^{!?}$-a-tum "Brauerin" in text no. 22 (I): 9.

60 Michel 2020, no. 206. The author follows precedent in leaving the term untranslated as it bears an unclear relationship to an Old Assyrian expression, *ina sab/pittum*. The spelling is consistent with the term for the beer merchant in other sources and the context arguably consistent with what we know of the beer merchant's activities as a financial intermediary.

61 Michel 2015, 175, n. 33 cites three texts.

local palace "beer offices" are well-documented at Chagar Bazar,[62] Tell Leilan,[63] and lightly documented at Tell Rimah[64] all in northern Mesopotamia, there is as yet no explicit mention of the involvement of a *sābûm* or *sābītum* in the coordination of materials and products at those sites. However, the *sābûm* also continues to be attested in the administrative record of the Middle Babylonian period, particularly cited at Yorghan Tepe (ancient Nuzi) in Northern Mesopotamia, and once as late as the Neo-Assyrian (8th century) record at Nimrud. Standard Babylonian (late 2nd and 1st millennium) scholarly and literary texts also amply reference the male beer merchant.

The administrative references make it clear that the Old Babylonian *sābītum*'s business was not restricted to simply hocking beer, but that she was involved more broadly in small-scale loans and business. Various translations of the professional title have been offered;[65] here we will refer to her for convenience as a beer merchant since her mercantile activities predominantly involve beer and her title may derive from a verb associated with drawing beer.[66]

The series of four laws in the collection of Hammurabi that address the beer merchant all refer explicitly to the *sābītum* as opposed to her male counterpart.[67] These clauses (108–111) follow on a section relating to the *tamkārum* (merchant) and *šamallûm* (trading agent). After clause 111, the theme of trading expeditions (*ḫarrānum*) and silver and grain exchanges is resumed, with reference to *awīlum* (free men) in four more clauses. The position of the clauses regarding the *sābītum*, as well as the pairing of the *sābītum* and *tamkārum* within a clause in the earlier Laws of Eshnunna,[68] suggests that the woman beer merchant represented a general female entrepreneurial counterpart to the *tamkārum*, although the latter is known to

62 Lacambre 2008; Lacambre / Millet Albà 2008.

63 Van de Mieroop 1994.

64 Dalley 1976.

65 "Alewife" (Stol 1994, 179); "bar-maid" and "tavern-keeper" (Abusch 2001, 617); "Innkeeper" has been used by several authors including Stol 2016, 363 and Roth 1997, 101, who, however, herself later rejected this term in favour of "tapster" (1999, 446, n. 6) for the reason that there has been no evidence presented that this figure's business included the running of establishments for overnight stays.

66 Another suitable translation may thus be "tapstress", although that could misleadingly imply a hired-hand rather than entrepreneurial activities.

67 Noting however that Law 110 refers (gender-)ambiguously to the "tavern" (E$_2$.KURUN.NA) but in the context of priestesses.

68 Law 15: "A *tamkārum* or a *sābītum* should not accept silver, grain, wool, oil, or anything else from a male or female slave" (adapted, Roth 1997, 61).

deal in both local trade and (especially) in foreign trading ventures.[69] Indeed the wider textual evidence indicates that the *sābītum* was active in local lending, that contracts could be witnessed in her tavern, and that one could use her to obtain amounts of silver, as in the aforementioned letter AbB 9, 240.

Many aspects of this figure remain opaque to us, including her manner of integration into palace and temple redistributive systems in the various regions and centuries in which she operated, her relationship to the male *sābûm*, and her possible range of social standings and position within a family. Was she a liminal figure in relation to family life? Some of her female contemporaries whose business activities were documented in cuneiform texts were personnel of temple communities, including the *nadītum* who did not typically marry and was not permitted to bear children into a family's inheritance structure. Stol suggests the *sābītum* might be marginal to the family not for purity reasons, but because she may have belonged to a category of "poor, especially single women who were trying to earn a little as a landlady" and whose taverns had "bad reputation[s]";[70] however, there is thin evidence to support this characterisation.

Hammurabi's Law 110 has been read to indicate that neither a *nadītum* nor an *ugbabtum* were allowed to patronize the brewer's house because of the alleged sexual and criminal connotations of that establishment in contrast to the purity requirements of those temple devotees.[71] However, this interpretation has been convincingly called into question.[72] For one, the *sābītum*'s association with the "tavern-brothel" (*aštammu*) and the goddess Inana's role as patroness of prostitution may be a modern conflation.[73] Simultaneously protected and regulated, her "house", i.e., a tavern, was indeed seen as dangerous by the authorities[74] due to the potential for thievery (*sarrūtum*) to be plotted there. De Graef draws attention to an inheritance document showing that a *nadītum* could own a *bīt sābîm* ("tavern"), and proposes a new interpretation of the law, which suggests *not* that such women could not operate or patronize these establishments, but that they must do so *within* the temple and state regulated area known as the *gagûm*:[75]

69 Leemans 1950, e.g., 36.

70 Stol 2016, 365.

71 See de Graef 2019, n. 10 for previous literature.

72 Roth 1999.

73 Lion 2013; Assante 1998, 70.

74 As Charpin 2005, 2 describes it, *sensible*.

75 De Graef 2019.

> Should a *nadītum* and/or *ugbabtum* woman who does not reside in the *gagûm* open a tavern or enter a tavern for beer, this woman shall be burnt.[76]

De Graef argues that the *gagûm* may have been a regulated district. Bresson's discussion of the Greek *agora*,[77] for example, highlights the benefits of institutional regulation of districts in which exchange occurs, which facilitates the reduction of transaction costs. While it is the *kārum* that is now described as a "market" in Babylonian cities, it may be that the *gagûm* as well was a space in which regulation of certain exchange activities could help reduce transaction costs (as well as tax avoidance), through its association with control over standardised measures including vessel capacities, and standardised weights that were frequently associated with temples, such as the temple of Shamash in Sippar (see below). Lion and Langlois highlight some revealing economic documents,[78] the latter from which we learn that the Babylonian *sābītum* paid *nēmettum* and possibly *igisû*[79] taxes to the palace, and transferred draff to feed livestock of the main temple in Sippar at the order of the palace.[80] They may have primarily received grain from the palace in order to make their beer.[81] In Babylonia of the early 2nd millennium, their industry appears to have been regulated by and integrated into both palace and temple institutions.

The woman beer merchant appears conspicuously across literary-legal compositions: in the Laws of X, Laws of Eshnunna, Laws of Hammurabi, and the Edict of Ammiṣaduqa. In fact, one of the few points of overlap between the Laws of Hammurabi and the Edict of Ammiṣaduqa (r. 1646–1626 BC) is the inclusion of clauses related to the *sābītum*,[82] a fact which may speak to the importance of this figure in social discourse across the early 2nd millennium BC. In the Edict, clauses 16 and 17 are statements of debt remission for both the *sābītum* regarding her debts to the palace and her customers' debts to her. Because she was offered debt forgiveness we can surmise that she – along with other "state agents" including *tamkārum*-merchants – was likely under the umbrella of the palace redistributive system and engaged in some non-commercial exchanges on the palace's behalf. Her position at this time, over a century after the reign of Hammurabi, is thus still supported and regulated by the state. After the Old Babylonian period, administrative references

76 Ibid., 79.

77 Bresson 2016, 234–246.

78 Lion 2013; Langlois 2016.

79 A recent discussion of these taxes is offered in Goodeeris 2020.

80 Lion 2013, 396.

81 Stol 2004, 769.

82 Finkelstein 1961.

to the *sābītum* have not been noted.[83]

When we encounter the woman beer merchants in literature outside of literary-legal texts, she is in decidedly high social positions, in particularly close connection with kingship. She is twice mentioned in reference to earlier eras, where she appears in association with the goddess Bau who was initially at home in the southern Mesopotamian city-state of Lagash. Firstly, one Ku_3-Bau "Holy Bau", described in Sumerian as a munus lu_2 $kurun_2$-na (the Sumerian equivalent of *sābītum*) appears as the king (lugal) of Kish herself whose dynasty preceded the Akkadian period by many centuries in the Sumerian King List.[84] The goddess Bau was also regarded as the spouse of Kish's patron deity Zababa. Secondly, a *sābītum*[85] speaks in the first person to the Ur III (c. 2100–2000) king Šu-Suen in a Sumerian balbale ("dialogue" hymn) for the goddess Bau in a composition known from the Old Babylonian period. The identity of this *sābītum* is unclear but she may have been either one Kubātum who is a wife of the king named in the hymn, or else a lukur-priestess representing the goddess Bau in a symbolic sexual union with the king (*Šu-suen A*).[86]

Finally, a nameless *sābītum* appears as a woman who imparts wisdom to king Gilgamesh in an Old Babylonian Akkadian episode related to the later epic. In the later epic, the *sābītum*'s dialogue lines are significantly redacted such that the wisdom theme evaporates and she functions primarily to direct Gilgamesh's way onwards; she is also now identified as minor goddess by the name ^{d}šiduri, presumably as the real-life professional *sābītum* was no longer a suitable reference for audiences.[87] The *sābītum*'s role in the Old Babylonian episode may hint at earlier traditions in which this professional (or her Sumerian counterpart munus (lu_2).kurun$(_2)$.na) held a cultic position, also perhaps alluded to in the Ur III hymn to king Šu-Suen mentioned above.[88] However this would seem to be a tradition far removed from the Old Babylonian beer merchant, according to the economic and legal references.

83 Hartman / Oppenheim 1950, 12; Assante 1998, 69–70.

84 This composition is known from late 3rd and early 2nd millennium (early Old Babylonian) witnesses. For an early edition, see Jacobsen 1939. An updated online translation is available on the Electronic Text Corpus of Sumerian Literature, URL: https://etcsl.orinst.ox.ac.uk/section2/b211.htm, last accessed: 23.05.2023.

85 Curiously for a Sumerian text, this is written syllabically as if Akkadian, *sa_3-bi-tum-ma.*

86 Sefati 1998, 344–352; cf. Widell 2011.

87 Abusch 1993; Assante 1998.

88 Relatedly, an early association between the *sābītum* and Bau in literary contexts is noteworthy given a possible link between Bau and sacred marriage rites as suggested by Sallaberger 1993.

8. Merchants and the weighing of silver

Ialongo et al. have argued through statistical analysis of the deviation of weight values across Western Eurasia from the 3rd through 2nd millennium BC, taken as a measure of information flow, that an integrated, self-regulating market or markets existed, in which "private merchants were the main agents responsible for the diffusion of weighing technology and for the creation and customary regulation of widespread weight systems."[89] Indeed, the cuneiform record suggests that weighing of silver and other goods in exchange contexts fell to various professionals, merchants, and craftsmen in the early and mid-third millennium BC,[90] and the situation does not seem to be substantially different in the early 2nd millennium BC. In the Old Babylonian period, the *tamkārum*-merchant and the *sābītum* are both mentioned in the context of weighing silver. An Old Babylonian letter (CT 52 = AbB 7, 53) from a landlord *nadītum* to her tenant farmer describes that the farmer had had some of the grain in his possession measured with a *tamkārum* and some with "his *sābītum*".[91] If Ialongo et al.'s conclusions hold, then market forces may have contributed in large part to the regulation of merchant weighing practices.

Nonetheless, studying the variability of stone weights in the archaeological and textual record led Powell to describe the "almost endless opportunity for fraud which the system offered."[92] Inaccuracies can occur both through the size of weights used and through the scale, including the methods in which a scale is used which may be "additive" or "subtractive".[93] In addition to the normal product quality assurance uncertainties in any given exchange,[94] the merchant also has other privileged knowledge relating to the mechanisms for weighing out silver using balances and grain through the use of standardized containers, thus she performs a secondary service as a weighmaster during an exchange. Similar asymmetries apply to other Old Babylonian exchanges, and in some contexts exchanges involve "sealed

89 Ialongo et al. 2021, 3. Cf. ibid., 1: "The origin of weight systems in Western Eurasia can be explained with the random propagation of error from a single value, with statistical dispersion remaining at low levels due to an uninterrupted process of self-regulation put in action by networks of merchants over roughly two millennia. We propose that if the information flow was efficient enough to regulate weight standards on a continental scale without public intervention, then it is also possible that the market could react efficiently to local price fluctuations."

90 Bartash 2017.

91 Lion 2013, 397.

92 Powell 1979, 83.

93 Joannès 1989.

94 Akerlof 1970.

silver", that is, silver weighed by a trusted authority and kept in bags with a sealing. This type of silver may have been frequently used in trade[95] and also may have been the palace's preferred form of receiving silver tribute.[96] Temple authorities could weigh silver, in particular both in Sippar and other Mesopotamian cities there are references to silver weighed by the weight stone of Shamash.[97]

Anxiety about the problem of trust in the weighing of silver and other commodities is expressed in a number of literary genres. Mentions of weight fraud appear as early as the reforms of Urukagina.[98] From an Old Babylonian Sumerian proverb collection[99] we read:

> 17. B 7: Scales made with sinews are a trap contrived of dishonesty; should a man then take a merchant (dam-gar$_3$-ra) for his friend?
>
> 17. B 8: You, merchant, how small you made the amount of silver! And how small you made the amount of barley!

Cultural concern regarding mercantile cheating is found across history and institutions are established for discouraging it.[100] In Babylonia, specific phraseology, comparing two transactions side-by-side links some formulations of the above theme from Old Babylonian texts into the later-attested *Shamash Hymn* and the ritual incantation text known as *Šurpu*, "burning".[101] That is, merchants are described as taking with one measure and giving out with another. The *Shamash Hymn* makes it clear that cheating by using fraudulent weights will result in a person's financial ruin:

> The merchant who practices trickery as he holds the corn measure,
> Who weighs out loans (or corn) by the minimum standard, but requires a large quantity in repayment,
> The curse of the people will overtake him before his time.[102]

Just as court cases often relied on obtaining true testimony by having plaintiffs swear by the gods, so the economic rationality of the individual Mesopotamian actors would – for one accepting the veracity of the *Shamash Hymn* – incorporate

95 Stol 2004, 903.

96 Földi 2014, 101.

97 Stol 1999.

98 Badamchi 2016, 12. For an edition of the reforms, Frayne 2008, 245–275.

99 URL: https://etcsl.orinst.ox.ac.uk/proverbs/t.6.1.17.html, last accessed: 01.05.2023, with minor differences in translation offered in Alster 1997, 239.

100 E.g., in classical Greek society, Bresson 2016, 235.

101 Simons 2017.

102 Lambert 1996, 133.

calculation on the consequences of fraudulent behaviour by attracting divine disapproval.

The law collections represent another set of institutional responses to the dishonest merchant. The stele of Hammurabi itself is topped with an image of the king standing before Shamash, the god of justice. Among Shamash's characteristics is that of metrology; cuneiform sources attest to a "true weight of Shamash" from the Old Babylonian period. Ascalone and Peynerol point out some iconographic evidence associating Shamash and scales and draw attention to weights found in temples dedicated to Shamash. Textual and archaeological lines of evidence thus illustrate a long-term Mesopotamian tradition in which metrology was associated with the notion of justice, with "moralizing" literature that linked individual optimal outcomes with adherence to divine principles of justice.[103]

Fraud certainly occurred, although early Mesopotamian merchants might have been tempered in such practices because they understood the importance of cultivating trust among their customers.[104] The merchant's alleged actions in LH 108 (and gap ~x, see below) may be consistent with the expectations of a rational actor as viewed within game theory; they may have an incentive to take advantage of their privileged knowledge of scale functioning and weight-stones to deceive their customers. Adopting a randomization strategy so as to involve deception in only some transactions can be profitable on average.[105] However, calculation of the utility of this strategy might differ in a setting influenced by the Laws of Hammurabi, in which the beer merchant may lose her life. Although this may tempt us to view LH 108 as a rational legal response to regulate a very serious problem of transaction costs, the treatment in the same law collection of male merchants engaged in weight fraud (discussed below) indicates that other variables need to be addressed.

9. Beer and the state

When Martu decided to join in the town's festivities and find a wife by which to bind himself to urban society, he exclaimed "Come, friends, let us go, let us go there, let us visit the beer-houses (e_2 kaš) of Ninab, let us go there."[106]

---

103 Ascalone and Peynerol 2001.

104 Lamberg-Karlovsky 2009, 23.

105 Moss 2010, 622.

106 Other literary hands were more skeptical. The *Instructions of Shurrupak* warn: "You should not choose a wife during a festival. Her inside is illusory (?); her outside is illusory (?). The silver on her is borrowed; the lapis lazuli on her is borrowed" (Electronic Corpus of Sumerian Literature, URL: https://etcsl.orinst.ox.ac.uk/section5/tr561.htm, last accessed: 01.05.2023).

Brewing activities are among those documented in the earliest cuneiform texts, from late 4th millennium Southern Mesopotamia.[107] A temple brewery (e_2 $bappir_3$) of the Early Dynastic periods (early through mid-3rd millennium BC) is known both archaeologically and textually from the Southern Mesopotamian city of Girsu.[108] It is well known that alcohol was "a fundamental element in the state-making arsenal"[109] and that beer was the most ubiquitous and important early Mesopotamian alcoholic beverage. Beer fell into the category of everyday subsistence needs but was also associated with socially marked situations such as ritual offering and feasting[110] and was known throughout early Mesopotamia in a wide variety of types and qualities. It was a typical product within early Mesopotamian redistributive or "rationing" systems, although in the various manifestations of redistributive behaviour beer was not as consistently provided as was grain, bread, oil, or wool.[111]

Neumann has shown through analysis of Ur III material (c. 2100–2000 BC) that in the centuries running up to the Old Babylonian period beer was among the "exceptional" subsistence distributions:

> Beer allotments [in the Ur III period] depended upon the special role played by the serving persons. Almost all of them were immediately connected with institutions of the central or provincial government. They did not belong to the ordinary workers, but rather had to perform special services. Some of them were higher rank, as for instance the generals. Aga_3-us_2 and Amorites may have formed a kind of royal guard ...[112]

He notes a text from Ur recording beer allotments to "Amorites (mar-tu) and other foreigners" (ibid.).

Perhaps significantly, it is precisely the incursion and incorporation of foreign groups into Old Babylonian society that Renger identifies as a stimulus to structural economic changes.[113] Many records of 2nd millennium beer allotments are known. For example, in the Kingdom of Upper Mesopotamia in the early 2nd millennium BC, the bureau of beer at Chagar Bazar tracks rations given to visiting dignitaries.[114]

---

107 Nissen et al. 1993.

108 Hansen 1992; Frayne 2008, 213–215 and 237–238; Ashby 2017.

109 Paulette 2021, 1.

110 Michalowski 1994.

111 Gelb 1965.

112 Neumann 1994, 329.

113 Renger 2005, 210.

114 Lacambre 2008.

Old Babylonian royal inscriptions frequently celebrate provisioning, including beer to workers involved in construction projects. An inscription of Sîn-iddinam commemorates the digging of a canal on the Tigris:

> When I dug the Tigris, the great river, the wages of each worker were:
> 1 gur of barley, 2 sila of bread, 4 sila of beer [kaš], 2 shekels of oil, in one day so they received this.[115]

Beer also featured in Mesopotamian cultures of hospitality. In the Akkadian-language *Counsels of Wisdom*[116] we read:

> Give food to eat, give beer (*kurunnu*) to drink,
> Provide what is asked for, supply food, and honour your guests!
> For this a man's god is happy with him;
> It is pleasing to Shamash [the Sun God] – he will reward him.[117]

The text may be addressed to a nobleman, and the beer specified in this passage is not the common *šikarum* but the "fine beer" called *kurunnum*, which is referenced in the Sumerian and Akkadian logographic writing of the *sābītum*'s title, munus lu_2 $kurun_{(2)}$.na, "woman of kurun-beer". Overall, evidence suggests that the symbolic significance of beer was likely a significant factor in the formulation of Hammurabi Law LH 108.

10. Beer and the domestic household

Despite the long history amongst the early Mesopotamian "great households" of organizing the production and distribution of beer for certain sectors of personnel, beer-brewing was also associated with the "private" (that is, kin-based household) domestic sphere where, as diverse cuneiform literature suggests, women may often have been home-brewers.[118] The overlap of private household and great institutional production of beer is a natural one to the extent that the great households can be seen as projections of smaller family-household units. Ninkasi is a rare example of a female Mesopotamian deity primarily associated with a craft, along with Nisaba as a goddess of the scribal arts, the latter eventually to be replaced by the male god Nabû. In the Sumerian literary text *Debate between Sheep and Grain,* Grain, who is described as "a beautiful girl radiating charm", argues for her superiority

115 Frayne 1990, E.4.2.9.2.

116 Lambert 1996, 96–106. This composition may have been composed as early as the Kassite period which followed on the Old Babylonian period.

117 Reynolds 2007, 171.

118 E.g., Michel 2009, 206–207.

over Sheep. Her self-praise includes a description of Ninkasi assisting the act of brewing:

> When the beer dough has been carefully prepared in the oven, and the mash tended in the oven, Ninkasi mixes them for me.[119]

A Sumerian[120] composition known as *Two Women B* deriving from the Old Babylonian scribal schools is a dialogue in which two women insult each other. The text may have served to guide young scribes in choosing a suitable wife. The composition informs us that women who work too much in menial labor tasks outside of the home, such as grinding grain for wages, are to be reviled. But equally, laziness or neglect of engaging in the proper domestic tasks is likewise undesirable, hence we find the insult:

> kaš sa$_{10}$-sa$_{10}$ aŋ$_{2}$-šeg$_{6}$-ŋa$_{2}$ tum$_{3}$-de$_{3}$ la-ba-ni-ib-la$_{2}$-la$_{2}$-e
> One can't stop her from constantly buying beer (and) bringing ready-made food.[121]

Thus, a proper wife for one of these urban scribes is one that would either regularly make beer to fulfil the needs of the family, or else (we may project) ensure that she has properly arranged for her servants to produce it. Renger has similarly identified textual evidence to suggest that in the Old Babylonian period, "under ordinary circumstances to eat bought bread seems to have been something despicable, something to be ashamed of."[122] The line from *Two Women B* recalls Hammurabi Law 143 in which a wayward married woman irresponsibly disposes of the household's wealth:

> If she is not guarded but is wayward, squanders her household possessions, and disparages her husband, they shall cast that woman into the water.[123]

---

119 URL: https://etcsl.orinst.ox.ac.uk/section5/tr532.htm, last accessed: 01.05.2023.

120 Partly in the "Emesal" dialect often for women's speech.

121 Matuszak 2016, 238. Updated translation from URL: http://oracc.museum.upenn.edu/dsst/pager, last accessed: 01.05.2023. The full context of the quotation emphasizes that the insult relates to mismanagement of household assets: "Don't you say 'everything is plenty', (even though in reality) you're incurring losses? Your husband has no clothes to wear, you yourself are wearing rags: Your butt sticks out from them. One litre of barley is all you find. One can't stop her from constantly buying beer (and) bringing ready-made food. And you, you belong to womankind?!"

122 Renger 1984, 85.

123 Adapted from Roth 1997, 108.

Here we should note that the profiteering female beer merchant in LH 108 and this wayward woman who spends the household's wealth share the same rare (and usually a woman's) punishment of being cast into the water. This should alert us to influences on the formulation of the beer merchant's punishment that are extraneous to rational calculation with respect to institutional management of transaction security, and instead may reflect a mixture of real legal traditions relating to transgressing women, but also potentially to the associative mindsets of the scholars compiling the literary-legal collection. The "wise" reader invoked by Hammurabi cited above might notice a connection between the punishment of the woman beer merchant who greedily seeks wealth through market exchange and that of the woman who wastefully spends it at the market.

These attitudes were surely some among many – only scraps of the broader discussions that individuals were having regarding the cultures of production, distribution, and exchange among households and their members. We may only raise the question as to whether the biting literary presentation of the profligate beer-buying wife in *Two Women B*, threatening the household's economic independence, was associated in popular or scholarly reflection to the woman beer merchant who participated in the arena of market exchange, seeking profit through the sale of beer to householders.

The apparent economic marginalization of the woman beer merchant after the Old Babylonian period parallels that of the other significant female economic actors of the time – the *nadītum* and lukur priestesses.[124] Were changes in society resulting in increased pressure on women to become less involved in certain spheres of economic activity outside the domestic household?

11. Law of Hammurabi 108

Although it is a popularly cited clause, ambiguities in the grammar, coupled with a poor understanding of this merchant's arenas of exchange, mean that a precise understanding of the law remains contested.[125] Translations disagree about whether the beer merchant is accused of one, two, or three separate transgressions. The law may be parsed as follows:

> *šumma sābītum* (^{munus}KURUN.NA) ^{I}*ana šīm šikarim âm lā imtaḫar* ^{II}ina *abnim rabītim kaspam imtaḫar* ^{III}*ū maḫīr šikarim ana maḫīr êm umtaṭṭi sābītam šuāti ukannūšī-ma ana mê inaddûši*

124 Brisch 2021.

125 Discussion of these difficulties appear in Driver and Miles 1952 / 1955; Finet 2002; Müller 2006; Haase 2007; Badamchi 2010, 171–174; 2016, 14–16; Démare-Lafont 1999, 418–422.

Protasis:
If a woman beer merchant (*sābītum*) ...
I has not accepted grain for the price of beer
II has accepted silver by a/the large stone weight
III and/or she has reduced the "exchange value" (*mahīrum*) of beer against the exchange value of grain

Apodosis:
... they shall convict that *sābītum* and they shall cast her into the water.

The conjunction connecting the second and third phrase can be either *u* "and" or *ū* "or". The first two phrases are lacking the common coordinating particle *-ma* between them, which might indicate their independence, but might equally be read as asyndetically joining them, giving particular emphasis to their relationship.[126]

In the first phrase the merchant does not accept grain for the purchase price (*šīmum*) of beer. This may be a transgression in itself, as the palace may have expected grain ration-receivers to be able to go to the *sābītum* to exchange their grain for beer.[127] The first phrase may furthermore serve to set up the situation in phrase two involving silver weighing in which she overcharges her customer.[128] By not accepting payment in grain using standardized containers,[129] the merchant was able to take advantage of the complicated systems of weights and scales used for weighing silver. The second phrase has usually been understood to represent a deception, and indeed the manipulation of scales and weights was a serious concern. However, it is also possible that the "large weight" referenced here was itself a legitimate measure for some contexts, since it is not described specifically as a "false weight". There are a number of ways that the use of a "large weight" might imply a deceitful or unfair weighing practice, but the context does not here make the mechanism clear. In fact, due to the inaccuracies of Mesopotamian scale systems for smaller measures, payment with silver in small quantities was not desirable.[130] Reference to

126 Huehnergard 2011, 51.

127 Renger 1984, 85, but cf. Démare-Lafont 1999, 418.

128 E.g., Roth 1997, 101.

129 E.g., de Boer 2013.

130 Powell 1999, 16: "the margin of error in small weights was about three per cent of the total mass. At the mass of a shekel, this would amount to about a day's pay in silver, so it is obvious that exchange of cheap commodities or small amounts of commodities for silver is not something to be expected. However, once the mass rises to the level of a shekel, which for Old Babylonian times represented a month's pay, the inhibitions to buy something for silver are naturally going to be less." LH 108 is silent about the general scale of the quantity of beer in the exchange, but it is unlikely to be as the modern reader

the accepted going rate (*mahīr(at) illaku*) for beer sales is made in the Laws of Eshnunna (c. 1770 BC) in relation to a *sābītum*:

> 41: If a foreigner (*ubarum*), a *napṭaru*, or a *mudû*[131] wishes to sell his beer, the woman beer merchant shall sell the beer for him at the going rate.[132]

The going rate may have depended primarily on the changes in grain value in relation to cycles of the harvest. It is not clear what forces or authorities were responsible for the going rate mentioned here and in other sources. Rates (also similarly *maḫīrat ibbaššû*, "present rate") are sometimes described in relation to particular cities. In a literary (that is, fictional) bi-lingual letter from king Shulgi of Ur to Ishbi-Erra,[133] we read:

> Take the gold and silver from his hand and buy up all the grain at the prevailing market rate (*maḫīrat ibbaššû*).[134]

In contrast, truly fixed prices are typically understood to be relevant to state transactions, not local ones. As opposed to grain, silver, oil, and wool, beer prices are less often stated as fixed in royal inscriptions and literary-legal texts of the third and early second millennium. The Laws of Eshnunna opens with exchange-rate fixing, with each item being set in equivalence to silver, beginning with barley and extending through raw materials including types of oil, lard, wool, and bitumen. Beer like other finished products is not included among these commodities, and beer to grain exchange rates are not stated elsewhere in either the Laws of Hammurabi or the Laws of Eshnunna. In the Hammurabi Law 111, as well as in a fragmentary earlier Sumerian law collection "the laws of X"[135] (c. 2050–1800 BC), the female beer

---

might at first assume a personal-consumption pint or two – it is likely that the beer merchants frequently dealt in bulk sales.

131 An *ubarum* is a "resident alien", a term attested also in Amorite. Westbrook 1994 suggests that a *napṭaru* is a "visitor" and the attested "house" of a *napṭaru* is an inn or a guesthouse. *Mudû*, from the verb "to know" is not understood in this context. In legal contexts, it is a reference to witnesses in a legal dispute. Roth 1997, 70 describes all three as "categories of persons outside of the common social and jural protective networks."

132 Adapted from Roth 1997, 65.

133 This letter was probably composed initially in Akkadian during the late Old or Middle Babylonian periods (Michalowski 2011, 387–388). Here, the writing is KI.LAM-at, for *maḫīrāt*, the feminine form of *maḫīrum*, see the *Chicago Assyrian Dictionary* vol. 10/1 (= Oppenheim / Reiner 1977), 98 for the "semantic and syntactic parallel uses" of the feminine and masculine nouns.

134 Michalowski 2011, 387.

135 Possibly a fragment belonging to the incomplete Laws of Ur-Nammu (Roth 1997, 36).

merchant is to receive 50 "litres" of grain at the harvest time for a certain kind of beer jug loaned at an unspecified earlier time. These two laws are related to the others regulating loan practices and interest rates. We can surmise that in practice, the price of beer depended not only on the seasonably variable price of grain, but also on the quality of the beer as a finished product, incorporating into the value the total amount of grain used as well as other ingredients and labor.

A crucial aspect of LH 108 may be clarified: in the third phrase, describing the merchant as having "reduced the value of beer"[136] is potentially misleading; she has *increased* the cost. The former phrasing stems from difficulty in translating the term *maḫīrum*, which is a reference to rate of a particular good that is *received*[137] as is indicated in the phrase *nadānum u maḫārum* to refer generally to "exchange", literally "giving and receiving".[138] Thus, a diminished *maḫīrum* for beer against the *maḫīrum* of grain means that less beer is received per amount of grain, with implicit reference to an acceptable exchange rate.

A few comments on *maḫīrum* are required here. A *bāb maḫīrim* "gate of m." may have been a location where transactions took place, and a *bīt maḫīrim* "house of m." likely describes simply a warehouse of goods, for example as owned or purchased by *nadītum* women and others in the city of Sippar.[139] *Maḫīrum* itself is often understood as a general term for "the market" as a conceptual arena of exchange, contrasting with the other "modes of exchange" as adopted in Mesopotamian studies from Polanyi. Although in practice these modes are not always easily to disentangle,[140] they have persevered in the literature, arguably because they have proven useful (if not perfect) for describing the exchanges presented in Mesopotamian sources. For the Old Babylonian period, market exchange contrasts with "redistribution" which refers to exchanges dictated by household membership obligations and rights, broadly speaking both taxation and tribute and the related redistributive payouts to dependents. It also contrasts with "reciprocity", which encompasses other heavily socially-defined exchanges that we may call gift-exchange (the latter may conceptually overlap with tribute as above). In Babylonia, the beer merchant was an agent within the palace or temple redistributive systems, and like other

136 Roth 1997; Similarly, Langlois 2016 and Démare-Lafont 2016, 315–316. Preferable translations of the phrase appear already in Driver / Miles 1968, 203; Renger 1984; Westbrook 2003; Müller 2006 and Badamchi 2016 (following Finet 2002).

137 Renger 1984, 78.

138 Van der Spek et al. 2018, 105.

139 Renger 1983, 77–78; Zaccagnini 1987, 424.

140 E.g., comments by Van de Mieroop 2004: 60 regarding the commercial nature of Amarna (Late Bronze Age) "gift exchange" (reciprocity).

merchants from both the third and early second millennia, her private entrepreneurial opportunities grew out of her service obligations and privileges (such as a supply of raw materials for her product).

Returning to the law, a final problem that remains is the relationship between the third phrase and the first two. Since grain was not accepted in the first phrase, the third phrase cannot be part of the same transgression if it refers to the actual receipt of too little beer for a given amount of grain. We do not need to imagine, however, that the third phrase describes *other* transactions, that is, a resulting market adjustment in exchange equivalencies based upon the beer merchant's behaviour in the previous phrase(s). This would of course be of interest in the context of the long-standing debates regarding the extent to which prices were determined by market forces in Mesopotamian economies. However, even if the third phrase of LH 108 is connected to the first two, we might understand it to describe the implicit beer: grain ratio to which the customer was subjected in the initially described transaction, via equivalencies of beer : grain : silver. Scribes were proficient at navigating exchange valuation with conversions of equivalency between products, particularly using either grain or silver as standard middle-measures.

Yet, the third phrase may well express a stand-alone transgression – namely, charging too much grain for beer – with the coordinating conjunction read as *ū* "or", particularly since *u* "and", in contradistinction to the coordinating particle *-ma*, normally links clauses that are reversible and non-resultative.[141] Thus, it is likely that two or three separate transgressions are given in LH 108, the first one or two involving inappropriate demand for and weighing of silver; and finally, selling beer for grain at too high a price. The final transgression, if independent, could suggest that the merchant may have simply demanded too a high a price rather than engaged in trickery.[142]

Although aspects of LH 108 remain ambiguous, it should be understood altogether to protect the beer merchant's customers from her: probably for *either* not accepting grain for beer, for weighing silver to the customer's disadvantage, or for charging too much grain for her beer – each transgression which could result in death by drowning.

12. A gender penalty gap?

Given the connections between metrology and justice outlined further above, it may thus be no surprise that weight fraud was deemed a very serious crime particularly

141 Huehnergard 2011, 49.

142 One of several complaints, incidentally, regularly documented in relation to 16th century English brewers (Bennett 1996, 140), see below.

in the context of a composition on a stele topped with an image of Shamash. Yet, the beer merchant's death penalty can be compared with that of the *tamkārum* who appears in the preceding section:

> gap ~ x If a merchant gives grain or silver as an interest-bearing loan and when he gives it as an interest-bearing loan he gives the silver according to the small weight or the grain according to the small seah-measure, but when he receives payment he receives the silver according to the large weight or the grain according to the large seah-measure, [that merchant] shall forfeit [anything that he gave].[143]

There is thus a significant difference between the punishments of the two merchants for what appear to be very similar offenses, for the *tamkārum* would stand to lose only his profit while the beer merchant may lose her life. This should remind us that although we may seek out explanations through a paradigm such as transaction cost economics for the development of institutions, those institutions will also have been considerably shaped by the unequal valuation of different members of society with respect to utility calculation.

Study of modern legal institutions through the lens of rational actor theory is undertaken in the field of law and economics, in which mainstream western social contract theory sees the individual as acting rationally with respect to utility maximization, and furthermore suggests that "common law has developed according to [an] implicit economic logic, even if judges and other legal actors have not consciously tried to fashion legal rules with economic theory in mind."[144] Notable criticism of this position comes from Subversive Contractarianism as presented in Pateman and Mills who highlight the problems with describing legal norms as rational, in light of observable racial and gender inequality.[145] Instead, they argue, social contracts disadvantage some groups by being premised on their unequal valuation in a number of senses (the value of their lives, their access to political power, and their intellectual ability) in comparison to the other contractual partners. The law collection of Hammurabi indeed presents a conception of society with unequal valuation of life for different social groups and (though perhaps less straightforwardly comparable) for men versus women. An illuminating study of European merchant guilds

143 Roth 1997, 98. This clause bears close resemblance to the phrasing of the later *Shamash Hymn* and *Šurpu* ritual text cited above, and the implied trickery may lie primarily in "taking by the small measure", wherein the merchant can multiple a margin of error by using an additive method on the scale (Joannès 1989, 138).

144 Finkelstein 2004, 1.

145 Pateman / Mills 2013.

(AD 1000–1800) suggests that although classical economic efficiency may be successfully evoked in an analytical narrative to explain the development of institutions and their interactions with merchants, careful attention should be paid to precisely whose financial benefit institutions may be formulated to maximize, and what sections of society and economy may be excluded or disadvantaged in the process.[146]

The situation for Old Babylonian merchants is complex and further documentation is needed to establish the shifting dynamics between the patron households, institutional policy, and merchants of different social standing. For example, a century after Hammurabi, king Ammiṣaduqa seems to have threatened the *tamkārum* and *sābītum* alike with the death penalty for the crime of falsifying weight measurements, as described in a fragmentarily preserved clause of the Edict of Ammiṣaduqa that lists the two merchants side-by-side.[147]

In seeking to explain the harsh penalty of the *sābītum* in Hammurabi law 108, Démare-Lafont suggests that her cheated customers are foreigners, relying on Law of Eshnunna 41 cited further above.[148] However, this law in fact references individuals who were selling their beer to the *sābītum*, not purchasing from her. Cuneiform texts attest to a variety of (apparently local) individuals engaging in business with the *sābītum*, and it is unclear whether the unidentified victims in LH 108 should be assumed to be foreigners. A *sābûm* in Sippar during the time of Ammiṣaduqa is documented providing beer to more than one *gala.mah* (high-status temple administrator) and a *rabi sikkatim*, perhaps the chief representative of the king stationed in Sippar.[149]

Given the predilection of the code to specify punishment according to the relative status of perpetrator and victim, the phrasing of law 108 may be seen to somewhat conspicuously to avoid the matter of the *sābītum*'s customers' identities, perhaps implying a diversity of clientele or conversely suggesting that they are of the same general class as she is. The anonymity of the social standing of one participant in the transaction might also be read in light of Carlo Zaccagnini's attempt at defining the "commercial mode of transaction" in ancient Mesopotamia, as opposed to gift-giving (reciprocity) and redistribution: the commercial mode featured the "non-existence or non-intervention of kinship and friendship ties and irrelevance of the partner's rank ... [and] explicit mention of 'silver' and 'prices' with reference to the goods that are transacted."[150]

146 Ogilvie 2011.

147 Démare-Lafont 2016, 316; cf. Kraus 1984.

148 Démare-Lafont 1999, 422.

149 BM (British Museum) 81810 (Richardson 2010, 48).

150 Zaccagnini 1987, 425–426.

It has been argued that the laws in this section of the collection, beginning with those involving merchant and *šamallûm* (trading agent) demonstrate a progression from international trade ventures among some-time state agents, to the local, to the tavern represented by the woman beer merchants, and finally "private" trade among *awīlum*-men in the section following Law 111.[151] The observation might also be used to suggest, contrary to the above, that the *sābītum*'s punishment is harsher because the customers she was cheating were from among the local population (as opposed to foreign traders as in Law of Eshnunna 41). It would also be reasonable to suggest that her activities might have implicated the palace's or local temple's own agents and profits. Finally, we may raise (if not answer) the question of whether the transgression of requiring payment in silver or taking too much silver may imply a concern on the part of the palace authorities with control over the circulation of silver, which was one of the primary forms of tax payment within the tribute economy.

Yet gender discrimination was also undoubtedly at play in the formulation of the punishment, recalling that it is specifically the female beer merchant referenced in the Laws of Hammurabi, while a male is also well known from economic documents. This should be combined with considerations of literary compositional motivations for Law 108, as mentioned above in relation to Law 143. For example, since execution by drowning is typically a woman's punishment, or is associated with men's crimes in relation to the purity of women (e.g., Law 155), we might wonder whether the Law 108 would be taken to imply that a *sābûm* would equally be drowned. This is probably irrelevant to the rhetoric intended by this section of the composition, where the king and his scribes were drawing on intertextuality as well as on attitudes related to exchange and the roles of women within household, temple, and palace-regulated spheres of economic activity. However, once the law had been included in Hammurabi's widely popular literary-legal composition, we cannot deny the potential influence it may have had on the business potentialities of the *sābītum*. While we should be careful to note that a divergence between the rulings of the Hammurabi collection and contemporary legal practice have been used to downplay the real-world impact of the collection, in terms of simple economic rationality in the modern conception, some influence of Hammurabi's laws would have presented the woman beer merchant with considerable pressure to refrain from deceptive profit-seeking practices, putting her at a disadvantage in comparison to other merchants. She likely also faced disproportionate danger of false

151 Roth 1999, 447.

accusation, and she was singled out from both the male *tamkārum*-merchant and probably the male beer merchant with respect to the severity of this pressure.

This brings us back to the question set out at the beginning of the study. What factors are relevant to explaining the cultural changes that brought the *sābītum* into and out of existence on either side of the Old Babylonian period? A similar question was raised by Bennett regarding the historical trajectory for independent brewsters (female brewer-merchants) in England from 1300 to 1600 AD, which was answered through an analytical narrative built on historical, cultural, and economic analysis.[152] Following the Black Plague, argues Bennett, lower grain prices and increased drinking habits contributed to making beer-brewing and selling more profitable and therefore to a growing industrialization of the trade. Due in part to legal and inheritance customs, this ultimately disadvantaged small-scale woman brewer-merchants who subsequently took up menial roles in larger male-headed brewing and ale-house enterprises. But other factors, although more difficult to quantify, she illustrates, probably also contributed to the decline of the brewster. In fact, in one particular, the brewster and the *sābītum* in LH 108 present an interesting parallel. Bennett observed that "most representations of the trade depict cheating brewers as women."[153] For example, a popular poem paints the brewster as an unscrupulous businesswoman who accepts payment in forms that she should not and drives customers into debt;[154] however, there was likely not a real and consistent discrepancy in the frequency of cheating along gender lines.[155] She concludes:

> Anxiety about cheating was displaced onto just one segment of the trade: women (and perhaps especially not-married women, who, if they lived without male masters or householders, seemed to be particularly unregulated and uncontrolled). In other words, descriptions of the false trading practices of a brewster such as Rose the Regrater both *expressed* and *aroused*

152 Bennett 1996.

153 Ibid., 138.

154 Ibid., 124.

155 A report filed by the aletasters, a regulatory body, in Oxford in 1324 listed approximately equal numbers of cheating single women and men (the latter who may in some cases have been in partnership with their wives); even though the result should be taken with due caution since "there is an immeasurable interpretive shortfall between transgression and legal response", the result at least does not confirm the impression given by the popular literature of the time (ibid., 137). By comparison, "in 1419–20 ... the guild's list of those selling with false measures included more women than men", a phenomenon which Bennett attributes mainly to women's decreasing membership in those member-protecting guilds (ibid., 63).

> the anxieties of ordinary people about their reliance for an essential food-stuff on a trade that could only be minimally regulated ... Stories about Rose the Regrater and other dishonest alewives might have inhibited a real ale-wife's ability to manipulate her trade in customary ways; since her customers anticipated being cheated, she was perhaps able to cheat them less effectively. These stories might also have discouraged customers from frequenting the premises of real alewives; since they expected an alewife to be especially dishonest, customers might have taken their trade, if given the choice, to a male brewer or tippler or, at least, to a married alewife well-governed by her husband.[156]

LH 108 may be argued to similarly express and arouse the anxieties of Babylonians, placing them particularly on the *women* in the brewing profession. However, in sharp contrast to the increasingly poor, vulgar, and ugly depictions of English brewsters between AD 1300 and 1600, outside of the law collections the few surviving literary depictions of *sābītum* are positive or neutral, presenting a figure of high status, and possibly alluding to this professional's cultic roles in some eras and locales. Even within the law collections, which identify the possible crimes stemming from a wide variety of professionals and classes, the *sābītum* herself is only especially negatively portrayed in the sense that she is singled out from her male counterpart, and in that her punishment for weight fraud is harsher than the merchant's. Furthermore, in Ammiṣaduqa's debt remission edict from a century after Hammurabi's time, she is still protected by inclusion among those whose debts are forgiven. In other respects, too, the cultural and economic circumstances of the *sābītum* are markedly different from the early brewster. Bennett's study is a relevant model in as much as it presents a fascinating possible gender-discrimination parallel.

13. Trouble brewing

The presentation of a *sābītum* in LH 108 as cheating her customers to increase her profit should be understood in light of a complex interplay of economic circumstances, social structures, cultural attitudes, and literary themes. Though the law provides some of the earliest written evidence for the existence of profit-seeking behaviour, it particularly highlights anxieties surrounding such behaviour in Babylonia. The beer merchant in LH 108 is undeniably depicted as acting rationally to her own financial benefit, but her methods are held up as an inversion of justice. Some of the evidence above may hint at a possible tension between Babylonian

156 Ibid., 138.

redistributive state ideology and the profit-seeking initiatives of Old Babylonian merchants.

However, her punishment is more severe than that for male merchants, and the male beer merchant in particular is not even mentioned. It seems likely that, as with her early modern European counterpart, the female beer merchant was scapegoated in the context of broader anxieties regarding developments in mercantile activity. The particular, selective condemnation of a woman's pursuit of profit (profit representing the classical economic sense of rational action; also "instrumental rational action"[157]) is striking in the context of claims that in western thought the "rational" is an explicitly male domain.[158] When rational actor theory is applied at the institutional level, the studies of Pateman and Mills, Ogilvie, and Bennett referenced above all indicate that in the search for historical explanation for institutional development, principles of "rationality" and "maximization" must be understood with respect to the benefit of a well-defined group, often at the expense of others. Historical examples show that women are among the groups who are valued "differently" and set apart in institutional utility calculation.

What this study primarily contributes is the example of the Babylonian semiotic situation, which, although gathered from snippets of evidence, cumulatively illustrates a society pointedly concerned with defining the appropriate boundaries of profit-seeking, and in which the *sābītum* for a time served as symbol of a socially threatening form of opportunistic profit-seeking. Her suitability as such symbol appears to incorporate several different aspects of her position in society. First, the literary evidence indicates that marriage and child-bearing were defining aspects of an individual's proper place in society, in contrast to boundless ambition. A *sābītum* explicitly plays a role in relating this moral in the *Old Babylonian Gilgamesh* story. The fact that she is a woman with some level of economic autonomy outside of patriarchal control – and possibly in fact unmarried – is certainly a relevant detail,[159] but one which must remain without further articulation until the *sābītum*'s position is better understood.[160] Second, her livelihood involved control over a

157 Poole 1990.

158 Lloyd 1984; England 1989; discussion in Anderson 2002 and Cudd 2002.

159 Cf. Budin 2021.

160 Returning again to rational actor theory's alleged conceptual "maleness" or its implicit androcentrism, here with respect to its emphasis on the "autonomy" of actors. That is, "autonomy" is argued to be gendered male in binary opposition to the female as "relational", particularly through their status as spouses and child-minders in the domestic space: thus "economists' assumptions are often unrealistic, and distorted in a way that in our cultural heritage is masculinist" (England 1989, 26). See alternately Cudd 2002

staple of the diet which also had a symbolic role in the integration of people into the social order, including via banqueting, libation, and rationing traditions associated with palace and temple households.

The evidence also indicates that regulation of her activities by palace authorities was a challenge. She may have operated (or had a tendency to operate) at the margins of the major socio-economic institutions of palace, temple, and domestic household, in an unfamiliar arena of growing "private" exchange. Such exchange, though an outgrowth of institutional resource management, contrasted with the redistributive principles central to early Mesopotamian social ideology in which goods were allotted in finite form based upon social position. This top-down and finite allocation of resources stands in contrast with the classical economic rational actor conception of individually-earned wealth from private market activity as a stimulus for action *ad infinitum,* that is assuming profit as a ceaseless goal which will drive the rational action indefinitely. The early southern Mesopotamian situation, wherein wealth distribution as a measure of social order was a significant feature of urban cultural identity, thus offers a particular challenge to the application of rational actor analysis. As evidenced by changing literary references, the *sābītum* as symbol for profit-seeking beyond appropriate limitation, and without appropriate integration into the social order, probably did not outlive the 2nd millennium BC, around the same time that the woman beer merchant also stopped appearing in economic documents and faded into the background of Mesopotamian history.

Bibliography

Abusch, Tzvi (1993): Gilgamesh's Request and Siduri's Denial. II: An Analysis and Interpretation of an Old Babylonian Fragment about Mourning and Celebration, in: The Journal of the Ancient Near Eastern Society 22, 3–17.

Abusch, Tzvi (2001): The Development and Meaning of the Epic of Gilgamesh: An Interpretive Essay, in: Journal of the American Oriental Society 121/4, 614–622.

Akerlof, George A. (1970): The Market for 'Lemons': Quality Uncertainty and the Market Mechanism, in: Quarterly Journal of Economics 84/3, 488–500.

Alster, Bendt (1997): Proverbs of Ancient Sumer: The World's Earliest Proverb Collection. 2 vols., Bethesda, MD.

Alster, Bendt (2005): Wisdom of Ancient Sumer, Bethesda, MD.

Anderson, Elizabeth ([2]2002): Should Feminists Reject Rational Choice Theory?, in: Antony, Louise M. / Witt, Charlotte E. (eds.), A Mind of One's Won. Feminist Essays on Reason and Objectivity, New York, 369–397.

with discussion of previous literature. The Babylonian example seems to echo some of these themes from western tradition.

Ankarloo, Daniel (2002): New Institutional Economics and Economic History, in: Capital & Class 26/3, 9–36.

Ascalone, Enrico / Peyronel, Luca (2001): Two Weights from Temple N at Tell Mardikh-Ebla, Syria: A Link between Metrology and Cultic Activities in the Second Millennium BC?, in: Journal of Cuneiform Studies 53, 1–12.

Ashby, Darren P. (2017): Late Third Millennium BCE Religious Architecture at Tell Al-Hiba, Ancient Lagash, PhD-thesis, University of Pennsylvania, URL: https://search.proquest.com/docview/1954691818?pq-origsite=primo, last accessed: 01.05.2023.

Assante, Julia A. (1998): The Kar.Kid/Harimtu, Prostitute or Single Woman? A Reconsideration of the Evidence, in: Ugarit-Forschungen 30, 5–96.

Badamchi, Hossein (2010): Theft and Related Offences in Early Mesopotamian Law, PhD-thesis, The Johns Hopkins University, Baltimore, URL: https://search.proquest.com/docview/759853999?pq-origsite=primo, last accessed: 01.05.2023.

Badamchi, Hossein (2016): Fraud and Forgery in Old Babylonian Law, in: Zeitschrift für Altorientalische und Biblische Rechtsgeschichte / Journal for Ancient Near Eastern and Biblical Law 22, 1–27.

Bartash, Vitali (2017): Supervising over Weighing in Early Dynastic and Sargonic Mesopotamia, in: De Boer, Rients / Dercksen, Jan G. (eds.), Private and State in the Ancient Near East. Proceedings of the 58th Rencontre Assyriologique Internationale at Leiden 16–20 July 2012, Winnona Lake, ID, 79–88.

Bennett, Judith M. (1996): Ale, Beer and Brewsters in England: Women's Work in a Changing World, 1300–1600, Oxford.

De Boer, Rients (2013): Measuring Barley with Šamaš in Old Babylonian Sippar, in: Akkadica 134, 103–116.

Bresson, Alain (2016): The Making of the Ancient Greek Economy. Trans. by Steven Randall, Princeton, NJ.

Brisch, Nicole (2021): The Marginalization of Priestesses in Ancient Mesopotamia, in: Abar, Aydin / D'Anna, Maria B. / Cyrus, Georg / Egbers, Vera / Huber, Barbara / Kainert, Christine / Köhler, Johannes / Ögüt, Birgül / Rol, Nolwen / Russo, Giulia / Schönicke, Julia / Tourtet, Francelin (eds.), Pearls, Politics and Pistachios. Essays in Anthropology and Memories on the Occasion of Susan Pollock's 65th Birthday, Heidelberg, 585–594.

Budin, Stephanie L. (2021): Freewomen, Patriarchal Authority, and the Accusation of Prostitution, London.

Charpin, Dominique (1980): Archives familiales et propiété privée en Babylonie ancienne: étude des documents de "Tell Sifr", Geneva (Hautes Études Orientales 12).

Charpin, Dominique (2005): Le statut des cabaretiers à l'époque paléo-babylonienne, in: Nouvelles Assyriologiques Brèves et Utilitaire 1, 97.

Charpin, Dominique (2008): Le roi et la terre dans le Proche-Orient du deuxième millénaire av. J.-C., in: Forlanini, Massimo (ed.), La richessa nel vicino Oriente antico. Atti del Convegno Internazionale Milano, 20 Gennaio 2007, Milan (Collana Origini 8), 63–87.

Charpin, Dominique (2010): Writing, Law and Kingship in Old Babylonian Mesopotamia. Trans. by Marie J. Todd, Chicago.

Dale, Gareth (2011): Lineages of Embeddedness: On the Antecedents and Successors of a Polanyian Concept, in: The American Journal of Economics and Sociology 70/2, 306–339.

Dale, Gareth (2013): 'Marketless Trading in Hammurabi's Time': A Re-Appraisal, in: Journal of the Economic and Social History of the Orient 56/2, 159–188.

De Graef, Katrien (2019): *In taberna quando sumus*. On Taverns, Nadītum Women, and the Gagûm in Old Babylonian Sippar, in: Budin, Stephanie L. / Cifarelli, Megan / Garcia-Ventura, Agnès / Millet Albà, Adelina (eds.), Gender and Methodology in the Ancient Near East: Approaches from Assyriology and Beyond, Barcelona (Barcino Monographica Orientalia 10), 77–115.

De Graef, Katrien (2020): Bad Moon Rising: The Changing Fortunes of Early Second-Millennium BCE Ur, in: Frame, Grant / Jeffers, Joshua / Pittman, Holly (eds.), Ur in the Twenty-First Century CE: Proceedings of the 62nd Rencontre Assyriologique Internationale at Philadelphia, July 11–15, 2016, University Park, 49–90.

(Démare)-Lafont, Sophie (1999): Femmes, Droit et Justice dans l'Antiquité orientale: Contribution à l'étude du droit pénal au Proche-Orient ancien, Fribourg / Göttingen (Orbis Biblicus et Orientalis 165).

(Démare)-Lafont, Sophie (2016): Women at Work in Mesopotamia: An Attempt at a Legal Perspective, in: Lion, Brigitte / Michel, Cécile (eds.), The Role of Women in Work and Society in the Ancient Near East, Berlin (Studies in Ancient Near Eastern Records 13), 310–327.

Driscoll, Eric Wesley (2021): Review of: Manning, Joseph G., The Open Sea: The Economic Life of the Ancient Mediterranean World From the Iron Age to the Rise of Rome, Princeton, NJ 2018, in: Bryn Mawr Classical Review, URL: https://bmcr.brynmawr.edu/2018/2018.12.02, last accessed: 20.12.2021.

Driver, Godfrey R. / Miles, John C. (1952): The Babylonian Laws. Vol. 1 : Legal Commentary. Vol. 2: Edited with Translation and Commentary, Oxford.

England, P. (1989): A Feminist Critique of Rational-Choice Theories: Implications for Sociology, in: The American Sociologist 20/1, 14–28.

Finet, André ([4]2002): Le code de Hammurabi, Paris (Littératures anciennes du Proche-Orient 6).

Finkelstein, Claire (2004): Legal Theory and the Rational Actor, in: Mele, Alfred R. / Rawling, Piers (eds.), The Oxford Handbook of Rationality, Oxford, 399–416.

Finkelstein, Jacob J. (1961): Ammiṣaduqa's Edict and the Babylonian 'Law Codes', in: Journal of Cuneiform Studies 15/3, 91–104.

Földi, Zsombor (2014): On Old Babylonian Palastgeschäft in Larsa. The Meaning of Sūtum and the 'Circulation' of Silver in State/Private Business, in: Csabai, Zoltán / Grüll, Tibor (eds.), Studies in Economic and Social History of the Ancient Near East in Memory of Péter Vargyas, Budapest / Pecs (Ancient Near Eastern and Mediterranean Studies 2), 79–118.

Foster, Benjamin R. (1977): Commercial Activity in Sargonic Mesopotamia, in: Iraq 39, 31–44.

Frayne, Douglas R. (1990): Old Babylonian Period (2003–1595 BC), Toronto (Royal Inscriptions of Mesopotamia: The Early Periods 4).

Frayne, Douglas R. (2008): Presargonic Period (2700–2350 BC), Toronto (The Royal Inscriptions of Mesopotamia: The Early Periods 1).

Garfinkle, Steven J. (2021): Entrepreneurs and Enterprise in Early Mesopotamia: A Study of Three Archives from the Third Dynasty of Ur (2112–2004 BCE), Bethesda, MD (Cornell University Studies in Assyriology and Sumerology 22).

George, Andrew R. (2003): The Babylonian Gilgamesh Epic: Introduction, Critical Edition and Cuneiform Texts, Oxford.

Gledhill, John / Larsen, Mogens (1982): The Polanyi Paradigm and a Dynamic Analysis of Archaic States, in: Renfrew, Colin / Rowlands, Michael J. / Abbott, Barbara Segraves (eds.), Theory and Explanation in Archaeology: The Southampton Conference, New York, 197–229.

Goddeeris, Anne (2002): Economy and Society in Northern Babylonia in the Early Old Babylonian Period (ca. 2000–1800 BC), Leuven (Orientalia Lovaniensia Analecta 109).

Goetze, Albrecht (1965): Tavern Keepers and the Like in Ancient Babylonia, in: Güterbock, Hans G. / Jacobsen, Thorkild (eds.), Studies in Honor of Benno Landsberger on his Seventy-Fifth Birthday, April 21, 1965, Chicago (Assyriological Studies 16), 211–215.

Graeber, David / Wengrow, David (2021): The Dawn of Everything. A New History of Humanity, New York.

Haase, Richard (2007): Schankwirtinnen in Babylon: Zu § 108 des Codex Hammurapi, in: Die Welt des Orients 37, 31–35.

Hartman, Louis F. / Oppenheim, A. Leo (1950): On Beer and Brewing Techniques in Ancient Mesopotamia, in: Journal of the American Oriental Society 70, 1–55.

Huehnergard, John ([3]2011): A Grammar of Akkadian, Winnona Lake, ID (Harvard Semitic Series 45).

Ialongo, Nicola / Hermann, Raphael / Rahmstorf, Lorenz (2021): Bronze Age Weight Systems as a Measure of Market Integration in Western Eurasia, Proceedings of the National Academy of Sciences 118/27, no. e2105873118.

Jacobsen, Thorkild (1939): The Sumerian King List, Chicago (Assyriological Studies 11).

Jursa, Michael (2010): Aspects of the Economic History of Babylonia in the First Millennium BC: Economic Geography, Economic Mentalities, Agriculture, the Use of Money and the Problem of Economic Growth, Münster (Alter Orient und Altes Testament 377).

Klein, Jacob (2017): The Concept of 'Misfortune' in Sumerian Wisdom Literature, in: Abusch, Tzvi (ed.), Fortune and Misfortune in the Ancient Near East: Proceedings of the 60th Rencontre Assyriologique Internationale Warsaw, 21–25 July 2014, Winnona Lake, ID, 25–38.

Kraus, Fritz Rudolf (1984): Königliche Verfügungen in altbabylonischer Zeit, Leiden.

Krebernik, Manfred (2001): Tall Bi'a/Tuttul II: Die Altorientalischen Schriftfunde, Saarbrücken.

Koliński, Rafał (2010): Between City Institutions and Markets: Mesopotamian Traders of the 2nd Millennium BC, in: Kogan, Leonid (ed.), Proceedings of the 53e Rencontre Assyriologique Internationale. Vol. 2: City Administration in the Ancient Near East, Winnona Lake, ID, 81–95.

Joannès, Francis (1989): La culture matérielle a Mari (IV): Les méthodes de pesée: A propos d'un ouvrage récent, in: Revue d'Assyriologie et d'archéologie orientale 83/2, 113–152.

Koyama, Mark (2018): Analytic Narratives, in: Blum, Matthias / Colwin, Christopher L. (eds.), An Economist's Guide to Economic History, Cham (Palgrave Studies in Economic History), 371–78.

Lacambre, Denis (2008): 10. Le bureau de la bière, in: Tunca, Önhan / Baghdo, Abd el-Massih Hanna (eds.), Chagar Bazar (Syrie) III: Les trouvailles épigraphiques et sigillographiques du chantier I (2000–2002), Louvain, 180–207.

Lacambre, Denis / Millet Albà, Adelina (2008): 2. Textes Administratifs, in: Tunca, Önhan / Baghdo, Abd el-Massih Hanna (eds.), Chagar Bazar (Syrie) III: Les trouvailles épigraphiques et sigillographiques du chantier I (2000–2002), Louvain, 19–122.

Lamberg-Karlovsky, Carl C. (1975): Third-Millennium Modes of Exchange and Modes of Production, in: Sabloff, Jeremy A. / Lamberg-Karlovsky, Carl C. (eds.), Ancient Civilizations and Trade, Albuquerque, 341–368.

Lamberg-Karlovsky, Carl C. (2009): Structure, Agency, and Commerce in the Ancient Near East, in: Iranica Antiqua 44, 47–88.

Lambert, Wilfred G. (1996): Babylonian Wisdom Literature, Winona Lake, ID.

Langlois, Anne-Isabelle (2016): The Female Tavern-Keeper in Mesopotamia: Some Aspects of Daily Life, in: Budin, Stephanie L. / Turfa, Jean M. (eds.), Women in Antiquity, London, 113–125.

Leemans, Wilhelmus F. (1950): The Old-Babylonian Merchant. His Business and His Social Position. Vol. 3, Leiden (Studia et Documenta ad Iura Orientis Antiqui Pertinentia).

Lion, B. (2013): Les Cabarets à l'époque Paleo-Babylonienne, in: Michel, Cécile (ed.), L'alimentation dans l'Orient ancien. Cuisines et dépendances, Nanterre (Cahiers des thèmes transversaux d'ArScAn XI), 393–400.

Liverani, Mario (1979): 'Irrational' Elements in the Amarna Trade, in: Liverani, Mario, Three Amarna Essays, Malibu, CA (Monographs on the Ancient Near East), 21–34.

Lloyd, Genevieve (1984): The Man of Reason. "Male" and "Female" in Western Philosophy, Minneapolis.

Manning, Joseph G. (2018): The Open Sea: The Economic Life of the Ancient Mediterranean World from the Iron Age to the Rise of Rome, Princeton, NJ.

Manzo, Gianluca (2013): Is Rational Choice Theory still a Rational Choice of Theory?: A Response to Opp, in: Social Science Information 52/3: 361–382.

Matuszak, Jana. 'She Is Not Fit for Womanhood': The Ideal Housewife According to Sumerian Literary Texts, in: Lion, Brigitte / Michel, Cécile (eds.), The Role of Women in Work and Society in the Ancient Near East, Berlin (Studies in Ancient Near Eastern Records 13), 228–254.

Matuszak, Jana (2021): Und du, du bist eine Frau?! Editio princeps und Analyse des sumerischen Streitgesprächs *Zwei Frauen B*, Berlin (Untersuchungen zur Assyriologie und vorderasiatischen Archäologie 16).

Michalowski, Piotr (1994): The Drinking Gods: Alcohol in Mesopotamian Ritual and Mythology, in: Milano, Lucio (ed.), Drinking in Ancient Societies: History and Culture of Drinks in the Ancient Near East, Papers of a Symposium Held in Rome, May 17–19, 1990, Padua, 27–44.

Michalowski, Piotr (2011): The Correspondence of the Kings of Ur: An Epistolary History of an Ancient Mesopotamian Kingdom, University Park (Mesopotamian Civilizations 15).

Michel, Cécile (2008): 'Tu aimes trop l'argent et méprises ta vie'. Le commerce lucratif des Assyriens en Anatolie centrale, in: Forlanini, Massimo (ed.), La richessa nel vicino Oriente antico. Atti del Convegno Internazionale Milano, 20 Gennaio 2007, Milan (Collana Origini 8), 37–62.

Michel, Cécile (2009): "Dis-moi ce que tu bois ..." Boissons et buveurs en haute Mésopotamie et Anatolie au début du IIe millénaire av. J.-C., in: Bottéro, Jean / Faivre, Xavier / Michel, Cécile / Lion, Brigitte (eds.), Et il y eut un esprit dans l'homme: Jean Bottéro e la Mésopotamie, Paris, 197–220.

Michel, Cécile (2015): Were There only Merchants at Aššur and Kaneš? Overview of Professions Attested in the Old Assyrian Sources, in: Albayrak, İrfan / Çayır, Murat / Erol, Hakan (eds.), Cahit Günbattı Armağan. Studies in Honour of Cahit Günbattı, Yayınevi, 171–184.

Michel, Cécile (2020): Women of Assur and Kanesh: Texts from the Archives of Assyrian Merchants, Atlanta.

Moss, Laurence S. (2010): Price Theory and the Study of Deception in the Exchange Process, in: American Journal of Economics and Sociology 69/1, 595–628.

Müller, Gerfrid G. W. (2006): Die Wirtschaft im Spiegel altorientalischer Rechtssatzungen, in: Hengstl, Joachim / Sick, Ulrich (eds.), Recht Gestern und Heute. Festschrift zum 85. Geburtstag von Richard Haase, Wiesbaden (Philipikka 13), 21–26.

Neumann, Hans (1994): Beer as a Means of Compensation for Work in Mesopotamia during the Ur III Period, in: Milano, Lucio (ed.), Drinking in Ancient Societies. History and Culture of Drinks in the Ancient Near East. Papers of a Symposium Held in Rome, May 17–19, 1990, Padua 1994, 321–333.

Nissen, Hans Jörg (1993): Archaic Bookkeeping: Early Writing and Techniques of Economic Administration in the Ancient Near East, Chicago, IL.

Nongbri, Brent (2008): Dislodging 'Embedded' Religion: A Brief Note on a Scholarly Trope, in: Numen 55, 440–460.

Ogilvie, Sheilagh (2011): Institutions and European Trade: Merchant Guilds, 1000–1800, Cambridge (Cambridge Studies in Economic History).

Oppenheim, A. Leo / Reiner, Erica (eds.) ([3]1977): The Assyrian Dictionary of the Oriental Institute of the University of Chicago. Vol. 10: M, Pt. 1. Chicago, IL.

Pateman, Carole / Mills, Charles W. 2013, The Contract and Domination, Cambridge, URL: https://public.ebookcentral.proquest.com/choice/publicfullrecord.aspx?p=1180907, last accessed: 01.05.2023.

Paulette, Tate (2021): Inebriation and the Early State: Beer and the Politics of Affect in Mesopotamia, in: Journal of Anthropological Archaeology 63, no. 101330.

Polanyi, Karl / Pearson, Harry W. / Arensberg, Conrad M. (1971): Trade and Market in the Early Empires: Economies in History and Theory, Chicago.

Polanyi, Karl (1957): The Great Transformation the Political and Economic Origins of Our Time, Boston.

Poole, R. Modernity (1990): Rationality and 'the Masculine', in: Threadgold Terry / Cranny-Francis, Anne (eds.), Feminine Masculine and Representation, Sydney, 48–61.

Powell, Marvin A. (1979): Ancient Mesopotamian Weight Metrology: Methods, Problems and Perspectives, Kevelaer / Neukirchen-Vluyn.

Powell, Marvin A. (1999): *Wir müssen alle unsere Nische nutzen*: Monies, Motives, and Methods in Babylonian Economics, in: Dercksen, Jan G. (ed.), Trade and Finance in Ancient Mesopotamia: Proceedings of the First MOS Symposium (Leiden, 1997), Istanbul, 5–23.

Reiner, Erica / Gelb, Ignace J. / Jacobsen, Thorkild / Brinkman, John A. / Civil, Miguel / Biggs, Robert D. (eds.) (1964): The Assyrian Dictionary of the Oriental Institute of the University of Chicago. Chicago, IL.

Renger, Johannes (1984): Patterns of Non-Institutional Trade and Non-Commercial Exchange in Ancient Mesopotamia at the Beginning of the Second Millennium B.C., in: Archi, Alfonso (ed.), Circulation of Goods in Non-Palatial Context in the Ancient Near East: Proceedings of the International Conference, Rome, 31–123.

Renger, Johannes (1994): On Economic Structures in Ancient Mesopotamia: Part One, in: Orientalia N.S. 63/3, 157–208.

Renger, Johannes (2005): Archaic versus Market Economy, in: Topoi 12/1, 207–214.

Reynolds, Frances (2007): Food and Drink in Babylonia, in: Leick, Gwendolyn (ed.), The Babylonian World, London, 171–184.

Richardson, Seth (2010): Texts from the Late Old Babylonian Period, Boston, MA (Journal of Cuneiform Studies. Supplemental Series 2).

Richardson, Seth (2012): Early Mesopotamia: The Presumptive State, in: Past & Present 215, 3–49.

Richardson, Seth (2016): Obedient Bellies: Hunger and Food Security in Ancient Mesopotamia, in: Journal of the Economic and Social History of the Orient 59/5, 750–792.

Rochburg, Francesca (2016): Before Nature: Cuneiform Knowledge and the History of Science, Chicago.

Roth, Martha T. ([2]1997): Law Collections from Mesopotamia and Asia Minor, Atlanta, GA (Writings from the Ancient World 6).

Roth, Martha T. (1999): The Priestess and the Tavern: LH [Par] 110, in: Böck, Barbara / Cancik-Kirschbaum, Eva Chr. / Richter, Thomas (eds.), Munuscula Mesopotamica: Festschrift für Johannes Renger, Münster (Alter Orient und Altes Testament 267), 445–464.

Rutar, Tibor (2019): For an Integrative Theory of Social Behaviour: Theorising with and beyond Rational Choice Theory, in: Journal for the Theory of Social Behaviour 49/3, 298–311.

Sallaberger, Walther (1993): Der kultische Kalender der Ur III-Zeit, Berlin (Untersuchungen zur Assyriologie und vorderasiatischen Archäologie 7).

Sefati, Yitschak (1998): Love Songs in Sumerian Literature: Critical Edition of the Dumuzi-Inanna Songs, Ramat-Gan (Bar-Ilan Studies in Near Eastern Languages and Culture. Publications of the Samuel N. Kramer Institute of Assyriology).

Sewell, William H. (2005): Logics of History. Social Theory and Social Transformation, Chicago (Chicago Studies in Practices of Meaning).

Simons, Francis J. M. (2019): Burn Your Way to Success: Studies in the Mesopotamian Ritual and Incantation Series Šurpu, PhD-thesis, University of Birmingham, URL: https://etheses.bham.ac.uk/id/eprint/9545, last accessed: 01.05.2023.

Steinbacher, Mitja / Raddant, Matthias / Karimi, Fariba / Camacho Cuena, Eva / Alfarano, Simone / Iori, Giulia / Lux, Thomas (2021): Advances in the Agent-Based Modeling of Economic and Social Behavior, in: SN Business & Economics 1: no. 99, URL: https://doi.org/10.1007/s43546-021-00103-3.

Stol, Marten (1981): Letters from Yale, Transliterated and Translated, Leiden (Altbabylonische Briefe in Umschrift und Übersetzung 9).

Stol, Marten (1994): Beer in Neo-Babylonian Times, in: Milano, Lucio (ed.), Drinking in Ancient Societies. History and Culture of Drinks in the Ancient Near East. Papers of a Symposium Held in Rome, May 17–19, 1990, Padua, 155–183.

Stol, Marten (1999): Mit dem Gewichtsstein des Šamaš, in: Böck, Barbara / Cancik-Kirschbaum, Eva Chr. / Richter, Thomas (eds.), Munuscula Mesopotamica: Festschrift für Johannes Renger, Münster (Alter Orient und Altes Testament 267), 573–590.

Stol, Marten (2004): Wirtschaft und Gesellschaft in Altbabylonischer Zeit, in: Attinger, Pascal / Sallaberger, Walther / Wäfler, Markus (eds.), Mesopotamien: Die Altbabylonische Zeit. Vol. 4, Fribourg (Orbis Biblicus et Orientalis 160), 643–973.

Stol, Marten (2016): Women in the Ancient Near East. Trans. by Helen Richardson-Hewitt and Mervyn E. J Richardson, Berlin.

Van De Mieroop, Marc (1992): Society and Enterprise in Old Babylonian Ur, Berlin (Berliner Beiträge zum Vorderen Orient 12).

Van De Mieroop, Marc (1994): The Tell Leilan Tablets 1991: A Preliminary Report, in: Orientalia N.S. 27/4, 305–344.

Van De Mieroop, Marc (1999): Cuneiform Texts and the Writing of History, London (Approaching the Ancient World).

Van De Mieroop, Marc (2004): Economic Theories and the Ancient Near East, in: Rollinger, Robert / Ulf, Christoph (eds.), Commerce and Monetary Systems in the Ancient World. Means of Transmission and Cultural Interaction. Proceedings of the Fifth Annual Symposium of the Assyrian and Babylonian Intellectual Heritage Project. Held in Innsbruck, Austria, October 3rd–8th, 2002, Stuttgart (Melammu Symposia 5), 54–64.

Van De Mieroop, Marc (2016): Philosophy Before the Greeks. The Pursuit of Truth in Ancient Babylonia, Princeton.

Van der Spek, Robartus J. / Dercksen, Jan G. / Jursa, Michael / Kleber, Kristin (2020): Silver and Money in the Ancient Near East, in: van der Spek, Robartus J. / van Leeuwen, Bas (eds.), Money, Currency and Crisis. In Search of Trust, 2000 BC to AD 2000, 102–131.

Verboven, Koenraad (2015): The Knights Who Say NIE: Can Neo-Institutional Economics Live up to its Expectation in Ancient History Research?, in: Erdkamp, Paul / Verboven, Koenraad (eds.), Structure and Performance in the Roman Economy: Models, Methods and Case Studies, Brussels (Collection Latomus 350), 33–57.

Westbrook, Raymond (1994): The Old Babylonian Term 'Napṭarum', in: Journal of Cuneiform Studies 46, 41–46.

Westbrook, Raymond (2003): A History of Ancient Near Eastern Law, Leiden.

Widell, Magnus (2011): Who's Who in 'A balbale to Bau for Šu-Suen' (Šu-Suen A), in: Journal of Near Eastern Studies 70/2, 289–302.

Wilcke, Claus (2007): Markt und Arbeit im Alten Orient am Ende des 3. Jahrtausends v. Chr., in: Reinhard, Wolfgang / Stagl, Justin (eds.), Menschen und Märkte: Studien zur Historischen Wirtschaftsanthropologie, Köln (Veröffentlichungen des Instituts für Historische Anthropologie e.V. 9), 72–133.

Zaccagnini, Carlo (1983): On Gift Exchange in the Old Babylonian Period, in: Carruba, Onofrio (ed.), Studi orientalistici in ricordo di Franco Pintore, Pavia (Studia Mediterranea 4), 189–253.

Zaccagnini, Carlo (1987): Markt, in: Reallexikon der Assyriologie 7, 421–426.
Zagarell, Allen (1986): Trade, Women, Class, and Society in Ancient Western Asia with CA Comment, in: Current Anthropology 27/5, 415–428.

A Rational God?

Rationality and Religion in the Ebabbar of Sippar, an Old Babylonian Temple

Thibaud Nicolas

Abstract: Could a god act as a rational economic actor? In this paper, we shall try to answer this seemingly odd question. In Ancient Mesopotamia, gods and goddesses were acting as individuals: that is the reason why this paper will try to explain how Šamaš, the Mesopotamian Sungod, was acting in the economic and financial fields. We will focus on the Ebabbar temple, built in Sippar in the first half of the second millennium BCE, in order to answer a simple and yet complex question: how rational could religion-based decisions be? There is evidence that ancient Mesopotamians had their own economic fictions, as we have ours. If they probably did not believe in a rational *homo oeconomicus*, this paper intends to show that the Sungod and his *paredra* Aya were often acting in a logical and rational way as they were lending silver, bargaining, and supplying the needy. This paper will also try to demonstrate that behind this economically active god we can find a social network of priests, notables and other individuals interacting in order to uphold the wealth and power of the Sungod. We will try to understand how rational their choices were. Finally, we will sketch the portray of a debt-based economy with its own coherence and rationality.

Keywords: Temples – Maximization – Debt – Charity – Ancient Near East – Sippar – Old Babylonian Period

In modern economies, the word 'rationality' usually refers to the neo-classical theory postulating that economic actors are *homines oeconomici*, acting with their own interests and profits in mind in order to maximize them. This approach is especially connected to the neoclassical economic theory which was refunded in the 1970's, when the monetarists developed a theory based on the concept of rational choices and expectations.[1] Yet, the theoretical framework of rational choices, based on Weber's theories developed in *Protestant Ethic and the Spirit of Capitalism* (Weber 1904–1905), sketched a portray of economic actors as rational *homines oenonmici* making

---

1 Muth 1961; Miller 1962; Friedman 1970.

transactions, exchanging, bargaining, interacting with a supply-maximization purpose.[2]

In neoclassical economic theory, rationality is based upon "axioms such as completeness, reflexivity, transitivity, and continuity. It treats a choice as rational if it is the one most likely to satisfy these preferences".[3] Moses I. Finley has applied that perception to the Ancient World in his 1973-book *The Ancient Economy*, and he developed the idea of a "peasant mentality".[4] According to Finley, ancients were completely missing even the concept of amortization, as he wrote: "investment in land in short was never in antiquity a matter of systematic, calculated policy, of what Weber called economic rationality." Then, they were mainly focusing on economic sufficiency. Nevertheless, according to Finley, even if the preoccupation for self-sufficiency was an important feature of the ancient economy, it was not the only purpose of transactions in the Ancient world and "the stress on taking steps to avoid cash outlays [...] must be explained within a framework of profit making."[5] Indeed, Finley's theory came mostly from Weber's theorization of the passage from *oikos* to the market economy: rationality is mainly understood to be about profit-making, with the aim to produce wealth and power for the profit-maker. This theory is based upon the idea of a competitive and insightful *homo oeconomicus*.

On the other hand, Karl Polanyi developed a substantivist theory of rationality. According to him, economic choices are embedded in a broader cultural and spiritual context. Rational choices do not take place in a vacuum and, as such, must always be correlated to the environment in which they are made. A religious decision therefore cannot be rational because it will always take place in a religious economy that has not been "disembedded": a quite paradoxical matter.

Moreover, our theoretical framework is based on modern theories and literature exclusively, for the simple reason that ancient Mesopotamians did not leave behind theoretical or reflexive writings. There is no Babylonian Aristotle, no Assyrian Anonymus Iamblichi, no Sumerian Cato. Yet, this theoretical framework must not prevent us from trying to understand how rational the economic actions driven by Ebabbar, the temple of Šamaš, and its clergymen were. It is difficult to use the term rationality when discussing a set of unconceptualized phenomena built over generations. However, we shall not feel limited by terminology but rather encouraged to question it – however fuzzy rationality may be as a concept. Therefore, we

2 Gates / Steane 2007.

3 Teraji 2018, 137.

4 "They had a 'peasant-like' passion for self-sufficiency on their estates, however extravagant they may have been in their urban outlays" (Finley 1973, 109).

5 Ibid., 109–110.

shall use in this paper the following definition of 'rationality', binding together Polanyian perspectives and Weberian ideas (and connecting them through their lowest common denominator): "the capacity of making choices in investments and transactions with the aim to develop appropriate means and reach a specific and anticipated purpose". Using this definition, this paper will assess whether the Sungod Šamaš and its clergy were rational actors.

1. Social, economic, and historical framework

In this article, we will mainly focus on the ancient City of Sippar, in central Mesopotamia, 50 kilometers from Baghdad. This town is widely recorded in ancient literature, not only in Mesopotamian texts but also in Greek chronicles such as Berossos'.[6] According to scholars, Sippar has two main characteristics: it is considered a twin city and a Sun city.

First, it has been associated by some ancient scholars with the biblical Sepharvaïm,[7] and therefore deemed a twin city in the North with Sippar-amnanum and in the South with Sippar-yahrurum.[8] Sippar's second characteristic was its great temple of the Sungod Šamaš, called the Ebabbar, which means "shiny house" in Sumerian, a shrine of great importance throughout all Babylonian History.[9]

This temple was a powerful and wealthy socio-economic organization. As such, it was also the core of major social networks based on debts. Indeed, the Mesopotamian economy during the Old-Babylonian period was mainly relying upon debts[10]. If we want to question the rationality behind such a process, we shall also question the usual definition of "economic rationality" based on the concepts of maximization and profit-seeking. Indeed, those debt-networks could be interpretated as part of a maximization's strategy but to understand clearly what kind of debts were

6 Verbrugghe / Wickersham 1996 is an extensive study on Berossos that deals notably with that issue.

7 2 Kings 17:24, 31; 18:34; 19:13; Isa 37:13. For this ancient identification, see Scheil 1895, 203–206. It has been also discussed (in English) in Rassam 1897, 408–409.

8 Charpin 1992; 2005b.

9 We will not discuss the Ebabbar during the first millennium BCE but will rather study its place and role in the Old Babylonian period (during the second millennium BCE). Focusing on this temple and its documentation will help us to draw meaningful conclusions about rational activities in a religious context. About the role of the Ebabbar during the Neo-Babylonian period, see esp. Bongenaar 1997 (with bibliography) or Zawadzki 2013; 2014.

10 For perspectives on ancient Mesopotamian economy and the importance of debts in it, see Renger 1995; Stol 2004; Neumann 2006; Démare-Lafont 2019; Mynářová / Alivernini 2020.

handled by the Ebabbar, we need to introduce a distinction established by French scholars Michel Aglietta and André Orléan between horizontal and vertical debts.[11] Horizontal debt binds an individual creditor to an individual debtor, it must be repaid in a specific time limit, and it is solved once repaid. This is the common way to understand the word debt in our contemporary economies. On the other hand, vertical debt is owed by the debtor to a society and its anthropological superstructures such as religious, political, and social organizations. They bind everyone together, and they cannot be fully repaid. In fact, even the organizations owning them were not expecting them to be repaid. It is in the light of this concept that we can study the rationality of the Ebabbar's dependents and members. Yet, to understand whether the Ebabbar's clergy and the god Šamaš were rational actors, we need to explain the economic framework of the Old-Babylonian Sippar.

Sippar was also a merchant-city, settled on the bank of an important channel connecting Tigris and Euphrates. The city was located at the crossroad of fluvial traffic and along a terrestrial commercial road leading from northern to southern Babylonia.[12] During the first half of the second millennium, the city grew and became prosperous due to its commercial activity and the fame of its Šamaš shrine. The Sungod cult was so famous that Babylonian kings took pride in making offerings to the Ebabbar on their year names.[13] The other important place in Sippar was its *gagûm*-cloister where learned and rich daughters[14] of Babylonian and Sipparian notables were nuns. It was so famous that even Babylonian kings could eventually give

11 Aglietta / Orléan 2002.

12 Harris 1975, 257–258; Charpin 1982; de Boer 2013; 2021.

13 In Mesopotamia, the date was given by a 'year name': indeed, each year was named after an important event, like a military victory, a religious or architectural achievement or a king's coronation. And when looking at Hammurabi's year's name, one can easily notice that while Šamaš is celebrated in the names of the years 26 and 43, Marduk is praised and glorified in the years Ha 30, Ha 32, Ha 37, and Ha 38. Yet, the major role of the Sungod in kingship, and notably in Hammurabi's kingship, has been studied by modern scholars (e.g., Tanret 2010 or Charpin 2013). Moreover, there was in Babylon a major temple of Šamaš called the Edikudkalamma. David Warburton has also provided some new thoughts on the question (Warburton 2021, 217–220). His main idea is notably that Hammurabi's importance as a king might have been too much overrated compared to Samsi-Addu. Yet, the question to know who was the strongest or the mightiest king of the Old-Babylonian period according to our modern criteria shall not interest us here. Indeed, when it comes to our topic, both Samsi-Addu and Hammurabi showed their devotion to the Sungod and that point emphasizes the fact that Šamaš was the "god of kingship".

14 Cf Lion 2001. On the texts coming from the files of those *nadītum*-nuns, see Barberon 2009.

a sister or a daughter to the *gagûm*-cloister.[15]

Although gods and kings dominated almost every aspect of Mesopotamians' lives, the importance of free enterprise at the beginning of the second millenium BCE. has been widely discussed.[16] Philippe Clancier, Francis Joanès, Bertrand Lafont, and Aline Tenu summarized it well: "one could have the impression, since the archaic Sumerian period and over the long term, of a linear progression, where we would have gradually passed from an economy dominated by temples (Sumerian city-states) to a palatial economy (Ur III), then to a private economy (Hammurabi): such a view of things would be wrong."[17] According to the authors, it is better "to admit a permanent tension between two distinct socio-economic spheres": on the one hand, individual plots within small communities governed by the socio-economic rules of reciprocity and, on the other hand, large areas with redistribution processes as the socio-economic basis.

The opinio communis in Assyriology consists in considering that from the Old-Babylonian period "the disengagement of the State in the direct management of the most important sector of economic activity, that of agricultural production, contributed to the development of the private sphere of the economy"[18]. Yet, the idea of traders and entrepreneurs revivifying an Old-Babylonian economy sclerosed by the extreme state interventionism of Ur's supposed third dynasty must be balanced. We shall remember Marc Van de Mieroop's words: "the wish to promote Mesopotamia's free entrepreneurs as the driving force of that economy is, I believe, driven by a desire to see in the past a fulfillment of present dreams."[19]

Clergymen also acted as private economic actors, and significant evidence supports the implication of members of Ebabbar's clergy specifically. Michel Tanret has clearly established that the administrators of the Ebabbar were conducting business in their own name, endeavoring to increase their real estate and making profit from it.[20] Nevertheless, these texts must be distinguished from the records where Ebabbar officials reported the business conducted on behalf of the temple.

15 De Graef 2016; 2018b; 2019.

16 Moreno García 2016, 15 gives a good bibliography about the increasing recourse to traders and agricultural entrepreneurs in the beginning of 2nd millenium BCE in Egypt.

17 Lafont / Tenu / Joannès / Clancier 2017, 378.

18 Ibid., 379.

19 Van de Mieroop 2005, 122. Indeed, many scholars worked on this "private" business during the Old-Babylonian period (e.g., Charpin 1982; Burggraaff 1995; Tyborowski 2003; Garfinkle 2008; Földi 2014) and they often concluded that they were the main motor of the economy (e.g., Bulgarelli 2011; Silver 1983; 2006; 2007).

20 Tanret 2010.

It is therefore clear that private entrepreneurs played a significant part in the Old-Babylonian economy. However, the temples and the palace remained the biggest households and, as such, crucial economic actors. The Ebabbar, for example, was a colossal landowner and employed many harvesters. For example, in CT 4, 25c, agricultural entrepreneurs called the *iššakkum* received large amounts of barley under the control of temple officials called *šatammum*. They oversaw the hiring of no fewer than 450 agricultural workers who were supposed to break up clods to prepare the fields for cultivation. We can also mention the text de Graef 2018 (AOAT 440), no. 9 which mentions the hiring of 46 agricultural workers under the supervision of an individual who is not named in the text but whose "affiliation" is identifiable thanks to a seal which de Graef reads as follows: "[...]-ni / ⌜DUMU⌝ [...]-(d)UTU / ÌR É.BABBAR.RA" which means "[...]-ni son of [...]-Šamaš, servant of the Ebabbar".

In fact, the "Ebabbar" is depicted in the texts as an active socio-economic organization. When a text refers to the temple, it refers to a place where operations are conducted or where supplies are stocked. Mentions of "Ebabbar" (é.babbar) or the "House of Šamaš" (é ^{d}utu) refer to the same organization and carry mostly material considerations. It refers to the temple as a geographical area and as a physical place. This temple was, in fact, a household held by a landlord: the god Šamaš. Moreover, texts state that temple officials lent silver, bought slaves, received barley, or traded the temple's wool, but that they did not keep the benefit from that sale for themselves.[21]

Another solid clue of the temple's implication in transactions is the presence amongst the contractors or witnesses of the Ebabbar's gods themselves. For example, in the text CT 6, 40c we can read that the god Šamaš himself gave some silver to someone called Kišušu to redeem a war prisoner. In another text, TCL 1, 68/69, he received in his house a former slave. He is not alone but helped by his *paredra*, Aya. There are many examples of such a situation because it is usual to find in a text the mention of a god or a goddess acting as a lender or a buyer.[22] Moreover, we find many mentions of gods or goddesses as witnesses in contracts.[23] So the god was an economic actor in ancient Near East, and his temple, his house, was an economic household. The differences between the households of a king, a god, a rich notable or a commoner were not structural: it was only a distinction based upon width and wealth, not an ontological one. A god and its clergy could act as rationally, or

21 Charpin 1982 and more recently Richardson 2010, 21–24.

22 Cf. Harris 1960; Charpin 2010; 2015.

23 E.g., MHET 2/2, 283; YOS 12, 451; Di 1966; 1848; CT 33, 41. This short list is not exhaustive at all.

irrationally, as any landowner: that is why we shall now examine how the members of the household of Šamaš behaved in the socioeconomic field.

2. A rational behavior?

2.1 Rational real estate strategy

We saw that Šamaš often hired large number of workers. That point reveals that the household of the Sungod, the temple Ebabbar, was a very important one, and as such the Sungod was a major landowner. We can also see it through the massive quantities of harvested barley recorded in the administrative documentation.[24] We can assume that the temple owned a great amount of arable land, even if we have only a few textual recordings of "temple-fields".[25] This is due to the specific circumstances of excavations in Sippar.[26] Nevertheless, we know that Sippar notables and the owners of important estates were buying preferentially in some specific irrigated districts, and we shall now try to understand if this behavior was based on a will to maximize their agricultural production.

It is impossible to know whether the temple dependents worked some fields through the tenure system and owned other fields personally. On the other hand, we are certain that the *nadītum*-nuns had their own fields since bringing a girl into the cloister was a heritage conservation strategy.[27] So when we see private fields and temple fields in close areas (as in the text YOS 13, 12), we can suppose that the temple's fields certainly adjoined those of its dependents (if they were private fields) and those of the *nadītum*-nuns. They also had to be next to the fields of the great families of Sippar since the fields of the *nadītum*-nuns were those of their families, and these families were the families of the notables of Sippar.[28]

Another example is found in BDHP 15 where the witnesses are no less than the gods Šamaš and Aya: in this one, a nun rents a field, and the neighboring lands are that of a priest and another field owned by the same nun. Another example is YOS 13, 12 (Ad 15) where many fields are listed and are very often the property of nuns or temple dependents (such as an "*ērib bītim*" or a great lamenter). We can therefore see that the fields owned by temple dependents could be grouped together in close areas.[29]

---

24 Harris 1975, 209–219.

25 We can notably quote CT 2, 50; 8, 30c; MHET 2/4, 549; Rositani RSO 82 Sup. 1, 116.

26 Indeed, the temple archives for the Old Babylonian period are yet undiscovered.

27 Démare-Lafont 2016, 241–256.

28 De Graef 2018.

29 "1,1.0.1 GÁN 6 SAR A.ŠÀ A.GÀR šu-ut-⸢ša⸣-(d)a-a /ša ša-lu-rum ša É (d)UTU" (ll. 34–35)

The notables of Sippar strived to regroup their possessions despite the difficulties this presented in view of the collapse of the cadaster. Indeed, the tenures were relatively scattered: Katrien de Graef speaks smartly of a "kaleidoscope" of properties to describe the tenures of the soldiers in Sippar-amnanum.[30] This mentality may be encountered elsewhere in Mesopotamia, among the merchants of Larsa, for example.[31]

By studying the texts recording the Ebabbar's agricultural activities, we realize that the irrigated districts where the temple had fields for certain were always the same ones, notably those named Tenunam, Tawir (a) tum, "the edges of the Sippar canal", Itiqtum, Gizanum, the district of Gula, Mu'ate, Tuhamum, and Šut-ša-Aya. The temple is not always clearly identified as the owner of the field, even if it sometimes is, but a study based upon prosopography or sigillography allows us to state that in those districts, temple dependents were acting not for themselves, but for the temple.

Indeed, specific witnesses lists or metrological features included in certain texts clearly show that the temple was harvesting those fields for its own benefit through its dependents. Moreover, epigraphic documentation from Sippar shows that those districts' fields were often bought by notables. Indeed, we find buyers such as the chief of merchants, *nadītum*-nuns, daughters of Sippar officials, high ranking administrative officials, or Ebabbar's priests.[32] This real estate buying policy is quite rational: the Ebabbar primarily bought fields in productive and prestigious districts, near the private fields of social partners to ensure they would help with harvesting. By doing so, the temple's social network was upholding its might and socioeconomic rank. We therefore see that the Ebabbar was not only trying to maximize its agricultural production but also to strengthen its social importance.

2.2 Rational trading strategy

Ebabbar's dependents and clergy were also always trying to obtain barley and silver. Yet, they were also lending or selling it on credit.[33] These two commodities were the

30 De Graef 2018. See also about those tenure fields de Jong Ellis 1977, 61–66 and Fiette 2018, 107–167.

31 Charpin 2003, 311–322.

32 Cf. Harris 1975, 378 (about Tenunam) or, more recently, Stol 1998 and de Graef 2007 (both about the district of Halhalla).

33 E.g., Richardson 2010, 22. The texts mentioned by Richardson show that the temple wanted silver in exchange for its wool. AbB 12, 173 reveals that the temple expected that some taxes be paid in silver. We can also mention the many texts where the Sungod (in

most traded ones in Central Mesopotamia and, as such, had high fiduciary value as fungible assets. These two goods could be traded against other commodities and were particularly sought after. A large part of the power held by Ebabbar came from its easy access to both those commodities. First, as the landowner of multiple fertile fields, it had access to barley. Secondly, as the recipient of important offerings, contributions (like the *igisûm*-contribution), and taxes, the Ebabbar had access to silver.[34] The wool sold by the Ebabbar was almost always bought in exchange for silver and the temple loaned silver or barley, with interest paid in silver.[35] Many loans to be repaid "with the interest of Šamaš" (probably around 20 %[36]) are recorded in our corpus. It seems that the Ebabbar pursued, as an economic organism, a policy to gain access to this precious metal.

A quick glance at the Mesopotamian economy reveals the obvious preoccupation of some people for profit. For example, Klaas R. Veenhof clearly demonstrated that Assyrian traders were seeking profit: trade was a source of income, and they would make investment decisions depending on potential revenue they could derive from it. The Ebabbar temple was also participating in business ventures, and its wealth as much as its preponderant role among the social networks of Sippar made the temple an important actor. As early as the end of the 19th century, the French Assyriologist Jules Oppert called Šamaš a "merchant god".[37] Oppenheim and other Assyriologists of the 1940s took up this idea and explained the temple's commercial power by the fact that it had large land holdings.[38] As these estates produced surpluses, they were subject to resale. The producers, within the temple, were remunerated either by a system of rations or, in rarer cases for specialized craftsmen, directly by remuneration. The temple also had slaves. Thanks to this unexpensive workforce and following the law of surplus value on capital, the temples grew in size and economic weight over time. Was it then a rational actor? It is known, nowadays, that trade and rationality are not always correlated and there is no evidence in cuneiform documentation that the trading business of the Ebabbar was purely rational. If the traders buying wool from the Ebabbar had obvious profit-seeking motives (as their letters show), for the Ebabbar that search for profit is not that clear.

---

fact, the temple) lend silver to people and demands a repayment in silver, for example, in VS 9, 83; VS 29, 183/184 or TCL 1, 113 (about a trade expedition).

34 AbB 12, 173; Di 1954; YOS 13, 374.

35 Charpin 1982; Richardson 2010.

36 Skaist 1994; Pecha 2018, 164–165.

37 Oppert 1897, 469–488.

38 Oppenheim 1944, 54–63.

On the other hand, the Ebabbar kept involved for a long time in a successful business, notably the trading of the temple's wool.[39]

2.3 Rational book-keeping methods

The Babylonian accounting documents found related to Sippar's Ebabbar are not always rational from today's point of view. Indeed, when we look at it closely, we realize that its main objective was to list the available supplies, much like an inventory, rather than making a prospective calculation. As explained by Michael Kozuh and John P. Nielsen, the Mesopotamian book-keeping practices were "a patchwork of overlapping interests, areas of responsibility, practicalities, and largely unpredictable abstractions of economic and administrative activity".[40]

Nevertheless, the predictive purpose of Babylonian accounting has been quite clearly demonstrated.[41] Kozuh has clearly explained this fact concerning the temples of the late-Babylonian period.[42] Concerning the Old-Babylonian period, Grégory Chambon was able to show – by studying the archives of Ilu-kan in the town of Mari in northern Mesopotamia – that they sometimes could have a provisional goal, even if it remained quite rare.[43] The fact that this practice is not general reveals one thing: the fundamental purpose of the Ebabbar's accounting efforts was to assess the potential wealth of this organism, and not to find a way to increase it. The economic ideal for ancient Babylonian temples was hoarding and redistribution.

To explain that point, we need here to discuss two documents from Sippar's warehouse. In the first one (CT 8, 21b), we can read that "X liters of barley have been withdrawn from the Y liters that are piled up in the warehouse to lend it to PN1". In the second one (CT 8, 10c) we learn that "Z liters of barley have been withdrawn from the Y liters that are available up in the warehouse to lend it to PN2." Those two texts concern the same warehouse: the only difference is that the first (CT 8, 21b) text has been written the eleventh day of the twelfth month on the year Aṣ 05 and the second text (CT 8, 10c) has been written the twelfth day of the same month on the same year. The warehouse had not been provided with grain between those two withdrawals and yet, the "Y" quantity does not change after the first withdrawal. Was it because Mesopotamians could not record precisely incomes and expenses? A quick glance throughout the massive administrative documentation shows that they were. So, if they keep recording that there are "Y" liters of barley

39 Charpin 1982.

40 Kozuh / Nielsen 2021, 154–155.

41 For the Old-Babylonian period, see notably Chambon 2011; 2018.

42 Kozuh 2014.

43 Chambon 2018.

available it is because in their mind, lent barley will be recovered and is therefore a potentially available liability. It could seem irrational to a modern accountant not to distinguish by any administrative scripture between *materially* and *virtually* available assets. Yet, immaterial is not irrational. On the contrary, it reveals a powerful capacity for abstraction – although quite different from our own.[44]

The Sipparian temple was mainly trying to reach two goals in the conduct of its business: hoarding and ostentation. And one of the better ways to show off its wealth was to redistribute it. On account of that, we can state that the temple was a rational actor, but not the kind of rationality expected from a *homo oeconomius* or a *deus oeconomicus*.

2.4 A banking temple?

For a tenant of classical theory, this economic behavior could swiftly call banking institutions to mind. The quintessential money handlers, bankers, and their institutions, are supposed to be seeking profit and maximization by analyzing situations rationally and making rational choices. Indeed, making the right choices and following the best advice is a major concern of ancient Babylonians. As Piccin showed in an article about the Mesopotamian "wisdom literature", planning, monitoring, and making the best choices were crucial aspects of the Babylonian economy.[45] Yet, still according to Michela Piccin, the best advice came from the gods.[46] They had to be heard from the divine world and could not come from the human mind.

That is one of the many reasons why gods and goddesses (and their sanctuaries) were often considered by ancient Babylonians as major actors of their socioeconomic processes. That might also explain a distortion in our vision of Mesopotamian

---

44 From that point of view, Mesopotamian non-monetary book-keeping can still be compared to Athenian accounting practices as described by S. Günther: "from a perspective of financial planning and budgetary accounting that the extant accounts are not sufficient to let every Athenian participate in the details of the budget since in- and outgoing assets, open account obligations etc. remain usually unclear. The inventories, usually without mentioning consumables, rather reflect a status quo but do not tell much about the income-expenditure-structure, investments, loans, or commitment authorizations. [...] Yet, this does not mean that they were published only for the sake of representation of the officials involved, the disclosure of correct record-keeping, the religious responsibility in case of accounts from sanctuaries, or the praxis of following examples of predecessors" (Günther 2021, 88–89). See also Davies 1994.

45 As she wrote: "wisdom language is also substantiated in terms of the semantic realm of careful planning and evaluating, with the ability to provide good advice occurring as a result." (Piccin 2021, 161)

46 Ibid., 162–163.

economy that led early scholars to consider the Ebabbar as a kind of ancient bank.[47] For example, in 1897, Jules Oppert wrote the following about the Ebabbar: "we can say, without being contradicted, that the house of high banking under the *firma* 'Sun God' is the oldest financial institution whose history has left us memory."[48] Later, the specialist of Sippar Rivkah Harris wrote in 1955 that "the temples alone had the resources needed to act as a bank, lending money and foodstuffs such as barley, peas and starch"[49] and reiterated it more precisely in 1960, in an article on temple loans where she states: "the prominence of Šamaš in the role of creditor, and therefore the prominence of his temple in this function is significant. It was the temple of Šamaš which, more than any other temple, served as a kind of bank."[50] However, Harris was a meticulous Assyriologist and her quote must be read precisely: she wrote "served as *a kind* of bank" (emphasis added). Indeed, we saw that the Ebabbar was capable of rational choices in its "investments" and the conduct of its business. We will, then, have to understand whether the temple of Šamaš, did – as modern banks do – seek profit, maximization, and growth.

The temple sought commodities such as silver and barley, but for what purpose? We need to understand why the Ebabbar was leading a policy of centralization/certification of silver ending with its redistribution. Was it a method of capturing flows with a view to stabilize the economy and redistribute the wealth within a non-centralized network-based system reticular system? Or was it on the contrary a return-on-investment policy aiming to enrich the temple and maximize its profits? Indeed, some scholars such as Morris Silver came to believe that palaces, temples, and other great organizations were seeking profit. He defended the idea that "palatial enterprise should not automatically be identified with public enterprise in which considerations of profitability are largely set aside. In fact, I have found no evidence, direct or indirect, demonstrating that Near Eastern palaces were not primarily motivated by profit in their production of textiles and other private goods."[51] It is this idea of profit-seeking and maximization that we must investigate now.

47 See, e.g., Bromberg 1942 (with bibliography).

48 "On peut dire, sans être contredit, que la maison de haute banque sous la *firma* 'Dieu-Soleil' est le plus antique établissement financier dont l'histoire nous ait laissé le souvenir" (Oppert 1897, 498).

49 Harris 1955, 38–39.

50 Harris 1960, 128.

51 Silver 2006, 11.

3. A profit-seeking behavior?

3.1 Profit-seeking in the Ancient Near East

Profit-seeking is a known phenomenon in Ancient Mesopotamia, as we explained earlier when we talked about the Assyrian traders during the Old Babylonian period.[52] That is why Mesopotamians had words to describe such preoccupations. One of the most well-known examples is the vocable *mahīrum* which has been widely discussed and means "market price". The study of this word has revealed that Old Assyrian traders negotiated the best prices (buying and selling) based on that *mahīru*-price. Their letters also reveal the important preoccupation of lowering the costs and expenses. Even their wives were involved in that business, and we see in their correspondence that they worried about the information spreading and their economic competition with other traders. Their strategies of commercial competition and cooperation have since been largely discussed and studied in other Assyriological papers.[53]

Another example, closer to Sippar, has been recently studied by Baptiste Fiette in his book about the archives of Šamaš-hazir. He explained how this Babylonian official exercising his charge in the southern Babylonian city of Larsa was trying to increase his personal wealth, notably through a real estate buying strategy.[54] His wife Zinu helped him and dealt ingeniously with business deals when her husband was away.[55] The list of examples could be much longer because rational behavior to maximize wealth can be observed in many acts of commoners, but Šamaš was not an ordinary economic actor.

The Ebabbar was, as we said, mainly the house of Šamaš, the Sungod. As such, he was also the god of justice who could see everything. He was then concerned with oaths, oracular consultations, and his temple could act as a justice court, even if the term (as we use it today) is anachronistic. Indeed, there were no justice courts such as ours in Mesopotamia, but meeting-places for magistrates, and the most important of these places in Sippar was the Ebabbar temple.[56] Moreover, Šamaš was the god of kingship, and we can see him giving the insignia of power to the kings in many iconographic representations such as Hammurabi's laws stela. He was the one

52 They are also well known because of what Polanyi took from the study of their texts (Polanyi 1944), notably his hypothesis of the absence of market in ancient Mesopotamia, a theory that has been since abandoned but has been widely commented. Cf. Veenhof 1972, followed by Veenhof 1997 and 2013.

53 E.g., *Michel* 2015, 7–78; Michel 2020; Eidem 2008, 31–42 (all three with bibliography).

54 Fiette 2018, 239–315.

55 Ibid., 317–319.

56 Charpin 2017, 69–76.

commanding rulers to be fair, gentle, and to protect the weak, entrusting the king to do the same thing and to be a human equivalent of himself.[57]

Moreover, the Ebabbar temple was meant to redistribute wealth in the well-known redistributive scheme appliable to *oikos*-economies. For the Old-Babylonian period, this idea has been widely developed by Marten Stol[58] and Dominique Charpin[59], notably from a philological point of view. On the other hand, Johannes Renger[60] has built a more theoretical approach. Their work now allows us to better understand the similarities in the functioning and general organization of what has come to be called "large organizations" or "great domains" held by gods, kings, and a few wealthy men.

That idea partly echoes the following statement by Renger: "What happened to the silver in circulation and not hoarded? It mostly served trade purposes, i.e., the acquisition of strategic goods and prestige objects. But there was practically no capital investment for productive purposes"[61]. From this can easily follow a demonstration of the fundamentally redistributive structure of the Mesopotamian economy: one did not buy to invest, within a large organization, but rather for reasons of prestige and social status. However, Silver, one of the main critics of Polanyian theory, rejected this point: according to him, the purchase of real estate and arable land is an investment. He writes:

> A basic problem with Renger's vision of the Mesopotamian economy is its uncritical nature. He takes redistribution by Mesopotamian institutions as a given. That is, Renger never analyses the questions of origin. How did a relative handful of individuals manage to acquire control over so much productive wealth? Who redistributed this wealth to the redistributors? Did the wealth originate in a "primitive accumulation" along the lines imagined by Marx and later implemented by Stalin? Was there a forced collectivization campaign? Command economies are not noted for the

57 Indeed, many papers had already been dedicated to Hammurabi as "king of justice" and his relationship with the Sungod as judge-god (see the good bibliography and historiography in Charpin 2013).

58 Notably in Stol 1982, 127–230; 2004.

59 See, e.g., Charpin 1985, 111–126, but also Charpin 2017 and 2020.

60 Renger 1994.

61 Renger 2005, 55–56. This issue of the hoarding of silver is a constant preoccupation of modern scholars, notably due to the fact that the weighing and hoarding of that precious metal is connected to the birth of coinage (e.g., Van Driel 2002; Thompson 2003; Gitin / Golani 2004; Pecha 2006; Garfinkle 2008; Peyronel 2010; Földi 2014; Jursa 2018). For a more complete bibliography and summary of that issue, cf. Heymans 2021, 55–113.

> creation of great societies [...] Indeed, even Lenin had to rely on markets to save his socialist experiment. Did the (alleged) redistributional economies of the fourth and third millennia rise on the ruins of earlier market behavior? Did the market economies of the earlier second millennium rise on the ruins of the redistributional (better regulatory) economy? [...] Similarly, Renger does not explain the rise of "tributary forms of economy" beginning in the second millennium. To develop a new vision of the Mesopotamian economy the economic forces driving such transformations need to be documented and understood. A final problem is that Renger does not attempt to integrate the (alleged) technological stagnation of Mesopotamia into his theory of a redistribution-dominated economy.[62]

The idea of Silver is that the Babylonian economic system focused on increasing its technological and financial level to endlessly maximize its profit. But was it so?

We know on the contrary that Mesopotamian economy was widely conservative and focused on hoarding. It can notably be observed in Ancient Mesopotamian sapiential literature with the *Debate between Silver and Copper*.[63] This text belongs to a literary genre appreciated by Mesopotamians, where virtues, animals, minerals, or anything else are arguing and boasting about their value and importance. In that specific debate, copper is proud about his importance in Mesopotamian craft and daily life, presenting itself as the main metal in term of utility. Nevertheless, silver does not intend to be so easily beaten and claims his supremacy based upon his importance for hoarding as a safety value and his role in the measuring process. It says:

62 Silver 2007, 107–108.

63 We read indeed in this sapiential text: "'Silver, you are forgotten in the soil inside the house. A scared mouse in a silent house. Silver, the palace is not your station! An obscure place, a grave, such is your station. Silver, banquets are not your assigned task – fasting is your assigned task. Silver, to make lead shine (?) is not an important achievement. The task of making divine statues is not likely to fall within your capabilities. Why do you keep attacking me like a dog? You snake, get back in the darkest part of the house and lie down in your grave!' Strong Copper cast his legitimate insults against Silver, and was full of hate against him – insults of a miserable dog, like water from a brackish well. He exerted his powers against him to harass him. And at this, Silver felt thoroughly harassed; it did not befit his dignity" (*Debate between Silver and Copper*, Segment D, 38–51, translation from the Electronic Text Corpus of Sumerian Literature, URL: https://etcsl.orinst.ox.ac.uk/section5/tr536.htm, last accessed: 01.05.2023). On hoarding in ancient Greece and Rome, cf. the paper by Leese in this volume.

> wedges are not written by you. The wooden shovels pile up the sheaves – match your measuring devices to the measuring stick![64] Just approach the cargo boat that [...] the canal banks, just keep knocking on the great door of the house at night! The stonecutter wrestles with stones and with beads – they are too hard and he has to stop because of you. Work away with your tines at the dirt by the oven instead.[65]

Thus, there is nothing surprising in the appetence of Ebabbar for hoarding. Renger explains that even if precious metals were mostly hoarded, the silver in circulation "served trade purposes, i.e., the acquisition of strategic goods and prestige objects. But there was practically no capital investment for productive purposes."[66] Yet, we can assume that this hoarding tendency was also due to Mesopotamians' limited access to information, which most likely impended confidence in the future – especially as optimism was not the dominant feature of the Mesopotamian mentality. There was little incentive to invest or spend but rather to hoard.

The limits of knowledge were also those of rational choices, a statement that might drive us to speak of limited rationality in the Mesopotamian economy. This recalls the model upheld by Herbert Simon and Daniel Kahneman of the bounded rationality. This model can be defined as "subjective, relative, procedural, limited and intuitive":[67] it could be a good definition of the Mesopotamian economic rationality. Nevertheless, if this definition can fit in an etic approach, we could also adopt an emic perspective and try to understand the role of the Ebabbar in the Babylonian economy from the Mesopotamian point of view.

3.2. Charity above profit: debts to bind together men and gods

The Ebabbar, for example, benefitted from an impressive position of economic domination because it was the main socioeconomic organization in the Sippar region. As such, it held important estates and capital and mostly chose not to increase it by loaning with high interests or adopting profit-maximizing strategies but rather to redistribute its wealth.

First, it is known that during the 1st millennium BCE the temple of Šamaš in Sippar cared for widows, orphans, and the poor.[68] For example, there are traces of

---

64 About this instrument and its use, cf. Wilcke 1983 and Chambon 2011, 169–170.

65 *Debate between Silver and Copper*, Segment D, 52–59 (translation from the Electronic Text Corpus of Sumerian Literature, URL: https://etcsl.orinst.ox.ac.uk/section5/tr536.htm, last accessed: 01.05.2023). See also Mittermayer 2019.

66 Renger 2005, 55–56.

67 Tran 2018, 54.

68 In the Late-Babylonian period, this fact is well attested. See, e.g., Van Driel 1998.

women welcomed into the temple to weave, and Louise Quillien has clearly shown that in later periods, it was common for the temple to welcome widows and, in exchange, for them to produce textile goods.[69] In the Old-Babylonian period, we see that most of the temple weavers were probably single women because they are never attached to a man's name, brother, father, or husband and are supplied with rations in the manner of temple dependents or beneficiaries of its charity. All this allows us to conclude that from Old to Neo-Babylonian period, the Ebabbar intended to help widows.

A large part of its socioeconomic role was indeed to help the poor. We know, for example, that the temple redeemed prisoners[70], welcomed war refugees who fled after the fall of southern Mesopotamian cities, notably refugees from Larsa.[71] The refugees in Sippar also benefitted from Šamaš's judgment in the Ebabbar. We have an example at the very beginning of the reign of Abi-ešuh in the trial BM 16764 studied by Michael Jursa where the chief of the merchants and the "judges of Larsa" release a *nadītum*-nun from a paternal debt.[72] The temple therefore regularly spent grain or silver to help the needy.

Another striking example are the so-called "charitable-loans". Indeed, in many recorded loans for which the god Šamaš is the creditor, the debt has to be repaid "*ina šalmu û balṭu*" which means "when he will be safe and in good health." Klaas R. Veenhof has demonstrated that those loans did not have a time-limit clause, which is a clear clue of their charitable aspect. Indeed, all the Old-Babylonian loans have usually a time-limit. It is often the "day of the harvesting" because Babylonian economy mainly relied on the agricultural calendar, which is quite a common pattern in ancient civilizations.[73]

Moreover, in some of them we can read sentences like "do not charge him interest",[74] which show that those loans were, in fact, gifts from the temple to the

69 Quillien 2018. Ouyang 2022 also proposed that temples of the Ur III period (2112–2004 BCE) gave shelter to the orphans.

70 We see it in CT 6, 40c, and the practice is further documented in the Code of Hammurabi. This process has also been studied in Charpin 2014.

71 This is notably demonstrated by the analysis of prosopography in van Koppen 1999, 77–78.

72 Jursa 1997.

73 Skaist 1994. About the "consumption" loan, see the recent Wilcke 2018. On ancient Greek, early modern European, and Chinese loan practices, cf. the paper by Schefold in this volume.

74 E.g., in the text TCL 1, 188 we can read (ll. 1–3) "10 GÍN KÙ.BABBAR / *hu-bu-ta-tum* / *ṣí-ib-ta ú-la i-šu*." That we could translate by "10 shekels of silver *without interests*, there must be no interest-rate took upon him."

needy. Moreover, usury was frowned upon in Babylonian wisdom as shown in sapiential texts such as the "great hymn to Šamaš"[75] or the "Dialogue of Pessimism"[76]. Yet, the charitable aspect of those loans had sometimes been discussed by some excellent scholars.[77] Nevertheless, the main opinion among Assyriologists, which we are inclined to follow, is to consider that the best explanation for the lack of a repayment-date in those loans is still Veenhof's.[78]

3.3. *A debt-based economy*

Thus, a large part of the socioeconomic activity of the Ebabbar was, in the end, to spread its wealth around. Is that behavior, are those choices, rational? If the purpose of the Ebabbar was to maximize its hoard, and reach a high level of return on investment, the temple would act as a modern bank or corporation. From that point of view, it would not be a rational choice to loan silver or barley to people who would not be able to repay it. Yet, even in modern economies, redistribution can be a rational choice. We will not delve into the issue here as it would be off-topic, but the case of the rationality of the welfare state has been subject to many studies.[79] Thus, we can consider that the Ebabbar was acting rationally while trying to stabilize the socioeconomic structure of ancient Sippar. Yet, we can also consider that this rationality was also obeying a religious and traditional motive: let the god Šamaš play his role of ward of the social balance and cosmic harmony.

75 Foster 2005, 631–633.

76 Ibid. 923–926.

77 Van de Mieroop 1992 criticized this theory. Yet, Antoine Jacquet challenged his reluctance: "For Van de Mieroop (BBVO 12, p. 94–95 and p. 206) the humanitarian/charitable dimension of gods' loans in Ur isn't clearly evident and he upholds the idea that loans were necessarily profitable for creditors, real persons as gods. Nevertheless, we cannot argue, with the text UET 5, 160 as only clue, that loan made by Šamaš or Nanna in Ur had no humanitarian/charitable purpose: indeed, in that text (www.archibab.fr/T13007), which is the basis of Van de Mieroop's argumentation, Nanna-zimu sells his house to Ṣilli-Addu in order to repay, with the sale's profit, a debt he owed to the temple of Nanna in the specific frame of the sale on credit of temple's wool, [...]. Nanna-zimu is not here the debtor but an intermediate trader ordered to sell the wool from the temple of Nanna and then to pay the temple with the sale's profit (this process is explained in D. Charpin, "Marchands du palais et marchands du temple à la fin de la I° dynastie de Babylone", JA 270, 1982, p. 25–65." (Jacquet 2020, 395, n. 177).

78 And this case is not unique (cf. Charpin 2005).

79 E.g., Mares 2009; Garland 2014 (for a synthesis, notably bibliographical); Petrakis / Kafka / Kostis / Valsamis 2021.

Here we come back to the distinction established by Aglietta and Orléan between vertical and horizontal debts. We saw that the Ebabbar could try to maximize its wealth through credit and created horizontal debts by doing so. Yet, the charitable loans and the offering system of the Ebabbar are typical non-profit and religious-based vertical debts. Indeed, the Šamaš temple aimed to structure the horizontal and vertical debt-network of the whole Sipparian society and to articulate them in a social system of which the temple was the nerve center. In Mesopotamia, everyone was in debt, directly or indirectly: humans owed an existential debt to the gods. Broadly speaking, it was all about debt, which is why we could refer to the Mesopotamian economy not as an *oikos*-economy but as a "debt-economy". However, these debts could be cancelled (in part) when they became too heavy through a royal edict of *mīšarum*.[80] Yet, the purpose of the Mesopotamian kings who issued an edict to cancel debts was not one of emancipatory justice. It was not a question, by removing outstanding debts, of making *tabula rasa* in order to build a new ideal future: it was quite the opposite. The purpose of an edict of *mīšarum* was to restore a "prior state". It was not done to prepare the future, but to return to an idealized past.[81] However, this ability to manage virtual sums, debts, as well as their cancellation or maintenance (because some debts were not affected by the edicts of *mīšarum*), shows a strong capacity for financial abstraction.[82] This capacity was not used to maximize profits, but to secure the social organization.

4. Conclusion

We saw that there were many situations where the temple was not motivated by profit and maximization. Most of the time, the temple acted to preserve the established order, perceived as fair, in an ideal of fixity and stability. One could take a cynical approach by saying that in this system the Ebabbar had great power and had interest in upholding it, but that might be slightly anachronistic. The Mesopotamian ideal was an ideal of stability and the role of the temples in fulfilling this ideal was imposed on them by the palace and by the religious representations of the believers. Then the purpose of most of their socioeconomic behaviors was not to obtain freedom for everyone but to ensure order and security for all.

From this point of view, even debt and its management might seem irrational from a modern point of view since many debts were not intended to be repaid but

80 On the *mīšarum*, see notably Bottéro 1961; Charpin 1990; Van De Mieroop 2002; Tanret 2012; Charpin 2000 (with previous bibliography); Fiette 2013.

81 Cf. Fiette 2013.

82 Charpin 1990; 2000. Cf. the paper on the ancient Israelite jubilee legislation by Højgaard in this volume.

only to exist. As they were vertical debts, their main purpose was to connect people with gods. For horizontal debts, the edicts of *mīšarum* cancelled only debts relating to emergency loans. The deep debt-network that was binding the various inhabitants of Sippar together was therefore not altered.

Yet should we say that the Ebabbar's clergy and the god Šamaš were irrational actors? On the contrary: they were very rational. We saw that the Ebabbar settled appropriate means to reach a specific and anticipated purpose, so, qualifying that behavior as rational is possible depending on the definition we chose for rationality. If we adopt an emic point of view, the man relying on the gods to secure social justice is rational. From the etic point of view, he is a fool. Nevertheless, we also saw that the "house of the Sungod" was really protecting this man needing help. Then, was he so irrational to rely on the god when the temples were effectively helping him? Moreover, if we adopt the neo-classical point of view about what is a rational behavior, based on the idea of maximization of the capital rather than satisfaction of the needs, then the charitable aspect of the socioeconomic behavior of the Ebabbar and Šamaš makes them look like fools.[83]

Indeed, the way the Ebabbar drove its business was not by focusing on maximizing its wealth, but rather on satisfying its needs. In a way, we find here a logic which recalls the definition of "bounded rationality" established by Simon and Kahneman. We cannot speak of "perfect rationality" concerning ancient actors, especially when it comes to religious businesses. We cannot talk of "perfect information" in the business conduct either[84] for evident reasons: religious matters are based on faith and, as such, on uncertainty and lack of information – driving us back to the unfinished story of Blaise Pascal's bet. The Ebabbar's behavior as a socioeconomic organization aimed to secure a social model relying upon an ideal of fixity where rational actors did not aim to get *more*, but to get *enough*. That rationality seems very different from ours, but not inferior.

---

83 Or, as George Tridimas summed it up recently, from another point of view: "From a consumer economics perspective, religion confers utility to individuals in the form of worship, explanations of the origin of things, comfort against suffering, dispensation of sins and promise of salvation. From an institutional analysis perspective, religion is a fundamental determinant of social interactions and economic performance. By sanctioning some values and banning others it affects individual ethics and social norms shaping actions and outcomes." (Tridimas 2021, 1).

84 That we could speak of "perfect rationality" and consider as acceptable the neo-classical theory about rationality for the modern world is not the concern of this article. Yet, for the ancient Mesopotamian economy, this concept is irrelevant.

Bibliography

Aglietta, Michel / Orléan, André (2002): La monnaie: entre violence et confiance, Paris.

Barberon, Lucille (2009): Les documents d'archives des religieuses en Babylonie ancienne. Usage, transmission et conservation, in: Topoi. Orient-Occident. Supplément 10, 273–288.

Bottéro, Jean (1961): Désordre économique et annulation des dettes en Mésopotamie à l'époque paléo-babylonienne, in: Journal of Journal of the Economic and Social History of the Orient 4, 113–164.

Bongenaar, Arminius (1997): The Neo-Babylonian Ebabbar Temple at Sippar: Its Administration and its Prosopography, Leiden (Publications de l'Institut historique et archéologique néerlandais de Stamboul 80).

Bromberg, Benjamin (1942): The Origin of Banking: Religious Finance in Babylonia, in: The Journal of the Economic History 2/1, 77–88.

Bulgarelli, Odoardo (2011): Financial and Economic Activity in Mesopotamia, in: Barjamovic, Gojko / Dahl, Jacob L. / Westenholtz, Joan G. / Koch, Ulla S. / Sommerfeld, Walter (eds.), Akkade is King: A Collection of Papers by Friends and Colleagues Presented to Aage Westenholz on the Occasion of his 70th Birthday, 15th of May 2009, Leiden (Publications de l'Institut historique et archéologique néerlandais de Stamboul 118), 37–53.

Burggraaff, Wim (1995): Belijatum: An Agricultural Entrepreneur in the Old Babylonian Period, in: Aula Orientalis 13, 161–167.

Chambon, Grégory (2011): BBVO 21. Normes et pratiques – L'homme, la mesure et l'écriture en Mésopotamie. Vol. I: Les mesures de capacité et de poids en Syrie Ancienne, d'Ébla à Émar, Gladbeck.

Chambon, Grégory (2018): Florilegium marianum XV. Les archives d'Ilu-kân: gestion et comptabilité du grain dans le palais de Mari, Paris (Mémoires de Notes Assyriologiques Brèves et Utilitaires 19).

Charpin, Dominique (1982): Marchands du palais et marchands du temple à la fin de la I° dynastie de Babylone, in: Journal Asiatique 270, 25–65.

Charpin, Dominique (1985): Le rôle économique du palais en Babylonie sous Hammurabi et ses successeurs, in: Lévy, Edmond (ed.), Le système palatial en Orient, en Grèce et à Rome, Leiden, 111–126.

Charpin, Dominique (1990): Les édits de "restauration" des rois babyloniens et leur application, in: Cahiers du Centre Glotz 1, 13–24.

Charpin, Dominique (1992): Le point sur les deux Sippar, in: Notes Assyriologiques Brèves et Utilitaires 1992, 84–85.

Charpin, Dominique (2000): Les prêteurs et le palais: les édits de *mīšarum* des rois de Babylone et leurs traces dans les archives privées, in: Bongenaar, Arminius C. V. M. (ed.), Interdependency of Institutions and Private Entrepreneurs, Leiden (MOS Studies 2 / Publications de l'Institut historique et archéologique néerlandais de Stamboul 87), 185–211.

Charpin, Dominique (2003): La politique immobilière des marchands de Larsa à la lumière des découvertes épigraphiques de 1987 et 1989, in: Huot, Jean-Louis (ed.), Larsa, travaux de 1987 et 1989 (Bibliothèque Archéologique et Historique 165), 311–322.

Charpin, Dominique (2004): Histoire politique du Proche-Orient amorrite (2002–1595), in: Orbis Biblicus et Orientalis 160/4, 25–480.

Charpin, Dominique (2005): Les dieux prêteurs dans le Proche-Orient amorrite (ca. 2000–1600 av. J.-C.), in: Topoi, Orient-Occident 12/13, 13–34.

Charpin, Dominique (2005b): Chroniques bibliographiques 5. Economie et société à Sippar et en Babylonie du Nord à l'époque, paléo-babylonienne, in: Revue d'Assyriologie et d'archéologie orientale 99, 133–176.

Charpin, Dominique (2010): Zur Funktion mesopotamischer Tempel, in: Wiener Offene Orientalistik 6, 103–122.

Charpin, Dominique (2013): "I Am the Sun of Babylon": Solar Aspects of Royal Power in Old Babylonian Mesopotamia, in: Hill, Jane / Jones, Philip / Morales, Antonio (eds.), Experiencing Power, Generating Authority: Cosmos, Politics, and the Ideology of Kingship in Ancient Egypt and Mesopotamia, Philadelphia, 65–96.

Charpin, Dominique (2014): Le prix de rachat des prisonniers de guerre d'après les archives paléo-babyloniennes, in: Csabai, Zoltán (ed.), Studies in Economic and Social History of the Ancient Near East in Memory of Péter Vargyas, Budapest (Ancient Near Eastern and Mediterranean Studies 2), 33–70.

Charpin, Dominique (2017): La vie méconnue des temples mésopotamiens, Paris.

Charpin, Dominique / Béranger, Marine / Fiette, Baptiste / Jacquet, Antoine (eds.) (2020): Archibab 4. Nouvelles recherches sur les archives d'Ur d'époque paléo-babylonienne, Paris (Mémoires de Notes Assyriologiques Brèves et Utilitaires 22).

Davies, John (1994): Accounts and Accountability in Classical Athens, in: Osborne, Robin / Hornblower, Simon (eds.), Ritual, Finance, Politics. Athenian Democratic Accounts Presented to David Lewis, Oxford, 201–212.

Démare-Lafont, Sophie (1997): Codification et subsidiarité dans les droits du Proche-Orient ancien, in: Lévy, Edmond (ed.), La codification des lois dans l'Antiquité, codification et subsidiarité, actes du colloque de Strasbourg, Strasbourg, 49–64.

Démare-Lafont, Sophie (2016): Vocations religieuses et stratégies successorales dans la Babylonie de Hammurabi, in: Bouineau, Jacques (ed.), Hommage à Marie-Luce Pavia. L'homme méditerranéen face à son destin, textes réunis par Burt Kasparian, Paris, 241–256.

Démare-Lafont, Sophie (2019): Debt in Ancient Mediterranean Societies (A Documentary Approach Legal Documents in Ancient Societies VII, Paris, August 27–29, 2015), Geneva (Hautes Études orientales 56).

De Boer, Rients (2013): Measuring Barley with Šamaš in Old Sippar, in: Akkadica 134/2, 103–116.

De Boer, Rients (2021): The Ikūn-pîša Letter Archive from Tell ed-Dêr, Louvain / Paris / Bristol (Publications de l'Institut historique et archéologique néerlandais de Stamboul 131).

De Graef, Katrien (2007): By the Rivers Dark: Halhalla, City of Soldiers and Priestesses, or: How Cuneiform Documents can Contribute to the Study and Reconstruction of Past Landscapes, in: Ooghe, Bart (ed.), Broadening Horizons: Multidisciplinary Approaches to Landscape Study, Newcastle upon Tyne, 184–204.

De Graef, Katrien (2016). «Cherchez La Femme!». The Economic Role of Women in Old Babylonian Sippar, in: Lion, Brigitte / Michel, Cécile (eds.), Role of Women in Work and Society in the Ancient Near East, Berlin / Boston, 270–295.

De Graef, Katrien (2018): "Kîma napišti māti eqlum ma ul tîdê?" Field Work in Old Babylonian Sippar, in: Garcia-Ventura, Agnès (ed.), What's in a Name? Terminology Related to the Work Force and Job Categories in the Ancient Near East, Münster (Alter Orient und Altes Testament 440), 189–241.

De Graef, Katrien (2018b): Puppets on a String? On Female Agency in Old Babylonian Economy, in: Svärd, Saana / Garcia-Ventura, Agnès (eds.), Studying Gender in the Ancient Near East, Philadelphia, 133–156.

De Graef, Katrien (2019): In Taberna Quando Sumus. On Taverns, Nadītum Women, and the Gagûm in Old Babylonian Sippar, in: Budin, Stephanie L. / Cifarelli, Megan / Garcia-Ventura, Agnes / Millet Albà, Adelina (eds.), Gender and Methodology in the Ancient Near East. Approaches from Assyriology and Beyond, Barcelona (Barcino Monographica Orientalia 10), 77–115.

De Jong Ellis, Maria (1977): Land of Dead rêdû's, in: De Jong Ellis, Maria (ed.), Essays on the Ancient Near East in Memory of Jacob J. Finkelstein, Hamden (Memoirs of the Connecticut Academy of Arts and Sciences 19), 61–66.

Eidem, Jasper (2008): Old Assyrian Trade in Northern Syria. The Evidence from Tell Leilan, Leiden (Publications de l'Institut historique et archéologique néerlandais de Stamboul 111), 31–42.

Fiette, Baptiste (2013): "Retour au sein maternel": une expression nouvelle pour les édits de restauration des rois amorrites, in: Notes Assyriologiques Brèves et Utilitaires 2013, 127–128.

Fiette, Baptiste (2018): Archibab 3. Le palais, la terre et les hommes: la gestion du domaine royal de Larsa d'après les archives de Šamaš-Hazir, Paris.

Finley, Moses (1973): The Ancient Economy, Berkeley.

Földi, Zsombor (2014): On Old Babylonian Palastgeschäft in Larsa. The Meaning of sūtum and the 'Circulation' of Silver in State/Private Business, in: Csabai, Zoltán (ed.), Studies in Economic and Social History of the Ancient Near East in Memory of Péter Vargyas, Budapest (Ancient Near Eastern and Mediterranean Studies 2), 79–117.

Foster, Benjamin (2005): Before the Muses: An Anthology of Akkadian Literature, Rockville.

Friedman, Milton (1970): A Theoretical Framework for Monetary Analysis, in: Journal of Political Economy 78/2, 193–238.

Garfinkle, Steven (2008): Silver and Gold: Merchants and the Economy of the Ur III State, in: Michalowski, Piotr (ed.), On Ur III Times: Studies in Honor of Marcel Sigrist, Boston, 63–70.

Garland, David (2014): The Welfare State: A Fundamental Dimension of Modern Government, in: European Journal of Sociology 55/3, 327–364.

Gates, Donald K. / Steane, Peter (2007): Historical Origins and Development of Economic Rationalism, in: Journal of Management History 13/4, 330–358.

Gitin, Seymour / Golani, Amir (2004): A Silver-based Monetary Economy in the Seventh Century BCE: A Response to Raz Kletter, in: Levant 36, 203–205.

Günther, Sven (2021): Trick and Treat? New Approaches to Forms and Narratives of Ancient Account Lists, in: Günther, Sven / Horowitz, Wayne / Widell, Magnus (eds.), Of Rabid Dogs, Hunchbacked Oxen, and Infertile Goats in Ancient Babylonia: Studies Presented to Wu Yuhong on the Occasion of his 70th Birthday, Changchun (Supplements to the Journal of Ancient Civilizations 7), 83–95.

Harris, Rivkah (1955): The Archive of the Sin Temple in Khafajah (Tutub), in: Journal of Cuneiform Studies 9, 91–120.

Harris, Rivkah (1960): Old Babylonian Temple Loans, in: Journal of Cuneiform Studies 14, 126–137.

Harris, Rivkah (1975): Ancient Sippar: A Demographic Study of an Old-Babylonian City (1894–1595 B.C.), Leiden (Publications de l'Institut historique et archéologique néerlandais de Stamboul 36).

Heymans, Elon D. (2021): The Origins of Money in the Iron Age Mediterranean World, Cambridge.

Jacquet, Antoine (2020): Contrats de prêts et créances dans les archives d'Ur d'époque paléo-babyloniennes, in: Charpin, Dominique et al. (eds.), Archibab 4, Nouvelles recherches sur les archives d'Ur d'époque paléo-babylonienne (Mémoires de Notes Assyriologiques Brèves et Utilitaires 22), Paris, 345–398.

Jursa, Michael (1997): "Als König Abi-ešuh gerechte Ordnung hergestellt hat": Eine bemerkenswerte altbabylonische Prozessurkunde, in: Revue d'Assyriologie et d'archéologie orientale 91, 135–145.

Jursa, Michael (2018): Money, Silver and Trust in Mesopotamia, in: Van der Spek, Robartus J. / Van Leuuwen, Bas (eds.), Money, Currency and Crisis, London, 111–112.

Kozuh, Michael (2014): The Sacrificial Economy. Assessors, Contractors, and Thieves in the Management of Sacrificial Sheep at the Eanna Temple of Uruk (ca. 625–520 B.C.), Winona Lake (Explorations in Ancient Near Eastern Civilizations 2).

Kozuh, Michael / Nielsen, John P. (2021): "Check the writing boards from the time of Nebuchadnezzar": An Inventory of Administrative Writing Boards in the Spurlock Museum of World Cultures, in: Revue d'Assyriologie et d'archéologie orientale 115, 143–158.

Lafont, Bertrand / Tenu, Aline /Joannès, Francis / Clancier, Philippe (2017): La Mésopotamie. De Gilgamesh à Artaban 3300–120 av. J.-C., Paris.

Lion, Brigitte (2001): Riches dames cloîtrées, in: Lunes 17, 67–75.

Mares, Isabella (2009): The Comparative Political Economy of the Welfare State, in: Lichbach, Mark I. / Zuckerman, Alan S. (eds.), Comparative Politics: Rationality, Culture, and Structure, Cambridge, 358–375.

Michel, Cécile (2015): Production and Trade in the Old Assyrian Period. in: Rivista di Storia Economica 1, 57–78.

Michel, Cécile (2020): Women of Assur and Kanesh: Texts from the Archives of Assyrian Merchants, Atlanta.

Miller, H. Laurence Jr. (1962): On the Chicago School of Economics, in: The Journal of Political Economy 70/1, 64–69.

Mittermayer, Catherine (2019): Was sprach der eine zum anderen? Argumentationsformen in den sumerischen Rangstreitgesprächen, Berlin / Boston (Untersuchungen zur Assyriologie und vorderasiatischen Archäologie 15).

Mynářová, Jana / Alivernini, Sergio (eds.) (2020): Economic Complexity in the Ancient Near East: Management of Resources and Taxation (Third–Second Millenium BC), Praha.

Moreno García, Juan Carlos (2016): Economies in Transition: Trade, "Money", Labour, and Nomads at the Turn of the 1st Millennium BC, in: Moreno García, Juan

Carlos (ed.), Dynamics of Production in the Ancient Near East, 1300–500 BC, Oxford, 1–39.

Muth, John F. (1961): Rational Expectations and the Theory of Price Movements, in: Hoover, Kevin D. (ed.), The New Classical Macroeconomics. Vol. 1, Camberley Surrey, 3–23.

Neumann, Hans (2006): Schuld und Sühne. Zu den religiös-weltanschaulichen Grundlagen und Implikationen altmesopotamischer Gesetzgebung und Rechtsprechung, in: Hengstl, Joachim / Sick, Ulrich (eds.), Recht gestern und heute. Festschrift zum 85. Geburtstag von Richard Haase, Wiesbaden (Philippika 13), 27–43.

Oppert, Jules (1897): Un dieu commerçant, in: Comptes-rendus des séances de l'Académie des Inscriptions et Belles-Lettres 41/5, 469–488.

Oppenheim, Léo (1944): The Mesopotamian Temple, in: The Biblical Archaeologist 7/3, 54–63.

Ouyang, Xiaoli (2022): Foundlings Raised in the Temple? The Meaning of dumu kar-ra in Ur III Umma, in: Dabir 9, 21–34.

Pecha, Lukáš (2006): Silver as Means of Payment in the Old Babylonian Period, in: Charvat, Petr / Lafont, Bertrand / Mynářová, Jana / Pecha, Lukáš (eds.), L'État, le pouvoir, les prestations et leurs formes en Mésopotamie ancienne. Actes du Colloque assyriologique franco-tchèque. Paris, 7–8 novembre 2002, Praha, 109–119.

Pecha, Lukáš (2006): The Material and Ideological Base of the Old Babylonian State: History, Economy, and Politics, Lanham.

Petrakis, Panagiotis / Kafka, Kyriaki / Kostis, Pantelis / Valsamis, Dionysis (2021): Greek Culture after the Financial Crisis and the Covid-19 Crisis, New York.

Peyronel, Luca (2014): Between Archaic Market and Gift Exchange: The Role of Silver in the Embedded Economies of the Ancient Near East During the Bronze Age, in: Carlà, Filippo / Gori, Maja (eds.), Gift Giving and the Embedded Economy in the Ancient World, Heidelberg, 355–356.

Piccin, Michela (2021): Vocabulary of Wisdom in *Ludlul bēl nēmeqi* and Babylonian Theodicy, in: Günther, Sven / Horowitz, Wayne / Widell, Magnus (eds.), Of Rabid Dogs, Hunchbacked Oxen, and Infertile Goats in Ancient Babylonia: Studies Presented to Wu Yuhong on the Occasion of his 70th Birthday, Changchun (Supplements to the Journal of Ancient Civilizations 7), 147–179.

Polanyi, Karl (1944): The Great Transformation, New York.

Quillien, Louise (2018): La prise en charge des veuves par le temple de Sippar par le temple de Sippar sous le règne de Darius Ier: étude du texte Dar. 43 (BM 60099), in: ARTA 2018.001, URL: https://journals.openedition.org/abstractaira nica/49991, last accessed: 01.05.2023.

Rassam, Hormuzd (1897): Asshur and the Land of Nimrod: Being an Account of the Discoveries Made in the Ancient Ruins of Nineveh, Asshur, Sepharvaim, Calah, etc. 2 vols., Cincinnati.

Renger, Johannes (1994): On Economic Structures in Ancient Mesopotamia, in: Orientalia N.S. 63, 157–208.

Renger, Johannes (2005): Archaic versus Market Economy, in: Topoi Orient-Occident 12–13/1, 207–214.

Richardson, Seth (2010): The Late Old Babylonion Period Texts, Boston (The Journal of Cuneiform Studies Supplemental Series 2).

Scheil, Victor (1895): Sippar-Sépharwaim, in: Revue biblique 4/2, 203–206.

Silver, Morris (1983): Karl Polanyi and Markets in the Ancient Near East: The Challenge of the Evidence, in: The Journal of Economic History 43/4, 795–829.

Silver, Morris (2006): Public, Palace, and Profit in the Ancient Near-East, in: Akkadica 127, 5–12.

Silver, Morris (2007): Redistribution and Markets in the Economy of Ancient Mesopotamia: Updating Polanyi, in: Antiguo Oriente 5, 89–112.

Skaist, Aaron (1994): The Old Babylonian Loan Contract. Its History and Geography, Ramat-Gan.

Stol, Marten (1982): State and Private Business in the Land of Larsa, in: Journal of Cuneiform Studies 34, 127–230.

Stol, Marten (2004): Wirtschaft und Gesellschaft in altbabylonischer Zeit, in: Charpin, Dominique / Edzard, Dietz Otto / Stol, Marten (eds.), Mesopotamien. Die altbabylonische Zeit, Fribourg / Göttingen (Orbis Biblicus et Orientalis 160/4), 641–975.

Tanret, Michel (2010): The Seal of the sanga. On the Old Babylonian sangas of Šamaš of Sippar-Jaḫrūrum and Sippar-Amnānum, Leiden (Cuneiform Monographs 40).

Tanret, Michel (2012): Of Wills and Bills... On Inherited Debts in the Ur-Utu Archive, in: Boiy, Tom et al. (eds.), The Ancient Near East, A Life! Festschrift Karel Van Lerberghe, Leuven / Paris / Walpole (Orientalia Lovaniensia Analecta 220), 585–598.

Teraji, Shinji (2018): Perspectives in Behavioral Economics and the Economics of Behavior. The Cognitive Basis of Institutions, Amsterdam.

Thompson, Charles, M. (2003): Sealed Silver in Iron Age Cisjordan and the "Invention" of Coinage, in: Oxford Journal of Archaeology 22, 67–96.

Tran, Laurène (2018): Herbert Simon et la rationalité limitée, in: Regards croisés sur l'économie 22, 54–57.

Tridimas, George (2021): Religion without Doctrine or Clergy: The Case of Ancient Greece, in: Journal of Institutional Economics, 1–15.

Tyborowski, Witold (2003): Šêp-Sin, a Private Businessman of the Old Babylonian Larsa, in: Die Welt des Orients 33, 68–88.

Van de Mieroop, Marc (2005): Cuneiform Texts and the Writing of History, London / New York.

Van Driel, Govert (1998): Care of the Elderly: The Neo-Babylonian Period, in: Stol, Marten / Vleeming, Sven P. (eds.), The Care of the Elderly in the Ancient Near East, Leiden / Boston / Köln (Studies in the History and Culture of the Ancient Near East 14), 161–197.

Van Driel, Govert (2002): Elusive Silver – In Search of a Role for a Market in an Agrarian Environment, Leiden (Publications de l'Institut historique et archéologique néerlandais de Stamboul 95).

Van Koppen, Franz (1999): Abum-waqar Overseer of the Merchants at Sippar, in: Notes Assyriologies Brèves et Utilitaires 1999, 77–78.

Veenhof, Klaas R. (1972): Aspects of Old Assyrian Trade and its Terminology, Leiden.

Veenhof, Klaas R. (1997): "Modern" Features in Old Assyrian Trade, in: Journal of the Economic and Social History of the Orient 40/4, 336–366.

Veenhof, Klaas R. (2013): The Archives of Old Assyrian Traders: Their Nature, Functions and Use, in: Faraguna, Michele (ed.), Archives and Archival Documents in Ancient Societies:, Trieste (Legal Documents in Ancient Societies IV), 27–71.

Verbrugghe, Gerald P. / Wickersham, John M. (1996): Berossos and Manetho, Introduced and Translated. Native Traditions in Ancient Mesopotamia and Egypt, Ann Arbor.

Warburton, David (2021): Šamšî-Adad as a Great King, in: Günther, Sven / Horowitz, Wayne / Widell, Magnus (eds.), Of Rabid Dogs, Hunchbacked Oxen, and Infertile Goats in Ancient Babylonia: Studies Presented to Wu Yuhong on the Occasion of his 70th Birthday, Changchun (Supplements to the Journal of Ancient Civilizations 7), 213–262.

Weber, Max (1905): The Protestant Ethic and the Spirit of Capitalism, London.

Wilcke, Claus (1983): Nachlese zu A. Poebels Babylonian Legal and Business Documents from the Time of the First Dynasty of Babylon Chiefly from Nippur (BE 6/2) Teil 1, in: Zeitschrift für Assyriologie und Vorderasiatische Archäologie 73/1, 48–66.

Wilcke, Claus (2018): *ḫubullum*, *ṣibtum* und *melqētum*. Zu Bezeichnungen konsumptiver Kredite in den altbabylonischen Edikten, in: Mollenbeck, Christin / Kleber, Kristin / Neumann, Georg / Paulus, Susanne (eds.), Grenzüberschreitungen.

Studien zur Kulturgeschichte des Alten Orients: Festschrift für Hans Neumann zum 65. Geburtstag am 9. Mai 2018, Münster (dubsar 5), 781–789.

Zawadzki, Stefan (2013): Neo-Babylonian Documents from Sippar Pertaining to the Cult, Poznán.

Zawadzki, Stefan (2014): "If you have a heep you have all you need". Sheep Husbandry and Wool in the Economy of the Neo-Babylonian Ebabbar Temple at Sippar, in: Bréniquet, Catherine / Michel, Cécile (eds.), Wool Economy in the Ancient Near East and the Aegean: from the Beginnings of Sheep Husbandry to Institutional Textile Industry, Oxford, 428–452.

Rational Actors and the Ancient Israelite Jubilee Legislation

Christian Canu Højgaard

Abstract: The Jubilee legislation of the Hebrew Bible has often been considered irrational and utopian. It prescribes general debt cancellation and manumission of bond slaves every fiftieth year. It is hard to align this economic practice with rational behavior as assumed in rational choice theory. The question to be pursued, then, is whether the ancients – and the Jubilee legislation in particular – can be considered rational. The paper argues with others that rationality is a social construct, and that it therefore needs to be examined with respect to its own historical, social, and literary setting. In particular, it is demonstrated how social network analysis and rhetorical criticism can be employed to scrutinize the rationality of ancient legislations.

Keywords: Rational Choice Theory – The Jubilee – Leviticus 25 – Social Network Analysis – Rhetorical Criticism

1. Introduction

Rational choice theory states that individuals when facing the choice between two or more options will choose the one that is most beneficial to them.[1] The theory has become axiomatic in modern economics, and even supposedly irrational behavior has been shown to be rational when other factors are considered.[2] But what about historical economics? Does rational choice theory have explanatory power when the object of inquiry is not modern households or consumers but ancient? The ancients had, in fact, economic practices that might seem odd in the eyes of the

---

1 More technically, it is assumed that consumers have "transitive preferences" (Regenwetter / Dana / Davis-Stober 2011). That is, if a consumer at any given time prefers some good (A) to some other good (B), and B is preferred to yet another good (C), it must be the case that A is preferred to C. By implication, we would find it irrational if C was preferred to A.

2 For example, it might be considered irrational if, all things held equal, demand of a good grows if its price increases because consumers would normally be expected to be less willing to buy the good at an increased price. However, the phenomenon is readily observed among collectors of stamps or coins who value the collectible not for their practical use, but for the rarity or uniqueness indicated by the price. This phenomenon is known as the "snob effect" (Ulen 1994, 490).

modern. One of those practices was a general debt cancellation which took place in the ancient Near East. Babylonian kings are known to have established *mīšarum,* "justice", which involved the absolution of debt, freeing of debt slaves, and return of land property sold as debt.[3] Ironically, in ancient Greece, such practice was apparently seen as unjust, because it made the property of citizens vanish.[4] It seems, then, that the ancients themselves did not share the same sense of rationality. Nevertheless, Babylonian kings had in fact political and economic incentive to establish *mīšarum* because "widespread enslavement or landlessness as a result of indebtedness could well lead to internal disruption and uprisings in the kingdom".[5]

General debt cancellation is also documented in the Hebrew Bible. At the impending attack of Nebuchadnezzar II on Jerusalem (587 BCE), the last king of Judah, Zedekiah, proclaimed *dᵊrôr*, "liberty", for all Hebrew slaves (Jer 34:8–10). Another release was proclaimed by the governor Nehemiah in Persian Yehud (Neh 5).[6] Apart from these occasional redemption events, the Hebrew Bible contains a curious legislation that prescribes a general debt release every fiftieth year, known as the Jubilee after the Hebrew word *yôvēl.*[7] According to the Jubilee legislation, all agricultural land and houses on agricultural land along with all Israelite bond servants were to be released every fiftieth year. It is difficult to imagine such practice given that there would be little economic incentive for people to lend money as the Jubilee approached due to cancellation of debt. If the ancients were driven by self-interested utility maximation, the Jubilee might very well be sympathetic but downright counterproductive. It is therefore not surprising that modern commentators have

3 Cf. the paper of Nicolas in this volume, in particular pp. 78–79.

4 Cf. Blok / Krul 2017, 638. Nevertheless, probably during his archonship in 594/3 BCE Solon of Athens imported the Near Eastern practice of general debt cancellation under the name of *seisachtheia* (Blok / Krul 2017). It became a one-time event, and debt cancellation seems to have been prohibited by law at some point after Solon.

5 Westbrook 1991, 47. Moreover, "By ordaining 'justice' for the land, particularly at the opening of his reign, a king demonstrated his quality as a ruler according to law (*šar mīšarim*)" (ibid.).

6 General debt cancellation is also attested in Ezek 46:17 and Isa 61.

7 The precise meaning of *yôvēl* is disputed. Some have claimed that the word is the nominal form of the root *ybl* which is etymologically related to *yābāl*, "stream" (Isa 30:25), *yᵊbûl*, "produce (of the earth)" (Lev 26:4), and perhaps even *tēbēl*, "earth" (1 Sam 2:8) (cf. Milgrom 2001, 2169). In the Hebrew Bible outside Lev 25, *yôvēl* always means "horn", probably a horn of a ram (Exod 19:13; Josh 6:4, 5, 6, 13). It is likely, then, that the Jubilee received its name because it was inaugurated by the blowing of horns, perhaps made of ram (Lev 25:9).

commonly considered the Jubilee as utopian or "some romantic manifesto".[8] It is the purpose of this paper to examine whether the Jubilee legislation is indeed a utopian manifest or whether it presupposes or fosters a different sort of rationality.

The paper is organized in three parts. Firstly, the Jubilee legislation and its place in current scholarship will be briefly introduced. Secondly, the economic aspects of the Jubilee will be outlined. Thirdly, the body of the paper discusses the rationality of the Jubilee legislation. Following the call of Mark Granovetter for considering the social dimensions of rationality, I shall examine different aspects of embeddedness, most importantly the social embeddedness of the actors portrayed in the Jubilee legislation but also the ideological and rhetorical framework embedding the text as a whole. In short, therefore, I shall present a method for scrutinizing rationality in ancient texts by combining social network analysis and rhetorical analysis.

2. The Jubilee legislation

The Jubilee legislation is preserved in the book of Leviticus, the third book of the Torah. As such, the Jubilee legislation is part of a whole collection of laws regarding cult and society. The Torah is composed of narratives as well as several collections of laws known as "codes", e.g., the Covenant Code (Exod 20:22–23:33), the Deuteronomic Code (Deut 12–26), and the Holiness Code (Lev 17–26), the latter in which the Jubilee is contained.[9]

The Holiness Code is a series of divine speeches mediated by the prophet Moses to the people of Israel. The physical setting according to the narrative itself is the desert of Sinai where the people stayed one year after the liberation from Egyptian slavery. The Jubilee legislation is preceded by a law on the sabbatical year (Lev 25:1–

---

8 Hartley 1992, 445; cf. Wenham 1979, 318; Milgrom 2001, 2214.

9 The word "code" is ill-chosen because ancient Near Eastern laws were not codes in the modern sense of the word. A code is a fixed and exhaustive collection of laws to which judges must refer when they decide on concrete cases. Although the Bible frequently mentions or alludes to the Torah, there is no mention of judges explicitly referring to the law to decide a case. Like the other ancient Near Eastern law collections, the biblical laws should be considered "common law", according to which "Law gradually develops through the distillation and continual restatement of legal doctrine through the decisions of courts. When a judge decides a particular case, he or she is empowered to reconstruct the general thrust of the law in consultation with previous judicial formulations. Critically, the judicial decision itself does not create binding law; no particular formulation of the law is final. As a system of legal thought, the common law is consciously and inherently incomplete, fluid and vague" (Berman 2017, 109–110). Some biblical scholars therefore use the designation "Holiness legislation" instead of Holiness Code (e.g., Stackert 2009; Schwartz 1999). I use "Holiness Code" for convenience.

7). Just as the Israelites were to rest every seventh day (i.e., the sabbath), the land was to lie fallow every seventh year. Fashioned according to this sabbatical model, the Jubilee was to take place every seventh sabbatical year, that is, every fiftieth year. In this year, all rural property that had been sold since the last Jubilee should be returned to the original owners, and all bond servants were set free from their debt.

As noted, the Jubilee legislation is part of a series of speeches attributed to the deity YHWH and mediated by Moses. According to biblical chronology, these events would have taken place somewhere between 15–13th century BCE. Most scholars, however, do not accept the internal biblical chronological evidence and date the text much later. In general, the dating of the Hebrew Bible is a complex issue, since there are no archives of manuscripts or reliefs similar to those found in Egypt and Mesopotamia. The earliest evidence, apart from a few early inscriptions, are the Dead Sea scrolls which date to the 3rd century BCE to 1st century CE as well as the Old Greek translation of which the earliest fragments date to the 2nd century BCE.[10] Consequently, source- and redaction criticism have been the common tools to date the biblical texts. Today, the majority of scholars date the Jubilee legislation to one of the last compositional stages of the Torah, more specifically to the 5th century BCE, or later, when the Jews had returned from Babylonian exile to the Persian province Yehud.[11] Another group of scholars attribute the majority of the Holiness Code to the era of Israelite monarchy, around the 8th century BCE.[12] Finally, a pre-monarchic date of origin has been proposed, that is, 12–11th century BCE.[13] Several criteria are important for dating the legislation including 1) the dependence on other biblical or extra-biblical material; 2) linguistic dating; and 3) the social organization implied by the text. Here, I will only mention the social particularities of the legislation because they are also related to the economic questions to be addressed.

The addressees of the legal speeches are *bənê yiśrāʔēl*, "the sons of Israel", a designation for the Israelite men in charge of their respective households.[14] The household, or extended family (*bêt ʔav*, lit. "father's house"), formed the basic social unit

10 Tov 2001.

11 Otto 1994; Nihan 2007. Early historical-critical scholars argued that the Holiness Code once formed an early, independent law code that was only later incorporated into the priestly laws of Leviticus (Graf 1866; Wellhausen 1927; originally published 1883). For an extensive review of previous research on the Holiness Code, cf. Sun 1990, 1–43; Tucker 2017, 10–28.

12 Kaufmann 1960; Joosten 1996; Milgrom 2003; Knohl 2007.

13 Schaeffer 1922; Hartley 1992; Bergsma 2007.

14 Joosten 1996, 31.

of the society. The composition of the *bêt ʾav* is not entirely clear, but "most likely it comprised all the living descendants of a single living ancestor ... with their families, servants, and so forth."[15] Each household was allocated a portion of land to be the permanent inheritance of the household. In fact, if the property was sold due to debt, the main purpose of the Jubilee was to return the inherited portion of land to the original owners (cf. below). The household was part of a *mišpāḥāʰ*, "kin group", whose primary function was arguably economic. It is from this social entity that an indebted Israelite might be redeemed according to the Jubilee legislation (e.g., Lev 25:48–49). The kin group also had military obligations and has therefore been described as "a protective association of extended families".[16] Within the society presumed by the Holiness Code, the highest level of social organization is the *ʿēdāh*, "congregation", which is concerned with cultic, agricultural, social, juridical, and political affairs.[17] Any mention of a king or central leader, apart from Moses, is absent, and there is no hint that the land should be under foreign dominance. There is a priestly class, but their domain is restricted to the cultic domain, and their main obligation is to handle the sacrifices of the people. The most complex social group in the Holiness Code is the resident foreigners, the so-called *gērîm*, "so-journers". This group is sometimes depicted as poor outsiders, but in the Jubilee legislation it is presented as wealthy inhabitants (Lev 25:47). The mixed picture of the resident foreigners has sometimes been taken as evidence of the compositional growth of the corpus.[18] In sum, the society pictured in the Holiness Code is a loosely organized society composed of mixed ethnic groups with no central administration. The most likely historical context for this legislation, then, is either the pre-monarchic or post-monarchic era. The legislation could be an attempt to address a new socio-economic situation after the return of the Jews from their Babylonian exile. Christophe Nihan, who argues for a post-exilic origin, concedes, however, that "It is very unlikely that the scribes who composed and transmitted the Holiness legislation, alongside the rest of the Torah, were ever in a position to effectively implement that

---

15 Wright 1990, 53.

16 Gottwald 1979, 301–305.

17 Joosten 1996, 39.

18 Bultmann 1992. Early critics claimed that the notion of *gēr* (translated here as "sojourner") underwent a transformation from a poor, landless Israelite in Deuteronomy to a proselyte in the Priestly literature, including the Holiness Code (Bertholet 1896). Today, it is more common to consider the *gēr* a designation of a social group consisting of resident foreigners that were most often poor but could acquire substantial wealth (Milgrom 2001, 2036).

legislation during the Persian period."[19] In pre-monarchic times one would not expect the mention of a king or a central administration. And biblical accounts in the books of Joshua and Judges describe tensions and conflicts between different ethnic groups settled in the land prior to the monarchy. To conclude, then, in light of the social structures implied by the legislation, a pre-monarchic date is preferable.

3. Jubilee economics

The Jubilee occurred only once every fiftieth year. Meanwhile, the Jubilee legislation prescribed other means of assisting indebted fellow countrymen. It appears that the major aim of the law was to assure each Israelite household a permanent plot of land despite of debt and poverty. It is less clear what motivated a legislation of this kind. Before turning to a general discussion of the purpose and rationality of the law, however, we need first summarize the concrete means listed in the legislation by which impoverished farmers could obtain credit and be released from debt. It has been shown that the legislation describes three successive stages of poverty, each with its own means of relieving the poor.[20] In all three stages, the Jubilee was only the final resort for the impoverished farmer.

Stage 1: A poverty-stricken man sells a part of his ancestral property (vv. 25–28)

The first stage envisions an indebted farmer who needs to acquire credit, possibly in the event of crop failure. To acquire credit, the farmer sells a part of his ancestral property to a fellow Israelite.[21] A next-of-kin may redeem the property so that the property remains within the clan. The property likely remains with the redeemer until the Jubilee in which the original owner may take possession of it.[22] If there is no kinsman, or he refuses to intervene, the original owner may – but probably not likely – acquire sufficient means on his own to redeem his property. If he fails to do so, the property has to be released in the Jubilee.

The main principle for obtaining credit and amortizing debt is stated in Lev 25:14–17: "When you make a sale to your neighbor or buy from your neighbor, you shall not cheat one another. When you buy from your neighbor, you shall pay only for the number of years since the Jubilee; the seller shall charge you only for the remaining crop years. If the years are more, you shall increase the price, and if the years are fewer, you shall diminish the price; for it is a certain number of harvests

19 Nihan 2011, 132.

20 Chirichigno 1993; Milgrom 2001; Nihan 2007.

21 Similar practice existed in other premodern societies, cf. the paper of Schefold in this volume.

22 Milgrom 2001, 2195.

that are being sold to you. You shall not cheat one another, but you shall fear your God; for I am the LORD your God."[23] In other words, the value of rural property is calculated in terms of crops, and the value depends on the time remaining until the next Jubilee. According to the law, the calculation is based on "the number of years *since* the Jubilee" – not *after* – but the reason may simply be that it was easier to remember the number of years elapsed since the last Jubilee than to keep track of the remaining years until the next Jubilee.[24] In any case, both buyer and seller are urged not to cheat one another.

Stage 2: The poverty-stricken man forfeits the remainder of his land (vv. 35–38)

If the property sold in stage 1 was not redeemed, and the poverty-stricken man found himself in need of an additional loan, he could take out a new loan by forfeiting the remainder of his land. Yet, he remains on his property, now as a tenant farmer working for the creditor. The usufruct of the land is still his, and it amortizes his loan. The creditor is not allowed to lend money for interests. At the end of the loan, the same amount of money or victuals are to be repaid. In fact, even if the value of the victuals had dropped by the end of the loan, the creditor may not demand its monetary value. To account for increasing prices, however, it may have been customary to demand the repay in kind (e.g., grain) rather than monetary value.[25]

Stage 3: The poverty-stricken man enters the household of the creditor (vv. 39–55)

In case the farmer cannot repay his debt as a tenant farmer (stage 2) and can no longer support himself and his family, he and his family enter the household of the creditor. In this case, the poverty-stricken man forfeits both his property and its usufruct, and he now lives as a *śākîr kĕtôšāb*, "resident laborer". He is not to be considered a slave but receives wages to pay off his debt. However, the law also envisions a situation where the poor farmer enters the household of a non-Israelite creditor. In this case, the poor fellow risks being forced into slavery, and the Israelite addressees of the law are urged to see to it that the non-Israelite does not treat him harshly (v. 53).[26]

---

23 If not indicated otherwise, all Bible quotations are taken from the New Revised Standard Version.

24 Milgrom 2001, 2178.

25 Ibid., 2211.

26 In addition, the addressees are twice commanded to ensure that native Israelites do not oppress their debtors (vv. 43 and 46).

In sum, the legislation makes a great effort to protect the wellbeing of indebted Israelite farmers. The Israelites are repeatedly exhorted not to take advantage of impoverished fellows, nor to treat them as slaves, certainly not as chattel slaves. The question remains what motivated a law of this sort other than, perhaps, compassion. Firstly, there is surely a religious motivation given the sanctity of the land in the Holiness Code and the covenantal connection between God, people, and land.[27] Outside the Holiness Code, it is prescribed how each household should be allocated a particular and permanent plot of land within the territory of their respective tribe (Num 26:52–56). The allocation of land is the realization of the land promises to the patriarchs: Abraham, Isaac, and Jacob (Gen 17:8; 26:3; 28:13). Within this theological outlook, the Jubilee is fundamentally meant to assure the possession of land for every single household among Jacob's descendants.

Secondly, in terms of economics, the Jubilee provided a "safety valve" for poor Israelites so "The effect of one person's economic collapse [would] be limited, roughly, to the next generation only".[28] The so-called safety valve, however, was not motivated by an egalitarian view on economics.[29] The Jubilee only applied to rural property, and estates in walled cities were not subject to redemption, so wealthy inhabitants could amass property in the cities (Lev 25:29–30).[30] Rather, the general debt release of the Jubilee was intended to attain economic efficiency by spreading out the wealth among the Israelites.[31] By prohibiting the permanent amassment of

27 Joosten 2010; Meyer 2015. The covenant is a major theme in the Torah (McCarthy 1978; Walton 1994). The concept of biblical covenants is apparently borrowed from the suzerain treaties of the ancient Near East. Within the biblical covenants, YHWH is portrayed as a suzerain lord and Israel as his vassal. However, not only Israel but each individual Israelite (or at least the patriarch of each household) is presented as a vassal of YHWH (Gane 2017, 46). The land constitutes the third party in the covenantal relationship between YHWH and Israel, because the land is ultimately YHWH's possession but is granted to Israel on the basis of the conditions stipulated by the law.

28 Wright 1990, 178.

29 Anderson 2005. According to Schaefer and Noell, "equality may be more a consequence than an aim of the laws; if equality had been their aim, the laws no doubt would have included provisions for the redistribution of flocks and income from foreign trade ventures, both of which were significant sources of wealth" (Schaefer / Noell 2005, 9–10).

30 The only exception is the city property of the Levites, one of the twelve tribes of Israel. The Levites were affiliated with the temple cult and were not allocated rural property apart from fields around selected cities. To assure the Levites permanent inheritance in the land, their original houses in particular cities were subject to the Jubilee redemption (Lev 25:32–34).

31 Rosenberg / Weiss 2010.

bond servants and agricultural property, the law aimed toward limiting the ability for individuals to monopolize the market. From an economic point of view, monopolies are undesirable, because they lead to decreased production of goods and increased prices due to little competition. Moreover, monopolists can reduce the wages because the workers have few other employment opportunities (known as monopsony). Thus, by limiting the ability to monopolize the market, the Jubilee legislation facilitates economic growth.[32] While Rosenberg and Weiss' account explains well the possible incentives of the legislator, it does not explain why wealthy citizens would lend money in the first place with the knowledge of an upcoming general debt release. As assumed in rational choice theory, if a voluntary exchange is to take place, it must be mutually beneficial, and there must be a cooperative surplus to be divided.[33] However, as the Jubilee approached, the cooperative surplus would decrease. If land were to be redeemed and bond servants released – and thereby the security for the creditor to regain his loan – creditors would be less likely to lend money. In fact, "loss of the means of security would lead to a drying-up of credit before the Jubilee or to conditions being inserted into contracts to make the debt fall due after the Jubilee year. If the law were really effective the size of loans available would decrease as the Jubilee approached and the value of security available accordingly shrank."[34]

In sum, while the Jubilee legislation would certainly be attractive for indebted farmers in need for restoration and for the legislator seeking economic efficiency, the effectiveness of the law rests on whether rational, wealthy farmers would be willing to lend money with little security. Thus, we are still faced with the question whether the Jubilee legislation was economically rational at all, or whether the legislation offered another sort of rationality diverting from a classical rational choice prediction. It is to this question that the remainder of this paper is dedicated.

4. Jubilee rationality

Much of classical and neoclassical economics consider rationality in terms of self-interested behavior largely independent of social relations. Rationality, however, is not so much about an innate human inclination to self-interest but rather interpersonal expectations of appropriate behavior.[35] Mark Granovetter has contended that what looks like irrational behavior may in fact be rational when situational

---

32 Cf. also Mason 1987.

33 Ulen 1994, 496.

34 Westbrook 1991, 51.

35 Manning 2012.

constraints are taken into consideration.[36] To clarify the rationality of the Jubilee legislation, we must therefore pay attention to the situational constraints of the text and the interpersonal interactions and expectations. More specifically, in what follows, I shall first present a social network analysis of the Jubilee legislation to determine the role and status of the poor Israelite farmer in the social community envisioned by the text. Secondly, I shall explore the rhetorical framework of the text to assess the text's own claims of rational behavior with respect to general debt cancellation.

5. The social characterization of the "brother"

It has been argued elsewhere that the actors or literary characters in the Holiness Code, including the Jubilee legislation, form a social network.[37] The interactions between the participants form ties, and the interactions thus constitute a network in which each participant is embedded. The social roles of the participants depend on their position in the network, and social network analysis can be applied to scrutinize these roles. Here, I shall only discuss the embeddedness and role of the poor farmer as a means to understand the rationality of the Jubilee legislation. The social network of the poor farmer (presented as "brother") is illustrated in Fig. 1 below.[38]

The brother is connected to three classes of participants: The Israelite community ("the Israelites" and "2MSg"), his family and clan ("brother's brother", "brother's uncle", and "clan"), and the sojourner who has settled down in the land of Israel. The sojourner is the same person as the "non-Israelite creditor" mentioned in stage 3 above. A social network analysis of the text has shown that the ties among the deity YHWH, the Israelite community, and the individually addressed Israelite ("2MSg") are much more frequent and stronger than the ties to the poor farmer. In fact, there is no recorded interaction between YHWH and the poor farmer although

36 Granovetter 1985. A recent migration study, for example, demonstrates the deficiency of a narrow, neoclassical approach to rationality. In classical utilitarian approaches, it is thought that "migration processes can be explained through the individual's weighing of the pros and cons of the proposed move", but it has been shown that "ethnic networks guarantee access to available job posts, especially recently-arrived immigrants" and "granting access to work is motivated/justified by solidarity, specifically ethnic solidarity" (Martes / Fazito 2010, 44).

37 Højgaard 2021.

38 The ties among the actors correspond to interactions realized as verbs in the Hebrew text. The network is created from a computational harvest of RDF-triplets with actor-event-undergoer information. In this graph, each tie may represent more than one interaction, each of which is directed from actor to undergoer, e.g., "You [actor] may not take interest in advance [event] from him [undergoer]" (Lev 25:36; my translation).

YHWH is the most central participant in the whole community and interacts recurrently with the Israelites. Thus, from a structural point of view, the poor farmer is outside the core of the community.

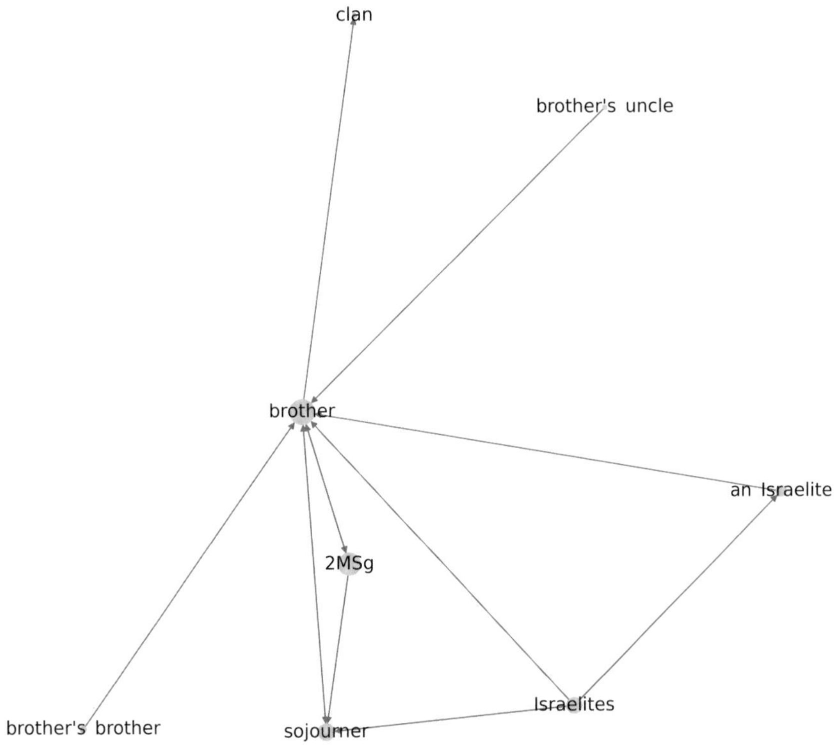

Fig. 1: The social network of the poor farmer (= "brother").

A closer look at the interactions themselves gives a clearer impression of the brother's position in the social network. The main challenge of doing so is the disparate nature of the interactions. Unlike regular social network analyses, where the network ties are most often binary (e.g., marriage, transaction, trust), the network analysis of the Jubilee legislation employs all sorts of interactions in order to glean as much information from the text as possible. Consequently, the interactions of the Jubilee network include both transactions, emotions, possessions, movements, and relationships. In order to analyze the interactions and their significance for the role of the "brother" in his social network, the interactions need to be quantifiable. That is, some method is needed to weigh, for example, a transaction over against an emotion. The solution is to conceptualize the interactions in terms of agency, that is, how much agency or effort is invested in a particular event.[39] In linguistics, agency

39 Højgaard 2021.

is related to motion, volition, sentiment, and causation.[40] Agency thus gives a clear measure of power because powerful agents are assumed to be able to intentionally instigate more active and causal events than weak participants. More particularly, agency can be conceptualized as a hierarchy ranging from -2 (passive or non-agentive) to 5 (very agentive).[41] Fig. 2 shows the mean agency scores of the "brother" in each of his relationships.[42]

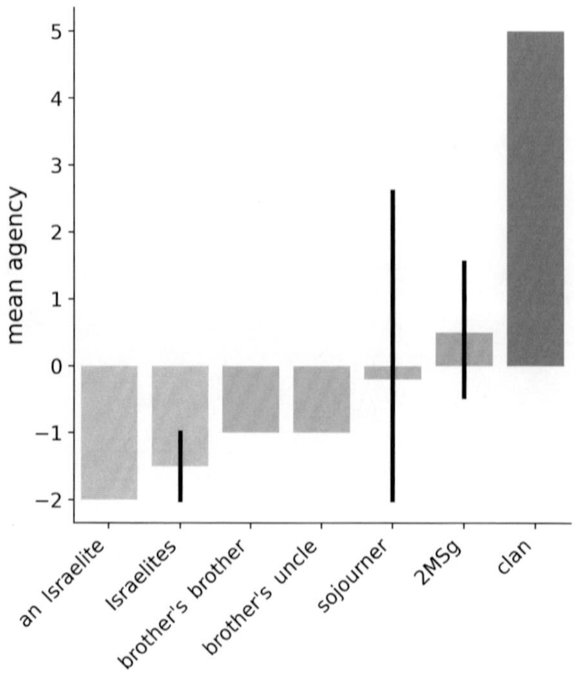

Fig. 2: Agency invested by the "brother" ranging from passive (-2) to very agentive (5). The graph includes confidence intervals (95 %).

40 E.g., Dowty 1991.

41 The agency range covers a hierarchy of semantic roles: Agent (value = 5), Force (4), Affected Agent (3), Instrument (2), Frustrative (1), Neutral (0), Volitional Undergoer (-1), and Patient (-2). Any interaction involves two participants, each of which being ascribed a semantic role from the hierarchy on the basis of a careful linguistic analysis of the interaction.

42 The mean agency score is computed by summing the agency scores ascribed to the "brother" in a particular relationship (e.g., with the "sojourner") and dividing by the number of interactions.

The poor farmer has only one very agentive interaction, namely, his interaction with the clan to which he returns after the Jubilee redemption (Lev 25:41). This agency score neatly illustrates the Jubilee as an act of empowerment because the poor farmer is empowered to return freely and independently to his clan. In the remaining relationships, the poor farmer invests only little agency. The Israelites are commanded not to oppress the brother (Lev 25:14), and the individually addressed Israelite or creditor ("2MSg") is urged to sustain the brother when he reaches out for help (Lev 25:35). He can buy his property but not in perpetuity (Lev 25:23). He may not lend him money for interests (Lev 25:36–37), neither may he treat him as a slave if the brother enters his household in case of increased debt (Lev 25:39). The poor farmer's family must be allowed to redeem him from his debt (Lev 25:49).

In sum, therefore, the poor farmer is pictured as a man who depends entirely upon the good will of his family, society, and even non-Israelite sojourners. In risk of losing his ancestral property, the farmer is at the fringe of society and in acute risk of sliding even further away. The main purpose of the Jubilee legislation is to constrain the agency of more well-being participants and direct their agency towards compassion for the poor farmer. It is curious, however, that the legislation does not employ legal sanctions to achieve this goal, and one wonders why the law expects rational actors to behave in this way. It should be noted at this point that it is a matter of dispute whether there is in fact a legal basis for the Jubilee legislation.[43] On the one hand, there is ample biblical evidence for local juridical procedures executed by the elders of the community at the town gate (e.g., Gen 23:18; Deut 17:5; 21:19; 25:7; Josh 20:4; Ruth 4:1). Obtainment of credit, repay of debt as well as the release of property and bond servants did not rely completely on independent agents' free will. On the other hand, the lack of concrete sanctions is striking when compared to other laws in the Torah (e.g., Exod 21–22; Deut 17). To answer the question of rationality, we must therefore consider another kind of embeddedness, namely the narrative and ideological embeddedness of the law and its rhetorical framework.

6. Jubilee rhetoric

Biblical scholars have noted a peculiarity of biblical law. Whereas Near Eastern laws primarily consist of impersonal case laws written in the grammatical 3rd person, the biblical laws abound with personal address. Within the narrative context of the Pentateuch, the laws are recorded as divine speeches mediated by Moses to the Israelite community. The personal address has a strong persuasive effect because it

43 Mason 1987.

establishes a direct link between speaker and hearers.[44] In effect, "Hearers and readers are likely to feel directly addressed and therefore obliged to respond."[45]

Another peculiarity is the presumably deliberate conflation of the divine legislator, YHWH, and his human mediator, Moses. While speaking on behalf of God, Moses not only refers to YHWH in the grammatical 3rd person but frequently employs 1st person references as if he was God himself.[46] In the Jubilee legislation, for example, Moses uses the words "I am YHWH your God" (Lev 25:38), the effect of which is the impression that YHWH speaks directly to the people. As a matter of fact, this utterance occurs most frequently in the Holiness Code of which the Jubilee legislation is part. The conflation of YHWH and Moses appears to be a rhetorical device that establishes an "encounter between the lawgiver and the law's addressees".[47]

Another rhetorical feature of the biblical laws is their embeddedness in a narrative. The Torah tells the story of Israel from the creation of the world to the impending entrance of the Israelites into the promised land. The laws, therefore, are not independent and fragmented but present themselves as the embodiment of the covenantal relationship between the people and their God. According to this story, the covenant was first established between YHWH and Abraham and was later reaffirmed after the exodus from Egyptian bondage. The covenant and the liberation constitute the theological underpinnings of the laws. The Jubilee legislation invokes this historical framework several times by confronting the addressees with YHWH's presence and participation in the law as well as reminding them of his liberating act from Egyptian bondage (Lev 25:38, 42, 55).

Finally, the Jubilee legislation employs a curious social characterization of the audience and their social world. The audience is literally called *bᵊnê yiśrāʾēl*, "the sons of Israel" (Lev 25:2), and *bêt yiśrāʾēl*, "the house of Israel" (Lev 17:3). That is, the people – albeit consisting of various tribes and clans – is portrayed as a family. According to this portrayal, their fellow countrymen are not only described as "fellows" or "fellow countrymen" but as *ʾaḥîm*, "brothers" (e.g., Lev 25:14). By doing so, the legislator instils a sense of immediacy and acuteness. The poor farmer is not only a man who happens to speak the same language or has distant family ties. Rather, he is portrayed as "your brother" who needs your help because you are family. The purpose of this characterization is to tighten the ties of the community because "People are reluctant to cheat those with whom they have formed a personal

44 Gane 2017, 84.

45 Watts 1999, 64.

46 Højgaard 2021, 61–65.

47 Bartor 2010, 25.

relationship."[48]

In sum, therefore, the Jubilee legislation is embedded in a distinctive literary context that appears to intentionally invoke a sense of direct encounter with YHWH. The foundation of this encounter is the historical redemption of Israel from Egyptian bondage known as the exodus, and the legislator employs this foundational story to enhance the rhetorical thrust of the law. It is my contention, therefore, that the Jubilee legislation compensates for legal sanctions by creating a strong sense of immediacy, belonging, and responsibility. The law-text constantly reminds the addressees of YHWH's presence and their moral obligations – not only towards their fellow countrymen but towards YHWH who is, after all, not that far away. Moreover, by alluding to the exodus, the legislation creates a sense of belonging and seeks to persuade the addressees towards the same compassion that YHWH showed for the people in the exodus. In other words, obedience is "elicited by appeal to the theological and moral sensibilities of the community".[49]

7. Conclusion

The Jubilee legislation with its prescription of a general debt cancellation every fiftieth year has most commonly been deemed utopian and irrational. As the Jubilee approached, actors driven by proclivity to self-interested utility maximation would be less likely to lend money because the debt would soon be cancelled. And without legal sanctions, they would not be likely to give up the property that functioned as their security to having the loans repaid.

However, since rationality is more appropriately considered in terms of interpersonal expectations and social constraints rather than some innate human quality, we cannot assume from the outset that the ancient Israelites were driven by self-interested utility maximation. In fact, the rhetorical thrust of the Jubilee legislation directs us to rethink ancient rationality. In this paper, I have shown that the poor Israelite farmer is depicted as a less-than powerful agent at the hands of more wealthy citizens. He is positioned at the margins of society and is in danger of even becoming dependent on non-Israelites. The overall thrust of the legislation, then, is to counter the increasing inequality and indebtedness, not by legal sanctions or enforcement, but by fostering a social sense of common history and identity. It seeks to direct the agency of powerful agents towards compassion for their poor fellow countrymen who are described not only as countrymen but as brothers. The portrayal of the fellows as brothers inculcates a sense of responsibility that must exceed simple financial interests. The sense of responsibility and solidarity is increased by

48 Ulen 1994, 495.

49 Fager 1993, 106.

the predominant use of direct address and Moses' speaking as if he was the divine legislator himself, thereby creating a strong sense of encounter between YHWH and the creditors. In effect, the creditor is not only confronted with his poor fellow as a brother but with YHWH himself who determines the destiny of the land – and the creditors.

In short, therefore, while the Jubilee may be considered utopian and irrational in the eyes of modern interpreters, the solidarity required of the original hearers of the law is completely rational within the horizon of the text itself. How could anyone not be gracious when faced with the poverty of one's brother?

Bibliography

Anderson, John E. (2005): A Biblical and Economic Analysis of Jubilee Property Provisions, in: Faith & Economics 46, 25–41.

Bartor, Assnat (2010): Reading Law as Narrative: A Study in the Casuistic Laws of the Pentateuch, Atlanta.

Bergsma, John S. (2007): The Jubilee from Leviticus to Qumran: A History of Interpretation, Leiden / Boston (Vetus Testamentum Supplements 115).

Berman, Joshua (2017): Inconsistency in the Torah: Ancient Literary Convention and the Limits of Source Criticism, New York.

Bertholet, Alfred (1896): Die Stellung der Israeliten und der Juden zu den Fremden, Freiburg i. Br. / Leipzig.

Blok, Josine / Krul, Julia (2017): Debt and its Aftermath: The Near Eastern Background to Solon's Seisachtheia, in: Hesperia 78/4, 607–643.

Braga Martes, Ana C. / Fazito, Dimitri (2010): Solidarity and Social Networks – Economic Sociology of International Migration and the Brazilian Case, in: Economic Sociology: The European Electronic Newsletter 11/3, 43–53.

Bultmann, Christoph (1992): Der Fremde im antiken Juda: Eine Untersuchung zum sozialen Typenbegriff "Ger" und seinem Bedeutungswandel in der alttestamentlichen Gesetzgebung, Göttingen.

Chirichigno, Gregory C. (1993): Debt-Slavery in Israel and the Ancient Near East, Sheffield.

Dowty, David R. (1991): Thematic Proto-Roles and Argument Selection, in: Language 67/3, 547–619.

Fager, Jeffrey A. (1993): Land Tenure and the Biblical Jubilee: Uncovering Hebrew Ethics through the Sociology of Knowledge, Sheffield.

Gane, Roy E. (2017): Old Testament Law for Christians: Original Context and Enduring Application, Grand Rapids.

Gottwald, Norman K. (1979): The Tribes of Yahweh: A Sociology of the Religion of Liberated Israel, 1350–1050 B.C.E, Maryknoll.

Graf, Karl Heinrich (1866): Die geschichtlichen Bücher des Alten Testaments: zwei historisch-kritische Untersuchungen, Leipzig.

Granovetter, Mark (1985): Economic Action and Social Structure: The Problem of Embeddedness, in: American Journal of Sociology 91/38, 481–510.

Hartley, John E. (1992): Leviticus, Dallas.

Højgaard, Christian C. (2021): Roles and Relations in Biblical Law: A Study of Participant Tracking, Semantic Roles, and Social Networks in Leviticus 17–26, PhD-thesis, Vrije University Amsterdam.

Joosten, Jan (1996): People and Land in the Holiness Code: An Exegetical Study of the Ideational Framework of the Law in Leviticus 17–26, Leiden (Vetus Testamentum Supplements 67).

Joosten, Jan (2010): La persuasion coopérative dans le discours sur la loi: pour une analyse de la rhétorique du Code de Sainteté, in: Lemaire, André (ed.), Congress Volume Ljubljana 2007, Leiden (Vetus Testamentum Supplements 133), 381–398.

Kaufmann, Yeḥezkel (1960): The Religion of Israel: From its Beginnings to the Babylonian Exile, Chicago.

Knohl, Israel (2007): The Sanctuary of Silence: The Priestly Torah and the Holiness School, Winona Lake.

Manning, Paul (2012): Economic Rationality and Corporate Social Irresponsibility: An Illustrative Review of Social Capital Theory, in: Corporate Social Irresponsibility: A Challenging Concept, Bingley (Critical Studies on Corporate Responsibility, Governance and Sustainability 4), 111–135.

Mason, John D. (1987): Biblical Teaching and Assisting the Poor, in: Transformation 4/2, 1–14.

McCarthy, Dennis J. ([2]1978): Treaty and Covenant: A Study in Form in the Ancient Oriental Documents and in the Old Testament, Rome.

Meyer, Esias E. (2015): People and Land in the Holiness Code: Who Is YHWH's Favourite?, in: Old Testament Essays 28/2, 433–450.

Milgrom, Jacob (2001): Leviticus 23–27, New York.

Milgrom, Jacob (2003): HR in Leviticus and Elsewhere in the Torah, in: Rendtorff, Rolf / Kugler, Robert A. / Bartel, Sarah Smith (eds.), The Book of Leviticus: Composition and Reception, Leiden (Vetus Testamentum Supplements 93), 24–40.

Nihan, Christophe (2007): From Priestly Torah to Pentateuch: A Study in the Composition of the Book of Leviticus, Tübingen.

Nihan, Christophe (2011): Resident Aliens and Natives in the Holiness Legislation, in: Achenbach, Reinhard / Albertz, Rainer / Wöhrle, Jakob (eds.), The Foreigner and the Law: Perspectives from the Hebrew Bible and the Ancient Near East, Wiesbaden (Beihefte zur Zeitschrift für altorientalische und biblische Rechtsgeschichte 16), 111–134.

Otto, Eckart (1994): Das Heiligkeitsgesetz Leviticus 17–26 in der Pentateuchredaktion, in: Mommer, Peter / Thiel, Winfried (eds.), Altes Testament – Forschung und Wirkung: Festschrift für Henning Graf Reventlow, Frankfurt am Main, 65–80.

Regenwetter, Michel / Dana, Jason / Davis-Stober, Clintin P. (2011): Transitivity of Preferences, in: Psychological Review 118/1, 42–56.

Rosenberg, Jacob / Weiss, Avi (2010): Land Concentration, Efficiency, Slavery, and the Jubilee, in: Levine, Aaron (ed.), The Oxford Handbook of Judaism and Economics, Oxford, 74–87.

Schaeffer, Henry (1922): Hebrew Tribal Economy and the Jubilee as Illustrated in Semitic and Indo-European Village Communities, Leipzig.

Schaefer, Kurt C. / Noell, Edd S. (2005): Contract Theory, Distributive Justice, and the Hebrew Sabbatical, in: Faith & Economics 45, 1–19.

Schwartz, Baruch J. (1999): The Holiness Legislation: Studies in the Priestly Code, Jerusalem.

Stackert, Jeffrey (2009): The Holiness Legislation and its Pentateuchal Sources: Revision, Supplementation, and Replacement, in: Shectman, Sarah / Baden, Joel S. (eds.), The Strata to the Priestly Writings: Contemporary Debate and Future Directions, Zürich, 187–204.

Stackert, Jeffrey (2011): The Sabbath of the Land in the Holiness Legislation: Combining Priestly and Non-Priestly Perspectives, in: The Catholic Biblical Quarterly 73/2, 239–250.

Sun, Henry T. C. (1990): An Investigation into the Compositional Integrity of the So-called Holiness Code (Leviticus 17–26), Claremont.

Tov, Emanuel ([2]2001): Textual Criticism of the Hebrew Bible, Assen.

Tucker, Paavo N. (2017): The Holiness Composition in the Book of Exodus, Tübingen.

Ulen, Thomas S. (1994): Rational Choice and the Economic Analysis of Law, in: Law & Social Inquiry 19/2, 487–522.

Walton, John H. (1994): Ancient Israelite Literature in Its Cultural Context: A Survey of Parallels Between Biblical and Ancient Near Eastern Texts, Grand Rapids.

Watts, James W. (1999): Reading Law: The Rhetorical Shaping of the Pentateuch, Sheffield.

Wellhausen, Julius ([6]1927): Prolegomena zur Geschichte Israels, Berlin / Leipzig.

Wenham, Gordon (1979): The Book of Leviticus, Grand Rapids.
Westbrook, Raymond (1991): Property and the Family in Biblical Law, Sheffield.
Wright, Christopher J. H. (1990): God's People in God's Land: Family, Land, and Property in the Old Testament, Grand Rapids.

A City Fit for Business

The Justice of Moneymaking in the *Republic's* Healthy City*

Daniel Silvermintz

Abstract: This article argues that the "healthy city" described at 369b–372e in Plato's *Republic* has been misunderstood by previous scholars as a Platonic ideal. Close reading of the passage reveals that all of the significant political proposals have not been determined by Socrates but rather by the acquisitive Adeimantus. While Socrates conceives of the city as a subsistence economy, Adeimantus adopts economic institutions for production and distribution that undermine the citizens' ability to restrict their consumption to necessities. Moreover, the healthy city's use of a market economy requires everyone in the city to practice a secondary art as moneymakers in violation of the founding principle that individuals should only practice a single occupation.

Keywords: Plato's *Republic* – Division of Labor – Political Economy – Reciprocal Justice

1. Introduction

Socrates famously proposes in Plato's *Republic* that the company imagine a perfectly just regime as an analogy for understanding the psychological implications of justice and injustice upon the soul. This exercise of theoretical regime building begins with the founding of the "healthy city" or "city of utmost necessity" described at *Resp.* 369b–372e. Although this first city quickly degenerates into a deviant regime afflicted by manifold vices, many scholars regard it as a Platonic ideal.[1] Additionally, economic historians have long appealed to this passage as evidence of Plato's endorsement of job specialization and market exchange.[2] In contrast, I contend that

---

* For valuable feedback, I thank J. Ranciere, J. Parens, S. Meikle, S. Molinelli, and S. Günther.

1 See Devereux 1979, 36–40; Annas 1981, 77; McKeen 2004; Rowe 2017; Green 2021. For the view that the first city is impossible, see Strauss 1964, 95; Bloom 1991, 346; Barney 2001, 220. My reading is closest to Reeve 1988, 176–178; Cross and Woozley 1964, 75–93; Schriefl 2018.

2 For example, see Trever 1916, 33–37; Haney 1922, 52; Roll 1942, 19; Schumpeter 1954, 56; Foley 1974; Lowry 1987, 72; Karayiannis 1990; Spiegel 1991, 246; Karamanlis 1997, 83–93;

Socrates does not consider the first city to be a desirable regime despite his judgment of it as healthy (*hugiēs*) and true (*alēthinē*) (*Resp.* 372e). In fact, when the passage is read carefully, one finds that most of the city's governing principles have not been decided by Socrates, but rather by the acquisitive Adeimantus.[3] This reading helps to explain the incongruity of implementing various economic institutions to maximize productivity when the citizens' consumption is regulated by a strict standard of necessity. I further contend that Socrates presents the healthy city in order to show Adeimantus the shortcomings of a regime that exists solely for the sake of ensuring the economic interests of its citizens. By analyzing the city's mode of production, distribution, and system of valuation, I demonstrate how the institutions implemented by Adeimantus undermine the city's standard of necessity, making the descent to the feverish city of luxuries an inevitable consequence of the city's first principles and not, as many scholars assume, a fall from grace.

2. Contextualizing the *Republic's* political proposals

Before commencing with a detailed examination of the healthy city, it is necessary to establish some interpretive principles for engaging with Plato's works. Despite Plato's voluminous writings, one must be cautious when attempting to identify his views since he never appears as a participant in the dialogues.[4] Although it is tempting to regard Socrates as Plato's mouthpiece, one should keep in mind that Plato is equally responsible for composing the speeches attributed to Socrates' interlocutors who offer vigorous challenges to his views. Plato clearly intends for the reader to pay particular attention to the arguments proffered by Socrates, but this does not mean that one should summarily dismiss arguments advanced by his interlocutors. Even if one is justified in granting Socrates' speeches a privileged status, one must nonetheless keep in mind that the dialogues represent an ongoing investigation rather than a statement of final conclusions. Any particular argument that is advanced by Socrates must therefore be contextualized by carefully considering its significance in light of a reading of the entire dialogue. The safest interpretive strategy is thus to attribute particular arguments to the specific character who advances

---

Sun 2005, 4–5; Reisman 2021, 16–20. Note the caution of several scholars of attributing modern economic concepts to the ancient Greeks: Schumpeter 1954, 53–54; Finley 1973, 3–4; Austin and Vidal-Naquet 1977, 3–17.

3 For the view that the first city is meant to appeal to Adeimantus, see Strauss 1964, 95 and Bloom 1991, 344 and 413. For the characterization of Adeimantus as a money-lover, see Schriefl 2018, 199.

4 This point is also made by Strauss 1964, 50; Bloom 1991, xxi; Sallis 1996, 2; Beversluis 2000, 19; Rosen 2008, 2. Also see Pl. *Leg.* 341c.

them while reserving more speculative conclusions about Plato's views to a dialectical reading of the work as a whole.

The need for contextualizing arguments is particularly important when evaluating the project of regime building in the central books of the *Republic*. Socrates is quite clear throughout the discussion that he does not intend these to be practical political proposals: "Much in our proposals look ridiculous if our words are to be realized in fact" (*Resp.* 452a).[5] When Socrates is later queried by Glaucon regarding the feasibility of the regime, he reminds him that they were only exploring politics in the first place in order to provide a model for examining the soul: "were not we, as we say, trying to create in words the pattern of a good state? ... Do you think, then, that our words are any the less well spoken if we find ourselves unable to prove that it is possible for a state to be governed in accordance with our words?" (*Resp.* 472e). Despite Socrates' repeated reminders of his reason for discussing the ideal regime, many scholars continue to dissociate the discussion of politics from its context as part of the ethical and psychological investigation.

Setting aside the issue of feasibility, one is left to consider whether or not the ideal regime actually provides a valid analogy for examining the soul. Although the central books of the *Republic* assume a homologous relationship between a city and an individual, Socrates himself suggests in a provocative passage that the investigation may ultimately reveal that they have been working under a false assumption:

> We supposed that, if we found some larger thing that contained justice and viewed it there, we should more easily discover its nature in the individual man. And we agreed that this larger thing is the city, and so we constructed the best city in our power, well knowing that in the good city it would of course be found. What, then, we thought we saw there we must refer back to the individual and, if it is confirmed, all will be well. But if something different manifests itself in the individual, we will return again to the state and test it there and it may be that, by examining them side by side and rubbing them against one another, as it were from the fire-sticks we may cause the spark of justice to flash forth. (*Resp.* 434d–435a)

Socrates thus intimates early on in the discussion that there may be a lack of correspondence between the city and the individual.[6] Despite initially claiming that each of the citizens within the city exhibit justice by maintaining job specialization, it later becomes evident that the philosopher-kings are the only individuals capable

5 Unless otherwise noted, passages of *Republic* are quoted from Shorey's translation 1969. Greek is quoted from Burnet 1903.

6 For discussion, see Sachs 1963.

of manifesting virtue. Since Platonic virtue requires the individual to practice philosophy, the rigid system of job specialization actually hinders virtue for all but the few philosopher-kings. With these interpretive principles in mind, I turn to a detailed examination of the economic institutions in the healthy city.

3. Is the healthy city a Socratic ideal?

Socrates begins the exercise of regime building by positing biological need as the motivating force impelling individuals to form a political association. Since individuals must satisfy various needs to preserve their lives, they seek out the assistance of others for help procuring necessary goods (*Resp.* 369b–c). Socrates' description of the lifestyle in the healthy city presumes that the citizens will continue to maintain a subsistence economy over time:

> Will they not make bread and wine and garments and shoes? And they will build themselves houses and carry on their work in summer for the most part unclad and unshod and in winter clothed and shod sufficiently? And for their nourishment they will provide meal from their barley and flour from their wheat, and kneading and cooking these they will serve noble cakes and loaves on some arrangement of reeds or clean leaves, and, reclined on rustic beds strewn with bryony and myrtle, they will feast with their children, drinking of their wine thereto, garlanded and singing hymns to the gods in pleasant fellowship, not begetting offspring beyond their means. (*Resp.* 372a–b)

One can certainly understand how many readers might regard the healthy city as an ideal given Socrates' account of the citizens peaceful and moderate lifestyle.

McKeen is one of the many scholars that idealize the healthy city. She begins her study with the following assessment: "At *Republic* 370c–372d, Plato presents us with a *polis* that is self-sufficient, peaceful, cooperative, and which provides a comfortable life for its inhabitants."[7] Focusing upon the merits of the healthy city, scholars such as McKeen lament its immediate descent into the feverish city.

The predilection for idealizing the healthy city is certainly understandable given Socrates' own assessment of it; however, one wonders if he is not ironic in his praise. Aristotle, at least, does not regard Socrates' city, which is solely comprised of artisans, as a serious proposal, dismissing it as, "witty but inadequate" (*kompsôs touto, ouch hikanôs de eirêtai*) (*Pol.* 1291a). In light of Aristotle's judgment, one ought to pay particular attention to Socrates' exact locution when describing the merits of the healthy city. He does not refer to the first city as the solitary example of a

---

7 McKeen 2004, 70.

"true city," but rather he offers the more modest claim that it is consistent with the truth of a city (*alêthinê polis*).[8] I take this to mean merely that the city of pigs satisfies the minimal conditions of a political association and thus is appropriately designated a "city of utmost necessity" (*anankaiotatê polis*) (*Resp.* 369d).[9] In fact, the city's economic institutions are its only signs of formal political structure.[10]

Readers readily associate the fevered city of luxuries with the erotically inclined Glaucon rather than the sober Socrates despite the fact that his contribution to the city is not much more than the request that Socrates provide the citizens with a more appetizing diet. In similar fashion, we should be as eager to distance the poverty-stricken Socrates from the city of necessity in light of its overemphasis on productivity. Although it may seem, on first reading, as if Socrates is responsible for determining the various enactments of the healthy city, I contend that Socrates is simply allowing Adeimantus to play out his acquisitive desires by helping him see the consequences of a city that is governed by economic rationality. One thus finds that Socrates precedes each of the proposals in the founding of the healthy city with a question directed at Adeimantus. Moreover, Adeimantus' vigorous objections to Socrates over the course of the dialogue suggest that he would not acquiesce unless he wholeheartedly agreed with him.[11] In fact, his objection at *Resp.* 419a–420a is so strong that Socrates treats it as if it were charges in a legal indictment (*katêgorias*) that must be responded to with a formal defense (*apologêsometha*).[12]

Adeimantus' acquisitive orientation is intimated at the beginning of the dialogue through his association with the family of the wealthy metic Cephalus.[13] Unlike his brother Glaucon, Adeimantus participates in the mob led by Cephalus' son Polemarchus, who threaten Socrates with violence if he does not do as they say (*Resp.* 327c). His disposition as a money-lover is further revealed in his strong opposition to the proposal prohibiting the guardians from possessing private property. Adeimantus contends that Socrates is denying the guardians' happiness, which he insists requires, "owning lands and building fine big houses and providing them with suitable furniture and winning the favor of the gods by private sacrifices and

8 Cf. Socrates' later judgment at *Resp.* 449a that the purged city is the only constitution deserving the name good (*agathên*) and right (*orthên*). For discussion, see Benardete 1989, 175, 200, and 211.

9 This point is also made by Cross and Woozley 1966, 82; Dorter 2006, 65; Bloom 1991, 346.

10 For the role of reciprocity as a bond of solidarity, see Grote 1888, 111–128; Cross and Woozley 1966, 79–80; Weinstein 2009, 445.

11 This point is also noted by Ferrari 2005, 21; Bloom 1991, 413; Blondell 2000, 132.

12 Also see *Resp.* 449d.

13 On the oddity of this relationship, see Ferrari 2005, 11.

enjoying ... gold and silver" (*Resp.* 419a).[14] One might note that Cephalus possesses all of the goods that Adeimantus associates with the happy individual: a large house, elaborate furnishings, and abundant riches for making ritual sacrifices.[15]

Adeimantus' association and admiration for the house of Cephalus, whose profits from the armaments industry are notorious, raises questions about the extent he is willing to go in pursuing the acquisitive life.[16] He is, in fact, quite explicit about his temptation to pursue injustice for the sake of gain, rehearsing the following justification: "If I am unjust and have procured myself a reputation for justice a godlike life is promised ... For a front and a show I must draw about myself a shadow-line of virtue, but trail behind me the fox of most sage Archilochus, shifty and bent on gain (*kerdalean*)" (*Resp.* 365c). Although Adeimantus attempts to disavow his praise of injustice at *Resp.* 367a, one wonders if he is not the "quick witted youth" that he describes at *Resp.* 365a as holding these views.[17] These glimpses into Adeimantus' character justify a closer examination of his role in founding the healthy city, particularly in light of some of the economic proposals that seem out of place in a regime that restricts its consumption to utmost necessities.

In Socrates' supposed state of nature, one finds all of the instruments and mechanisms of a market economy: cost-benefit rationality, division of labor, job specialization, a monetary system, retail trade, imports and exports, and a designated marketplace.[18] The greater significance of these details is evident if one considers that the entire argument is motivated by Socrates' attempt to prove that justice is, contrary to Thrasymachus' claims, more profitable than injustice (*Resp.* 345a, 354a). Unfortunately, the sophist's immoralist teaching has already influenced his impressionable audience as both Glaucon and Adeimantus come to his defense. Socrates attempts to purge them of their acquisitive aspirations by allowing them to conceive of imaginary cities in which they can pursue their desires without restraint. If Adeimantus seeks monetary gain, then Socrates will allow him to conceive of a city whose economizing orientation makes it fit for pigs.[19] Likewise, if Glaucon demands

14 The passage is a rhetorical question.

15 For the association of Cephalus with the first city and the producing class in the *kallipolis*, see Barney 2001, 217. Also see Hinsch 2021, 103, 171, 188, and 543–544.

16 Cephalus' shield factory was one of the largest operations of the period employing more than one hundred workers (Lys. 12.19; Glotz 1926, 163, 166, 182, 185, 205–206, and 266–267; Finley 1973, 48, 72, and 137; Gifford 2001, 35–106).

17 For support that Adeimantus aligns himself with the views at *Resp.* 364a–c, see Blondell 2000, 132.

18 See Schofield 1999, 69–81; Lowry 1987, 103–108; Taylor 2001, 273; Föllinger 2016, 34–35.

19 For Socrates' influence on Adeimantus, see *Resp.* 551e–552e.

indulgences, then Socrates will allow him to conceive of a city whose insatiable appetite for consumables will only be satisfied by the conquest of its neighbors (*Resp.* 373d–e).[20] One might then understand Socrates' subsequent introduction of the philosopher-king, who loves wisdom over material possessions, as his attempt to reorient the brothers' misdirected sense of gain.[21] I now turn to an examination of the various proposals instituted in the healthy city with the suspicion that these reflect the values of the acquisitive Adeimantus.

4. Citizen as economic agent

Adeimantus' influence on the first regime begins with the city's founding. Rather than conceiving of the city as an association forged between self-sufficient households, Socrates gets Adeimantus to agree that individuals are inherently incapable of providing for their own needs. Socrates offers the following account of the city's founding: "The origin of the city ... is to be found in the fact that we do not severally suffice for our own needs, but each of us lacks many things" (*Resp.* 369b). In light of this conception of the individual, Socrates proceeds to formulate that the community arises out of the need to form partnerships for the sake of exchange: "Then, one man calling in another for one service and another for another, we, being in need of many things, gather many into one place of abode as associates and helpers, and to this dwelling together we give the name city or state (*polin*)" (*Resp.* 369c). Socrates notes that the citizens only benefit each other as an unintended consequence of their pursuit of self-interest: "And between one man and another there is an interchange of giving, if it so happens, and taking, because each supposes this to be better (*ameinon*) for himself" (*Resp.* 369c). Despite his noble lineage, Adeimantus unquestioningly accepts Socrates' conception that the people in their ideal regime will be self-serving.

Adeimantus' role as architect of the healthy city becomes even more apparent when one examines his responsibility in determining the city's mode of production. At this point in the argument, Socrates presents Adeimantus with two rival economic systems and asks him to consider which of the two he finds more advantageous:

> Shall the farmer, who is one, provide food for four and spend fourfold time and toil on the production of food and share it with the others, or shall he

20 Cf. Burnyeat 1999, 231; Barney 2001, 214. Cf. *Resp.* 548d where Socrates rejects Adeimantus' characterization of Glaucon as a victory-lover. See Bloom 1991, 345 and 347.

21 For the distinction between these two notions of acquisitiveness, see Pl. *Hipparch.* 231a–c; Grote 1888, 120; Balot 2001, 237; Ferrari 2008, 34.

> take no thought for them and provide a fourth portion of the food for himself alone in a quarter of the time and employ the other three-quarters, the one in the provision of a house, the other of a garment, the other of shoes, and not have the bother of associating with other people, but, himself for himself, mind his own affairs (*ta hautou prattein*)? (*Resp.* 369e–370a)[22]

Adeimantus responds with the contention that an economic system based upon job specialization would be easier, and Socrates bolsters his conviction with the following assessment of the benefits that will be derived from this decision: "The result, then, is that more things are produced, and better and more easily when one man performs one task according to his nature, at the right moment, and at leisure from other occupations" (*Resp.* 370c). Despite recognizing its economic benefits, Socrates is clearly not a proponent of job specialization given its ability to hinder individuals from manifesting their personal virtue.[23]

One is led to believe that the luxurious city is founded in response to Glaucon's request to add relishes to the citizens' diet; however, Adeimantus' decision at the city's founding to produce finer quality goods through job specialization indicates that the potential for producing luxury goods had existed from its inception. The ability to produce surplus goods not only violates the city's founding principles, it completely shifts their psychological orientation as participants in a subsistence economy. One should keep in mind that the seemingly moderate individuals that make up the healthy city quickly become the gluttonous citizens of the feverish city and ultimately the money-loving class of the *kallipolis*.[24]

The implications of Adeimantus' decision to produce and exchange goods through a nexus of interdependent artisans might be examined by consideration of the alternative and more natural mode of producing and distributing goods in the household economy.[25] As Aristotle points out, "In the primary association therefore

22 The phrase "*ta hautou prattein*" is repeated at *Resp.* 433a and thereafter with the opposing meaning that each citizen should only work at a single occupation within the city. See Pl. *Chrm.* 167a; Donovan 2003.

23 For the view that Plato does not endorse job specialization, see Reeve 1988, 172; Silvermintz 2010. Cf. Shorey's note on *Resp.* 370a for the view that the question posed to Adeimantus is rhetorical.

24 For the view that there is no acquisitive motive in the healthy city, see Devereux 1979, 38; Bloom 1991, 344. Cf. Barney 2001, who argues that the naive reading of the citizens in the healthy city as innately moderate runs contrary to Platonic psychology.

25 See Hanson 1999, 66–67; Donovan 2003, 2; Schofield 1999, 72; Barney 2001, 212; Booth 1993; Hinsch 2021. Cf. Greco 2009, 60.

(I mean the household) there is no function for trade" (*Pol.* 1257a).[26] Goods are shared rather than exchanged in the household because the individual's well-being is inseparable from the welfare of the other family members. Parents feed, clothe, shelter, and protect their children knowing that they will not receive any direct compensation for their efforts. This orientation to others extends, to a lesser degree, in the tribe and village.

In contrast to the householder, the citizens of the healthy city are presented as autonomous agents calculating their self-interest.[27] Remarkably, the description of the healthy city is almost entirely lacking any discussion of the family – the sole reference emphasizing the economizing orientation of the citizens, who are careful not to beget "offspring beyond their means" (*Resp.* 372b). Benardete notes the city's atomistic character: "It is a wholly selfish association and in principle does not require any living together except for the sake of the greatest efficiency of exchange and distribution."[28] If judged by the standard set by Glaucon, the city of pigs does not appear to have made any headway in advancing a non-utilitarian conception of justice.[29] On the contrary, it substantiates Glaucon's claim that individuals are inherently self-serving.

5. The commercial system

Having determined the city's mode of production, Adeimantus is again made responsible for determining its mode of distribution. Socrates asks him, "But again, within the city itself how will they share (*metadôsousin*) with one another the products of their labor?" (*Resp.* 371b), intimating that the citizens might "share" their productions in the manner of the household economy. Adeimantus, however, completely disregards Socrates' suggestion, emphatically declaring that it is "obvious" (*dêlon*) that goods should be exchanged through a system of buying (*ônoumenoi*) and selling (*pôlountes*) (*Resp.* 371b) – as if this were the only conceivable means of distribution.[30] Just as Socrates, against his better judgment, will concede to Glaucon's request for relishes to be added to the city's diet (*Resp.* 372e), he appeases Adeimantus by establishing a marketplace (*agora*) and a unit of currency (*nomisma*) despite his

26 Quoted from Rackham's translation 1944. For discussion, see Meikle 1995, 49; Crespo 2013, 16.

27 Cf. Green 2021, 61–66.

28 Benardete 1989, 49.

29 For support, see Annas 1981, 78; Hemmenway 1999, 280. Cf. Devereux 1979, 40, who believes the first city displays a genuine sense of cooperation.

30 Cf. Weinstein 2009, 444–445, who notes the abrupt shift from sharing of goods to market exchange.

own anxiety about how money corrupts the individual.[31] Socrates' concern about the corrosive effects of handling money is so great that he completely prohibits his guardians from possessing any private property, let alone gold and silver.[32] In light of Socrates' concern regarding this issue, one cannot easily dismiss the decision to implement a commercial system as an innocuous means for circulating goods.[33]

After adopting the commercial system as the city's mode of distribution, Socrates obtains Adeimantus' consent that the city has been completed and reminds him of their original aim in founding the city. Socrates asks Adeimantus, "Where, then, can justice and injustice be found in it? And along with which of the constituents that we have considered does it come into the state?" (*Resp.* 371e). One should note that Socrates' question indicates that Adeimantus will find injustice along with justice in this seemingly ideal city. Although some scholars find Adeimantus' response vague, he seems to identify the business dealings as the locus for judging the city's ethics: "'I cannot conceive, Socrates,' he said, 'unless it be in some need (*chreia*) that those very constituents have of one another'" (*Resp.* 372a).[34] The significance of Adeimantus' assessment is evident when one considers that it immediately follows from the introduction of the commercial system as the means for individuals to meet their need within the city.[35] Although Socrates suggest that they should proceed by investigating the ethics of the healthy city's commercial system, Glaucon's interruption demanding a higher standard of living in the healthy city prevents this discussion from taking place (*Resp.* 372c).

Let us then take up Socrates' challenge to examine the justice and injustice of the city's business dealings. Rather than appraising the worth of goods by considering how they respond to biological needs, the commercial system assigns an arbitrary value to all goods as designated by their market price. The disconnected, and often inverted, relationship between these two systems of valuation is obvious when considering the biological need for water with the unnecessary desire for diamonds. Benardete notes how the commercial system in the healthy city acts to dissociate value from need: "They [the retailers] must decide on what a fair price is,

31 For discussion, see Günther 2017, 131–144.

32 For discussion, see Schofield 1999, 79–80; Arruzza 2011; Hinsch 2021, 187–188.

33 Cf. Seaford 2004, 259, who casually assumes Plato's assessment of currency as a valid means for facilitating exchange at *Resp.* 371b based on the discussion at *Leg.* 918b. See also Weinstein 2009, 454–455; Baily 2013, 6–8; Noutsopoulos 2015, 139; Föllinger 2016, 36–38; Russon 2021, 55–56.

34 On the vagueness of Adeimantus' response, see Devereux 1979, 37; Cross and Woozley 1966, 83.

35 Cf. *Resp.* 333b.

for as long as the city is governed by the equality of needs, the exchange of one house for one cloak or one-fourth of the harvest for one pair of shoes will hold; but as soon as there is money, things equally useful must be fractioned into units that establish their exchangeability apart from use."[36] I have previously noted that the city's mode of production could potentially undermine the adherence to the principle of necessity; however, exchange through commerce poses a more serious threat insofar as it requires a system of valuation that is completely divorced from utility.

Several of Socrates' interlocutors had previously noted how an unjust person can use unfair practices to his advantage. Thrasymachus (*Resp.* 343d) and Glaucon (*Resp.* 360d, 362a–b) both observed that the unjust individual profits more than the just individual in a business transaction. Glaucon raises even greater concern regarding unjust business practices since he believes that all people are naturally unjust: "no one is just of his own will but only from constraint, in the belief that justice is not his personal good, inasmuch as every man, when he supposes himself to have the power to do wrong, does wrong" (*Resp.* 360c). Moreover, if the aim of business is to generate wealth – as Socrates admits it to be (*Resp.* 346c–d) – and unjust practices generate greater profits, then one might think that being unjust in the marketplace is simply what it means to do business. Polemarchus seems to confirm this in suggesting that the just person is the one most needed – and presumably the hardest to find – when brokering a financial transaction (*Resp.* 333b). In light of these arguments, one wonders about Adeimantus' motives in adopting the commercial system given his acknowledgement of the benefits of being deceitful for the sake of gain (*Resp.* 365c).

If Adeimantus is indeed sincere about using commerce as a fair means of distribution, then there should be equity between the two parties in the transaction. This requires that goods, which are fundamentally incommensurable, could somehow be equated. When founding the ideal regime in the *Laws*, the Athenian Stranger addresses the issue of unjust business practices by appointing a class of civil servants responsible for equitably brokering all transactions: "For how can any man be anything but a benefactor (*euergetês*) if he renders even and symmetrical the distribution of any kind of goods which before was unsymmetrical and uneven? And this is, we must say, the effect produced by the power of money, and we must declare that the merchant (*emporos*) is ordained for this purpose" (*Leg.* 918b).[37] For the Stranger,

36 Benardete 1989, 50 (my interpolation).

37 Quoted from Bury's translation 1926. See Föllinger 2016, 44; Reisman 2021, 179–180.

the ideal merchant is not only public minded in his own actions, but plays an essential role in ensuring the justice of all of the other citizens.[38]

Although the Stranger's public minded merchant may provide for equity in business, one should keep in mind Socrates' critique of this conception of justice at the outset of the *Republic*. Cephalus, the famed armaments manufacturer, initiates the formal philosophic inquiry with the suggestion that justice is nothing other than paying one's debts (*Resp.* 331b). Polemarchus' attempts to bolster his father's conception with the amended notion that one should give to each what is owed (*Resp.* 332a). Socrates refutes Cephalus by noting that it would be unjust to return a weapon to its owner if he were not in his right state of mind (*Resp.* 331c–d).[39] He widens the scope of his criticism of equity in his refutation of Polemarchus by arguing that giving someone money could be just as injurious as providing him with a weapon when the person uses the funds to harm himself or others (*Resp.* 332b). Regardless if it is possible to exchange goods equitably, Socrates demands a higher standard of justice in his ideal regime.

Although the Athenian Stranger may have overvalued equity in his attempt to justify financial transactions, there may nonetheless be a salutary role for commerce within the city. As with other arts, one presumes there is a proper role for business when it is employed to achieve nature's ends. Just as the genuine physician acts to restore the natural standard of health in the patient, business might be pursued in order to redistribute the goods that would be provided within the self-sufficient household. This is, of course, the approach adopted by Aristotle in distinguishing natural and unnatural forms of acquisition. For Aristotle, acquisition is natural when it operates in a subsidiary role to the art of household management: "One kind of acquisition therefore in the order of nature is a part of the household art, in accordance with which either there must be forthcoming or else that art must procure to be forthcoming a supply of those goods, capable of accumulation, which are necessary for life (*zôên anankaiôn*) and useful (*chrêsimôn*) for the community of city or household" (*Pol.* 1256b).[40] Our concern regarding the healthy city's economy was prompted by Adeimantus' rejection of the self-sufficient household in favor of a network of interdependent artisans. Sharing this concern, Aristotle attempts to restore the integrity of the household by situating the acquisitive art under the

---

38 Benardete 1989, 50–51. Plato likely is thinking of the *agoranomos*, who were appointed to fix prices and monitor commercial exchanges in the agora.

39 The commercial implications of Socrates' refutation of Cephalus are evident given his business dealings in the armaments industry. The irony of Socrates' hypothetical is noted by Gifford 2001, 75; Barney 2001, 210; Rudebusch 2002, 75.

40 See Meikle 1995, 43–67; Crespo 2013, 12–77.

command of household management. As the commanding art, household management would then dictate to the acquisitive art precisely what goods are needed and to what extent they are required in order to maintain the well-being of the household.

Having established the subsidiary status of acquisition, Aristotle tries to legitimate commerce as simply another means for procuring necessary goods.[41] He thus finds no difference between the forms of acquisition consistent with a self-sufficient life (shepherding, fishing, farming, hunting) and production for the sake of exchange: "Take for example a shoe – there is its wear as a shoe and there is its use as an article of exchange; for both are ways of using a shoe, inasmuch as even he that barters a shoe for money or food with the customer that wants a shoe uses it as a shoe, though not for the use peculiar to a shoe, since shoes have not come into existence for the purpose of barter" (*Pol.* 1257a).[42] Although Aristotle initially treats monetary transactions as comparable to barter (the shoe may be exchanged for money or for food), he concludes the passage by affirming that "The art of trade is not by nature a part of the art of wealth-getting" (*Pol.* 1257a). Barter is a limited activity that is pursued only for the sake of providing for one's needs; in contrast, commerce is pursued without limit under the assumption that one has insatiable needs. Solon thus notes that people pursue acquisition without bounds (Sol. fr. 13.71).[43] Glaucon concurs, affirming that it is inevitable that the citizens will disregard necessary wants in pursuit of unlimited wealth-getting (*Resp.* 373d–e).[44]

Although Socrates indicates that the citizens will regulate their consumption according to the strict standard of necessity, they nonetheless demonstrate the value they place on surplus when accepting remuneration for their labor even when their immediate needs are met.[45] The citizens accept symbolic tokens as a medium of commerce because they believe that they will be able to exchange them at some time in the future for things that are useful and needed.[46] Money thus disassociates individuals' identification with their biological needs by having them calculate their indeterminate future needs. Aristotle notes: "Now money serves us as a guarantee of exchange in the future: supposing we need nothing at the moment, it ensures

41 For discussion, see Brandt 2022, 65–98.

42 For discussion, see Meikle 1995, 43–67; Pridatt 2012, 5–21; Crespo 2013, 12–77; Hinsch 2021, 237

43 For discussion, see Aristot. *Pol.* 1256b–1258a; Balot 2001.

44 Cf. *Leg.* 918d. See Balot 2001, 34–43 and 234–248; Bailey 2013, 2; Noutsopoulos 2015, 145; Föllinger 2016, 36 and 39–48.

45 This point is also made by Ranciere 2004, 269; Rosen 2008, 74; Föllinger 2016, 34.

46 For discussion of currency as a symbolic token, see Seaford 2004, 143.

that exchange shall be possible when a need arises, for it meets the requirement of something we can produce in payment so as to obtain the thing we need" (*Eth. Nic.* 1133b).[47] Although Aristotle attempts to model commercial exchange along the lines of barter, his discussion of unnatural acquisition in *Politics* suggests that this is a futile effort. Rather than reminding the exchangers of the natural limits of what is necessary, the use of currency as a representative of indefinite need constructs a notion of unlimited and unbounded desires.

While some scholars find the healthy city to be an example of a regime that does not regard money as an end-in-itself, it is difficult to imagine how one can use money as part of a market economy without adopting its system of assessing values. Bloom poignantly notes money's role in redefining all values, "Money, or what we would call the economic system, is a sort of architectonic principle; for in ordinary cities the amount of money paid for the products of the arts determines what arts are practiced, how they are practiced, and what kind of men practice them."[48] Despite Bloom's contention that the citizens in the healthy city lack a sense of acquisitiveness, he provides a persuasive account of how the commercial system inevitably shapes their worldview.

6. Citizen as moneymaker

Although the analysis has been critical of Adeimantus' adoption of job specialization within the healthy city so far, one must also account for Socrates' appeal to this principle as revealing civic justice. After watching the healthy city undergo several regime changes, Socrates declares that the principle of justice for which they have been seeking was actually present at the city's inception: "For what we laid down in the beginning as a universal requirement when we were founding our city, this I think, or some form of this, is justice. And what we did lay down, and often said, you recall, was that each one man must perform one social service in the state for which his nature is best adapted" (*Resp.* 433a). Socrates' acknowledgement of the producers' justice is not surprising given his frequent appeal to the genuine artisan as an analogy for conceiving of the virtuous individual. He had, for example, used this approach with Polemarchus, asking him to compare the domain of just actions with the work proper to medicine and cooking: "In the same way tell me the art that renders what to whom would be denominated justice" (*Resp.* 332d). Rather than merely using the arts as an analogy, Socrates makes the bold claim that the artisans in the healthy city embody justice merely by performing their job.

47 Quoted from Rackham's translation 1926. For discussion, see Meikle 1995, 21–28.

48 Bloom 1991, 333.

Socrates laid the foundation for his defense of job specialization in his earlier discussion with Thrasymachus. Attempting to refute Thrasymachus' conception that justice always profits the stronger party, Socrates draws on the arts to argue that the producer serves the consumer's interest despite their obvious power imbalance: "no art considers or enjoins the advantage of the stronger but every art that of the weaker which is ruled by it" (*Resp.* 332d). Appealing to the artisans' technical knowledge and professional integrity as a check on their actions, Socrates establishes a basis for justice in commercial dealings. Socrates' point is best illustrated by considering the relationship of the physician and patient. Although the physician could easily take advantage of the patient's enfeebled state, his commitment to his profession entreats him to disregard his own good in favor of the patient's well-being. Socrates asks Thrasymachus, "Can we deny ... that neither does any physician in so far as he is a physician seek or enjoin the advantage of the physician but that of the patient? For we have agreed that the physician, precisely speaking, is a ruler and governor of bodies and not a moneymaker" (*Resp.* 342d).

Socrates thus establishes the justice of the artisan class by conceiving of them as selflessly performing their labors for the consumer's benefit. The problem with this conception is that people are not innately selfless. On the contrary, Socrates himself recognized that the founders of the healthy city were solely driven by self-interested motives to forge association with others in order to benefit themselves (*Resp.* 369c). Glaucon further contends that people are greedy (*pleonexian*) by nature and would take what belongs to another if they could get away with it (*Resp.* 359c). Since nobody would labor without some sort of remuneration, Socrates establishes with Thrasymachus that all artisans must engage in a second art in addition to their specialized profession:

> But if we are to consider it 'precisely' medicine produces health but the fee-earning art the pay, and architecture a house but the fee-earning art (*mistharnêtikê*) accompanying it the fee, and so with all the others, each performs its own task and benefits that over which it is set, but unless pay is added to it is there any benefit which the craftsman receives from the craft? (*Resp.* 346d)[49]

Despite establishing in the exchange with Thrasymachus that all artisans must engage in two professions (their specialized art and the universal art of wage-earning),

49 For discussion of the wage earner's art, see Lerner 1974, 43; Strauss 1964, 24 and 80–81; Bloom 1991, 331–333; Benardete 1989, 24; Reeve 1988, 19–20; Noutsopoulos 2015, 148–154; Hinsch 2021, 190.

he later insists that justice is the practice of a single job (*Resp.* 370c, 374a–c, 397e, 433a, 443c).

Socrates never explains how the artisans are to overcome the quandary in which they are forbidden from practicing a second job, yet will only benefit from their labors when they violate this principle. Moreover, as Bloom notes, the practice of the wage-earning art poses a constant threat to the artisans' professional integrity when engaging in their primary occupation: "What is the doctor to do who is offered a bribe for harming his patient? His two arts each make rigorous and contradictory claims upon him, and there is no evident principle for choosing which should be preferred."[50] Following on Bloom's observation, one should keep in mind that the individuals forging the healthy city were solely motivated by calculating their self-interest (*Resp.* 369c).

Socrates' best attempt at addressing the artisans' dilemma is to appeal to their specialized knowledge as a check on their pursuit of self-interest. Since Socrates conceives of the artisans as possessing knowledge, he believes that their actions would always be in accordance with the principles of their profession. While the moneymaker seeks to increase his wealth without limit, the specialized artisans' actions are constrained by their knowledge and training. Socrates thus notes that a professional would try to correct a nonprofessional, but not someone else possessing knowledge: "Do you think then, my friend, that any musician in the tuning of a lyre would want to overreach (*pleonektein*) another musician in the tightening and relaxing of the strings or would claim and think fit to exceed or outdo (*pleon*) him?" (*Resp.* 349e). One should note the ethical overtones of Socrates' words when illustrating his argument. Although Socrates literally means that the string of an instrument will only be in tune when pulled to a precise degree of tautness, his term (*pleonektein*) for indicating that the musician has placed the instrument out of tune is often used in an ethical context. This is, in fact, the same term that Glaucon uses at *Resp.* 359c to argue that everyone is naturally greedy. While Socrates agrees with Glaucon that all people lacking knowledge are greedy without limit, for "The bad man and the ignoramus will overreach both like and unlike" (*Resp.* 350a–b), he contends that the possession of knowledge places this inclination in check.

In assessing Socrates' argument, one must keep in mind that the technical knowledge possessed by the artisans only grants them virtue within the limited scope pertaining to their specialized field. Having initially considered craft knowledge as constitutive of virtue, Socrates ultimately qualifies it as distinct from the sort of architectonic knowledge claimed by *phronesis*: "For it is not by ignorance

50 Bloom 1991, 332. On this same point, see Irwin 1977, 181.

but by knowledge that men counsel well ... But there are many and manifold knowledge's or sciences in the city ... Is it then owing to the science of her carpenters that a city is to be called wise and well advised?" (*Resp.* 428b–c). Socrates argues the point even more boldly during his defense speech, chastising the artisans for thinking that knowledge of their trade grants them authority to pontificate on ethical matters (*Ap.* 22c).

Since craft knowledge is distinct from practical wisdom, one cannot be assured how the artisans will put their knowledge to use. In fact, Socrates acknowledges that the artisans' knowledge makes them the most capable of applying their expertise in an unjust manner (*Resp.* 333e–334b). Misapplying their respective knowledge and training, the physician could easily kill the patient and the captain could adeptly sink the ship.[51]

The moral ambiguity of the artisan is heightened in the class of citizens that are solely involved in commercial dealings. With the establishment of a marketplace to conduct business, several occupations are introduced within the healthy city that threaten the civic order as a result of their lack of any specialized training or code of conduct. The retailer, hireling, importer and exporter are solely moneymakers without knowledge of a craft that might ensure their integrity.[52] In addition to the traders and merchants, Socrates curiously introduces a class of day laborers (*misthôtoi*) whose lack of innate aptitude leads them to take whatever work they can get their hands on. Their lack of mental discernment and single-minded pursuit of pay (*misthos*) makes them equally likely to serve noble as ignoble causes.

Like the decision to exchange goods with a system of currency, the introduction of a class of retailers seems like an innocuous method for facilitating trade; however, one should not ignore the consequences of either of these proposals. Socrates suggests that instead of idling in the marketplace waiting for customers, the artisans are able to employ the services of the retailer (*kapēlōs*) as an intermediary responsible for reselling their products (*Resp.* 371c–d). There is certainly no indication that these shopkeepers will operate in the benevolent manner prescribed by the Athenian Stranger; on the contrary, these individuals are entrusted with assessing the values of all consumables regardless of the fact that they do not possess any knowledge of what may be in the best interest of the city. Socrates' companion in the *Hipparchus* highlights the absence of public mindedness of one pursuing gain by arguing that he attempts to turn a profit (*kerdainein*) out of things that are absolutely worthless (*mêdenos axiôn*) (*Hipparch.* 225a). A similar analysis leads Hemmenway to

51 For discussion, see Hemmenway 1999, 270; Dorter 2005, 28.

52 Benardete 1989, 50 notes that the retailer is the first citizen in the healthy city that does not make anything.

identify this class of citizens as the cause of the healthy city's degeneration into the feverish city: "What would keep these money handlers or professional exchangers honest is not an expertise or knowledge they have, and therein lies the essential difference from the other artisans; this is precisely where, if anywhere, injustice would make its way into the Healthy City."[53] The shopkeepers' role in causing the descent into the feverish city is even more apparent when one considers how they might generate more sales by selling luxury goods within the city of necessity.

In spite of the city's supposed commitment to consuming only bare necessities, the healthy city's mode of production has always had the potential for producing luxury goods. Socrates, in fact, acknowledges that job specialization will be employed to produce goods of finer quality as the city attempts to forge business partnerships with neighboring cities through an export industry (*Resp.* 371a).[54] Obviously, the exporter will not be very fruitful if he attempts to sell the typical merchandise consumed by the city of necessity to a foreign market accustomed to a higher standard of living.[55] Socrates is thus forced to concede that the exports must meet the standards expected of the potential market:

> And again, if our servitor goes forth empty-handed, not taking with him any of the things needed by those from whom they procure what they themselves require, he will come back with empty hands ... Then their home production must not merely suffice for themselves but in quality and quantity meet the needs of those of whom they have need. (*Resp.* 370e–371a)

If the exporters are to be successful in their business endeavors, they must obviously traffic goods that meet the standards expected in other cities even if this should transgress what is allowed in the healthy city.[56] The exporters must, moreover, not only be cognizant of the accepted standards demanded by the foreign customers, but they must also be able to convince the artisans in the healthy city to produce these goods. Socrates confirms this, remarking that the export business will require that other kinds of artisans (*allôn dêmiourgôn*) will need to be introduced. Although one is led to believe that the citizens in the healthy city are able to maintain their rustic lifestyle because they have no temptations and no firsthand

53 Hemmenway 1999, 279. A similar point is made by Wallach 2001, 152. For the derogatory view of the retailer, see Günther 2017, 143.

54 Cf. Pl. *Lg.* 705a.

55 For discussion, see Weinstein 2009, 451; Bresson 2016, 49–50.

56 See Föllinger 2016, 34, who notes that the healthy city is not (as many imagine) a subsistence economy.

experience of luxury goods, the reality is that the exporting business has made them producers of the very goods that they are forbidden from consuming. Is one then to believe that the weaver, who spends her days producing finely embroidered gowns for the export business, will continue to don a simple garment and maintain her belief that clothes are simply to protect one from the elements?

7. Maximizing profits

Although it may seem odd to consider the citizens of the healthy city, with their meager existence, as economic agents rationally calculating their actions to maximize their profits, this is precisely what emerges when one strips away the rhetoric of a simple-minded people protected by providence.[57] McKeen sums up the rationalism of the citizens in this city in the following manner: "The community, in effect, is a mutual benefit society unified by individuals, operating from considerations of enlightened self-interest."[58] While McKeen describes the citizens as cooperative, one must weigh this against her judgment that their actions are motivated by self-interest.[59]

Reeve is one of the few scholars to recognize that the city of pigs solely exists for ensuring the economic interests of its citizens. He writes: "The First Polis is that part of the *Kallipolis* in which money-lovers, and only money-lovers, are made as happy as it is possible for them to be."[60] In support of Reeve's claim, one might note that while the citizens of the city of pigs take measures so that they do not fall into poverty, they do not make any similar provision concerning individuals becoming excessively wealthy.[61] One presumes that the citizens of the healthy city have no need for a great store of riches when their lifestyle is so simple; however, I have noted how notions of excess might enter the city as a result of its mode of production and distribution. Moreover, Socrates' account of oligarchic individuals, who pursue gain without limit despite restricting their consumption to what is absolutely necessary, suggests that acquisitiveness may not necessarily be motivated by a desire to consume:

---

57 This point is also made by Cross and Woozley 1966, 80; Annas 1981, 78. Cf. Weinstein 2009, 441, who believes that the first city shares goods prior to the establishment of the market at *Resp.* 371b.

58 McKeen 2004, 71.

59 Cf. Hemmenway 1999, 275.

60 Reeve 1988, 176.

61 Cf. the guardians' concern that the producing class in the purged city do not become impoverished or excessively wealthy (*Resp.* 421d–e).

> Would he [the oligarchic individual] not, in the first place, resemble it [the oligarchic city] in prizing wealth above everything? ... And also by being thrifty and laborious, satisfying only his own necessary appetites and desires and not providing for expenditure on other things, but subduing his other appetites as vain and unprofitable? ... He would be a squalid fellow ... looking for a surplus of profit in everything. (*Resp.* 554a–b)[62]

If Reeve is correct, then the moderation exhibited by the citizens in the healthy city is, like the oligarch, only an instrumental result of their desire to acquire riches. Their lack of commitment to moderation is, moreover, decisively revealed as they show no resistance to indulging in all of the luxuries introduced by the feverish city.

The problematic nature of the first city's virtue is further confirmed by Socrates' analysis of the producing class within the perfected city. Since this is the one group whose lineage can be traced back to the original city, one is justified in drawing upon an analysis of their psychological disposition in the purged city.[63] Although the individuals comprising the producing class have experienced several regime changes, their activities as artisans and moneymakers have not changed.[64] In fact, as previously noted, the constancy of this class throughout the political turmoil of the various regime changes allows Socrates to look to the division of labor in the first city when searching for justice in the perfected city (*Resp.* 432d). Besides their willing submission to the rule of the guardians, the producing class does not display much more of a sense of virtue in the perfected city than what it had exhibited in the first city.[65]

Let us then consider Socrates' assessment of the producing class as a valid diagnosis of the first city. Socrates begins his search for the various virtues by assuming that the parts of the city each exemplify a distinctive virtue. Having first associated wisdom (*sophos*) with the ruling class and courage (*andreios*) with the auxiliary class, one assumes that Socrates will associate moderation (*sôphrosunê*) with the remaining class of producers.[66] Although *sôphrosunê* means that one is self-controlled and the master of himself (*kreittô hautou*) (*Resp.* 430e), the producing class only achieves moderation by having regulations imposed upon them by the ruling classes. Socrates claims that moderation is present throughout the perfected city, yet

62 My interpolation.

63 For the view that the first city is subsumed in the later regimes, see Benardete 1989, 54; Reeve 1988, 172.

64 For support, see Reeve 1988, 172. Cf. Benardete 1989, 89; Bloom 1991, 348; Hemmenway 1999, 279.

65 For discussion, see Schriefl 2018, 209.

66 Cf. *Resp.* 432a.

acknowledges that there is "a domination of the desires in the multitude" (*Resp.* 431d). The claim that the perfect city is self-controlled ultimately amounts to nothing more than the willing subjugation of the immoderate majority (*Resp.* 432a).[67]

8. Conclusion

The preceding analysis has shown that the citizens of the healthy city are neither genuinely cooperative nor moderate, but rather motivated by a self-interested pursuit of gain. I contend that Socrates allows Adeimantus to determine the city's economic institutions in order to show him the corrosive effects of founding a regime that is solely motivated to ensuring the economic interests of its citizens. He goes so far as to claim in his account of the oligarchic individual that the pursuit of wealth and the pursuit of virtue are, like the scales on a balance, directly opposed to one another (*Resp.* 550e). Alternatively, he hopes to redirect Adeimantus and the other ambitious young men from the insatiable desire for money and goods to the love of wisdom as philosopher-kings.

Bibliography

Annas, Julia (1981): An Introduction to Plato's *Republic*, Oxford.

Arruzza, Cinzia (2011): The Private and the Common in Plato's *Republic*, in: History of Political Thought 32/2, 215–233.

Austin, Michel M. / Vidal-Naquet, Pierre (1977): Economic and Social History of Ancient Greece, Berkeley.

Baily, Alan I. (2013): *Ousia Aphanes*: Justice and Commerce in Light Of Plato's *Republic*, I and II, in: Expositions 7/2, 1–27.

Balot, Ryan K. (2001): Greed and Injustice in Classical Athens, Princeton.

Barney, Rachel (2001): Platonism, Moral Nostalgia, and the City of Pigs, in: Proceedings of the Boston Area Colloquium in Ancient Philosophy 17, 207–227.

Benardete, Seth (1989): Socrates' Second Sailing: On Plato's *Republic*, Chicago.

Beversluis, John (2000): Cross-Examining Socrates: A Defense of the Interlocutors in Plato's Early Dialogues, Cambridge.

Blondell, Ruby (2000): Letting Plato Speak for Himself: Character and Method in the Republic, in: Press, Gerald (ed.), Who Speaks for Plato? Studies in Platonic Anonymity, Lanham, 127–146.

Bloom, Allan (1991): Interpretive Essay, in: Bloom, Allan (trans.), The *Republic* of Plato, New York, 307–436.

67 For similar suspicions of the first city's moderation, see Barney 2001, 219–220; cf. Des-Lauriers 2001, 234–235. For discussion of Plato's top-down model of economic rationality, see the paper by Willms in this volume.

Booth, William J. (1993): Households: On the Moral Architecture of the Economy, Ithaca.

Brandt, Sven-Phillip (2022): Αὐτάρκεια as a Framework? The Concept of αὐτάρκεια in Late Classical Athens, in: Günther, Elisabeth / Günther, Sven (eds.), Frames and Framing in Antiquity I. Selected Papers from the First Frames and Framing in Antiquity Conference, 16–18 October 2020, Changchun (Supplements to the Journal of Ancient Civilizations 9), 65–98.

Bresson, Alain (2016): Aristotle and Foreign Trade, in: Harris, Edward M. / Lewis, David M. / Woolmer, Mark (eds.), The Ancient Greek Economy: Markets, Households, and City-States, New York, 41–65.

Burnet, John (ed.) (1903): Platonis Opera. 5 vols., Oxford (Scriptorum Classicorum Bibliotheca Oxoniensis).

Burnyeat, Miles F. (1999): Culture and Society in Plato's *Republic*, in: The Tanner Lectures on Human Values 20, 217–324.

Bury, Robert G. (trans.) (1926): Plato, *Laws*. 2 vols., Cambridge (Loeb Classical Library 187 & 192).

Crespo, Ricardo F. (2013): A Re-Assessment of Aristotle's Economic Thought, London.

Cross, Robert C. and Woozley, Anthony D. (1966): Plato's *Republic*: A Philosophic Commentary, New York.

DesLauriers, Marguerite (2001): Comments on Barney, in: Proceedings of the Boston Area Colloquium in Ancient Philosophy 17, 228–235.

Devereux, Daniel (1979): Socrates' First City in the *Republic*, in: Apeiron 13, 36–40.

Donovan, Brian (2003): The Do-It-Yourselfer in Plato's *Republic*, in: American Journal of Philology 124, 1–18.

Dorter, Kenneth (2006): The Transformation of Plato's *Republic*, Lanham.

Ferrari, Giovanni R. F. (2005): City and Soul in Plato's *Republic*, Chicago.

Finley, Moses I. (1973): The Ancient Economy, Berkeley.

Föllinger, Sabine (2016): Ökonomie bei Platon, Berlin.

Foley, Vernard (1974): The Division of Labor in Plato and Smith, in: History of Political Economy 6/2, 220–242.

Gifford, Mark (2001): Dramatic Dialectic in *Republic* I, in: Oxford Studies in Ancient Philosophy 20, 35–106.

Glotz, Gustave (1926): Ancient Greece at Work, New York.

Greco, Anna (2009): On the Economy of Specialization and Division of Labor in Plato's *Republic*, in: Polis: The Journal for Ancient Greek and Roman Political Thought 26, 52–72.

Green, Jerry (2021): The First City and First Soul in Plato's *Republic*, in: Rhizomata 9/1, 50–83.

Grote, George (1888): Plato and the Other Companions of Sokrates, London.

Günther, Sven (2017): (K)einer neuen Theorie wert? Neues zur Antiken Wirtschaftsgeschichte anhand Dig. 50,11,2 (Callist. 3 cognit.), in: Gymnasium 124/2, 131–144.

Haney, Louis H. (1922): History of Economic Thought: A Critical Account of the Origin and Development of the Economic Theories of the Leading Thinkers in the Leading Nations, New York.

Hanson, Victor D. (1999): The Other Greeks: The Family Farm and the Agrarian Roots of Western Civilization, Berkeley.

Hemmenway, Scott R. (1999): The Techne-Analogy in Socrates' Healthy City: Justice and the Craftsman in the *Republic*, in: Ancient Philosophy 19, 267–284.

Hinsch, Moritz (2021): Ökonomik und Hauswirtschaft im klassischen Griechenland, Stuttgart (Historia-Einzelschriften 265).

Irwin, Terence (1977): Plato's Moral Theory: The Early and Middle Dialogues, Oxford.

Karasmanis, Vassilis (1997): The Economic Man in Plato's *Republic*, in: Boudouris, Konstantinos (ed.) Plato's Political Philosophy and Contemporary Democratic Theory. Vol. I, Athens, 83–93.

Karayiannis, Anastassios D. (1990): The Platonic Ethico-Economic Structure of Society, in: Quaderni di Storia dell'Economia Politica 8/1, 3–45.

Lerner, Ralph (trans.) (1974): Averroes on Plato's *Republic*, Ithaca.

Lowry, Scott T. (1987): The Archeology of Economic Ideas, Durham.

McKeen, Catherine (2004): Swillsburg City Limits ('The City of Pigs': *Republic* 370c–372d), in: Polis: The Journal of the Society for Greek Political Thought 21/1, 70–92.

McNulty, Paul J. (1975): A Note on the Division of Labor in Plato and Smith, in: History of Political Economy 7/3, 372–378.

Meikle, Scott (1995): Aristotle's Economic Thought, Oxford.

Noutsopoulos, Thomas (2015): The Role of Money in Plato's *Republic*, Book I: A Materialist Approach, in: Historical Materialism 23/2, 131–156.

Priddat, Birger (2012): Aristoteles über Markt und Geld, in: Günther, Sven (ed.), Ordnungsrahmen antiker Ökonomien. Ordnungskonzepte und Steuerungsmechanismen antiker Wirtschaftssysteme im Vergleich, Wiesbaden (Philippika 53), 5–21.

Rackham, Harris (trans.) (1926): Aristotle, *Nicomachean Ethics*, Cambridge (Loeb Classical Library 73).

Rackham, Harris (trans.) (1944): Aristotle, *Politics*, Cambridge (Loeb Classical Library 264).
Ranciere, Jacques (2004): The Order of the City, in: Critical Inquiry 30, 267–291.
Reeve, Charles D. C. (1988): Philosopher-Kings: The Argument of Plato's *Republic*, Princeton.
Reisman, David (2021): Plato's Economics: Republic and Control, Cheltenham.
Roll, Eric (1942): A History of Economic Thought, New York.
Rosen, Stanley (2008): Plato's *Republic*: A Study, New Haven.
Rowe, Christopher (2017): The City of Pigs: A Key Passage in Plato's *Republic*, in: Philosophie Antique 17, 55–71.
Rudebusch, George (2002): Dramatic Prefiguration in Plato's *Republic*, in: Philosophy and Literature 26/1, 75–83.
Russon, John (2021): Politics, Money, and Persuasion: Democracy and Opinion in Plato's *Republic*, Bloomington.
Sachs, David (1963): A Fallacy in Plato's *Republic*, in: Philosophical Review 72/2, 141–158.
Sallis, John (1996): Being and Logos: Reading the Platonic Dialogues, Bloomington.
Schofield, Malcolm (1999): Saving the City: Philosopher-Kings and Other Classical Paradigms, London.
Schriefl, Anna (2018): Plato on the Incompatibility of Wealth and Justice: The Property Arrangements in the *Republic*, in: History of Political Thought 39/2, 193–215.
Schumpeter, Joseph (1954): History of Economic Analysis, Oxford.
Seaford, Richard (2004): Money and the Early Greek Mind: Homer, Philosophy, Tragedy, Cambridge.
Shorey, Paul (trans.) (1969): Plato, *Republic*, Cambridge (Loeb Classical Library 276).
Silvermintz, Daniel (2010): Plato's Supposed Defense of the Division of Labor: A Re-Examination of the Role of Job Specialization in the *Republic*, in: History of Political Economy 42/4, 747–772.
Spiegel, Henry W. (1991): The Growth of Economic Thought, Durham.
Strauss, Leo (1964): The City and Man, Chicago.
Sun, Guang-Zhen (2005): Readings in the Economics of the Division of Labor: The Classical Tradition, Hackensack.
Trever, Albert A. (1916): A History of Greek Economic Thought, Chicago.
Taylor, Alfred E. (2001): Plato: The Man and his Work, New York.
Wallach, John (2001): The Platonic Political Art: A Study of Critical Reason and Democracy, University Park.

Weinstein, Joshua (2009): The Market in Plato's *Republic*, in: Classical Philology 104/4, 439–458.

Adam Smith, Plato, and the Stoics

The Birth of Modern Economic Rationality and the Classical Heritage

Lothar Willms

Abstract: This paper argues that Plato and Adam Smith represent two different modes of economic and social rationality and that Smith's mode finds no match in ancient Stoics. This difference is part of his contribution to the constitution of modern economics. His mode of social rationality widely presupposes that people are able to behave as rational actors in both economy and ethics whereas Plato's model requires intensive education and institutional initiation before people are qualified to act according to his particular pattern of rationality. Whereas Plato yields a hierarchic top-down organization in society, economy, politics, and psychology, Smith in both *The Wealth of Nations* (1776) and his ethical treatise *The Theory of Moral Sentiments* (1759) favours a horizontal and bottom-up model in economy, ethics, and psychology that is based on the individuals' (peer-to-peer inter)action. Stoic theories such as proficients, cosmopolitanism, *oikeiôsis*, and providence worked as ingredients and ferments to this new model that enhanced the confidence in the individuals' fruitful cooperation. Transferring them from ethics and the cosmos to the economic system and complementing them by a model of self-regulatory interaction was Smith's achievement.

Keywords: Smith – Plato – Stoics – Rationality – Top-down – Bottom-up

1. Introduction

Rationality is a delicate topic, not only in everyday discussions where the charge of irrationality amounts to a popular killer phrase, but also in the Humanities and Social Sciences which have produced a plethora of competing definitions. The main dilemma which has hitherto prevented a general agreement on one and single concept of rationality is the fact that many concepts of rationality imply that rationality consists in conformity to parameters that are assumed to be objective and outside the human mind. Arguments are sound and rational because they are grounded on things that are assumed to exist. Actions are rational because their ends are worthwhile. However, these criteria tacitly imply a subjective idea of the material and social world that is individually contingent and still contingent to space and time even if it is shared by most members of the respective group.[1] This objective-subjective dilemma is the consequence of the modern age breakdown of a generally accepted worldview that had granted a congruence between mind and matter via idealism and revelation as did Platonism, Aristotelianism, and Scholasticism. Shifting the criterion to the individual has been the logical consequence. On the theoretical side, it thus becomes possible for discourse analysis and the history of ideas to scrutinize individual or collective concepts of rationality. On the practical level, Max Weber has proposed a model that describes two types of individual rational behaviour (purposive or instrumental rationality and value-oriented rationality).[2] Herein, instrumental rationality asks whether individuals choose the means appropriate for reaching their purposes and thereby uses the same criterion as does the rational actor model in economics, whereas value-oriented rationality is led by ethical or esthetical norms that are posited as absolute, independently from their realization.[3]

The organizers of the conference have chosen two most viable definitions, the individual concept of rationality and purpose-oriented rationality, and I am happy to build on them by investigating the concepts of rationality and the deeper rationale of Plato's and Adam Smith's economic thought with a focus on purposive and value-oriented rationality. My approach is inspired by, and allows for a reappraisal of, a voluminous monograph by Schmitt that detects two different models of rationality in Plato and the modern age that are differentiated by their respective epistemological operation and criterion (distinctiveness and distinction in Plato and Aristotle vs. empirical induction in Hellenistic philosophical schools and in the modern age, the former being a philosophy of distinction, the latter a philosophy of representation) and deals with Smith as a proponent of Stoic inspired modern age rationality.[4] Exploring the limits and the right use of reason for reaching knowl-

---

1 Such generally shared assumptions also shape economic (inter-)action and have been investigated in antiquity under the auspices of the New Institutional Economics and Erving Goffman's theory of frames (for details and further reading, see Günther 2017, 133–134).

2 Weber 1964, vol. 1, 17–18. For details of Weber's complex theory of rationality, see Kalberg 1980.

3 For the sake of relevance and consistency, further elaborations of the concept of rationality such as bounded rationality, a subtype of purpose rationality, or the *homo oeconomicus*, a complex topic (cf. Manstetten 2002) especially in the comparison of Plato and Smith (cf. Schmitt 2008, 434–441; Föllinger 2016, 49–62) or in the analysis of Plato (Bösherz 2019; Müller 2019), that presupposes the same instrumental paradigm as purposive rationality, will be not included in the analysis of Smith and Plato.

4 Schmitt 2008, i–vii, 5, 100–106, and 433–441.

edge, epistemology is an elegant (meta-)approach for investigating rationality that concerns the logic of people's thought and action, and yet one may doubt whether epistemological patterns are appropriate templates for encompassing economy and economics that deal with human behaviour.

I also hope both to enrich and profit from the research on Plato's economic thought that has emerged in the last two decades.[5] A conspicuous share of this scholarship operates within the theoretical framework of New Institutional Economics.[6] Within this approach, the difference between Plato's and the modern model has been acknowledged[7] and named as top-down vs. bottom-up.[8] In order to specify a description of this difference, I shall apply a structuralist-inspired heuristic instrument and map Plato's and Smith's economic thought and their respective anthropological and psychological premises on the grid of a horizontal and vertical axis. This grid that will be used here for the first time to compare Plato's and Smith's economic ideas is a tried and tested heuristic device in the humanities that has found its way into the study of Antiquity.[9] It offers the huge advantage of allowing both a neutral and comprehensive description and a deeper analysis of the characteristics and pervasive common denominators as well as of various granular features of both thinkers, which scholars have established through meticulous piecemeal investigation. In particular, research in Classical Philology and Ancient Philosophy has hitherto focused on individual background, such as Stoic influence on Smith and Plato's ethical focus and pedagogical ambitions.

My paper is organized in a classical chronological order that best suits the history of ideas, thus helping avoid anachronisms and discern possible historical developments. In both authors, I shall apply the grid after a stocktaking of the most relevant passages. In a first step, I shall ask how Plato judged the chances of individual rational behaviour in economy and which measures he devised as a consequence of this judgement. In a second step, I shall look for the backgrounds of Plato's judgements on individual rational behaviour in his philosophy and outline Plato's concept of rationality in the social world and its intertwinement with his epistemology and psychology. In the part on Plato, I shall demonstrate that the founder of the Academy favours a top-down model in epistemology, psychology, as well as in

5 E.g., Schofield 1999; Föllinger 2016; Föllinger / Korn 2019.

6 Föllinger 2016, 20–23, Föllinger / Korn 2019, 3–14. For a critical appraisal of this approach, see Günther 2017, 133–135.

7 Föllinger / Korn 2019, 13–14.

8 Günther 2020, 260–261.

9 Segal 1981, 227-228 (Oedipus Tyrannus); Willms 2020, esp. 439–443 (with further readings and details) (Hor. *Od.* 1.1; 2.20; 3.30).

political and socio-economic organization. Like with *Plato politicus*,[10] this fundamental pattern has been marginal in the interpretation of *Plato oeconomicus*.

My second part will be devoted to Adam Smith. His seminal work *The Wealth of Nations* (1776) is widely acclaimed as a foundational text of classical economics.[11] There is a predilection among classicists for using Adam Smith (1723–1790) as a foil in the interpretation of Plato's economic ideas[12] or of Plato's societal conception and the epistemology and anthropology from which it derives.[13] In this perspective, Plato appears as the proponent of a comprehensive social rationality in which economy is embedded, whereas Smith, whose economic ideas were substantially inspired by Stoicism, is presented as the author of a reductionist rationality and anthropology that prevails in modern economics and that focuses exclusively on the *homo oeconomicus* and goal-oriented rationality. In my comparison of the two thinkers' models of rationality, I shall take a different approach that focuses on patterns of interactional organization and the underlying anthropological models. I shall demonstrate that Smith holds the view that individuals are able to be rational actors in economy and elucidate the presuppositions and practical consequences of his assumption. It will turn out that Smith favours a horizontal and bottom-up model in economy, ethics, and psychology. Both the horizontal bottom-up and vertical top-down model that can be discerned in Smith's and Plato's thought respectively are

10 For a concise outline, see Willms 2008.

11 Söllner 2015, 24.

12 Föllinger 2016, 45–48.

13 Schmitt 2008, 431–441. Neither of these brief comparisons addresses the fundamental literary difference between the two authors' works. Plato hides himself behind the mask of polycentric dialogues whereas Smith features overtly as the author of elegant disquisitions. And yet, this difference is limited to the literary form. Both text corpora belong to the argumentative text type, and though being a single speaker, Smith offers no less elaborate argument, whereas Plato, albeit dividing the argument on different personae, is not less conclusive than Smith. The evident contrast between the horizontal peer-to-peer interaction of Plato's dialogues and the vertical top-down paradigm they favor is best explained, in view of Socrates' fate, as a mimicry of his democratic egalitarian environment in Athens, which strongly pro-pagated a horizontal model and was extremely sensitive towards any threat that could be deemed as tyranny. By the same token, the detail differences between the *Republic* and *Laws* that reflect a different perspective and take (the *Laws* discussing practical and institutional issues which the *Republic* had left unaddressed), but share the same epistemological and anthropological premises (Schmitt 2000, 75) are no insurmountable obstacle for investigating the top-down rationale that will be demonstrated in both political treatises. The proof of the pudding is in the eating.

two structural rationales that describe the organizational logic of cultural phenomena. The concept of a structural rationale offers a new facet to the rationality debate that transcends the subjective-objective opposition. In a last step, I shall investigate whether and to which extent Smith's economic model of fruitful peer-to-peer interaction is inspired by Stoic influence and which role the reception of Stoicism played in the birth of modern economic rationality that we can observe in Smith.

2. Plato

2.1 Rational actors?

Both the *Republic* and the *Laws* recognize the necessity and beneficial effect of economy and productive economic activities at the level of the city-state. The *Republic* grounds the birth and growth of the city in material requirements and the need for labour division (*Resp.* 369b–374a). The *Laws* acknowledges the function of money and retail trade of bringing things to where they are needed (*Lg.* 918a–c):

> καπηλεία γὰρ κατὰ πόλιν πᾶσα γέγονεν οὐ βλάβης ἕνεκα τό γε κατὰ φύσιν, πᾶν δὲ τοὐναντίον· πῶς γὰρ οὐκ εὐεργέτης πᾶς ὃς ἂν οὐσίαν χρημάτων ὡντινωνοῦν ἀσύμμετρον οὖσαν καὶ ἀνώμαλον ὁμαλήν τε καὶ σύμμετρον ἀπεργάζηται; τοῦτο ἡμῖν χρὴ φάναι καὶ τὴν τοῦ νομίσματος ἀπεργάζεσθαι δύναμιν, καὶ τὸν ἔμπορον ἐπὶ τούτῳ τετάχθαι δεῖ λέγειν. καὶ μισθωτὸς καὶ πανδοκεὺς καὶ ἄλλα, τὰ μὲν εὐσχημονέστερα, τὰ δὲ ἀσχημονέστερα γιγνόμενα, τοῦτό γε πάντα δύναται, πᾶσιν ἐπικουρίαν ταῖς χρείαις ἐξευπορεῖν καὶ ὁμαλότητα ταῖς οὐσίαις.
> All retailing – at any rate in its natural form – exists in a city not with a view to doing any harm, but precisely the opposite. Anyone who can convert a disproportionate and uneven distribution of goods into one which is even and proportionate must be a public benefactor. Bringing this about, we need to emphasise, is the reason why we have money, and precisely this is the trader's role; we need to point that out. Likewise hired labourers, innkeepers, and various others of greater or lesser respectability, all have precisely this function – to provide general fulfilment of needs, and an even distribution of property. (trans. Schofield / Griffith 2016)

Both dialogues, however, are pervaded by serious apprehensions about the morally corrupting effect that especially commercial activities would bring about for people involved in them as they would inspire the will for more (πλεονεξία). This premise is the dominant theoretical background of Plato's approach towards economic activity and can be labelled, with all due caution, as anthropological pessimism:[14] in the *Republic* (359c), "Glaucon presupposes a deep-seated human impulse toward πλεονεξία" that looms even over the just one:[15]

> δόντες ἐξουσίαν ἑκατέρῳ ποιεῖν ὅτι ἂν βούληται, τῷ τε δικαίῳ καὶ τῷ ἀδίκῳ, εἶτ' ἐπακολουθήσαιμεν θεώμενοι ποῖ ἡ ἐπιθυμία ἑκάτερον ἄξει. ἐπ' αὐτοφώρῳ οὖν λάβοιμεν ἂν τὸν δίκαιον τῷ ἀδίκῳ εἰς ταὐτὸν ἰόντα διὰ τὴν πλεονεξίαν, ὃ πᾶσα φύσις διώκειν πέφυκεν ὡς ἀγαθόν, νόμῳ δὲ βίᾳ παράγεται ἐπὶ τὴν τοῦ ἴσου τιμήν.
>
> Imagine giving to each of them, the just and the unjust, the power to do whatever they wish, and then following each of them, watching where their desire will lead them. We should then catch the just person red-handed going after the same thing as the unjust man, which everyone naturally pursues as a good thing because of his greed but is forcibly deflected by the law into respect for equality. (trans. Emlyn-Jones / Preddy 2013)

The same idea about a deep-seated human propensity to greed recurs in the *Laws* (*Lg.* 918c9–d8):

> Ὦ φίλε Κλεινία, σμικρὸν γένος ἀνθρώπων καὶ φύσει ὀλίγον καὶ ἄκρᾳ τροφῇ τεθραμμένον, ὅταν εἰς χρείας τε καὶ ἐπιθυμίας τινῶν ἐμπίπτῃ, καρτερεῖν πρὸς τὸ μέτριον δυνατόν ἐστι, καὶ ὅταν ἐξῇ χρήματα λαβεῖν πολλά, νήφει καὶ πρότερον αἱρεῖται τοῦ πολλοῦ τὸ τοῦ μέτρου ἐχόμενον· τὰ δὲ τῶν ἀνθρώπων πλήθη πᾶν τοὐναντίον ἔχει τούτοις, δεόμενά τε ἀμέτρως δεῖται καὶ ἐξὸν κερδαίνειν τὰ μέτρια ἀπλήστως αἱρεῖται κερδαίνειν· διὸ πάντα τὰ περὶ τὴν καπηλείαν καὶ ἐμπορίαν καὶ πανδοκείαν γένη διαβέβληταί τε καὶ ἐν αἰσχροῖς γέγονεν ὀνείδεσιν.
>
> My dear Cleinias, it is a small subset of the human race – few by birth, and brought up with the finest possible upbringing – who, when they encounter needs and desires for various things have the strength of mind for what is moderate, and when given the opportunity of making a lot of money will soberly choose what is in due proportion in preference to a lot. The general run of mankind is the exact opposite of these people; when they have wants, their wants are inordinate, and given the opportunity of making reasonable profit, they are, from choice, insatiable in their hunger for gain. That is why the retailing, trading, and innkeeping classes as a whole are

14 For a different approach, see Föllinger 2016, 40–41.

15 Pendrick 2002, 65.

> criticized and subjected to demeaning abuse. (trans. Schofield / Griffith 2016)

This claim is subsequently illustrated in the *Republic* by the example of Gyges who, thanks to a ring he had found by chance which bestowed invisibility upon him, rose to be king of Lydia (*Resp.* 359c–360b). The *Laws* stay in the present, still using a fictional economic situation for illustrating the recklessness of greed (*Lg.* 918d8–919b4):

> ἐπεὶ εἴ τις, ὃ μή ποτε γένοιτο οὐδ' ἔσται, προσαναγκάσειε – γελοῖον μὲν εἰπεῖν, ὅμως δὲ εἰρήσεται – πανδοκεῦσαι τοὺς πανταχῇ ἀρίστους ἄνδρας ἐπί τινα χρόνον ἢ καπηλεύειν ἤ τι τῶν τοιούτων πράττειν, ἢ καὶ γυναῖκας ἔκ τινος ἀνάγκης εἱμαρμένης τοῦ τοιούτου μετασχεῖν τρόπου, γνοίημεν ἂν ὡς φίλον καὶ ἀγαπητόν ἐστιν ἕκαστον τούτων καί, εἰ κατὰ λόγον ἀδιάφθορον γίγνοιτο, ἐν μητρὸς ἂν καὶ τροφοῦ σχήματι τιμῷτο τὰ τοιαῦτα πάντα. νῦν δὲ ὁπόταν εἰς ἐρήμους τις καπηλείας ἕνεκα τόπους καὶ πανταχόσε μήκη ἔχοντας ὁδῶν ἱδρυσάμενος οἰκήσεις, ἐν ἀπορίᾳ γιγνομένους καταλύσεσιν ἀγαπηταῖς δεχόμενος, ἢ ὑπὸ χειμώνων ἀγρίων βίᾳ ἐλαυνομένοις, εὐδιεινὴν γαλήνην παρασχὼν ἢ πνίγεσιν ἀναψυχήν, τὰ μετὰ ταῦτα οὐχ ὡς ἑταίρους δεξάμενος φιλικὰ παράσχῃ ξένια ἑπόμενα ταῖς ὑποδοχαῖς, ὡς δ' ἐχθροὺς αἰχμαλώτους κεχειρωμένους ἀπολυτρώσῃ τῶν μακροτάτων καὶ ἀδίκων καὶ ἀκαθάρτων λύτρων, ταῦτά ἐστι καὶ τὰ τοιαῦτα ἐν ξύμπασι τοῖς τοιούτοις [ὀρθῶς][16] ἁμαρτανόμενα τὰς διαβολὰς τῇ τῆς ἀπορίας ἐπικουρήσει παρεσκευακότα. τούτων οὖν χρὴ φάρμακον ἀεὶ τέμνειν τὸν νομοθέτην.
> Mind you, if – perish the thought, and it's not going to happen – but if someone (it may sound a daft thing to say, but I am going to say it anyway) were to compel the best men everywhere to start being innkeepers for a certain period of time, or retailers, or to carry on some activity of that sort, or if women, for that matter, by some compulsion of fate, had to play their part in a way of life of this kind, then we would realise how welcome and

16 ὀρθῶς is kept in Burnet's Oxford edition, but secluded in Bury's Loeb edition (1926, vol. 2, 408) and England's commentary (1921, vol. 2, 523), both following Wagner. One scholar transposes ὀρθῶς after ἁμαρτανόμενα. Schöpsdau to whom I owe this overview opts for αἰσχρῶς which is transmitted in the margin of O (2011, 476–477). An approving comment such as ὀρθῶς is not necessary and absent from the initial claim about innkeepers' bad reputation (*Lg.* 918d6–8) which the mental experiment is meant to justify and which this final conclusion confirms. It is, however, quite likely that such a comment which the tenor of the text suggests was slipped in by a later copist, as argues England 1921, vol. 2, 523.

> desirable each of these occupations is. And if they were conducted along honest lines, all these kinds of activities would be viewed in the same light as a mother or a nurse. As things are now, by contrast, someone sets up shop in some uninhabited spot, miles from anywhere; he takes in people who have nowhere to stay, gives them lodging and welcome – or for those driven violently by fierce storms, providing them with a peaceful haven, or a cool refuge from the torrid heat. But after that, does he receive them as friends, and give them the gifts with which friends accompany their hospitality? No, he treats them as if they were a defeated enemy, prisoners of war, holding them to ransom at a sky-high, unjust, and outrageous price. It is these malpractices, and others like them, which in any establishment of this kind give relieving people in distress a bad name. Well, those are the ills against which our lawgiver has to be constantly preparing remedies. (trans. Schofield / Griffith 2016)

In this mental experiment, the righteous people are able to preserve their moral integrity even when getting the opportunity of enriching themselves as innkeepers or retailers, whereas the *Republic* had insisted that the ring of Gyges would corrupt even a just person (*Resp.* 360b–c). Still, both passages share the central idea that, when given the opportunity, the vast majority of humans indulge a propensity to get as much economic capital as possible regardless of moral infractions. Although Plato insists on the choice people have between moral integrity and greedy behaviour, this choice is usually perfunctory since greed compels most people to choose gain. Plato's concept of πλεονεξία thus leaves little room for free will and moral responsibility in most people. It is innkeepers or retailers to whom their profession offers a particular easy opportunity of realizing this general human inclination. Plato's complex model does not ascribe an innate moral flaw to a group of people, but blames their negative behaviour on the social circumstances of their profession that lead them to give way to an inclination common in all humans. This immoral behaviour explains the bad reputation from which the business of retailers, long distance commerce and innkeepers would suffer in general (*Lg.* 918d6–8). Thus, in Plato's model, the unrestrained striving for economic capital impairs not only people's moral, but also their social integrity and the integrity of the city. In the *Republic*, the will for more is the ultimate reason why the polis passes from the healthy to the opulent state since some people would not be satisfied with the frugal life style and ask for luxury (*Resp.* 372d8–373a4). Moreover, within the deeper logic of Plato's philosophy, greedy behaviour is most irrational as all morally flawed acts impair the integrity of the soul, which occupies the supreme position in the hierarchy of Plato's ethics.

2.2 Political consequences

The deep-rooted concerns about the morally corrupting effects of material well-being and commercial activity prevent Plato from perceiving the individual that has not undergone philosophical re-education as a rational economic actor[17] and have two consequences for economic politics: a preference for a frugal lifestyle in society and for public interventions in economy. Since Plato is not confident about a sufficient capacity of rational action among most individuals, he delegates the responsibility for social rationality to the laws that are also meant to shape the moral character of the inhabitants[18] or the philosopher-kings (in his *Republic*) who are supposed to be immune against irrationality.

In his account of the birth and growth of the city from needs and division of labour, Plato favours the frugal state as healthy and true over the opulent one (*Resp.* 372e6–8).[19] This symmetric opposition is completed by equating the frugal and healthy city[20] to the just, whereas the opulent and diseased city is unjust (*Resp.* 372e).[21] Since Plato does not recognize the desire for amenities that go beyond physical survival, the new states he designs are less inclined to satisfy them and more prepared to ignore or repress them. When devising the frugal lifestyle for the

17 This tendency appears still in a scholar who explicitly endorses Plato's views against Stoicism and the allegedly Stoic inspired modern age and who denounces the Smith-inspired *homo oeconomicus* as a dangerous model as it would presuppose perfect rationality in every human being at any time (Schmitt 2008, 438–429). Schmitt (2019, 81) spells out the disenfranchising implication of this argument by citing Richard Thaler's idea of "nudging" as a consequence of the rational deficits of many economic agents. And yet, perfect rationality is an ideal concept that is highly indebted to Platonic thought. Schmitt provides no evidence that any proponent of the *homo oeconomicus* concept has ever claimed it and instead ignores that, in response to various heuristic challenges, economics has modified and refined the concept of the maximization of one parameter by more complex models that take into account situational parameters and the cost of information (so-called "bounded rationality") without denying the economic agents' rationality (Simon 1959, 256).

18 See Pradeau 2010, 132–160.

19 ἡ μὲν οὖν ἀληθινὴ πόλις δοκεῖ μοι εἶναι ἣν διεληλύθαμεν, ὥσπερ ὑγιής τις· εἰ δ' αὖ βούλεσθε καὶ φλεγμαίνουσαν πόλιν θεωρήσωμεν, οὐδὲν ἀποκωλύει. / "Now the genuine state seems to me to be the one we've dealt with and gone through in detail as a healthy one. But again if you want, we can look at an inflamed one. There's nothing to stop us." (trans. Emlyn-Jones / Preddy 2013).

20 For a detailed discussion of Plato's healthy city, see the paper by Silvermintz in this volume.

21 Schofield 1999, 77.

guardians of his ideal city, Socrates comments that his "interlocutors have been purging what they earlier described as a city of luxury" (*Resp.* 399e4–5: διακαθαίροντες)[22] and exhorts to complete the purging (*Resp.* 399e7: καθαίρωμεν). The verb for "purging" which denotes a frugal lifestyle in this passage is the central codeword of Plato's radical programme of ridding the city of any elements, deemed superfluous or offensive, including humans (*Plt.* 293d5; *Lg.* 735b–736a; *Resp.* 501a; cf. *Resp.* 540d–541a).[23]

Plato's answer to the innate greed is a strict and severe regulation of economic activity, especially in the commercial sector. In the conclusion of the above-quoted passage from the *Laws* (see section 2.1) that justifies the necessity of the lawgiver's rigid intervention into economic life by the innkeeper's greedy and merciless behaviour, Plato uses aggressive medical language (*Lg.* 919b2–4: φάρμακον, τέμνειν) which recurs in fantasies of purging an existing city instead of founding a reformed one (*Lg.* 735d–e). Moreover, the phrasing "giving each of them, [...] the power to do whatever they wish" (*Resp.* 359c1: δόντες ἐξουσίαν ἑκατέρῳ ποιεῖν ὅτι ἂν βούληται) in the description of the fatal consequences of unrestrained πλεονεξία matches exactly the permissive definition of freedom in democracy, which is given in the *Republic* (*Resp.* 557b4–6)[24] to which is ascribed similarly fatal consequences for the state, since democracy slips into tyranny by the excess of its main feature, unbridled individual freedom (*Resp.* 562b–569c). These parallels demonstrate that the criticism of profession-related greed and the following strict regulation of economic life are not intended to protect people from exploitation, but reflect Plato's pessimistic anthropology and are part of a radical programme of social reorganization which this view inspires.

Trade and commerce are reduced in the *Laws* by public administration to a degree that satisfies the necessary needs of this polis (*Lg.* 920b) which is chiefly a farmers' republic.[25] We find three types of restrictions of economic interaction: first, economic life is controlled by public administration and institutions, i.e., by an additional third party which is usually absent or shifted to the background and present in measures framing economic interaction. Second, the number of economic agents and their locations for economic interaction are drastically limited, and third, the

22 Ibid., 74.

23 For details, see Willms 2008, 158–161.

24 Οὐκοῦν πρῶτον μὲν δὴ ἐλεύθεροι, καὶ ἐλευθερίας ἡ πόλις μεστὴ καὶ παρρησίας γίγνεται, καὶ ἐξουσία ἐν αὐτῇ ποιεῖν ὅτι τις βούλεται; / "First of all, aren't people free, and doesn't the state abound in freedom and freedom of speech, and isn't there the means to do whatever one wishes?" (trans. Emlyn-Jones / Preddy 2013).

25 Spahn 1984, 316.

influence of their interaction on economic life is practically abolished. Craftsmen, traders, and retailers become functionaries of the polis.[26] The axis of economic activity which shapes the features of economy (who produces which product and sells it at which price to whom) is thus shifted from horizontal interaction to vertical, top-down determination. The owners of the 5,040 land lots, i.e., the body of farmers or rather landlord citizens, are forbidden by law from being trader (ἔμπορος) or retailer (κάπηλος) (*Lg.* 919d). No indigenous citizen is allowed to practice a craft (*Lg.* 846d). Retailing (καπηλεύσειν) is permitted only to alien residents (μέτοικοι) and foreigners (ξένοι) (*Lg.* 920a). Wages for craftsmen and hired workers as well as prices are determined by the authorities (*Lg.* 847b, 920c) and not by the interplay of supply and demand. Foreigners (ξένοι) have to leave after twenty years, or when their fortune exceeds the census for the third class, taking with them their fortune (*Lg.* 915b), probably because Plato feared the moral corruption by greed provoked by the afflux of wealth. To those with the status of alien residents (μετοίκησις) a similar rule applies: they have to leave after 20 years with their fortunes, but can stay under certain circumstances (*Lg.* 850a–b). Local removal is a default measure in Plato's political models for getting rid of people whose influence is deemed detrimental to collective integrity, such as mimetic poets (*Resp.* 398a1–9)[27] and certain religious dissidents (*Lg.* 909a8–c6), a polite ushering out for the former and a sentencing to life incarceration in a remote place for the latter. Local distancing recurs with the port that should be kept at a safe distance for avoiding moral corruption (*Lg.* 704b–705c). This plan implies a negative view of the function as an economic hub and gateway for mobility and various kinds of exchange which Piraeus had and which made the Athenian port an ancient predecessor of Special Economic Zones[28] and, as in the case of the social instrument that is labelled by the euphemism "colony" and meant to get rid of poor people who are willing to follow a leader against the rich (*Lg.* 735e-736a), it puts a given institution into the service of moral disciplining.

Plato's regulations of economic interaction encompass still the more means of payment and the possession of precious metals that have no practical use, but risk provoking greed and discord. This is the logical consequence of his focus on satisfying physical, material needs and his fear of moral corruption provoked by greed. In the *Republic*, guardians and philosophers are the only classes that are forbidden the possession of gold and silver as these precious metals jeopardize their moral integrity (*Resp.* 416e4–417a5). In the *Laws*, private individuals are forbidden the

26 Ibid., 317.

27 For a detailed analysis, see Dalfen 1974, 176–85.

28 On which see Günther 2016.

possession of gold and silver.[29] Taking interest, making money (*Lg.* 743d2–4), and the accumulation of money are banned since they affect social integrity. The use of money is reduced to purchasing everyday products and services (*Lg.* 741e1–742a5):

> χρηματισμὸς γὰρ οὔτ' ἔνεστι σφόδρα ἐν τῇ τοιαύτῃ κατασκευῇ, ξυνέπεταί τε αὐτῇ μηδὲ δεῖν μηδ' ἐξεῖναι χρηματίζεσθαι τῶν ἀνελευθέρων χρηματισμῶν μηδενὶ μηδένα, καθ' ὅσον ἐπονείδιστος λεγομένη βαναυσία ἦθος ἀποτρέπει ἐλεύθερον, μηδὲ τὸ παράπαν ἀξιοῦν ἐκ τῶν τοιούτων ξυλλέγειν χρήματα. πρὸς τούτοις δ' ἔτι νόμος ἕπεται πᾶσι τούτοις, μηδ' ἐξεῖναι χρυσὸν μηδὲ ἄργυρον κεκτῆσθαι μηδένα μηδενὶ ἰδιώτῃ, νόμισμα δὲ ἕνεκα ἀλλαγῆς τῆς καθ' ἡμέραν, ἣν δημιουργοῖς τε ἀλλάττεσθαι σχεδὸν ἀναγκαῖον, καὶ πᾶσιν ὁπόσων χρεία τῶν τοιούτων μισθοὺς μισθωτοῖς, δούλοις καὶ ἐποίκοις, ἀποτίνειν.
>
> An economic system of this kind leaves no room for the excess of money-making,[30] and it follows that there is no need – in fact it is not permitted – for anyone to indulge simply in vulgar money-making, given that what we disparagingly refer to as slaving away for money is a perversion of a free spirit,[31] and that in general no one should feel entitled to accumulate money by this kind of activity. What is more, all this would logically be backed up by a law that no private individual be permitted to own any gold or silver, only the currency needed for the day-to-day dealings they are more or less bound to have with workmen, and for paying wages to all those whose payment is in the form of wages – slaves or immigrants. (trans. Schofield / Griffith 2016)

The use of this currency is limited to Magnesia. International currency (which would allow the purchase of refined products unavailable in the frugal regime and possibly stir covetousness and decadence) is put under restrictive control by the state and is only available for journeys abroad (*Lg.* 742a7–c2). Plato's local currency

---

29 For the morally corrupting effect of the greed of money, see above, section 2.1.

30 Bury 1926, vol. 1, 371. "undue pursuit of money" (Schofield / Griffith 2016, 189).

31 Sauvé Meyer 2003, 210: "the kind called 'mechanical' carry ill repute and undermine the character of a free person." Schöpsdau 2003, 47: "insofern ja die als erniedrigend geltende Handwerksarbeit ein edles Gemüt abstößt." In many passages from Plato and Aristotle, manual activity (βαναυσία) is deemed unworthy of a free person (ἀνελεύθερον) (Schöpsdau 2003, 321). Bury 1926, vol. 1, 371: "inasmuch as what is called contemptible vulgarity perverts a liberal character"; Apelt 1916, vol. 1, 165: "denn das schon dem Namen nach verächtliche Banausentum läßt keine edle Sinnesart aufkommen"; Saunders 1976, 211: "you know how a gentleman's character is coarsened by manual labour, which is generally admitted to be degrading".

offers few incentives for economic efficiency and swiftness which have to be substituted for by control and sanctions. Craftsmen who for negligence (διὰ κάκην) fail to provide a product within the period stipulated are liable for a fine to the divinity who is their patron (i.e., Hephaestus and Athena) and liable for the price of the product with which they cheated the customer and should produce the product in the period stipulated for free. If the customer does not pay the appropriate wage within the period stipulated he is liable to the double of the wage plus interests (*Lg.* 921a1–d3).[32] The sanctions against the craftsman are more detailed and harsher, and they are accompanied by conjectures about the craftsman's religious speculations that his divine patron would be lenient which expose the craftsman's *naïveté*. These psychological speculations and the craftsman's suspected laziness point to a profound distrust of the morals of an underclass group that performs physical work. With retailers, the derogatory stance which Plato takes towards working-class people operates via qualification: retailers are those who are weaklings and who are useless in a well-governed city. Their job is saving time for farmers and craftsmen who would be unable to perform their job if they were forced to sell their products at the market themselves (*Resp.* 371c–d). The negative picture of the retailers in Plato stands out in comparison with his depiction of long-distance traders, which is ambivalent and not pervasively negative.[33] The top-down rationale that characterizes Plato's social and psychological models thus recurs in the prestige of these two professions and aligns with their respective social positions. Ancient literature offers the same distribution of the assessment of both kinds of traders, reflecting the upper-class origin of its authors.[34] The top-down rationale thus finds a match in the social background of the group that authored this judgement. It is complemented by the origin of the disregarded people. Banking, small trading, and retailing were practiced in Antiquity by groups that had relatively little power.[35] Even authors of economic views with a background in the new money-oriented business shared the condemnation of money making, wealth, and its acquisition that was expressed by the authors who were traditional landlords – and despite their condemnation often practiced the modern forms of income in addition.[36] Moreover, the disrespect which Plato displays for craftsmen finds a match in the attitude of his upper-class fellows.

---

32 This passage has not been included in Schriefl 2019, who offers a detailed discussion of workers' virtue in Plato.

33 Günther 2017, 143.

34 Ibid., 143–144.

35 Eich 2006, 41.

36 Hinsch 2021, 111–114.

Ancient landlords used to talk with disdain about craftsmen, small farmers, and slaves,[37] and the rich displayed an ostentatious disdain for craftsmen.[38]

2.3 Concept of rationality and the top-down rationale

It is worthwhile to remind ourselves that assessing concepts of rationality in ancient texts faces certain onomasiological problems that do not always allow us to identify modern concepts at face value or offer bullet-proof lexical evidence. With this caveat, we can state that Plato has a holistic and objectivist idea of rationality that is rooted in his epistemology and ontology, and in particular in his doctrine of ideas, and that informs his views on rationality in the social sphere. The universal and uniform character of Plato's concept of rationality thus deserves the label "philosophical".

The impact of Plato's theoretical concept of reason and rationality in the *Laws* is less pervasive because this constitutional model is meant to be only the second best after the *Republic*, dismissing the most specific epistemological and ontological features of his philosophy. Nevertheless, both models equally pledge rationality as characteristic of their constitution. In the *Laws*, the polis that is about to be founded should be free, reasonable, and a friend to itself (ὅτι πόλιν ἐλευθέραν τε εἶναι δεῖ καὶ ἔμφρονα καὶ ἑαυτῇ φίλην [*Lg.* 693b4]). *Lg.* 701d puts in this triadic enumeration νοῦν ἕξει instead of ἔμφρων. Ethical rationality thus warrants collective integrity. This nexus appears in another enumeration that presupposes the unity of self-control, practical wisdom, and collective integrity (*Lg.* 693c2–3: σωφρονεῖν, φρόνησις, φιλία). The eminent status of the city's moral constitution is the theoretical background for Plato's concern about the morally corrupting effects of commercial activities in the *Laws*. This focus on virtue and self-control is rooted in Plato's ethics and anthropology.

In the *Republic*, practical virtues and wisdom are characteristics of the lowest class. However, wisdom which is more intellectual and exclusive is the highest single virtue in the city and the soul (*Resp.* 428b–429a). Since only a few are gifted enough to cultivate wisdom, collective rationality is granted by the rule of the philosopher-kings (*Resp.* 474c1–3) and by the exclusion of the mass from political decisions (*Resp.* 428b–d) on account of their nature and degrading practical activity (*Resp.* 495d–e). These regulations apply a top-down model of government on the city that gives all power over the rest of the population to the philosopher-kings.

The rule of the philosopher-kings and the entire top-down model of paternalist social organization are buttressed by Plato's doctrine of ideas. The Allegory of the

37 Eich 2006, 41.

38 Ibid.

Cave which is meant to illustrate this epistemological model opposes the ignorant mass to one enlightened person who has seen the truth (*Resp.* 514a–517a). This social distribution of intellectual and moral competence is the perfect justification of the rule of a happy few over the ignorant majority of people.[39] The physical location of the cave below and the real world above (*Resp.* 516e4, 517a3) suggests the superiority of the person who has seen the real world and also the top-down organization of Plato's political models. The ignorant mass would not believe the enlightened person should he return into the cave and instead seek to kill him if he tried to unbound them to lead them upward (*Resp.* 517a4–6). This unreceptive and even aggressive reaction to the person who brings the truth suggests that the people who possess the truth can only rule by force and persuasion[40] (or even deceit[41]).

The Allegory of the Cave strongly suggests that Plato favours massive regulation of economic practice because he assumes that few people have the right knowledge. The correlation of the degree of certainty assumed in epistemology and the eagerness to economic interventionism is mirrored by the Sophists who held sceptical views in epistemology and included economic calculation into their curriculum[42] and devised no restrictions for, but instead advocated and recommended the circulation of economic capital.[43]

The psychological basis for the restrictive programme and the demonization of the mass of humans as driven by reckless striving for non-ideal benefit (πλεονεξία) that characterizes Plato's economic analysis is a three-layered model of the soul that posits as its lowest part an element that is the seat of desires (ἐπιθυμητικόν) and most irrational. The demoniac and subhuman character of this element is epitomized by a simile of the three-layered soul where it corresponds to a many-headed monster, whereas the second element, the element of courage and passion (θυμοειδές), is illustrated by a lion, and only the reasoning faculty (λογιστικόν), which is identified as the governing part of the soul (ἡγεμονικόν) in Plato's model, is represented by a human being (*Resp.* 588b10–e3). This colourful equation has a strong political bearing since the classes of the *Republic* are equated to parts of the soul (*Resp.* 441c4–6, 580d2–4). As the philosopher-kings who possess wisdom by nature and grant the entire state's wise character correspond to the inner human which should rule the rest of the soul, they are entitled and qualified by nature to rule the two lower classes, in particular the mass of people which correspond to the chimaera-like multifarious desire and are

39 Voigtländer 1980, 406–407 and 415.

40 *Grg.* 517b–c; *Resp.* 519e4; *Lg.* 711c4, 718b3; *Plt.* 304d4.

41 E.g., the myth of metals (*Resp.* 414b–415c).

42 Soverini 1998, 51–52.

43 See Spahn 2003, 43–45.

unqualified by nature (*Resp.* 428b1–429a3, 443c4–8, 473c11–d6, 474c1–3) and represent the many under the democratic regime.[44] In particular, craftsmen who cannot control the animalic parts of their soul are supposed to serve a better person who is dominated by the divine in order to be ruled at least indirectly by this principle (*Resp.* 590c–d).

The monstrous proliferation of economic desires and deviant activities is spelled out in the *Republic*. Economic legislation, into which the *Laws* would delve, is rejected (*Resp.* 425c10–e2) with the argument that lawgivers would fight a hydra in the economic field (*Resp.* 426e3–7). The oppressive implication of Platonic psychology is thus clearly inscribed into the wording, the imagery, and the text of the *Republic* and is not just a modern Stoicizing misreading that projects the Stoics' rigid suppression of passions onto the way in which the mind is meant to rule the desires in Plato.[45] There is further textual evidence in Plato. The brutal and bloody bridling of the horse in the chariot allegory in the *Phaedrus* (253e–254e), which represents the covetous element of the soul, clearly demonstrates the symmetry of Platonic psychology and its social implications in which violence is not only exerted by the concupiscent part of the soul, but also deployed to its repression. Plato's pessimist anthropology contains, in addition to innate greed, another theorem which goes in the same direction and suggests a rigid regulation of people, for he assumes that humans are disinclined to accept slavery and are to being regulated (*Lg.* 777b4–c1):

> ἐπειδὴ δύσκολόν ἐστι τὸ θρέμμα ἄνθρωπος καὶ πρὸς τὴν ἀναγκαίαν διόρισιν, τὸ δοῦλόν τε ἔργῳ διορίζεσθαι καὶ ἐλεύθερον καὶ δεσπότην, οὐδαμῶς εὔχρηστον ἐθέλει εἶναί τε καὶ γίγνεσθαι φαίνεται, χαλεπὸν δὴ τὸ κτῆμα·
> [S]ince a human being is a troublesome creature, and since, when it comes to the essential distinction which has to be made in practice between the slave and his free master, it looks as if he is never likely to be, or to become, cooperative, he is decidedly an awkward thing to own. (trans. Schofield / Griffith 2016).

This unwillingness of accepting rule finds a match in the behaviour of the undocile Greek woman in Aeschylus' *Persians* who unlike the Asiatic woman refuses to pull Xerxes' chariot (*Pers.* 194–199). Plato's model of a tripartite soul in the *Republic* is viewed as a hermeneutic progress vis-à-vis discussions of lack of self-control in the *Protagoras*.[46] The further history of Greek philosophy yields a tendency towards unification and rationalization. Whereas Aristotle posited two elements of the soul, the

44 Cf. O'Mahoney 2008, 277.

45 Schmitt 2008, 424–425.

46 Müller 2019, 54–59.

rational and the irrational (*Eth. Nic.* 1102b13–18), the Stoics assumed a unified soul. In this model, passions are not only the product of false judgements of the rational governing part, but also affect it as a whole. This model is less conflictual than the tripartite Platonic model where passions appear as a victory of the lower part of the soul over its rational element.[47] The Stoic horizontal model in psychology is paired with a preference for horizontal cooperation in society and a critical distance from unilateral top-down organization. A vast dialogic practice of philosophical persuasion and mental training in the Imperial Era attests to this. Marcus Aurelius even rejected hoping for Plato's Republic and instead suggested being happy with the smallest steps forward (M. Aur. 9.29.5), and Epictetus lessoned (in a probably fictive dialogue) a high imperial functionary (Lat. *corrector*) that he should treat the citizens like rational beings and point out their advantage (τὰ συμφέροντα) instead of threatening them with physical violence (Epict. 3.7.31–33). Whereas Aristotle justified the institution of slavery and reflected on its practical organization (*Pol.* 1252a31–b12, 1253b14–1255b40, 1259b17–1260b7), Stoics, albeit never embracing legal abolitionism, took a critical distance from this omnipresent institution in Antiquity and tended to ease the slave's status in theory and practice.[48] Whilst Aristotle claimed a class of humans who were slaves by nature (*Pol.* 1253b14–1255b15, esp. 1254a13–17), Seneca insists that slaves were humans and friends of lower extraction (*Ep.* 47.1).

3. Adam Smith

3.1 Rational actors

Adam Smith offers a picture that is diametrically opposed to Plato's. He construes economy bottom-up from horizontal peer-to-peer interaction and is confident about the individual's competence in making the best economic decisions, consequently advocating limiting public intervention in economic life. One reason for this was a divergent assessment of desires that to Plato require regulation. Whereas Plato was anxious about the morally and socially corrupting effect of greed, Smith acknowledged at least in the economic sphere that desires that cannot be satisfied and are unlimited operate as motors of economic development (*The Wealth of Nations* 1.11.c.7).[49] A second reason concerns moral qualification. Smith assumed that whereas perfect virtue is reserved to a happy few, apposite ethical behaviour (propriety) required an average degree of self-command that can be found even among "the most worthless of mankind" (*The Theory of Moral Sentiments* 1.1.5.7). This

47 Daraki-Mallet 1978, 88–89; Reydams-Schils 2005, 25–26.

48 For details, see Manning 1989; Erskine 1990, 43–63; Garnsey 1996, 128–152.

49 Manstetten 2002, 264.

assumption is borrowed from the Stoic theory of proficients who had not reached perfect virtue, but would be able to fulfil moral duties (*officia*, καθήκοντα), a theory with which Smith was familiar (*The Theory of Moral Sentiments* 7.2.1.42).[50]

Smith's construing of economy from horizontal peer-to-peer interaction is most obvious in a classical and often quoted passage (*Wealth of Nations* 1.2.2):

> In almost every other race of animals, each individual, when it is grown up to maturity, is entirely independent, and in its natural state has occasion for the assistance of no other living creature. But man has almost constant occasion for the help of his brethren, and it is in vain for him to expect it from their benevolence only. He will be more likely to prevail if he can interest their self-love in his favour, and shew them that it is for their own advantage to do for him what he requires of them. Whoever offers to another a bargain of any kind, proposes to do this. Give me that which I want, and you shall have this which you want, is the meaning of every such offer; and it is in this manner that we obtain from one another the far greater part of those good offices which we stand in need of. It is not from the benevolence of the butcher, the brewer, or the baker, that we expect our dinner, but from their regard to their own interest. We address ourselves, not to their humanity but to their self-love, and never talk to them of our own necessities but of their advantages.

By making individual self-interest the motor of economics, this passage implies the assumption that every economic agent is able to act in a rational way in the economic field and to take the best economic decisions for himself. Smith's reduction of economic activity to economic interests is no sign of immoralism, let alone apology for reckless economic egoism, but part of the constitution of economics as an autonomous discipline that excludes alien aspects and asks about the mechanisms, as indicated in the title of his work and spelled out in the above-quoted passage, for how prosperity can be achieved,[51] especially for the lower classes.[52] Crucial for this purpose is the combination of self-interest with social interaction and negotiation. This framing creates a complex interdependent and self-regulatory mechanism of exchange that is operated via social negotiation of partners on a formally equal level and grants the individual's needs by rooting them in the fellow human's self-interest. The latter creates a mechanism that guarantees their satisfaction. The peer-to-peer interaction only takes place on free and equal terms (which is the very opposite

50 Waszek 1984, 591 and 593.

51 Manstetten 2002, 39.

52 Cf. Ballestrem 2001, 154 and *Wealth of Nations* 1.8.36.

of Plato's regulation of putatively lazy craftsmen) and thereby grants the maximum satisfaction of both partners. Moreover, it is operated in a dialogic form ("Give me that which I want, and you shall have this which you want") that extends the dialogic character of Smith thought from ethics[53] to economy and implies reciprocity. The complex mechanism of interaction constitutes a system of checks and balances that reduces the risk of unilateral egoism.

Smith's second economic basic assumption for achieving prosperity is the claim that individuals unintentionally add to public welfare by pursuing their own interest (*Wealth of Nations* 4.2.9):

> As every individual, therefore, endeavours as much as he can both to employ his capital in the support of domestick industry, and so to direct that industry that its produce may be of the greatest value; every individual necessarily labours to render the annual revenue of the society as great as he can. He generally, indeed, neither intends to promote the public interest, nor knows how much he is promoting it. By preferring the support of domestick to that of foreign industry, he intends only his own security; and by directing that industry in such a manner as its produce may be of the greatest value, he intends only his own gain, and he is in this, as in many other cases, led by an invisible hand to promote an end which was no part of his intention. Nor is it always the worse for the society that it was no part of it. By pursuing his own interest, he frequently promotes that of the society more effectually than when he really intends to promote it. I have never known much good done by those who affected to trade for the publick good. It is an affectation, indeed, not very common among merchants, and very few words need be employed in dissuading them from it.

Whereas the confidence in self-interest implied a trust on the individual's conscious and intentional instrumental rationality, this claim clearly limits the range of the individual's conscious and intentional horizon and instead postulates a systemic rationality of their actions – what Plato achieves by a legal and institutional framework.

Both of Smith's basic assumptions, however, agree on the beneficial effect of the individuals' economic activity for public wealth. The economic competence of the economic agent is the implicit prerequisite for Smith's outright refusal of public intervention into the decisions about the use of private capital since such investment decisions would exceed the lawgiver's qualification (*Wealth of Nations* 4.2.10):

53 See next section 3.2.

> The statesman, who should attempt to direct private people in what manner they ought to employ their capitals, would not only load himself with a most unnecessary attention, but assume an authority which could safely be trusted, not only to no single person, but to no council or senate whatever, and which would nowhere be so dangerous as in the hands of a man who had folly and presumption enough to fancy himself fit to exercise it.

In a more extended passage, Smith insists on the impracticability of a central and official administration of the economy (*Wealth of Nations* 4.9.51):

> All systems, either of preference or of restraint, therefore, being thus completely taken away, the obvious and simple system of natural liberty establishes itself of its own accord. Every man, as long as he does not violate the laws of justice, is left perfectly free to pursue his own interest his own way, and to bring both his industry and capital into competition with those of any other man, or order of men. The sovereign is completely discharged from a duty, in the attempting to perform which he must always be exposed to innumerable delusions, and for the proper performance of which, no human wisdom or knowledge could ever be sufficient; the duty of superintending the industry of private people, and of directing it towards the employments most suitable to the interests of the society.

Smith's plea for economic liberty because of its beneficial effect is – needless to say – inspired by his trust in the synergy of peer-to-peer interaction and the unintentional promotion of common prosperity by the individual. Consequently, he limits public agency immediately afterwards to extra-economic tasks that cannot be performed by private initiative and interaction (*Wealth of Nations* 4.9.51):

> According to the system of natural liberty, the sovereign has only three duties to attend to; three duties of great importance, indeed, but plain and intelligible to common understandings: first, the duty of protecting the society from the violence and invasion of other independent societies; secondly, the duty of protecting, as far as possible, every member of the society from the injustice or oppression of every other member of it, or the duty of establishing an exact administration of justice; and, thirdly, the duty of erecting and maintaining certain publick works, and certain publick institutions, which it can never be for the interest of any individual, or small number of individuals to erect and maintain; because the profit could never repay the expense to any individual, or small number of individuals, though it may frequently do much more than repay it to a great society.

This programme is the very opposite of Plato's generous interventionism and dirigism, but Smith's delineation of the spheres of economy and politics aligns with Plato's formula of justice: everybody should do what is his (*Resp.* 433a–b). Statesmen do politics and make laws, and businessmen do business and make money. The theoretical background for this programme is the assumption that an action does not need an altruistic or collective motivation to benefit other people and that a healthy state of society can be achieved without good intentions in view of society. From the point of view of intellectual history, this insight marks a considerable progress vis-à-vis models that presupposed that healthy effects required good intentions and that consequently inspired a moral approach to economy and justified corrective interventions by an official side. Smith's division of the nature of intention and consequence finds a match in the paradox of Bernard Mandeville's *Fable of the Bees* that private vice would be the source of public prosperity, as indicated by the work's subtitle *Private Vices, Publick Benefits* and spelled out in the fable's moral after detailing the fatal consequences of purging the hive from its vices:[54]

> To make a Great an Honest Hive
> T'enjoy the World's Conveniencies,
> Be fam'd in War, yet live in Ease,
> Without great Vices, is a vain
> Eutopia seated in the Brain.
> Fraud, Luxury and Pride must live,
> While we the Benefits receive. [...]
> So Vice is beneficial found,
> When it's by Justice lopt and bound.

The first sentence is a downright rejection of the practicability of a programme of frugalist and moralist purifying as devised by Plato in his *Republic* and *Laws*, the last clause a clear regulative framing of legitimate private striving by principles of justice as in Smith (*Wealth of Nations* 4.9.51). Within this framework, both thinkers of the Enlightenment behold society and economy as a system that regulates itself in synergy and not as the sum of individual economic decisions and operations.

3.2 Horizontal and bottom-up rationale in psychology and ethics

In Smith, the peer-to-peer organizational pattern is not limited to economics, but recurs in a central figure of his ethics, the impartial spectator,[55] whom he imagines

---

54 Mandeville 1957, 36–37 (1732, 23–24).

55 On which see Raphael 2007.

as an instance that should moderate people's passions (*The Theory of Moral Sentiments* 7.2.1.44):

> By Nature the events which immediately affect that little department in which we ourselves have some little management and direction, which immediately affect ourselves, our friends, our country, are the events which interest us the most, and which chiefly excite our desires and aversions, our hopes and fears, our joys and sorrows. Should those passions be, what they are very apt to be, too vehement, Nature has provided a proper remedy and correction. The real or even the imaginary presence of the impartial spectator, the authority of the man within the breast, is always at hand to overawe them into the proper tone and temper of moderation.

The impartial spectator makes interpersonal interaction, on which Smith relies for the functioning of economy, also the warrant for ethics to work. It is worthwhile to note that horizontal peer-to-peer construction and dialogic performance bridge the two social disciplines, creating a structural coherence of Smith's social theory and underpinning its pervasive peer-to-peer character.[56] Moreover, and this is my second point, the impartial spectator and his interpersonal interaction rely on the doubling of the interacting person since the impartial spectator is the respective person itself that assumes the perspective of an external spectator of his or her own proposed action.[57] This doubling or internalization of a second person is patent in the model of self-control in which the impartial spectator is embedded and where he occupies the intermediary position between two persons, a real, external spectator and God as omnipresent spectator, who are distinct from the respective person and not imagined by him like the impartial spectator (*The Theory of Moral Sentiments* 3.2.31–33). By focusing his own actions by personal self-doubling, the impartial spectator offers an elaborate model of self-reflection. A dialogic disciplining occurs first in the *Odyssey*, where the hero calms his outraged heart (Hom. *Od.* 20.17–24):

> στῆθος δὲ πλήξας κραδίην ἠνίπαπε μύθῳ·
> "τέτλαθι δή, κραδίη· καὶ κύντερον ἄλλο ποτ' ἔτλης,
> ἤματι τῷ, ὅτε μοι μένος ἄσχετος ἤσθιε Κύκλωψ
> ἰφθίμους ἑτάρους· σὺ δ' ἐτόλμας, ὄφρα σε μῆτις
> ἐξάγαγ' ἐξ ἄντροιο ὀϊόμενον θανέεσθαι."
> ὣς ἔφατ', ἐν στήθεσσι καθαπτόμενος φίλον ἦτορ·

56 *Pace* Schmitt 2008, 435 who acknowledges the dialogic character of Smith's anthropology only in his ethics in relation to other people and opposes it to the self-interest-led human of his economics.

57 Raphael / Macfie 1976, 16.

> τῷ δὲ μάλ' ἐν πείσῃ κραδίη μένε τετληυῖα
> νωλεμέως· ἀτὰρ αὐτὸς ἑλίσσετο ἔνθα καὶ ἔνθα.
> He struck himself on the chest and spoke to his heart and scolded it:
> 'Bear up, my heart. You have had worse to endure before this
> on that day when the irresistible Cyclops ate up
> my strong companions, but you endured it until intelligence
> got you out of the cave, though you expected to perish.'
> So he spoke, addressing his own dear heart within his chest [Lattimore: him];
> and the heart in great obedience endured and stood it
> without complaint, but the man himself was twisting and turning.
> (trans. Lattimore 1999)

Whereas Smith's impartial spectator corresponds to the conscience and Freudian "super-ego",[58] Odysseus' heart represents mental layers below the "ego". This flipping of roles from the *Odyssey* to Smith certainly reflects Christian dominance, but also Stoic influence, such as Stoic ideas of conscience[59] since "the man within the breast" of Smith finds a predecessor in the Stoic "guardian-spirit seated within his breast" (M. Ant. 3.16.3). Moreover, theatricality, which the concept of the spectator implies, was claimed as useful already by the Stoics for dialogic moral education.[60]

Internal interaction and doubling are two characteristic features of the impartial spectator that stand out in comparison with Plato's psychology and its implication for social organization. The inner human or controlling and reasoning part remains under permanent threat by the desires whose lurking power is illustrated by an equation to a multi-headed beast. This psychology justifies the hierarchy of the three classes in the *Republic*. Once again, the top-down character of Plato's social theory and ethical psychology stands out against the peer-to-peer, relational, and horizontal organization of these two spheres by Adam Smith.

The role and position of the inner human being in both thinkers makes this difference most patent. In Plato, this "I" rules over intimidating animalic figures and represents the core of the human person; in Smith the "man within the breast" sits beside and coaches the "ego". The impartial spectator interacts with the "ego" as do the two economic partners in *The Wealth of Nations* on a horizontal level and in a bilateral manner. Plato's psychology is contrastingly vertical and, lacking internal

58 For a contrastive comparison of both concepts, see Raphael 1991, 53–56.

59 Schmitt 2008, 435–436.

60 Cf. the endorsing and programmatic quotation from Epicurus (fr. 129 Arr.) that concludes Seneca's letter on gladiator games (*Ep.* 7.11): *'haec' inquit 'ego non multis, sed tibi; satis enim magnum alter alteri theatrum sumus.'* / "I write this not for the many, but for you; each of us is enough audience for the other." (trans. Gummere 1917).

check of the "ego", suggests external control. In Smith, the impartial spectator renders this control by another person pragmatically superfluous as this figure is a purified doubling of the respective person.

The bottom-up pattern of Adam Smith's social organization is most salient on the largest level, that of humanity, for which he recommends a cosmopolitan attitude in ethics to the individual (*The Theory of Moral Sentiments* 3.3.11):

> Among the moralists who endeavour to correct the natural inequality of our passive feelings by diminishing our sensibility to what peculiarly concerns ourselves, we may count all the ancient sects of philosophers, but particularly the ancient Stoics. Man, according to the Stoics, ought to regard himself, not as something separated and detached, but as a citizen of the world, a member of the vast commonwealth of nature. To the interest of this great community, he ought at all times to be willing that his own little interest should be sacrificed. Whatever concerns himself, ought to affect him no more than whatever concerns any other equally important part of this immense system.

This passage provides material proof that Smith's bottom-up model was influenced by his familiarity with Stoic philosophy and connects to our next question, the role of Stoic influence in the formation of Smith's economic theory.

3.3 Stoic influence and the birth of modern economics

Scholars have identified various ancient inspirations of Smith's economic theory and his ethics. Smith has been suggested as a gateway to modern economy for Plato's ideas on justice and order and for his focus on mathematics.[61] Parallels and influences have been discussed between Plato's and Smith's theory of the division of labour,[62] and Aristotle's and Smith's theory of value have become the subject of an analytical and contrastive comparison.[63] Stoic ideas have been ascribed the deepest formational impact and have found the most attention.[64] Stoic influence has been suspected in particular in Smith's economic core tenets, such as his approval of self-interest and his claim about the congruence of private striving and public benefit as well as his confidence about the beneficial and self-regulatory effects of

61 Lowry 2008, 13.

62 Vivenza 2001, 126–140.

63 Ibid., 141–158.

64 For details and further reading, see Föllinger 2008, esp. 1063, n. 1; Schmitt 2008, 426–432; Raphael / Macfie 1976, 5–10.

economic interaction that is free from public intervention.[65] The former can be correlated to the Stoic theory of *oikeiôsis*, the latter offers a certain affinity with the Stoic concept of a divine *logos* that permeates and organizes the universe in its role as providence for the best, even turning individually detrimental phenomena and wicked people into beneficial effects for the universe. There is textual evidence that Smith was familiar with both tenets. A critical assessment of Smith's sources for Stoic doctrine has not found sufficient attention in previous comparative research.[66] It goes without saying that Smith's ideas about Stoic doctrine are a contingent stage in the history of ideas and do not necessarily match the elaborate results which modern reconstruction and detailed *Quellenforschung* on these fragmentary and indirectly transmitted sources for Early and Middle Stoicism has brought about since the end of the 19th century.[67] In addition to Smith's economic core tenets, I shall examine the origin of Smith's concept of fair play that finds a striking match in Cicero's account about Chrysippus in *De finibus*, a treatise to which Smith devoted a part of his lecture course each year.[68] I shall limit myself to these points which represent the two types of direct classical influence outlined by Vivenza (as opposed to indirect influence transmitted via modern sources)[69] and offer the highest degree of evidence, and which are to favour Smith's preference for peer-to-peer interaction and bottom-up social organization.[70] By a comparative close reading of relevant passages from Smith and the Stoics I shall assess two main questions: how evident and

---

65 Raphael 1991, 86–87; Schmitt 2008, 427–437; Föllinger 2008, 1070–1076; 2016, 46. To this core, Smith would have attached Aristotelian and Epicurean elements (Vivenza 2001, 185–90; cf. Vivenza 1999).

66 The fundamental methodological question of Smith's Stoic sources is addressed only in Raphael / Macfie 1976, 5–10 and not discussed in Schmitt 2008, 426–441 and Föllinger 2008, even though the former strongly insists on Smith's intellectual dependence on Stoic thought.

67 This potential gap, which adds a methodological *caveat* similar to the dialogical form for Plato's tenets, has gone unobserved in most comparative studies as well (Schmitt 2008; Föllinger 2008).

68 Vivenza 2001, 3.

69 Ibid., 2–5.

70 The potential influence of Stoic natural law theory that was adapted and developed further in the Early Modern Age (cf. Raphael 1991, 87–89; Föllinger 2008, 1067–1070) as well as the potential reception of the Stoic concept of "system" (cf. *The Theory of Moral Sentiments* 3.3.11; *Wealth of Nations* 4.9.51) which was most influential (Hager 1998, 824) are too thorny and remote from this paper's topic and will therefore stay out of consideration.

deep is Stoic influence on Smith's economic thought, and what stands out as his theoretical achievements in economic theory in dealing with Stoic ideas?

Grounding economy in self-love (*Wealth of Nations* 1.2.2) might be indebted to ancient ideas like φιλαυτία or, more specifically, the Stoic concept of *oikeiôsis*.[71] There is material proof for this assumption, as demonstrated by Föllinger.[72] Stoics acknowledged a primary propensity of any living being to what is favourable to it.[73] This Stoic principle of self-care is twice cited in *The Theory of Moral Sentiments*. The first passage is so faithful and detailed a rendering of the Stoic doctrine of *oikeiôsis* that it could feature in today's manual of the history of ancient philosophy[74] (*The Theory of Moral Sentiments* 7.2.1.15):

> According to Zeno, the founder of the Stoical doctrine, every animal was by nature recommended to its own care, and was endowed with the principle of self-love, that it might endeavour to preserve, not only its existence, but all the different parts of its nature, in the best and most perfect state of which they were capable.

Smith's creative licence in the reception of the theory of *oikeiôsis* is much stronger in the second passage (*The Theory of Moral Sentiments* 6.2.1.1):

> Every man, as the Stoics used to say, is first and principally recommended to his own care; and every man is certainly, in every respect, fitter and abler to take care of himself than of any other person. Every man feels his own pleasures and his own pains more sensibly than those of other people. The former are the original sensations; the latter the reflected or sympathetic images of those sensations. The former may be said to be the substance; the latter the shadow.

Here, the reference to the Stoics is no more than an incidental and parenthetical vignette to Smith's ideas that is meant to increase their acceptance by an authority from antiquity. Self-care strictly speaking is a subjective adaptation by Smith, as we shall see below. Smith underpins the principle of self-care by further aspects of subjectivity that are absent from the canonical Stoic argument (*SVF* 3.178–189) and reflect the increasing modern focus on this phenomenon, as shown above. Smith's further arguments from subjectivity focus on practical aspects when claiming that

71 Cf. Schmitt 2008, 429.

72 Föllinger 2008, 1070–1071.

73 E.g., Epict. 2.22.15–16. For further instances, see Föllinger 2008, 1071, n. 32.

74 Raphael / Macfie 1976, 272 refer to Cic. *Fin.* 3.(16–18, 20–21, 23) (= *SVF* 3.182, 186–189) and Diog. Laert. 7.85 (= *SVF* 3.178) as parallels.

every individual is fitter to take care for himself, a view that would recur in his socioeconomic analyses (*The Wealth of Nations* 2.2.2.1):

> Every man is, no doubt, by nature, first and principally recommended to his own care; and as he is fitter to take care of himself than of any other person, it is fit and right that it should be so.

This argument as well as the entire focus on self-care is absent from Stoic orthodoxy (*SVF* 3.178–189) that highlights self-preservation. Smith may have elaborated the idea of self-care from Cicero's phrasing of the theory of *oikeiôsis* (*Fin.* 3.16):

> *Placet his ... simulatque natum sit animal ... ipsum sibi conciliari et commendari ad se conservandum.*
> Those [...] have the following view: Every animal, as soon as it is born [...] is concerned with itself, and feels an impulse to preserve itself. (trans. Woolf 2001, with modifications from Rackham 1931).

The verb *commendari* which recurs in *recommend* of Smith's account of Zeno's doctrine and points towards self-care of the entrusted individual suggests this influence. Furthermore, Cicero's passage illustrates that in addition to self-care, shifting the theorem of *oikeiôsis* from biology and individual development to anthropology and the static human condition is another feature of Smith's adaptation of the Stoic theorem of *oikeiôsis* that stands out.

The decisive point in the context of Smith's reception of the theory of *oikeiôsis* and self-care is not the possible genealogy of this concept, but its transposition to social sciences, and, in particular, making it in *The Wealth of Nations* (1.2.2) the cornerstone of economic politics without moral(istic) ado. Stoics had confined this principle to anthropology and ethics where they made it the stepping-stone for psychagogic self-care and moral behaviour and kept a critical distance from wealth, which is still reflected in Seneca's auto-apologetic contortions (*Vit. Beat.* 21–28), whereas Smith outlines the beneficial effects of the rich for prosperity (*The Theory of Moral Sentiments* 4.1.10). Despite the shift of self-care from the soul to material well-being both concepts of self-care are fundamentally different from the modern (and colloquial) notion of "egoism" by which the Stoics' and Smith's concept is labelled[75] as this term implies a reckless pursuit of superficial advantage which corresponds to the Platonizing concept of greed and insatiability, but is alien from the concept of self-care which implies self-responsibility and is inspired by an empirical and individualistic approach.

75 Föllinger 2008, 1074; 2016, 47; Schmitt 2008, 433–435; 2019, 80.

If the Stoic inspired approval of self-care as natural supports autonomous individual economic action, the claim that by pursuing his own interests, the individual benefits the community supports the concept of autonomous peer-to-peer interaction to which it ascribes a positive effect on society. The evidence for a Stoic origin of the congruence thesis, however, is weaker than with self-interest. Unlike with self-interest, Smith nowhere ascribes this nexus to the Stoics. He merely demonstrates a general acquaintance with the Stoic concept of providence that concerns not only its ethical implication which Smith approves and identifies in limiting our interest in external things to those directed by providence (*The Theory of Moral Sentiments* 7.2.1.46), but also, more pertinent for the economic field, its beneficial pervading of cosmic events (*The Theory of Moral Sentiments* 1.2.3.4):

> The ancient stoics were of opinion, that as the world was governed by the all-ruling providence of a wise, powerful, and good God, every single event ought to be regarded, as making a necessary part of the plan of the universe, and as tending to promote the general order and happiness of the whole: that the vices and follies of mankind, therefore, made as necessary a part of this plan as their wisdom or their virtue; and by that eternal art which educes good from ill, were made to tend equally to the prosperity and perfection of the great system of nature.

In this benevolent cosmic plan, even human vices play a positive role. Human vices which are ascribed a positive effect might be associated by contemporary and modern readers with self-interest, yet they are something essentially different as vices have per se, and not occasionally, a negative association. The only common feature is thus a paradoxically positive social outcome of a morally neutral or negative human action that is authored by an abstract factor (providence with the Stoics, the invisible hand in Smith). The automatic social benefit of the individual striving for things that are useful for him is spelled out in a Stoic text (Epict. 1.19.11–15) in which scholars have merely spotted parallels with Smith[76] without claiming that Smith had it in mind when phrasing his theses about self-interest:[77]

> Τοῦτο οὐκ ἔστιν φίλαυτον· γέγονε γὰρ οὕτως τὸ ζῷον· αὑτοῦ ἕνεκα πάντα ποιεῖ. καὶ γὰρ ὁ ἥλιος αὑτοῦ ἕνεκα πάντα ποιεῖ καὶ τὸ λοιπὸν αὐτὸς ὁ Ζεύς. ἀλλ' ὅταν θέλῃ εἶναι Ὑέτιος καὶ Ἐπικάρπιος καὶ πατὴρ ἀνδρῶν τε θεῶν τε, ὁρᾷς ὅτι τούτων τῶν ἔργων καὶ τῶν προσηγοριῶν οὐ δύναται τυχεῖν, ἂν μὴ είς τὸ κοινὸν ὠφέλιμος ᾖ. καθόλου τε τοιαύτην <τὴν> φύσιν τοῦ λογικοῦ

76 Föllinger 2008, 1073–1074.

77 Vivenza 2001, 62.

> ζῴου κατεσκεύασεν, ἵνα μηδενὸς τῶν ἰδίων ἀγαθῶν δύνηται τυγχάνειν, <ἂν> μή τι εἰς τὸ κοινὸν ὠφέλιμον προσφέρηται. οὕτως οὐκέτι ἀκοινώνητον γίνεται τὸ πάντα αὑτοῦ ἕνεκα ποιεῖν. ἐπεὶ τί ἐκδέχῃ; ἵνα τις ἀποστῇ αὑτοῦ καὶ τοῦ ἰδίου συμφέροντος; καὶ πῶς ἔτι μία καὶ ἡ αὐτὴ ἀρχὴ πᾶσιν ἔσται ἡ πρὸς αὑτὰ οἰκείωσις;
>
> This is not mere self-love, because it lies in the nature of every living creature that it does everything for its own sake. Why, even the sun does everything for its own sake, and so indeed Zeus himself. But when Zeus himself wishes to be the Rain-giver or Fruit-bringer and father of gods and men, you can see that he cannot achieve these works, or win these appellations unless he contributes to the common benefit. And in general, he has so constituted the nature of the rational being that he cannot attain any of his own particular goods without contributing to the common benefit. And so in the end it is not antisocial to do everything for one's own sake. After all, what do you expect? That one should show no concern for oneself and one's benefit? How, in that case, could all living creatures have one and the same principle of action, namely attachment to themselves? (trans. Hard 2014, with modifications from Oldfather 1925)

Since, however, Epictetus was, alongside Marcus Aurelius, one of the best-known Stoics as the works of both were extant and abundantly translated into English during the 18th century, it is plausible – albeit not granted – that Smith was familiar with this text although his *Discourses* were less popular than the succinct *Handbook*.[78] *The Theory of Moral Sentiments* offers evidence that he was at least acquainted with Epictetus (7.2.1.35). Smith evokes the Phrygian philosopher and Marcus Aurelius as main proponents for the two basic tenets of Stoic ethics, the submission under fate and the contentment with the given situation, respectively. The semantic difference between the text from Epictetus' *Discourses* and Smith does not exclude that Smith wrote his text with Epictetus' in mind, but offers another instance of Smith's creative reception of the Stoic theory of *oikeiôsis*. In Epictetus, τὸ συμφέρον, which means "beneficial" or "conducive" and recurs in other instances of this theorem (1.22.13, 2.22.15–16), is defined by the creature's integrity and essential thriving. Like the philosophical framework by which Plato assesses economy, it is an

78 From the Renaissance onwards, the *Handbook* had seen several translations into English (James Sandford [1567], John Healey [1610], John Davies [1670], Ellis Walker [1692], George Stanhope [1694], anonymous verse translation [1707], William Bond [1736]) whilst the first translation of the *Discourses* dates to Smith's time (Elisabeth Carter [1758]).

ontological and essential category both in Epictetus and Stoic orthodoxy that characterizes virtue and the good.[79] Smith's self-interest, on the contrary, aims at what is profitable and hence enhances economic well-being.

In the only two instances, each in the *Wealth of Nations* (4.2.9, text see above, section 3.1) and *The Theory of Moral Sentiments* (4.1.10), in which Smith claims that by pursuing their profit in economy individuals would necessarily and without knowing or intending promote the interest of society, he uses the phrase "invisible hand" for characterizing the necessity and unintentional and unknowing nature of this nexus. The term "providence" which he used elsewhere in the account of Stoic doctrine features only in the passage from *The Theory of Moral Sentiments* (4.1.10):

> The rich only select from the heap what is most precious and agreeable. They consume little more than the poor, and in spite of their natural selfishness and rapacity, though they mean only their own conveniency, though the sole end which they propose from the labours of all the thousands whom they employ, be the gratification of their own vain and insatiable desires, they divide with the poor the produce of all their improvements. They are led by an invisible hand to make nearly the same distribution of the necessaries of life, which would have been made, had the earth been divided into equal portions among all its inhabitants, and thus without intending it, without knowing it, advance the interest of the society, and afford means to the multiplication of the species. When Providence divided the earth among a few lordly masters, it neither forgot nor abandoned those who seemed to have been left out in the partition. These last too enjoy their share of all that it produces. In what constitutes the real happiness of human life, they are in no respect inferior to those who would seem so much above them. In ease of body and peace of mind, all the different ranks of life are nearly upon a level, and the beggar, who suns himself by the side of the highway, possesses that security which kings are fighting for.

From a strict textual point of view, providence is merely the author of the benevolent distribution of the general amenities of the life on earth which the poor would enjoy like the privileged, and not of the preceding equal distribution of goods which the rich's economic activity would bring about unintentionally. Stoicism never ascribed Providence dividing the earth between the "a few lordly masters" and "those who seemed to have been left out in the partition" as does Smith here.

79 For details, see Willms 2011/2012, 952–956.

The phrase "invisible hand" features first in Smith[80] in a passage that reports ancient polytheistic ideas (*History of Astronomy* 3.2)[81] and thus is never associated by Smith with the Stoic concept of providence. This expression stems with much more likelihood from Smith's own time, where the phrase "invisible hand of providence" is attested,[82] which suggests a Christian origin since the wide public was not familiar with Stoic philosophy. Besides making his abstract and paradoxical claim accessible by a common religious parlance,[83] Smith's main motive for choosing the figurative phrase "invisible hand" was his rejection of contemporary mercantilism[84] that practiced public interventions into economic life in order to foster economic development. Smith's expression "invisible hand" directly builds on this concept as it suggests that this goal could be reached without a human agent by an abstract mechanism inherent in the economy.

The result of this critical re-appraisal of a Stoic origin of Smith's claim that the pursuit of individual interests unintentionally promotes the common weal remains meagre and sobering. It recurs in a Stoic text with which Smith was likely to be familiar and where it is ascribed to Zeus, but never in his account of Stoic doctrine where providence is ascribed only a similar morally paradoxical mechanism. Providence is absent from the passages in which Smith claims the conduciveness of individual striving for profit for society. Instead, he uses the phrase "invisible hand" that has no Stoic, but rather a contemporary background. The picture of complementary evidence which this critical appraisal has brought about thus merely suggests, but provides no bullet-proof evidence for, a scenario in which Smith used this simile for phrasing a mechanism that he had transferred from Stoic cosmology and anthropology to economics. The presence of Zeus in his first instance of the invisible hand and in Epictetus' account of the providentially arranged coincidence of individual and cosmic benefit provides only a clue for this transfer and the imbuing of the invisible hand by the Stoic concept.

---

80 Macfie 1971, 595, Raphael / Macfie (in Smith 1976), 184, n. 7.

81 "[I]n Polytheistic religions, among savages, as well as in the early ages of Heathen antiquity, it is the irregular events of nature only that are ascribed to the agency and power of their goods. Fire burns, and water refreshes; heavy bodies descend, and lighter substances fly upwards, by the necessity of their own nature; nor was the invisible hand of Jupiter ever apprehended to be employed in those matters. But thunder and lightning, storms and sunshine, those more irregular events, were ascribed to his favour, or his anger."

82 Raphael 1991, 86.

83 Ibid.

84 *The Wealth of Nations* 4.1–8 (almost a quarter of the entire inquiry [Ballestrem 2001, 166]). Cf. Manstetten 2002, 260; Ballestrem 2001, 166–176.

While the idea of interaction which is a prominent innovation by Smith is absent from Stoic providence, he transferred the coincidence of individual and collective benefit from cosmology to economics. The progressive abstraction and absorption of originally Stoic ideas and their shift from ethics and cosmology in *The Theory of Moral Sentiments* to pure economics without theological implication in the *Wealth of Nations* go hand in hand. To this evaporation of premodern residues, Smith's adoption of modern scientific methodology and epistemology added that required a coherent and regular description of all relevant phenomena, as elucidated by Kant and best exemplified in Smith's eyes in Newton's astronomy.[85] It has been argued that modern economic theory omitting the theological and cosmological premises which these theorems presupposed in Stoicism would undermine these theses.[86] This reservation targets in particular the claim of the economic agent's rationality that features also in Smith.[87] And yet, the case of the providential congruence of individual and cosmic interests which Smith transposes into economy is different. Here, Smith's integrating of self-interest into complex interaction which is totally absent from the Stoic theory of *oikeiôsis* and their version of the congruence of individual and collective interests offers a secular and intra-economic mechanism that is able to explain how the self-interest of more than one individual can be harmonized. On the level of theory and hermeneutic instruments, social interaction thus offers an analytical substitute for the providential arrangement which, admittedly, still might be covered in the immediate context of this thesis by the simile of the invisible hand.

The biggest impact of Stoic thought on Smith's economic thought and support of his approval of economic interaction may lie in a field that has hitherto been dwarfed by the invisible hand and the cosmological and anthropological parallels. Smith's advocating of economic liberty and pursuing one's interests had been put under the reservation of not doing injustice in *Wealth of Nations* (4.9.51). His confidence in the beneficial effects of individual economic striving and peer-to-peer interaction goes along with a similar restriction of striving for one's benefit by an ethics of fair play in *The Theory of Moral Sentiments* (2.2.2.1):

> If he would act so as that the impartial spectator may enter into the principles of his conduct, which is what of all things he has the greatest desire to do, he must, upon this, as upon all other occasions, humble the arrogance of his self-love, and bring it down to something which other men can

---

85 Manstetten 2002, 42–43.

86 Schmitt 2008, 437.

87 Ibid., 437–439.

> go along with. They will indulge it so far as to allow him to be more anxious about, and to pursue with more earnest assiduity, his own happiness than that of any other person. Thus far, whenever they place themselves in his situation, they will readily go along with him. In the race for wealth, and honours, and preferments, he may run as hard as he can, and strain every nerve and every muscle, in order to outstrip all his competitors. But if he should justle, or throw down any of them, the indulgence of the spectators is entirely at an end. It is a violation of fair play, which they cannot admit of.

Smith's idea that striving for one's own advantage is legitimate as long as it does not impair competitors and its illustration by the image of the race find such an exact match in a passage from Cicero (*Off.* 3.42 = *SVF* 3.689) that scholars have duly assumed that they were borrowed from this ancient text:[88]

> *Nec tamen nostrae nobis utilitates omittendae sunt aliisque tradendae, cum his ipsi egeamus, sed suae cuique utilitati, quod sine alterius iniuria fiat, serviendum est. Scite Chrysippus, ut multa: 'qui stadium' inquit, 'currit, eniti et contendere debet quam maxime possit ut vincat, supplantare eum quicum certet aut manu depellere nullo modo debet; sic in vita sibi quemque petere quod pertineat ad usum non iniquum est, alteri deripere ius non est.'*
> However, we are not to neglect benefits to ourselves and surrender them to others when we ourselves need them. Rather, each should attend to what benefits him himself, so far as may be done without injustice to another. Among Chrysippus' many neat remarks was the following: When a man runs in the stadium he ought to struggle and strive with all his might to be victorious, but he ought not to trip his fellow-competitor or to push him over. (trans. Griffin / Atkins 1991)

This critical stocktaking of Stoic influence on Adam Smith's economic thought has thus demonstrated that the Scottish scholar has faithfully adopted the Stoic qualification of the pursuit of one's advantage by fair play and shifted the approval of self-care from anthropology to economics. The idea, that by pursuing their own interests the individuals benefit the community, might be of Stoic inspiration, but we have no evidence that Smith was familiar with it whilst the (in)famous "invisible hand" that Smith uses to phrase this claim is of contemporary origin. The evidence for Stoic influence decreases from ethics to systemic economics. This is not only due to the fact that Stoics had an elaborate ethics, but no economic theory and that

88 Vivenza 2001, 3–4; Föllinger 2008, 1077–1078.

Smith would have to transpose cosmological concepts to economics, but simply to lack of material evidence.

4. Conclusion

This comparative overview enables us to draw the strings together. Subsuming Plato's approach to economic behaviour in Max Weber's terms under value-oriented rationality and Adam Smith under purposive or instrumental rationality would be too schematic as this labelling misses deeper structures of social organization and underlying anthropological assumptions. Instead, Plato and Smith represent two models of rationality which are delineated by the vertical and horizontal axes of social organization and the distribution of rational endowment among individuals. Making the individual the cornerstone of social organization and building society from the interaction of individuals is the hallmark of Adam Smith's economics and social theory. This horizontal and bottom-up organization stands out against Plato's vertical model of top-down regulation. Smith's model is dynamic and evolutionary; Plato's is rather static since individual activity has always to be checked and controlled by a third party. Smith makes the individual a full-fledged, albeit not perfect subject that is endowed with sufficient reason and morality whereas Plato makes it an object. The reason for this difference is anthropology, at least in Plato who assumes that the vast mass of people is unable to control the greed innate in the human race and requires checking by the happy few. Whereas the textual context roots Plato's economic policy in these anthropological tenets, there is no evidence for such an immediate motivation in Smith, but just a structural correspondence, as his ethics and anthropology are built on the individual and human-like interactions (impartial spectator) as well. Prosperity is granted by the interaction of individuals and their economic competence. Locating the intended collective state in the social system and social interaction is the decisive conceptual progress of Smith in comparison with Plato, who entrusted it to pre-defined and detailed public institutions and/or a group of people and thereby relied on their rationality and integrity which he denied to the mass of people ruled by them. This vertical rule is absolute and performs control whereas Smith's negotiating interactors control each other. It is paralleled and supported by the doctrine of ideas that operates in a top-down deductive mode and yields elitist implications. Smith has no such elaborate epistemology as Plato, but his approach is definitely much more inductive. Valuing the information of individual items in cognition doubtless favoured trusting the competence of individuals in social theory. The axis model thus confirms and rephrases Schmitt's epistemological opposition of Platonic distinctive vs. Hellenistic and modern empirical rationality on a more abstract and general level and highlights its social implications.

Smith's peer-to-peer model was favoured as well in varying degrees by his contact with Stoic philosophy, although the evidence is less certain than often claimed in scholarship and requires further accurate and detailed research as to his sources.[89] In ethics, his impartial spectator offers parallels with the Stoic concepts of δαίμων and of theatricality in psychagogy and his plea for fair play was borrowed from the Stoics. His economic claim about the automatic congruence of the individuals' striving for their benefit and the unintentional promotion of the common weal finds a match in Epictetus' account of the theory of *oikeiôsis* whilst the phrase "invisible hand" by which he characterizes this nexus has contemporary sources, and the Stoic concept of providence to which Smith ascribes a similar effect elsewhere cannot be identified with certainty in the context of Smith's versions of the coincidence thesis. Positing self-care as the anthropological baseline is Smith's only economic tenet that finds an exact match in the Stoic theorems (here the theory of *oikeiôsis*) which he reports in his writings.

Two points which both have been ignored by Platonizing comparative readings stand out as his intellectual achievement. The first is identifying social interaction as secular mechanism in economy that grants by checks and balances economic functioning and rationality. The second is eliminating any personal, ethical, or psychagogic elements, by which the aforementioned nexus are imbued in Stoic philosophy, and distilling the abstract mechanisms that are diagnosed in impersonal social and economic processes where Stoics did not identify them. Abstraction and transfer to economics are thus Smith's main achievements that enabled his new economic theories and are a side-piece to the secularization and emancipation from inherited Christian ideas which Enlightenment performed at that time. This embeddedness into intellectual world history implies that Smith's views, far from being canonized as eternal truths, invite for further thought.

89 Ricken's survey article about Stoic reception deals only with Smith's reception of points of Stoic ethics which are irrelevant for his economic theory (2003, 308–309). Schmitt 2019, 72, n. 5 offers no evidence from Smith for Stoic influence on his economic theory, additional to that discussed in this article or prior research (Föllinger 2008) which he cites in support of his thesis alongside his own monograph passim (2008). Waszek 1984 whom Schmitt 2019, 80 cites without indicating relevant pages for Stoic influence on Smith's two main works (as to maximizing profit and fair competition being two sides of the same medal) demonstrates the influence of the Stoic doctrines of κατορθώματα vs. καθήκοντα on Smith's ethics.

Bibliography

Apelt, Otto (trans.) (1916): Platons Gesetze. 2 vols., Leipzig.

Arrighetti, Graziano (ed.) (1973): Epicuro. Opere, Turin.

Ballestrem, Karl Graf (2001): Adam Smith, Munich.

Bösherz, Philipp (2019): Der ‚*homo oeconomicus*' und Anreize zu wertorientiertem Handeln, in: Föllinger, Sabine / Korn, Evelyn (eds.), Von besten und zweitbesten Regeln. Platonische und aktuelle Perspektiven auf individuelles und staatliches Wohlergehen, Wiesbaden (Philippika 137), 229–243.

Burnet, John (ed.) (1900–1907): Platonis opera. 5 vols., Oxford.

Bury, Robert Gr. (trans.) (1926): Plato, *Laws*. 2 vols., Cambridge, MA.

Bywater, John (ed.) (1894): Aristotelis Ethica Nicomachea, Oxford.

Dalfen, Joachim (1974): Polis und Poiesis. Die Auseinandersetzung mit der Dichtung bei Platon und seinen Zeitgenossen, Munich.

Dalfen, Joachim (ed.) (1987): Marcus Aurelius. Ad se ipsum libri XII, Leipzig.

Daraki-Mallet, Maria (1978): Les fonctions psychologiques du Logos in: Brunschwig, Jacques (ed.), Les Stoïciens et leur logique. Actes du colloque de Chantilly, 18–22 septembre 1976, Paris, 87–119.

Dorandi, Tiziano (ed.) (2013): Diogenes Laertius. Lives of Eminent Philosophers, Cambridge (Cambridge Classical Texts and Commentaries 50).

Eich, Arnim (2006): Die politische Ökonomie des antiken Griechenland, Cologne (Passauer historische Forschungen 14).

Emlyn-Jones, Chris / Preddy, William (eds. / trans.) (2013): Plato, *Republic*. 2 vols., Cambridge, MA.

England, Edwin B. (ed. / comm.) (1921): The Laws of Plato. 2 vols., Manchester.

Erskine, Andrew (1990): The Hellenistic Stoa. Political Thought and Action, London.

Föllinger, Sabine (2008): Der Einfluß der stoischen Philosophie auf die Grundlagen der modernen Wirtschaftstheorie bei Adam Smith, in: Neymeyr, Barbara / Schmidt, Jochen /Zimmermann, Bernhard (eds.), Stoizismus in der europäischen Philosophie, Literatur, Kunst und Politik. Eine Kulturgeschichte von der Antike bis zur Moderne. Vol. 2, Berlin / New York, 1063–1079.

Föllinger, Sabine (2016): Ökonomie bei Platon, Berlin.

Föllinger, Sabine / Korn, Evelyn (eds.) (2019): Von besten und zweitbesten Regeln. Platonische und aktuelle Perspektiven auf individuelles und staatliches Wohlergehen, Wiesbaden (Philippika 137).

Garnsey, Peter (1996): Ideas of Slavery from Aristotle to Augustine, Cambridge / New York (The W. B. Stanford Memorial Lectures).

Günther, Sven (2016): Sonderwirtschaftszonen. Antike Konzeptionen und Konstruktionen am Beispiel des athenischen Piräus, in: Droß-Krüpe, Kerstin / Föllinger,

Sabine / Ruffing, Kai (eds.), Antike Wirtschaft und ihre kulturelle Prägung / The Cultural Shaping of the Ancient Economy, Wiesbaden (Philippika 98), 113–130.

Günther, Sven (2017): (K)einer neuen Theorie wert? Neues zur antiken Wirtschaftsgeschichte anhand Dig. 50,11,2 (Callist. 3 cognit.), in: Gymnasium 124, 131–144.

Günther, Sven (2020): Review of: Föllinger, Sabine / Korn, Evelyn (eds.): Von besten und zweitbesten Regeln. Platonische und aktuelle Perspektiven auf individuelles und staatliches Wohlergehen, Wiesbaden 2019 (Philippika 137), in: Marburger Beiträge zur antiken Handels-, Wirtschafts- und Sozialgeschichte 38, 260–264.

Griffin, Miriam T. / Atkins, E. Margaret (trans.) (1991): Cicero, *On Duties*, Cambridge.

Gummere, Richard M. (trans.) (1917 / 1920 / 1925): Seneca. Ad Lucilium epistulae morales. 3 vols., Cambridge, MA.

Hager, Fritz-Peter (1998): System; Systematik; systematisch. Antike, in: Historisches Wörterbuch der Philosophie 10, 823–824.

Hard, Robin (trans.) (2014): Epictetus. Discourses, Fragments, Handbook. With an Introduction and Notes by Christopher Gill, Oxford.

Hinsch, Moritz (2021): Ökonomik und Hauswirtschaft im klassischen Griechenland, Stuttgart (Historia-Einzelschriften 265).

Kalberg, Stephen (1980): Max Weber's Types of Rationality: Cornerstones for the Analysis of Rationalization Processes in History, in: The American Journal of Sociology 85/5, 1145–1179.

Lattimore, Richmond (trans.) (1999): The Odyssey of Homer, repr. New York.

Lowry, S. Todd (2008): Ancient and Medieval Economics, in: Samuels, Warren J. / Biddle, Jeff E. / Davis, John B. (eds.), A Companion to the History of Economic Thought, Malden, MA, 11–27.

Macfie, Alec L. (1971): The Invisible Hand of Jupiter, in: Journal of the History of Ideas 32, 595–599.

O'Mahoney, Paul (2008): Plato's Chimera: The Transitional Polis in Republic, in: Polis: The Journal for Ancient Greek Political Thought 25/2, 268–284.

Mandeville, Bernard de ([2]1957): The Fable of the Bees, or Private Vices, Publick Benefits [1732], with a Commentary Critical, Historical, and Explanatory by Frederick B. Kaye, Oxford.

Manning, Charles E. (1989): Stoicism and Slavery in the Roman Empire, in: Aufstieg und Niedergang der Römischen Welt 2.36/3, 1518–1543.

Manstetten, Reiner (2002): Das Menschenbild der Ökonomie. Der *homo oeconomicus* und die Anthropologie von Adam Smith, Freiburg / Munich (Alber-Reihe Thesen 7).

Müller, Jörn (2019): Platon und der *homo oeconomicus*, in: Föllinger, Sabine / Korn, Evelyn (eds.), Von besten und zweitbesten Regeln. Platonische und aktuelle Perspektiven auf individuelles und staatliches Wohlergehen, Wiesbaden (Philippika 137), 43–70.

Oldfather, William A. (ed. / trans.) (1925 / 1928): Epictetus. The Discourses as Reported by Arrian, the Manual, and Fragments. 2 vols., Cambridge, MA.

Pendrick, Gerard J. (ed.) (2002): Antiphon the Sophist. The Fragments, Cambridge.

Pradeau, Jean-François ([2]2010): Platon et la cité, Paris.

Rackham, Harris (trans.) ([2]1931): Cicero. De finibus bonorum et malorum, Cambridge, MA.

Raphael, David D. / Macfie, Alec L. (1976): Introduction, in: Smith, Adam: The Theory of Moral Sentiments [1759]. Ed. by David D. Raphael and Alec L. Macfie, Oxford, 1–52.

Raphael, David D. (1991): Adam Smith, Frankfurt am Main.

Raphael, David D. (2007): The Impartial Spectator. Adam Smith's Moral Philosophy, Oxford.

Reydams-Schils, Gretchen (2005): The Roman Stoics. Self, Responsibility, and Affection, Chicago.

Reynolds, Leighton D. (ed.) (1965): L. Annaei Senecae Ad Lucilium epistulae morales. 2 vols., Oxford.

Reynolds, Leighton D. (ed.) (1977): L. Annaei Senecae Dialogorum libri XII, Oxford.

Reynolds, Leighton D. (ed.) (1998): M. Tulli Ciceronis De finibus bonorum et malorum, Oxford.

Ricken, Friedo (2003): Stoizismus, in: Der Neue Pauly 15/3, 297–311.

Ross, William David (ed.) (1957): Aristotelis Politica, Oxford.

Saunders, Trevor J. (trans.) (1976): Plato, *The Laws*, London.

Sauvé Meyer, Susan (2003): The Moral Dangers of Labour and Commerce in Plato's *Laws*, in: Scolnicov, Samuel / Brisson, Luc (eds.), Plato's *Laws*: From Theory into Practice. Proceedings of the VI Symposium Platonicum. Selected Papers, Sankt Augustin (International Plato Studies 15), 207–214.

Schmitt, Arbogast (2000): Der Einzelne und die Gemeinschaft in der Dichtung Homers und in der Staatstheorie bei Platon. Zur Ableitung der Staatstheorie aus der Psychologie (vorgelegt am 19. Juni 2000), Stuttgart (Sitzungsberichte der Wissenschaftlichen Gesellschaft an der Johann-Wolfgang-Goethe-Universität Frankfurt am Main 38/2).

Schmitt, Arbogast ([2]2008): Die Moderne und Platon. Zwei Grundformen europäischer Rationalität, Stuttgart.

Schmitt, Arbogast (2019): Selbsterhaltung oder Selbstverwirklichung? Über die unterschiedliche Suche nach einem guten Leben in den hellenistischen Philosophenschulen und bei Platon und Aristoteles, in: Föllinger, Sabine / Korn, Evelyn (eds.), Von besten und zweitbesten Regeln. Platonische und aktuelle Perspektiven auf individuelles und staatliches Wohlergehen, Wiesbaden (Philippika 137), 71–101.

Schöpsdau, Klaus (trans. / comm.) (2003): Platon, Nomoi (Gesetze) Buch IV–VII, Göttingen (Platon Werke Übersetzung und Kommentar 9/2.2).

Schöpsdau, Klaus (trans. / comm.) (2011): Platon, Nomoi (Gesetze) Buch VIII–XII, Göttingen (Platon Werke Übersetzung und Kommentar 9/2.3).

Schofield, Malcolm (1999): Plato on the Economy, in: Schofield, Malcolm, Saving the City. Philosopher-Kings and other Classical Paradigms, London / New York, 69–81.

Schofield, Malcolm (ed.) / Griffith, Tom (trans.) (2016): Plato, *The Laws*, Cambridge.

Schriefl, Anna (2019): Sind die Erwerbstätigen in Platons Politeia tugendhaft?, in: Föllinger, Sabine / Korn, Evelyn (eds.), Von besten und zweitbesten Regeln. Platonische und aktuelle Perspektiven auf individuelles und staatliches Wohlergehen, Wiesbaden (Philippika 137), 213–227.

Segal, Charles (1981): Tragedy and Civilization. An Interpretation of Sophocles, Cambridge, MA.

Simon, Herbert S. (1959): Theories of Decision-Making in Economics and Behavorial Science, in: The American Economic Review 49/3, 253–283.

Slings, Simon R. (ed.) (2003): Plato: Respublica, Oxford.

Smith, Adam (1976): The Theory of Moral Sentiments [1759]. Ed. by David D. Raphael and Alec L. Macfie, Oxford.

Smith, Adam (1981): An Inquiry into the Nature and Causes of the Wealth of Nations [1776]. Ed. by Roy H. Campbell and Andrew S. Skinner. Textual editor William B. Todd. 2 vols., Indianapolis.

Smith, Adam (1980): History of Astronomy [1795]. In: Wightman, William P. D. / Bryce, John C. (eds.), Essays on Philosophical Subjects with Dugald Stewart's Account of Adam Smith, ed. by Ian Simpson Ross, Oxford.

Söllner, Fritz ([4]2015): Die Geschichte des ökonomischen Denkens, Berlin / Heidelberg.

Soverini, Luca (1998): Il Sofista e l'Agora. Sapienti, economia e vita quotidiana nella Grecia classica, Pisa.

Spahn, Peter (2003): Sophistik und Ökonomie, in: Piepenbrink, Karen (ed.), Philosophie und Lebenswelt in der Antike, Darmstadt, 36–51.

Vivenza, Gloria (1999): Ancora sullo stoicismo di Adam Smith, in: Studi Storici Luigi Simeoni 49, 97–126.

Vivenza, Gloria (2001): Adam Smith and the Classics. The Classical Heritage in Adam Smith's Thought, Oxford.

Voigtländer, Hanns-Dieter (1980): Der Philosoph und die Vielen, Wiesbaden.

Waszek, Norbert (1984): Two Concepts of Morality: A Distinction of Adam Smith's Ethics and its Stoic Origin, in: Journal of the History of Ideas 45, 591–606.

Weber, Max (1964): Wirtschaft und Gesellschaft [1922]. 2 vols., Cologne / Berlin.

West, Martin L. (ed.) ([2]1998): Aeschylus. Tragoediae cum incerti poetae Prometheo, Stuttgart.

West, Martin L. (ed.) (2017): Homerus: Odyssea, Berlin / Boston.

Willms, Lothar (2008): Platon, Popper und die Integrität – Versuch eines Neuansatzes mit Giorgio Agamben, in: Eckl, Andreas / Kaufmann, Clemens (eds.), Politischer Platonismus, Würzburg, 151–165.

Willms, Lothar (2011/2012): Epiktets Diatribe *Über die Freiheit* (4.1) – Einleitung, Übersetzung und Kommentar. 2 vols., Heidelberg (Wissenschaftliche Kommentare zu griechischen und lateinischen Klassikern).

Willms, Lothar (2020): Zur Poetologie des Aufstiegs und der materialen Permanenz der poetischen *memoria* in Horaz' Oden, in: Latomus 79, 438–487.

Winterbottom, Michael (ed.) (1994): M. Tulli Ciceronis De officiis, Oxford.

Woolf, Raphael (trans.) / Annas, Julia (ed.) (2001): Cicero, *On Moral Ends*, Cambridge.

Hoarding and Rationality in the Ancient Economy[1]

Michael Leese

Abstract: Economic historians have often pointed to the irrational and unproductive "hoarding" of wealth as a major factor that inhibited the development of the premodern economy. Because profits were not continuously reinvested in further productive enterprise, as is characteristic of the modern industrial-capitalist system, the premodern economy did not mobilize capital in such a way that would encourage an efficient economic system that fostered growth and the circulation of money. Scholars have often cited evidence from ancient Greece and Rome to support this view of widespread hoarding of capital in the ancient economy. A reconsideration of this evidence, however, actually supports the opposite interpretation – that business owners in Greco-Roman antiquity invested their capital much like modern capitalists. Furthermore, the similarities between the ancient and modern economic systems play out at the macroeconomic level as well, with liquidity crises and problems of trust (as described by the Anonymus Iamblichi), and institutions that counteracted hoarding in a variety of ways. As in the modern economy, ancient circulation problems arose during abnormal circumstances, as a result of private and public actions that were eventually addressed through state intervention.

Keywords: Marxism – Keynesian Economics – Rationality – Monetary Circulation – Liquidity – Financial Crises – NIE

1. Introduction

Within the study of the ancient economy, "hoarding" is an important issue with a strange history. After a period of sustained attention in the scholarly literature, interest suddenly waned and quietly disappeared. This statement will immediately surprise some readers; the surviving coin hoards that abound in the archaeological record have been thoroughly studied and published by numismatists. But the semantic range of the term "hoarding" encompasses a variety of ideas, and in economic history, hoarding is traditionally treated as a somewhat different phenomenon – one of the major factors that inhibited further economic development in the

1 I would like to thank Donald W. Jones for detailed comments on an earlier draft of this paper, as well as Edward Harris and the anonymous reviewers for their helpful suggestions for the last stage of revision.

premodern world. In big-picture accounts of long-term economic progress and the modernization of the West, hoarding refers to the unproductive stockpiling of money by premodern peoples. This practice moreover occurred on an almost pandemic scale – so widespread that it effectively acted as a check on economic development by removing specie from circulation and depriving people of the ability to invest in profitable activities. Indeed some historians have even argued that hoarding of wealth by private individuals in the ground, lockboxes, and treasuries was one of the defining characteristics of ancient peoples' economic *mentalité*, an irrational avoidance of risky but productive enterprise. It has therefore been interpreted as a sign of economic irrationality and specifically a unique type of behavior that distinguishes the performance of the ancient economy from that of modern capitalism. In essence, hoarding has been considered symptomatic of many of the causes of underdevelopment within premodern economic systems.

If hoarding had been practiced in antiquity to the point that it constricted the money supply and therefore prevented profitable investment opportunities, this fact alone would have significant consequences for our interpretation of the role of individual behavior as a driving force within big-picture theories of long-term economic change. But despite its potentially fundamental role in explaining how the ancient economy functioned, scholars have recently moved away from the issue of hoarding in Greco-Roman economic history.[2] Adding confusion, the conversations on hoarding have been largely bifurcated, as Harris has recently argued about the surprising scarcity of discussion about these conceptual differences between numismatists and economic historians.[3] As it becomes more common to address the larger

2 Among most recent big-picture treatments of ancient Greek economic behavior, for example, hoarding is not treated directly as scholars' focus is on its opposite, *chrêmatistikê*, the active investment of money for the generation of profit. See, e.g., Eich 2006; Hinsch 2021; Leese 2021. Bresson 2016 mentions hoarding by the Persian royal treasury (ibid., 267) but not by private individuals in ancient Greece, a point I will return to later. Ober 2008, 48–52 does interpret coin hoards in light of economic performance, but few scholars explicitly address the issue in economic history, except briefly Harris / Lewis 2016, 6.

3 Harris 2019: "Recent Developments in the Study of the Economy of Ancient Greece: Implications for Numismatics," lecture delivered December 2019. The most recent magisterial overview of coin hoards and hoarding by the *Oxford Roman Economy Project* does not mention the economic history concept, as illustrated by the exhaustive discussion of the issues in numismatics by Howgego / Wilson 2022. Particularly suggestive and illuminating is their observation that assertions about velocity and circulation cannot be made without extensive further study of coin hoard deposition processes and distribution patterns (ibid., 16).

problem of economic rationality, however, hoarding will inevitably return to the scholarship as an important aspect of ancient behavior and mentality.

Therefore, in this paper I will conduct a reassessment of the evidence for hoarding by private individuals in the ancient economy, focusing primarily on the Greek evidence because of space limitations; based on estate inventories and anecdotal accounts, it seems that this practice was actually not substantial enough to inhibit investment or impede the circulation of money in the economy. Rather, individual hoarding was insignificant in comparison with the extant evidence for the "productive" employment of money, i.e., that which yielded a profit from interest, rent, or the manufacturing of goods. Moreover, that cash for which we do have evidence being in private hands, usually at the time of someone's death, appears not to have been irrationally hoarded, but rather designated for rational purposes.

On the other hand, hoarding by institutional bodies such as temples is far more visible in the evidence from ancient Greece, which at first glance would seemingly have greater consequences for the performance of the economic system. Nevertheless, although the sums dedicated in sanctuaries were substantial, this may not have caused serious money supply problems, as there was a number of temples which lent out large amounts of money at interest, thereby keeping it in circulation. In the patterns discernable in the evidence preserved from antiquity, it was only the actions of the central Roman republican and imperial state that were visibly able to affect the money supply to the degree that they impacted the systemic efficiency of the overall economy; hoarding by individuals and temples was far less significant and did not have any observably comparable effect on the performance of the economic system.

Because hoarding has been so rarely addressed in the scholarship of the past couple decades, to some it may seem to be a non-issue. But the stakes could not be higher if such an elementally unique type of behavior powered the ancient economy. Furthermore, a focused treatment of hoarding brings to light major assumptions about the theoretical underpinning of much scholarship on the ancient economy and the broader field of economic history as a discipline more generally. Some Marxist views in particular have been extremely influential and largely remain unchallenged, because they are often not explicitly acknowledged, unpacked, and traced throughout the history of subsequent scholarship.

This paper argues that these theoretical currents need to be overtly addressed and supplemented with the widest possible variety of theory and perspectives in order to achieve a more nuanced approach. Hoarding can be examined more accurately by incorporating Keynesian and depression-era economists' emphasis on the notion of liquidity preference.[4]

Previous treatments of hoarding in the ancient Greek economy

Because of the wide range of issues that can be referred to by the term "hoarding," it is first necessary to define it precisely before proceeding.[5] In economic history, hoarding is essentially the unproductive amassing of capital, the opposite of the continuous reinvestment of profits into further productive enterprise familiar to anyone who has read Marx's *Das Kapital*. Hoarding is seen as antithetical to a rational capitalistic mentality, stunting growth, and restricting the expansion of economic activity.

As a practice hoarding is depicted as strongly contrasting with the behavior of modern capitalists, in a polarized opposition. Its explanatory force is therefore akin to big-picture theories of economic change caused by psychological transformations such as Weber's *Protestantische Ethik und Geist des Kapitalismus*. Such modernization accounts place prime causal force on the new mental habits associated with modern capitalism. If premodern individuals did not behave like modern rational actors, this would be enough to explain the "stagnation" of the ancient economy, and certainly if they did not invest their money in profitable enterprise but rather kept it in lockboxes safe but unproductive. By creating unique patterns of microeconomic behavior and individual decision-making in the ancient economy, a psychological impulse to hoard money would have profound implications for our understanding of the performance of the economic system as a whole. Such an economy would be quite different from our own indeed.

But few scholars have directly engaged with this issue in the study of the ancient economy. Those who have, particularly in discussions of the ancient Greek situation, have done so as part of their attempts to incorporate classical antiquity into the long-term theories of development that have been proposed by experts of later periods of economic history.[6] In these accounts, the hoarding of private wealth

4 Recent discussions of the application of Keynesian economics to the ancient world can be found in Elliott 2020; Jones 2021, 234–248.

5 The term hoarding can refer to a wide variety of behaviors, from storing grain to sell in times of scarcity and high price (for which see Sharfman 2006) to stuffing money into a mattress out of distrust for banks. The difference between these phenomena is vast. See problems of even defining the relatively limited practices termed "hoarding" in the field of economics: Robinson 1938; Emmer 1959. See also discussions by Dornbusch 1973; Hartley 1990.

6 On the Roman side of things the scholarly tradition has developed somewhat differently.

was prevalent throughout the premodern world, characteristic of an economically "irrational" mentality that contrasts with the behavior of modern capitalist actors:

> the most powerful motives behind hoarding were social attitudes which served to restrict the opportunities for semi-systematic lending at interest ... [there was an] almost complete absence of productive credit ... lenders combined loans at interest with interest-free *eranos* loans: yet another illustration of behaviour that would be judged 'irrational' from the point of view of much modern economic theory. The Athenians themselves never show any awareness that extensive hoarding of cash might be economically inefficient.[7]

Millett combines a wide array of issues in this statement, effectively summarizing in one passage this model of individual economic behavior and its consequences for performance of the overall system: irrational hoarding created economic inefficiency. Similar views are expressed by Meikle, who likewise links hoarding to an economically irrational approach to investment decisions:

> It needs to be explained why the Greeks preferred to bury their exchange value, rather than to invest it profitably as an 'economically rational' person would do today ... there was no productive credit in the ancient world ... no lending or borrowing for establishing or expanding productive enterprises ... the Greeks were hoarders because there was no possibility of the productive investment of money.[8]

Here the association between irrationality and the propensity to hoard is reiterated, with even more forceful insistence on the lack of opportunities for productive investment into continuously profitable enterprise. The preference to "bury exchange value" is antithetical to an economically rational strategy, which was simply not available to the ancient Greeks due to an absence of productive investment opportunities.

> A modern bank is primarily a credit institution which aims at encouraging economic activity. Athenian banks, by contrast, worked on a small scale ... much of the moneyed wealth which existed never came into their hands

---

Hoarding is discussed as an economic concept in Roman monetary supply at least as far back as Kaufman 1932, but subsequent scholars have not entirely followed the example of their Hellenist colleagues. Recent exceptions, however, include Elliott 2020, 159–170.

7 Millett 1991, 169–170.

8 Meikle 1995, 160–162.

> but remained most of the time hoarded away and not put to productive uses.[9]

These last authors add a more precise focus: the undeniable differences between ancient and modern banking institutions must have shaped the ancient Greek economy in significant and unique ways. Here even banks are said to have hoarded, unlike modern banks which are the primary agents of circulation in the economy. These scholars therefore point in the same general direction, adding larger institutions like banks to the general behavior of individuals, further compounding the problem of unproductive hoarding.

These are strong claims that penetrate to the heart of economic performance in ancient Greece. Hoarding was responsible for economic inefficiency and impeded economic development and monetary circulation. It was motivated by "social attitudes" and the absence of investment opportunities which resulted in a very particular type of economic system: one that was frozen in place by a unique *mentalité* and limited opportunities for investment. The views expressed here still (as far as I am aware) represent the state of the field regarding hoarding and economic rationality in the ancient economy. No scholars have systematically or explicitly followed up to examine their validity or their consequences for understanding the performance of the economy.[10] Therefore, they are in need of reassessment, and the best place to start is the theoretical models that inform them.

First, they are clearly Marxist-influenced perspectives that retroject an assumed model of precapitalist behavior onto the ancient world. Unmistakable echoes can be found in Marx's own words:

> The ancients never thought of transforming surplus-product into capital. Or at least only to a very limited extent. The fact that the hoarding of treasure in the narrow sense was widespread among them shows how much surplus-product lay completely idle ... it was amassed in the hands of a few persons, who, incidentally, did not know what to do with it.[11]

Therefore, Marx himself probably laid the groundwork for the later development of the ideas cited above, and subsequent economic history is full of examples of this type of explanation for premodern economic stagnation.

---

9 Austin / Vidal-Naquet 1980, 149.

10 This is not to say that scholars have not considered problems of money supply from an economic perspective. For a helpful overview of how monetary theory and money supply post Keynes and Milton Friedman can be applied to classical antiquity, see Elliott 2020; Jones 2014, 312–323.

11 Marx, *Theories of Surplus Value* (translated by Tucker 1978, 460).

One of the more sophisticated articulations of this perspective is in Jones' *The European Miracle*, in which the hoarding mentality is described in terms of the economic concept of "liquidity preference".[12] The willingness of the entire premodern world to invest in profitable enterprise was constrained by the high risks of productive business activity: the modern economy's takeoff was enabled by a "slowly falling liquidity preference";[13] "Continental nobles lived in a universe of high liquidity preference and ... low productive investment";[14] Asian economies in general could be summed up as "largely agrarian economies ... [with a] tiny, circumscribed and often inessential trade sphere ... where natural and social risks were high, so were liquidity preferences and hoarding".[15] Such accounts of the "Rise of the West" see modern European achievements as essentially alien to premodern and non-western economic systems.

But Jones was working in an authoritative tradition – Keynes himself stated the contrast between the modern and premodern economies in precisely these terms: "the destruction of the inducement to invest by an excessive liquidity-preference was the outstanding evil, the prime impediment to the growth of wealth, in the ancient and medieval worlds."[16] Although seemingly extreme oversimplifications, these views nevertheless are reproduced in various forms throughout much of economic history; in many accounts, prevailing conditions prior to the modern industrial capitalist system did not encourage productive investment, so people simply preferred to hold onto their cash, much like stashing it in a mattress. The ancients were constrained by what amounts to a "buried treasure mentality".

While fascinating, however, such an explanation is not supported by the evidence for individual behavior. At first glance, this interpretation certainly *appears* possible. Thousands of ancient coin hoards have been discovered throughout Greece and Rome,[17] and substantial sums of money are attested in the possession of a number of wealthy individuals. Some of the recorded hoards in the Greek and Roman worlds are quite large. However, many coin hoards were buried for emergency purposes, and therefore cannot be taken for regular practice.[18] As Howgego observes, the coin hoards which are preserved for the Roman world are biased towards

12 Jones 2003.

13 Ibid., 94.

14 Ibid., 133.

15 Ibid., 165.

16 Keynes 2018 (1936), 313.

17 Kraay 1964; Thompson et al. 1973; Schönert-Geiss 1974; Ehrhardt 1975; Crawford 1969a.

18 See Howgego / Wilson 2022 for a detailed overview of the methodological problems with interpreting coin hoards.

unstable times since they were never recovered and therefore cannot be taken as an indication of normal practices.[19] As Elliott puts it, during crises "even the simple act of hoarding in this period was likely done temporarily – perhaps as a form of short term hedging behavior."[20] Therefore, hoarding is not a constant practice characteristic of the ancient economy, but was heavily affected by prevailing circumstances.

Hoards may actually be indices of increased, not reduced, precious metal in the money supply. Eich's interpretation of ancient Greek coin hoard distribution emphasizes the regional *circulation* of city coinage, where the hoards themselves are not seen as evidence for lack of circulation;[21] rather, hoards constitute the only measure by which coin movement can be gauged, snapshots in time of circulation that was arrested unintentionally. Ober interprets the rise in the number of coin hoards from the sixth to the fourth century BCE as the result the progressively *greater* volume of money in circulation, where more people could afford to save income in the form of cash as part of increased mine output and gradual rises in standards of living.[22] Greater frequency of hoards is a quantitative proxy for economic prosperity and growth over time, for "currency performance" rather than of increased petrification of the money supply.[23]

Moreover, coin hoards are skewed preservations of source material not representative of the typical uses of money in everyday life, as seen for example in the large amounts of small change for daily use among people in ancient Greece and Rome;[24] the evidence of hoards is therefore not an accurate index of monetary circulation. Perhaps even more decisively, there was considerable variation in the hoarding practices across the Roman empire both in time and space.[25] Such temporal and geographical heterogeneity within the ancient economy strongly undermines arguments for any shared pre-modern unproductive mentality.

---

19 Howgego 1992, 3; for the hoarding which took place during the turbulence of the Late Republican Civil Wars, see Crawford 1969b. Goldman 2022 confirms in his analysis of hoards in Judea under Roman rule that although savings hoards are certainly present during periods of peace, there is a spike in hoards during times of crisis, which therefore can be interpreted as deposited and/or unrecovered because of emergency circumstances.

20 Elliott 2020, 159.

21 Eich 2006, 122–149.

22 Ober 2016, 83–84.

23 Ober 2008, 48–52.

24 See, e.g., Kim 2002.

25 Howgego / Wilson 2022, 8–13.

Furthermore, although there is no clear idea about how much coin circulated in the economy at any one time, it seems that based on the amount of coin that has been found buried, savings hoards in the ground probably did not represent a significant drain on the total money supply. While quantification of total money supply via minting output is subject to extremely large margins of error, it nonetheless provides a sense of the scale of coin circulation in ancient Greece in the absence of official records. Just one issue of Athenian owls during the earliest peak minting period in the 490s and 480s BCE consisted of at least five million minted tetradrachmas, and in the 440s Athens was minting anywhere between one million and nine million silver tetradrachmas per year.[26] More recent estimates of the amount of silver mined in the Laureion every year approach 1,500 talents annually in the mid-fifth century, or nine million drachmas.[27] At a minimum, 1.2 million tetradrachmas were minted annually at peak periods.[28] Therefore, the evidence we have of coin hoards in the Classical period is insignificant in respect to the total volume of coinage in circulation at this time. Furthermore, the fact that many of the largest hoards could have been deposited in times of crisis makes it very difficult to claim that habitual hoarding for savings purposes seriously impacted the money supply and its velocity in any observable way.

Ancient evidence for hoarding, savings, and investment

It is undeniable that many Greeks buried their coin as a means of savings, however, and a key passage of Xenophon seems at first glance to support the notion that they preferred to use their wealth in this way.

> καὶ γὰρ δὴ ἔπιπλα μέν, ἐπειδὰν ἱκανά τις κτήσηται τῇ οἰκίᾳ, οὐ μάλα ἔτι προσωνοῦνται: ἀργύριον δὲ οὐδείς πω οὕτω πολὺ ἐκτήσατο ὥστε μηκέτι προσδεῖσθαι: ἀλλ' ἤν τισι γένηται παμπληθές, τὸ περιττεῦον κατορύττοντες οὐδὲν ἧττον ἥδονται ἢ χρώμενοι αὐτῷ.
> As for furniture, whenever someone acquires enough for his house, he will certainly not keep buying more in addition; but with coined money, nobody yet has ever accumulated so much that they no longer continue to desire any more. On the contrary, if people get a large amount of it, they gain no less pleasure in burying the surplus than in using it. (Xen. *Vect.* 4.7)

---

26 Kroll 2009, 196–198; for a detailed discussion of the problems with mint quantification and the total output of the Athenian mints during the fifth century, see Figueira 1998, 180–197.

27 See Bresson 2019 for arguments supporting this figure.

28 Flament 2019, 201.

This passage initially appears to confirm that Greeks had a widespread desire to hoard in the sense of burying money in the ground. But when considered in light of its broader context and unpacked to reveal its full implications, it becomes clear that Xenophon is describing a far more complex (though perhaps less interesting) set of behaviors.

First, this statement follows his now-famous discussion of a market system whose prices fluctuate according to supply and demand. In this economy, the actors do not simply hoard their money but instead repurpose it according to profitability. In response to changes in price (based on supply and demand), those who are able to do so will alter their production to the more profitable opportunities that are available; those who do not are ruined. The latter, who would apparently seem to resemble the kind of static behavior implied by a "hoarding mentality", are not presented as the norm, but are one subset of individual whose inflexibility is not to be emulated. Those who are dynamic and responsive in the face of changing circumstances are the example used to demonstrate the way Greeks (or Athenians more specifically, perhaps) typically behave. In neither case, however, is hoarding presented as the default, rule of thumb approach to the situation. Engaging in the production of goods for profit, even if one is not able to weather the storm of protracted price deflation, is the normal behavior.

Xenophon then proceeds to describe how coined money has a unique relationship to supply and demand. It is in the context of that explanation that he makes the statement about burying money bringing as much pleasure as using it. But here the context is again instructive. The never-ending demand for money is seen as being in contrast to the limits on demand that govern other goods. What Xenophon is describing here is not an irrational desire to hoard but rather diminishing marginal utility. Endlessly filling one's house with furniture would be characteristic of an irrational behavior, much like the "hoarding" commonly depicted in modern reality television; Xenophon recognizes that such behavior is associated with an aberrant personality type, as do modern observers of the same phenomenon. Money, on the other hand, can be accumulated endlessly without the same physical spatial limitations and social reproach. The never-ending desire to acquire silver coin had an upward-sloping demand curve, in economic terms.[29] Unlike chairs, it can be converted into almost any other form, whether goods or services, so the diminishing marginal utility of money follows an entirely different pattern.

It would be a bizarre paradox if money's very invention simply hindered its own circulation. Aristotle certainly did not consider this to be the case when he discusses

29 For the unique demand curve for money, see Jones 2014, 311–312.

the reasons motivating the creation of coinage.[30] Money increases the possibilities for gain and exchange; it does not impede circulation or encourage its own hoarding. Instead of creating economic inefficiency by constricting its own supply, money was seen as being an improvement over putatively older systems of barter, precisely because it increases transaction velocity. Coinage spawned a profusion of lending and exchange-based arts (*chrêmatistikê*) which thrived with its invention. Flament provides compelling arguments that the very mining and minting of coinage stimulated economic activity, including the charcoal, grain, and oil trade.[31] Money therefore facilitates rather than restricts exchange and productivity,[32] in Aristotle's view, far from the static image of an economic system rendered inefficient by a frozen money supply.

The limited nature of hoarding is also suggested by a passage in the pseudo-Aristotelian *Oikonomika*: καὶ πλείω τὰ κάρπιμα εἶναι τῶν ἀκάρπων, καὶ τὰς ἐργασίας οὕτω νενεμῆσθαι ὅπως μὴ ἅμα κινδυνεύσωσιν ἅπασαι / "more property should be productive than idle, but the properties should be distributed such that they are not all at risk together at the same time" (1344b28–29). Here the preference is unequivocally for productivity since the author advocates investing the majority of assets in profitable activities. Although this passage could be taken to say that some property should not be exposed to danger of loss, a more important clue to the author's message must be unpacked from the verb νενεμῆσθαι. The properties should be "distributed" with the result that they are not risked together simultaneously. Some property could lie idle or unproductive, but the owner manages them according to a different prevailing overall strategy: diversification. This is a significant insight into the way in which assets are conceptualized in *oikonomia*. They ought to be profitable as much as possible, but not so concentrated into an individual risky venture that one's entire fortune is in danger of being destroyed in a single disaster. Far from depicting a hoarding situation, this passage actually reveals a far more complex and sophisticated understanding of risk versus profit calculations.[33] Some property might lie idle (ἀκάρπων) of course, but this should be the minority, and this comment might also be specifically in reference to fallow earth on an agricultural estate,

30 *Pol.* 1257a–b; *Eth. Nic.* 1133a–b. For a discussion of these passages, see Meikle 1995, *passim*; Schaps 2003, 5–16; von Reden 2010, 2–7.

31 Flament 2019.

32 Cf. the discussion by Priddat 2012, who interprets Aristotle's views similarly: "Geld dient dazu, die Transaktionen, die für den Lebensunterhalt nötig sind, zu ermöglichen. Es ist ein Transaktionsmedium" (ibid., 7).

33 For discussion of diversification as well as the balancing of risk and profit in ancient Greek *oikonomia*, see Leese 2021, 57–95.

not money. In any case, hoarding would certainly *not* be the preferred use of wealth in the mind of this author.

Hoarding seems to be an aberration when viewed from the *polis* level as well. Sparta is the clearest example of an overall society that deviates from the rules that govern other economic systems, and as far as the circulation of precious metals is concerned, it is precisely the necessity of hoarding money in the house that distinguished it from other *poleis*. As Plutarch articulates it, looking back as a Greek living during the Roman imperial period, the prohibition against a precious metal-based coinage created a peculiar outcome in Sparta: such wealth had to be "stored up in the house and not invested productively" (ἐγκατῳκοδομημένης καὶ ἀργούσης).[34] This hoarding of wealth was the artificial result of state institutions intervening into the type of monetary systems that characterized Greek and Roman societies in general; the preference typically was to remove it from the house and mobilize it for other purposes, whether productive or consumptive.[35]

Diversity in behavior with respect to spending and saving also itself strongly suggests that traits associated with hoarding would belong to only some personality types and not to others. Aristotle, Plato, and Theophrastus describe a wide variety of personality types that all tended to seek, spend, or save money in different ways. Book 4 of the *Nicomachean Ethics* opens with a discussion of the virtue of liberality (*eleutheriotês*), which Aristotle defines as moderation with respect to wealth (*chrêmata*). What follows is a lengthy account of the details associated with the moderate spending and pursuit of wealth, as well as the personality types that were seen as excessive in these activities, including meanness (*aneleutheria*) and prodigality (*asôtia*); the latter in Greek is "lack of saving", literally the opposite of hoarding.[36] Hoarding in Plato's *Republic* is one personality trait that ebbs and flows between generations, and shifts dynamically according to external circumstances.[37] The oligarchic personalities described in this discussion are precisely the sorts of individual who piles up wealth endlessly in the house, which makes them distinct from other Greeks.[38] The fact that each of these characters has different attitudes and practices regarding spending and saving is revealing per se: there was no common overarching mentality in ancient Greece that tended towards hoarding.

---

34 Plut. *Lyc.* 9.3.

35 The same situation is advocated in the discussion of the ideal but fantastical utopian state at Pl. *Leg.* 742a.

36 Aristot. *Eth. Nic.* 1119b22–1125b9. See also at 1107b; *Eth. Eud.* 1231b28–1233b15; *Virt. et Vit., passim.*

37 Pl. *Resp.* 545a–591d.

38 Pl. *Resp.* 548a–b; 550d; 554a.

Furthermore, hoarded coin is extremely rare within the property that is attested to have been held by actual ancient Greek individuals in their estate inventories. Indeed, in comparison with the proportion of wealth in estates that is committed to profitable, productive purposes, that which is "hoarded" in cash seems much less substantial than investment in productive enterprises. Profitable investments clearly predominate in the evidence for individual economic preferences.[39]

I examine below a selection of estates which have been preserved in the extant source material and enumerated their constituent elements. This list is by no means exhaustive, but the mixture of manufacturing, lending-based, and agricultural estates will give some breadth of overview across the different types of economic activity available in the ancient Greek world.

The first belongs to the orator Demosthenes' father, of the same name.[40] Demosthenes the Elder possessed a diversified estate that consisted of mainly a sword (*machaira*) factory, a smaller workshop dedicated to producing couches, and money on loan and deposited with bankers:

1. Dem. 27–28: Demosthenes' Father

Personal effects:
House 3,000 dr.
Furniture and Jewelry 10,000 dr.

Manufacturing capital:
32 or 33 slave sword-makers 19,000 dr. (3,000 dr. profit/yr.)
20 slave couch-makers 4,000 dr. (1,200 dr. profit/yr.)
Ivory, iron, wood 8,000 dr.
Dye and copper 7,000 dr.

Interest-bearing loans:
6,000 lent at 12 % interest (700 dr. profit/yr.)
7,000 dr. lent on maritime loans 25–30 % interest (1,750–2,100 dr/yr.)

Loans, unknown if yielding interest:
3,000 dr. in banks
6,000 dr. lent out in sums of 200 or 300 dr.
1,600 dr. lent to Demomeles

39 "Productive" here is defined as yielding a profit from its employment, whether invested in the production of goods, lent out at interest, or in the form of income-yielding capital of some sort (productive slaves, house to be rented out, etc.). For a detailed discussion of the varieties of capital, see Bourdieu 2001 and Keynes 1936, 210–221.

40 For a more in-depth analysis of this estate, see Leese 2021, 67–78.

<u>*8,000 dr. cash at house*</u>

→ 82,600 dr. total
8,000 dr. "hoarded" cash (<10 %)
51,000 dr. at least productively invested (6,650–7,000 dr./yr.) (62 %)

Less than ten percent of the estate's value consisted of cash in hand, so even at face value the evidence for hoarding is outweighed by the clear indications of profitable investment. Indeed, the amount of liquidity, 8,000 dr., is almost tripled by the total sum of the money out on loan or deposited with other people, 23,600 dr. in total. The vast majority of the property in this estate was being used for productive purposes, just as is advocated by Pseudo-Aristotle above. The materials on hand for the factories would have been essential to maintain their smooth operation after Demosthenes the Elder's death, especially since the estate was being entrusted to the management of guardians. The lifecycle of this business owner is therefore of the utmost importance for interpreting the composition of the estate. Rather than being seen as typical levels of raw material and cash on hand, these amounts were arranged by the estate owner prior to his death in anticipation of the problems of passing his property on to his heirs.[41] The cash left behind would have been essential to ensure the continued operation of the factories as well. Money, after all, is an indispensable part of production functions in modern firms. Without it, productivity would grind to a halt, and profitability would eventually suffer to the point of risking the workshops' collapse. Although it may be tempting to interpret the sum of cash in this estate as being evidence of hoarding, the rest of the assets were distributed in a manner that is rather suggestive of profit-maximization and a view to continuous productivity.[42]

The orator Lysias' estate, as described in the speech *Against Eratosthenes*, provides a similar example of cash found, this time in a treasure chest: "three talents of silver, four hundred Cyzicene staters, a hundred darics and four silver cups."[43] This hoard sounds significant except when it is considered within the context of his

41 Acton 2014, 266 says this stockpile is evidence of irrational behavior, but this ignores the lifecycle, i.e., arrangements made in anticipation of death. Overall, however, he argues that Athenian manufacturing followed rational, profit-maximizing principles (ibid., 290).

42 Weber 1976, 207 interprets this situation as hoarding as well, but does not consider the fact that cash is needed on hand for operations and that the vast majority of the wealth was engaged in profitable enterprise.

43 Lys. 12.11.

overall fortune, which was said to have been sold for 70 talents.[44] In this light, the total amount of wealth dwarfs the sums found in the lockbox. Though tempting to cite as evidence of hoarding, because this cash was part of an estate with a large workshop, as seen with Demosthenes the Elder above, it could likewise be considered as part of the factory's production function rather than an unproductive hoard. The produce of the factory, 700 shields, when applying the best price known, 20 drachmas for a shield awarded to a victor (from early third-century Keos),[45] would have been worth about 14,000 drachmas or two and one-third talents. Here the shields alone, stockpiled and waiting to be sold, almost equaled the money seized from the lockbox.

The estate of the trader/moneylender Diodotus in Lysias' speech *Against Diogeiton* similarly undermines the assumption that the Greeks practiced widespread hoarding.[46] Diodotus left 30,000 dr. on deposit with his brother to care for family; 46,000 dr. lent on maritime loans yielding 25–30 % interest (11,500–13,800 dr./yr.); 10,000 dr. lent on other loans probably at 8 % interest (800dr./yr.); 2,000 dr. lent out in Chersonese (bringing in grain as interest); and finally 2,200 dr. in cash at the house, making 88,000 dr. total. At first glance it is tempting to interpret the large sums of cash listed in the estate as unproductive hoarding. But the six talents deposited by Diodotus with his brother, Diogeiton, is clearly a case of a man taking extraordinary measures to provide for his family's welfare in the event of his death as he leaves for war. As with Demosthenes the Elder therefore, the lifecycle of this estate owner is an important methodological consideration. It is impossible to know how the money had been used prior to this, but the broader context of Diodotus' career provides a more reliable index of how he typically would have used his wealth. 58,000 dr. was out on loan, all of it yielding interest, and the vast majority bringing the high rates of maritime loans. Out of a total of 88,000 dr., most was lent for maritime ventures, with profits of two talents of cash annually. Not only are these high-risk investments, but they demonstrate a clear concern with sustained profitability, the uninterrupted continuous reinvestment into additional productive enterprise at the heart of the definition of rational capitalistic activity mentioned above. Indeed, if these loans are any indication of how Diodotus preferred to use his money, he seems to have wanted to expand his lending and trading business rather than just bury his coin in the ground. In fact, if one excludes the six talent deposit, which was clearly made to take care of his family after his death, the only cash that could be reasonably claimed to be hoarded was the 2,200 dr. in the house,

44 *P.Oxy.* 13.1606.

45 *SIG*[3] 958, l. 31.

46 Lys. 32.4–15. See more at Leese 2021, 127–131.

which would only amount to 2.5 % of the overall estate. By contrast, 58,000 dr. at least was productively invested, i.e., 66 % of the property. If the money deposited with Diogeiton had been repurposed from other profitable enterprises, this rate of productive investment would be even higher.

The last two estates are primarily agricultural, but here also the risk-averse mentality often ascribed to farmers did not encourage the hoarding of cash.[47] Stratocles' estate consisted of a15,000 dr. *agros* at Thria rented for 1200 dr./yr.; 3,500 dr. for two houses rented for 300 dr./yr.; 4,000 dr. lent at 18 % interest (720 dr./yr.); 1,000 dr. lent at no interest (*eranos*); 4,900 dr. in furniture, sheep, barley, wine, fruits; 900 dr. cash at the house.[48] Out of 28,400 dr. total, 900 dr. was "hoarded" cash (3 %), while 22,500 dr. at least was productively invested (79 %). Stratocles' estate consisted of mainly land and real estate, livestock, and agricultural produce. He also had a large amount of cash, however, but the majority was not hoarded. The 900 dr. of cash in the estate was a paltry 3 %, and dwarfed by the 5,000 dr. lent, most of it at interest. Even the land and real estate was dedicated to productive purposes, yielding 1,500 dr./yr., a quarter of a talent. Ciron possessed an *agros* at Phlya worth one talent; a house in city, rented to a tenant worth 2000 dr.; a house in city which he inhabited himself and slave manufacturers worth 1300 dr.; considerable sums lent out on interest.[49] His property therefore was also primarily in agricultural land and houses, with an unknown but considerable amount out on loan, and no mention whatsoever of cash hoarded.

In each of these estates, the amount of cash held by their owners was only a very small percentage of their total wealth, while the rest was predominantly engaged in profit-yielding activities.[50] Therefore, because the hoarded cash consisted of a smaller proportion of personal wealth than productively invested money, the claim that ancient Greek individuals preferred to hoard instead of profitably invest their money must be considered false or at least an oversimplification. As far as the available evidence attests, wealthy Greeks certainly did not always hoard large amounts of cash and much of their wealth was actually engaged in profit-generating activities, either in production and manufacture or in interest-bearing loans. Therefore, the "hoarding" which we can observe in individual estates in ancient Greece need not be interpreted as a necessary action taken by individuals with nothing else

47 See more at Leese 2021, 78–83.

48 Is. 11.42–43.

49 Is. 8.35.

50 Thompson 1978. See also Thompson 1982 for the examples of productive credit which are attested in the extant literature (though he omits maritime loans from his list).

to do with their money. On the contrary, much of the wealth of which estates consisted was invested in productive enterprise, with far smaller sums held in cash.

More importantly, it seems that we can see a fundamental principle of modern economic theory functioning in the ancient world, Keynes' notion of "liquidity preference":

> the rate of interest at any time, being the reward for parting with liquidity, is a measure of the unwillingness of those who possess money to part with their liquid control over it ... up to a point it is worth while to sacrifice a certain amount of interest for the convenience of liquidity ... but, given that the rate of interest is never negative, why should anyone prefer to hold his wealth in a form which yields little or no interest to holding it in a form which yields interest?[51]

In the modern economy, hoarding, here reframed as the propensity to hold cash as liquidity, is intimately connected to and dependent upon interest rates, which are the reward for giving up the security and convenience of a "fistful of dollars". Thus, in today's world, it is necessary also to consider such factors as money supply, stability of banks, demand for money, and interest rates in order to understand its dynamics properly. And just like today, interest did encourage individuals in ancient Greece to give up the security of their cash holdings in return for the potential for profit. Otherwise individuals would not have lent money and risked losing it.

There were many interest-bearing and income-generating activities of the type described by Keynes available to the ancient Greeks. Demosthenes' father's maritime loans and the 58,000 drachmas lent out at interest in Lysias 32 are ample enough evidence to prove that Greeks did not simply hoard because they lacked any investment opportunities. The enormous amount of grain imported annually by the Athenian polis in the fourth century (800,000–1 million *medimnoi*) depended greatly upon the profitable investment of wealth in interest-bearing maritime loans, which created an incentive to de-hoard and therefore drive the circulation of money and goods throughout the Eastern Mediterranean.[52] At the rate of 6 dr./*medimnos* this would require between 4.8 million and 6 million drachmas every year, just for Athens.[53] Loans for other goods would have similarly stimulated the movement of goods

51 Keynes 2018 (1936), 147.

52 For the scale of grain imports into mid-fourth century Athens, see Moreno 2007, 32–33; Bresson 2016, 411.

53 For the average of 6 dr./*medimnos*, see Moreno 2007, 326.

and cash throughout these regions.[54] Cash was paid in innumerable market transactions,[55] and prices proliferate in the source material.

Institutions that counteracted hoarding

Even if individuals did hoard in larger amounts than attested in the examples cited above, there is no clear evidence that this money would have actually remained frozen in place to create systemic inefficiency; with the peculiar institutions that shaped the ancient economy, money would have circulated in somewhat different ways than we perceive today. Von Reden has made powerful arguments that effectively illustrate the role of market and non-market institutions in encouraging the dynamic fluidity of monetary circulation in the ancient economy.[56] Any hoarding tendencies would have been affected by such institutions. Reconsidering the issue from this perspective, it becomes clear that the ancient money supply would likely be characterized more as dynamic fluidity than static immobility.

Interest, *tokos*, was just one of the institutions in the ancient Greek world that counteracted the effects of hoarding. Athenian jury and *ekklêsia* pay, as well as wages for magistrates in the fourth century served to circulate wealth at this time,[57] especially if one considers the amount of trade which took place in the Piraeus with foreigners from other parts of the Aegean.[58] Lower amounts of money circulating from bank deposits, given the lesser importance of the ancient Greek banking sphere, may have led many to seek funds from relatives or friends,[59] whose wealth was often given in the form of loans and circulated in the population much like the money of banks and corporations today. Many individuals who held significant amounts of liquidity would have mobilized this wealth, whether at their own initiative or not, for social and economic purposes. *Eranos* loans, for example, provided access to "hoarded" funds when needed by others.[60] This institution has often been interpreted as a socially-embedded practice, i.e., one that operated outside the realm of the competitive profit-seeking spheres of the economy. But its economic

---

54 For other goods, see, e.g., Reger 1994 and Bissa 2009.

55 Figueira 1986 and Leese 2017.

56 Von Reden 2010.

57 See, e.g., Pritchard 2014.

58 Shipton 1997 also argues strongly for the effective circulation of money in the Athenian and Aegean economy.

59 For the question of how much bank money could have added to the overall money supply in ancient Greece, see Shipton 1997 and 2008; Cohen 2008.

60 Millett 1991. For more recent overviews of this institution, see Thomsen 2015; Faraguna 2012.

importance is undeniable as part of the complex system of informal credit that operated in the ancient world. As far as hoarding is concerned, the need for even non-productive (e.g., consumptive or non-profit-oriented) activities would have motivated individuals to mobilize their wealth and put in in circulation for the purchase of goods or services. Therefore, institutions did not need to be explicitly geared towards the creation of profit or the production of surplus in order to act as anti-hoarding mechanisms.

Other institutions more traditionally associated with the market could liquidate assets very quickly and get cash out of lenders. Financial instruments such as *hypothêkê* and *prasis epi lysei* functioned much in the same way as the modern mortgage, as Harris has convincingly argued.[61] The conceptualization of a piece of property as being divisible in such a manner that a portion of it could be used as security for a loan is of the utmost importance; in such a system, even land, the least mobile of what Marx would refer to as "fixed capital" could be envisioned as interchangeable with money. Such liquidity enabled immobile property to be converted into cash, and the incentive of receiving property as security in case of default was another important motivation for individuals to put their money into circulation. Other instruments such as *enechuron*, which are akin to pawnbroking in the modern economy, served a similar function of allowing tangible pieces of property to be transformed into monetary form, so here again institutions existed that encouraged liquidity. As with *eranos* much hypothecation would have been for what could be interpreted as "consumptive" purposes so nonmarket activities could also play a significant role in de-hoarding.

Outside of the market, partible inheritance and dowry would have served to disperse hoards of cash every generation and with the marriage of every daughter.[62] Taxation was another institution preventing hoarding. In Athens *eisphorai* and liturgies forced the wealthiest members of society to mobilize their wealth in cash-generating activities, creating a dynamic monetized economic system that moved money throughout the Athenian economy, as argued by Osborne.[63] Von Reden explicitly states that these institutions prevented hoarding of specie.[64] Hopkins, of course, famously made taxes central to the model he proposed for the stimulus to

61 As argued by Harris 2008 and 2013. See also the classical study by Harris 1988 and more recently Thür 2014 on these institutions.

62 Leese 2022.

63 Osborne 1991. For an extensive recent overview of complex range of issues involved with the financial demands of the *polis*, including costs and the number of eligible individuals, see Rohde 2019, 189–215.

64 Von Reden 2010, 40.

monetary circulation in the Roman empire.[65] Taxation also points to rational reasons for holding onto liquidity. In this respect, the presence of cash in the extant estate lists may actually follow rational, growth-oriented principles. Indeed, liquidity was a sensible choice for private citizens looking to avoid the burdens of *eisphorai* and liturgies.[66] In Athens liturgies were assessed according to "visible" wealth, and the possession of liquidity could have been a rational, self-interested means of avoiding taxation by the state. In fact, the best means for exposing even the extent of "visible" property a person owned required the concerted effort by individuals in the process of *antidosis,* and it is clear in our sources that it was almost impossible to catch *aphanês* wealth.[67] Nor were citizens hiding their wealth from state demands only in Athens: Dionysius' taxation of sheep and cattle caused Syracusan citizens to cease rearing livestock to avoid taxes, but as soon as he rescinded the tax, they immediately began to transfer their cash into cattle as a store of wealth free from taxation.[68] Livestock are a visible form of wealth which Syracusans preferred to liquidate as soon as it became less profitable than holding the same value in the form of cash. Tax avoidance shows how the preference for cash was fluid and responsive to institutional change, rather than part of a monolithic mentality.

Tax dodging also reveals the growth- and production-oriented actions of ancient Greek estate owners; profit seems to have been the primary aim of *oikonomoi* in general when the prevailing conditions in the wider society were permissive.[69] The testimony of the Anonymus Iamblichi indicates that the overall quantity of the supply of money was less important in encouraging profit-oriented investment than the level of trust:[70]

> In the first place, trust arises from *eunomia*, and this benefits all people greatly and is one of the great goods. For as a result of it, money becomes available, and so even if there is little it is sufficient, since it is in circulation, but without it not even a great deal of money would be enough. Fortunes and misfortunes in money and life are managed most suitably for people as a result of *eunomia.* For those enjoying good fortune can use it in safety and without danger of plots ... There are many other goods found in *eunomia* that assist life, and also from it comes consolation for our

65 Hopkins 1980; see, however, the critique by Duncan-Jones 1990, 38–47.

66 Cohen 1992; Christ 2006. See also Rohde 2019, 200–203.

67 See Dem. 42 (*Against Phaenippus*).

68 [Aristot.] *Oec.* 2.1349b.

69 See Hinsch 2021 and Leese 2021 for in-depth analyses of profit- and wealth-maximizing strategies of ancient Athenian estate owners.

70 For a similar reading of this source, see Günther 2023.

> difficulties. These are the evils that come from *anomia* ... Because of mistrust and lack of mutual dealings they hoard money and do not make it available, so it becomes rare even if there is much.[71]

Hoarding in this author's eyes is not seen as a fixed pattern of behavior but as constantly evolving, dynamically shifting as a function of trust. Without it, transactions decrease and individuals hold onto their cash for fear of losing it. The author's description of the relationship between risk, the likelihood of repayment (or profit), and the willingness of individuals to extend their money in the hope of making productive investments is almost a textbook articulation of Keynesian economics' concepts of liquidity preference: profit is the incentive to de-hoard and liquidate holdings. But profit is impossible without trust. The decision to save money or invest it in profitable enterprise is dependent on a wide variety of external parameters, and is not simply an innate characteristic of individuals, broader cultural inclinations, or premodern economies in general. Incentives for savings versus investment, especially in the form of interest rates as discussed by Keynes above, therefore provide a more accurate framework to explain the desire to hold or de-hoard money, than models based on behavioral dichotomies between modern and premodern systems.

This nuanced perspective, reframing hoarding as liquidity preference based on the evidence of ancient Greek estate inventories and the similarities between Keynes and Anonymus Iamblichi, is clearly preferable to absolute, Marxist-inspired claims such as "with the appearance of a credit system, hoarding simply disappears."[72] Hoarding is not merely an ancient phenomenon, but is widespread in the modern economy as well.[73] As Great Depression economists demonstrated, the hoarding that crippled the world economy during that time was a special case, unique to the specific conditions of that scenario. This crisis in particular brought the problem of hoarding to the fore in economists' discussions as they frantically tried to rescue the world from the collapse of its economic system.[74] Entire chapters

71 Anonymus Iamblichi, fr. 7.1–8. Translation by McKirahan and Curd in Curd 2011, 158–159.

72 Meikle 1995, 162.

73 For a detailed demonstration of how the work of modern economists can be relevant for the study of pre-modern economic behavior, see the discussion of thrift, savings, and investment in Gudeman 1990, 171–182. Economic anthropologists have pointed the way to the cross-cultural comparison of hoarding by demonstrating that, just as is practiced in "primitive" or premodern "householding," the stockpiling of liquidity is not unknown in the present day either – see, e.g., Gudeman 2009; Peebles 2009.

74 See especially the well-known debate over hoarding between two of the most

of Keynes' *General Theory of Employment, Interest, and Money* are devoted to hoarding during this period.

Nor is such action to be considered irrational. With low trust in credit and the banking system, corporations must ensure that they have the necessary cash to cover everyday operations while credit institutions remain unstable. During the Banker's Panic of 1907, both banks and corporations were found to be hoarding significant sums of cash due to runs on the banks and the uncertainty of obtaining needed funds to cover daily expenses.[75] In the aftermath of the recent Great Recession, corporate hoarding of cash increased substantially due to the lack of trust in the credit system.[76] Moreover, the "gold bubble" which simultaneously grew reveals that investors were increasingly interested in acquiring low-risk liquid assets to supplement their productive investments. In such a situation, liquid cash reserves are an attractive alternative because of the security they provide. Likewise, ancient Greek banks are known to have experienced failures, so perhaps the cash that was held by individuals was seen as a secure alternative to a potentially unstable investment.[77]

In the case of Demosthenes' father, rather than place all his money in banks and risk-laden investments, it would have made a great deal of sense to have a significant amount of secure cash on hand to guarantee the proper functioning of his estate and income-generating activities. His slaves would have needed to be fed without a farm to provide them with food, and his factories would have needed to be supplied with sufficient materials to ensure their smooth operation. Lysias' factory would have also needed a plentiful amount of cash to maintain profitability, especially with the enormous scale of its productive capacity. As mentioned above, cash

distinguished economists at this time, John Maynard Keynes and Dennis Robertson: Robertson 1933; Keynes 1936. For an overview of the problems in defining hoarding, see Robinson 1938.

75 Andrew 1908.

76 According to a *Wall Street Journal* article by Jeff Bater, published December 9, 2010, US nonfinancial corporations held 1.93 trillion dollars in cash reserves, 7.4 % of total assets, at the end of the third quarter of 2010, up from 1.8 billion dollars the previous quarter, URL: http://online.wsj.com/article/SB10001424052748703766704576009501161973480.html, last accessed 28.04.2023. This is not, oddly enough, far off the percentages attested in ancient Greece for individuals above.

77 Bank failures are discussed at length in Dem. 49.68. Many Greeks did of course deposit money in bankers' hands, and may have received interest in return, though this is a very problematic question. See Shipton 1997 for the evidence that private banks paid interest on loans. The role of banks in the Athenian economy is much disputed, for which see Millett 1991; Cohen 1992; Shipton 2008.

is an important part of modern firms' production functions. Productivity and therefore profit suffer without enough liquidity to supply the needs of labor, capital, and raw materials; this fact alone would explain why these factory owners held such substantial liquidity.

Furthermore, a plentiful supply of cash on hand could facilitate the purchase of additional productive enterprises, such as the sword factory which Demosthenes' father received on default of a loan made on the security of the factory. Such windfall acquisitions could not be taken advantage of without cash reserves on hand.[78] If someone were waiting for potential investments, it would make more sense to hold onto cash with the hope of capitalizing on the most profitable opportunities than to simply jump at the first property that came along.

The definition of rational choice is to survey the possible options for investment and to choose the one that brings the greatest return.[79] This involves a process of comparison and deliberation, a period of time in which one has money in their possession while deciding what to choose. If one simply grabs a property as soon as it becomes available, it is at the opportunity cost of a potentially more profitable venture. Therefore, having cash in hand is an essential aspect of the economically rational decision-making process. One cannot decide to purchase something without money, and even if credit is accessible, one cannot avail oneself of this without the ability to produce enough money to repay with interest.

Just as a similar rationale for emergency hoarding in ancient Greece and Rome can also be seen in modern economic crises (though motivated by different factors), there were rational reasons to hold onto cash, so liquidity could have been a deliberate and reasonable choice in many situations in classical antiquity. Although Jones is right above to discuss hoarding in the sense of liquidity preference, he still does so from the perspective of the great shift to modernity that sees previous history as being characterized by a universally shared hoarding mentality. In antiquity, instead of being crippled by fear of investment as a default state of mind, opportunities for profit ebbed and flowed in a dynamic manner in response to market conditions, such as price fluctuations with changes in supply and demand, climatic variation, political discord, and military threats. Legal and political institutions were not static, either, and constantly affected property rights in different ways.

Temple hoarding

One area in which the ancient economy unequivocally differed from the modern, however, is in the economic effects of institutions, and it is in religious sanctuaries

78 See Finley 1973, 118–119 for the windfall nature of much of ancient acquisition.

79 See Leese 2021, 3–13 for detailed discussion.

that the best evidence for potentially excessive hoarding may be found.[80] A large quantity of precious metals is known to have been dedicated at Delphi, Delos, Olympia, and other sites in Greece, which would have been thereby removed from circulation, and perhaps therefore caused serious problems for the money supply. Religious offerings are an undeniable unique characteristic of the ancient Greek and Roman economy in which cultural practices affected access to precious metals, as agricultural and commercial profits were converted into precious objects and frozen in solid form, seemingly inaccessible to the public. This institutional particularity clearly distinguishes the ancient from the modern economy. From this perspective, Austin and Vidal-Naquet are right to emphasize the much less significant role banks played in the economic system.

Religious dedications could, however, be accessed and utilized in special situations, such as the Corinthian proposal in 431 BCE to borrow coin from Delphi and Olympia;[81] the Athenian melting of the gold Nikai and the golden pieces of the Athena statue in the Parthenon;[82] the Phocian plunder of Delphi in the Third Sacred War;[83] Dionysius I's supposed plundering of wealth from religious sanctuaries on a more casual basis.[84] The Athenian *polis* borrowed money from the Acropolis treasures for wage payments and construction projects. The total amount of borrowed wealth placed into circulation by Athens amounted to 5,599 Talents between 433/2 and 423/2 BCE.[85] As Hecataeus' recommendation to use the treasures dedicated at the Panionion during the Ionian Revolt shows, however, it may not have been automatically assumed by ancient Greeks that they could have access to such wealth. Davies makes an interesting argument for an increased willingness by Greeks over time to consider temple funds as being available for their use, as they made more frequently attested requests into the classical period for the gods to grant them access to their wealth.[86] If this higher rate of Greeks seeking to borrow from divinities as preserved in the source material is an accurate reflection of the diachronic rise

80 I would like to thank Graham Claytor for directing me to the importance of this issue.

81 Thuc. 1.121.3.

82 Hellanicus *FGrH* 323a F26; Philochorus *FGrH* 328 F144. See Fornara 1977, no. 164B for commentary, as well as Harding 2008, 136–137.

83 Diod. 16.56.6 says that the total amount melted down and minted by the Phocians was 10,000 talents worth of gold and silver, much of which came from bullion and large dedications.

84 [Aristot.] *Oec.* 2.1353b.

85 Shipton 1997, 405.

86 Davies 2001.

in precious metals laid up at sanctuaries, religious dedications may have indeed been responsible for a reduction in the money supply in the long run.

Nevertheless, the fact that temples also increasingly acted as major lending institutions over time would have countered the effect of a diachronically growing quantity of dedications. Temples' role as major economic players distinguishes the ancient from the modern economy, where banking and financial institutions are the primary agents of circulating wealth.[87] In this sense, temples provided access to cash which otherwise would have been immobilized. The accounts of the Temple of Nemesis at Rhamnous attest significant lending activity.[88] The first entry (ll. 1–9) records 37,000 drachmas lent in 200 dr. increments,[89] which would imply that up to 185 borrowers were given access to these funds. Also in lines 9–14, 12,729 dr. are listed as being held in addition (*to allo argurio tes Nemeseos*), making 49,729.5 dr. in total. If this is the case, then 74.4 % of the *argurion* at the temple was being lent out, and just over a quarter remained hoarded. In the final entry, lines 32–38, 14,400 dr. is lent to 300 dr. borrowers (48 max.), and 37,000 dr. is lent to 200 dr. borrowers (185 again), 51,400 out of a total of 56,606 dr. in *argurion*. This would mean that 90.8 % of this temple's total *argurion* was lent out, presumably at interest, though there is no mention of this in the inscription. Other temples are known to have regularly lent to individual borrowers, especially the sanctuary of Apollo at Delos, in 434–432 BCE, loans of 9 talents 20 dr. at 10 % interest for 5 years are recorded with the total after interest amounting to more than 13 talents.[90] From 377/6–374/3 BCE, a large number of loans were made out to cities at a total of 260,600 drachmas in capital (43 Talents, 2,600 drachmas) bringing in more than 4 talents in interest.[91] These inscriptions show that, like individuals, temples were not content just to hoard their wealth but often invested it in profit-making enterprise, in the form of interest-bearing loans and rent-producing land.[92]

---

87 For temple finance in ancient Greece, see von Reden 2010, 156–185.

88 *IG* I³ 248. See Fornara 1977, no. 90B; Finley 1952, 284–285; Bogaert 1968, 93–94; Osborne / Rhodes 2017, no. 134.

89 The lending of fixed amounts is also attested at Delos and in Dem. 27–28 by Demosthenes' father.

90 *IG* I² 377; Fornara 1977, no. 121; Tod 1933–1948, no. 54; Bogaert 1968, 127.

91 *IG* II² 1635; Tod 1933–1948, 125.

92 See Bogaert 1968, 279–304 for a comprehensive treatment of Greek temple banking. See also von Reden 2010, 168–174 for temple lending. For a succinct but thorough overview of temple banking from the classical into the Hellenistic period, when there is evidence of lending from dozens of sanctuaries, see Chankowski 2011.

Not every sanctuary seems to have engaged in regular lending at interest, however, and even such large Panhellenic centers as Delphi may not have circulated much of their hoarded wealth.[93] This is particularly telling since the 10,000 talents said to have been melted down and minted by the Phocians in the Third Sacred War must be at least somewhat suggestive of the amount of non-circulating wealth sitting in the sanctuary.[94] Since the total property of the Athenians was valued at 5,750 talents in the same century (though this figure is likely an underestimate),[95] this would appear to be a significant amount of hoarded wealth that could represent a major drain on monetary circulation. Athens' annual public revenue seems to have been 1,200 talents in the Age of Lycurgus, and 9,700 talents in total were held in reserves on the Acropolis just prior to the Peloponnesian War. But 10,000 talents amassed at Delphi would only amount to 100 talents removed from circulation per year for a century, hardly enough to cripple the economy. Davies would cut that figure by half or more, making it even less, i.e., 40–50 talents a year, with the excellent point that when the temple of Apollo needed to be rebuilt, the Delphians did not seem to be wading through mountains of available cash at the sanctuary when they were seeking funds for this purpose.[96]

Perhaps more significantly, much of the money hoarded at Delphi was not dedicated by typical Greeks as part of their everyday religious practice but actually by fabulously wealthy foreign kings like Croesus – Diodorus says that 4,000 talents coined by the Phocians came from Croesus' gold dedications alone, and that much of the 6,000 other talents of silver was dedicated by Croesus as well.[97] Tyrants also made some of the most expensive offerings, like Cypselus' large golden statue at Olympia.[98] Therefore, the fact that many of the dedications at the religious sanctuaries were royal thanks offerings must make one pause before concluding that they represent a constant drain on normal monetary circulation.

Finally, individuals were often unable to make substantial precious metal dedications without adversely affecting their personal finances, so the rate and value of offerings was not a constant drain on circulation but could be variable in response to money supply problems, or adjusted according to the fluctuating value of metals and coinage and the relative prosperity or lack thereof in different times and places. Indeed, Greeks are known to have modified their dedication practices with changing

93 Bogaert 1968, 106–107.

94 Diod. 16.56.

95 Pol. 2.67.

96 Davies 2007.

97 Diod. 16.56.6–7. See Mikalson 2003, 224, n. 21.

98 Strab. *Geogr*. 8.6.20.

circumstances, even abstaining from required sacrifices when deemed necessary during shortages of cattle.[99] It may be that the dedications made at Delphi were subject to curtailment and expansion in times of scarcity or glut. Ceramic and carved stone offerings could take the place of precious metals as well, so there was elasticity in the materials available that would allow Greeks to use silver for money while also not completely withdrawing from the economy of divine reciprocity. Delphi has a much less well-published record of its lending activities, but still kept extensive records and seems to have mobilized its wealth for productive purposes to a certain extent. Although the earliest evidence for the sanctuary providing loans to the Alcmaeonids is not particularly solid,[100] later inscriptions explicitly specify that royal dedications would be lent out at interest.[101] Dedications at sanctuaries did not automatically remove them from the economy – temples were enormously influential institutions within their loyal economic systems. They employed independent contractors for building and maintenance projects, leased out lands to collect rents, lent money at interest for profit, and stimulated economic activity beyond their local communities as well, from craft production to agriculture and livestock rearing. Therefore, hoarding by temples may not have had a significantly depressing effect on the economy or even the money supply.

Indeed, hoarding at Greek temples paled in comparison to the amount of precious metal reserves stored by the Great King of Persia. The wealth recovered by Alexander at Susiane was recorded by Diodorus to be 49,000 talents of bullion and coin (Diod. 17.66.1–2); that at Persepolis, 120,000 talents (Diod. 17.71.2); and at Ecbatana 180,000 talents (Diod. 17.80.3). This precious metal amounts to 350,000 talents in total. Bresson remarks on the excessive hoarding of the Persian royal treasury with the implication that such massive removal of money from circulation was in stark contrast with normal behavior of individuals and institutions in the Greek world: "in the Persian World, silver and gold thus entered the central royal treasury as a tribute, but for the most part they did not emerge from it again. They were essentially destined to be removed from circulation."[102] Therefore if any hoarding would have been detrimental to economic efficiency and the money supply, it would have been that of kings. Rather than a universal mentality to hoard characterizing the behavior of Greek individuals, the main threat to the circulation of money in the

99 Philochorus, *FGrH* 328 F169A & B. See Harding 2008, 264a–b.

100 Dem. 21.144.

101 E.g., the dedication of Attalus II, for which see Jacquemin / Mulliez / Rougemont 2012, no. 168.

102 Bresson 2016, 267.

ancient world would therefore more likely have come from the institutional power of the state.[103]

Even if metals were hoarded inaccessibly at sanctuaries, Greek *poleis* did have recourse to measures that could counteract even the most debilitating conditions. With shortages of coinage during the Peloponnesian War, rather than freezing economic activity with a shrinking money supply, the Athenians turned to a fiduciary currency, the bronze coinage.[104] Scrips were also issued by generals such as Timotheus in times of scarce access to coin.[105] Therefore, currency was able to circulate and economic activity was able to continue even when precious metals were short because cities could enact legislation to counteract shortages in money supply. For example, a city could issue a fiduciary currency forcing citizens to de-hoard silver and used this as a loan to be repaid gradually over time, as was said to have been done by Clazomenae and perhaps also Syracuse.[106] Also, it is possible that cities were aware that the value of money changed relative to other goods and could be controlled and manipulated to solve money-supply problems. Aristotle recognized that the value of money fluctuates,[107] and Pseudo-Aristotle says that one job of monarchies is to control the value of their currency.[108] The state as an institution could enact effective policies to offset the detrimental effects of hoarding if it ever became too problematic.

The Roman material likewise suggests that the power of the state rather than the behavior of individuals had the most significant impact on the availability and circulation of money in the economy. The best-attested examples of constricted money supply in the ancient world certainly come from the Roman period, such as the so-called Financial Crisis of AD 33, a situation that is explicitly described by Tacitus as being a shortage of money, "*inopia rei nummariae*."[109] Many scholars have interpreted this episode as similar to the sort of monetary crisis that occurred during the Great Depression, that hoarding by Tiberius reduced the amount of cash

103 Bresson 2019, 147 estimates that only about 2,500 talents of cash was held in private hands in Athens at the beginning of the Peloponnesian War whereas the state had amassed a stockpile of 10,000 talents.

104 See Aristoph. *Ran.* 718–737 and *Eccl.* 813–822; the Scholiast to Aristoph. *Ran.* 725, says this coinage was issued in 406/5 BCE. Credit would also have been an important instrument to circumvent money supply problems, as argued by Harris 2006 and Cohen 2008.

105 [Aristot.] *Oec.* 2.1350a.

106 [Aristot.] *Oec.* 2.1348b–1349a.

107 Aristot. *Eth. Nic.* 1133b.

108 [Aristot.] *Oec.* 2.1345b21–23: τὸ νόμισμα λέγω ποῖον καὶ πότε τίμιον ἢ εὔωνον ποιητέον.

109 Tac. *Ann.* 6.16–17.

circulating in the economy.[110] The treasury was swollen with the wealth of confiscated estates, "*signatum argentum fisco vel aerario attinebatur*", so perhaps it was only at the scale of the central imperial fisc that hoarding could have significantly impacted the money supply. But this excessive stockpiling of cash was exacerbated by the sudden enactment of extraordinary legal measures that coincided in unprecedented (and unpredictable) ways to cause the crisis. When an outdated law against usury was suddenly and unexpectedly enforced and the Senate ordered them to invest two-thirds of their capital in land throughout Italy, the moneylenders called in their loans all at once, then hoarded their cash to purchase land.[111] Debtors were then forced to sell land at great loss of value because of the sudden mass sale and demands for repayment by creditors. Tiberius then intervened by distributing 100 million sesterces in banks (*mensas*) for three-year interest-free loans to those furnishing double the security. Trust was restored and gradually even private creditors reappeared: "*refecta fides et paulatim privati creditores reperti.*" The shortage of money resulted from the complex series of consequences resulting from individuals' response to institutional actions by the state. Therefore, even hoarding by the emperors may not have been sufficient to cause the kind of constriction that could create economic inefficiency in normal circumstances.

Indeed, the bird's-eye view provided by financial crises in the Roman world supports the impression that the ancient world was not crippled by pandemic hoarding but rather that liquidity crunches were irregular aberrations. The episodes of monetary problems that are attested in Rome were usually precipitated by sudden crises, such as the outbreak of civil war between Caesar and Pompey that spurred creditors to recall their loans all at once.[112] These types of credit crises were not caused by the everyday reluctance to extend money on loans because of high risks immanent in the economic system in general, but rather the opposite: the investment of cash at such a widespread level that it turned into a dangerous overextension of money in the face of a sudden and unexpected shock. In this respect, Roman liquidity crises are more akin to the types of modern debt crises, such as the

110 See, e.g., Thornton and Thornton 1990, 659–662. See, however, Elliott 2015 for an overview of earlier approaches to this crisis and critique of much of the mainstream treatment in previous scholarship. This is not to say, however, that this crisis cannot be understood in terms of modern economic theory, including rationality, as argued by Elliott 2020, 90–95, Temin 2013, 124–151, and most recently Jones 2021, 248–249. Cf. Remesal Rodriguez in this volume, p. 223.

111 For moneylenders in Roman society, including the *creditores* and *faeneratores*, see Verboven 2008.

112 For a succinct overview of Roman financial crises, see Andreau 1999, 100–111.

one that led to Shays' Rebellion in the early United States following the Revolutionary War, where a similar chain of events occurred during the credit crunch, and is described as following the same types of processes at the individual and macroeconomic level as the Roman Financial Crisis of AD 33.[113] Therefore, the Roman evidence is instructive and decisively so – hoarding was not a common enough practice that it froze the normal workings of the economic system, but was rather a marginal phenomenon. Liquidity crises were extraordinary situations, and were not caused by too little money being lent but rather too much. The emphasis on trust (*fides*) in Tacitus' account echoes that of the Anonymus Iamblichi and Keynesian economics.

Conclusions

In conclusion, the hoarding of specie did not uniquely characterize the ancient economy but should be compared to and understood in terms of modern economic theories of money supply, interest rates, and the stability of the banking system. In terms of liquidity preference, maintaining a certain level of liquidity could be rational from an economic perspective for practical and security reasons, just as it can be today. As Ober puts it, there could be "economically rational reasons" for ancient Greeks to choose to hold into coinage.[114] Marxist views of unproductive hoarding must be replaced (or at least complemented) by Keynesian and depression-era theories of liquidity preference alongside New Institutional Economics. An institutional focus, in which cash flows are examined in conjunction with attested behaviors of real-life individuals, provides a valuable perspective on economic performance. These issues also reveal hidden assumptions that have shaped the field. One reason for the intensity of the debate over the ancient economy is that implicitly-held theoretical stances, such as Marxist views of premodern vs. capitalistic economic behavior, have not been overtly unpacked and analyzed for their influence. Such causal paradigms still exert a tremendous pull on the discourse of the scholarship, and until they are addressed at the level of minute issues, many of these fundamental assumptions will continue to influence scholars' approach to how the economic system can even be described as functioning. The similar processes that characterized ancient and modern debt and liquidity crises alone are sufficient to show that hoarding was not so different in antiquity to act as a brake on economic development. The continuity that unites economic systems across artificially constructed temporal divisions can provide fascinating new insights into long-term economic change and development.

---

113 See, e.g., the in-depth description by Szatmary 1980 and Holton 2007.

114 Ober 2008, 49.

Bibliography

Acton, Peter (2014): Poiesis: Manufacturing in Classical Athens, Oxford.

Andreau, Jean (1999): Banking and Business in the Roman World, Cambridge.

Andrew, A. Piatt (1908): Hoarding in the Panic of 1907, in: The Quarterly Journal of Economics 22/2, 290–299.

Austin, Michel M. / Vidal-Naquet, Pierre (1980): Economic and Social History of Ancient Greece, Berkeley.

Bissa, Errietta (2009): Governmental Intervention in Foreign Trade in Archaic and Classical Greece, Leiden (Mnemosyne Supplements 312).

Bogaert, Raymond (1968): Banques et banquiers dans les cités grecques, Leiden.

Bourdieu, Pierre (2001): The Forms of Capital, in: Granovetter, Mark / Swedberg, Richard (eds.), The Sociology of Economic Life, Boulder, CO, 96–111.

Bresson, Alain (2016): The Making of the Ancient Greek Economy: Institutions, Markets, and Growth in the City-States, Princeton.

Bresson, Alain (2019): The Athenian Money Supply in the Late Archaic and Early Classical Period, in: Journal of Ancient Civilizations 34/2, 135–154.

Chankowski, Véronique (2011): Divine Financiers. Cults as Consumers and Generators of Value, in: Archibald, Zosia / Davies, John K. / Gabrielsen, Vincent (eds.), The Economies of Hellenistic Societies, Third to First Centuries BC, Oxford, 142–165.

Christ, Matthew R. (2006): The Bad Citizen at Athens, Cambridge.

Cohen, Edward E. (1992): Athenian Economy and Society: A Banking Perspective, Princeton.

Cohen, Edward E. (2008): Elasticity of the Money Supply at Athens, in: Harris, William (ed.), The Monetary Systems of the Greeks and Romans, Oxford, 66–84.

Crawford, Michael H. (1969a): Roman Republican Coin Hoards, London.

Crawford, Michael H. (1969b): Coin Hoards and the Pattern of Violence in the Late Republic, in: Papers of the British School at Rome 37, 76–81.

Curd, Patricia (ed.) ([2]2011): A Presocratics Reader, Cambridge.

Davies, John K. (2001): Temples, Credit, and the Circulation of Money, in: Meadows, Andrew / Shipton, Kirsty (eds.), Money and Its Uses in the Ancient Greek World, Oxford, 117–128.

Davies, John K. (2005): Linear and Non-linear Flow Models for Ancient Economies, in: Manning, John G. / Morris, Ian (eds.), The Ancient Economy. Evidence and Models, Stanford, 127–156.

Davies, John K. (2007): The Phokian Hierosylia at Delphi: Quantities and Consequences, in: Sekunda, Nicholas (ed), Corolla Cosma Rodewald. Monograph Series Akanthina 2, Gdansk, 75–96.

Dornbusch, Rudiger (1973): Currency Depreciation, Hoarding, and Relative Prices, in: The Journal of Political Economy 81/4, 893–915.

Duncan-Jones, Richard (1990): Structure and Scale in the Roman Economy, Cambridge.

Ehrhardt, Christopher (1975): Greek Treasure Trove: Hoards and Hoarders, in: The New Zealand Numismatic Journal 13, 169–173.

Eich, Armin (2006): Die politische Ökonomie des antiken Griechenland (6.–3. Jahrhundert v. Chr.), Köln (Passauer historische Forschungen 14).

Elliott, Colin (2015): The Crisis of A.D. 33: Past and Present, in: Journal of Ancient History 3/2, 267–281.

Elliott, Colin (2020): Economic Theory and the Roman Monetary Economy, Cambridge.

Emmer, Robert (1959): A Concept of Hoarding, in: The Review of Economics and Statistics 41/2, 162–169.

Faraguna, Michele (2012): Diritto, economia, società: riflessioni su eranos tra età omerica e mondo ellenistico, in: Legras, Bernard (ed.), Transferts culturels et droits dans le monde grec et hellénistique, Paris, 129–153.

Figueira, Thomas J. (1986): Sitopolai and Sitophylakes in Lysias' 'Against the Grain Dealers:' Governmental Intervention in the Athenian Economy, in: Phoenix 40, 149–171.

Figueira, Thomas J. (1998): The Power of Money: Coinage and Politics in the Athenian Empire, Philadelphia.

Finley, Moses I. (1952): Studies in Land and Credit in Ancient Athens, 500–200 B.C.: The *horos*-inscriptions, New Brunswick, NJ.

Finley, Moses I. (1973): The Ancient Economy, Berkeley.

Flament, Christophe (2019): The Athenian Coinage, from Mines to Markets, in: Journal of Ancient Civilizations 34/2, 189–210.

Fornara, Charles W. (1977): Archaic Times to the End of the Peloponnesian War, Baltimore.

Goldman, Joshua (2022): Coin Hoarding in Roman Palestine: 63 BC to AD 300, in: Mairat, Jerome / Wilson, Andrew / Howgego, Chris (eds.), Coin Hoards and Hoarding in the Roman World, Oxford, 208–220.

Gudeman, Stephen (1990): Conversations in Colombia: The Domestic Economy in Life and Text, Cambridge.

Gudeman, Stephen (2009): Hoarding Wealth: When Virtue Becomes Vice: A Response to Elyachar / Maurer, Applbaum and Peebles, in: Anthropology Today 25/2, 25–26.

Günther, Sven (2023): Let Money Circulate, for the sake of the Commonwealth! A Note on the Echo of Anonymus Iamblichi fragment 7 in Xenophon's Works, in: Reinard, Patrick / Rollinger, Christian (eds.), *Cum magna fide?* Vertrauen und Wirtschaft in der griechisch-römischen Antike / Trust and the Ancient Economy, Gutenberg (Scripta Mercaturae-Beihefte 3), 167–176.

Harding, Phillip (2008): The Story of Athens: The Fragments of the Local Chronicles of Attika, London.

Harris, Edward M. (1988): When is a Sale not a Sale? Athenian Terminology for Real Security Revisited, in: Classical Quarterly 38, 351–381.

Harris, Edward M. (2008): Response to Gerhard Thür, in: Harris, Edward M. / Thür, Gerhard (eds.), Symposion 2007. Vorträge zur griechischen und hellenistischen Rechtsgeschichte, Wien, 189–202.

Harris, Edward M. (2013): Finley's Studies in Land and Credit Sixty Years Later, in: Dike 16, 123–146.

Harris, Edward M. / Lewis, David M. (2016): Introduction, in: Harris, Edward M. / Lewis, David M. / Woolmer, Mark (eds.), Markets, Households, and City-States in the Ancient Greek Economy, Cambridge, 1–40.

Harris, William (2006): A Revisionist View of Roman Money, in: Journal of Roman Studies 96, 1–24.

Hartley, Peter R. (1990): Hoarding in General Equilibrium, in: Economica N.S. 57/228, 467–483.

Hinsch, Moritz (2021): Ökonomik und Hauswirtschaft im klassischen Griechenland, Stuttgart (Historia-Einzelschriften 265).

Holton, Woody (2007): Unruly Americans and the Origins of the Constitution, New York.

Hopkins, Keith (1980): Taxes and Trade in the Roman Empire (200 B.C. – A.D. 400), in: The Journal of Roman Studies 70, 101–125.

Howgego, Christopher (1992): The Supply and Use of Money in the Roman World: 200 B.C. to A.D. 300, in: Journal of Roman Studies 82, 1–31.

Howgego, Chris / Wilson, Andrew (2022): Introduction: Coin Hoards and Hoarding in the Roman World, in: Mairat, Jerome / Wilson, Andrew / Howgego, Chris (eds.), Coin Hoards and Hoarding in the Roman World, Oxford, 3–22.

Jacquemin, Anne / Mulliez, Dominique / Rougemont, Georges (2012): Choix d'inscriptions de Delphes, traduites et commentées, Athens (Etudes épigraphiques 5).

Jones, Eric (2003): The European Miracle: Environments, Economies and Geopolitics in the History of Europe and Asia, Cambridge.

Jones, Donald W. (2014): Economic Theory and the Ancient Mediterranean, Malden, MA.

Jones, Donald W. (2021): Four Economic Topics for Studies of Antiquity: Agriculture, Trade, Population, and the Behavior of Aggregate Economies, Oxford.

Kaufman, David B. (1932): Hoarding by the Romans, in: The Classical Journal 27/9, 684–686.

Keynes, John Maynard (2018 [1936]): The General Theory of Employment, Interest and Money. With Introduction by Paul Krugman and Afterword by Robert Skidelsky, Cham.

Kim, Henry S. (2002): Small Change and the Moneyed Economy, in: Cartledge, Paul / Cohen, Edward E./ Foxhall, Lin (eds.), Money, Labour and Land. Approaches to the Economics of Ancient Greece, New York, 44–51.

Kraay, Colin (1964): Hoards, Small Change, and the Origin of Coinage, in: Journal of the Hellenistic Studies 84, 76–91.

Kroll, John H. (2009): What about Coinage? in: Ma, John et al. (eds.), Interpreting the Athenian Empire, London, 195–210.

Leese, Michael (2017): Kapêloi and Economic Rationality in Fourth-Century BCE Athens, in: Illinois Classical Studies 42/1, 41–59.

Leese, Michael (2021): Making Money in Ancient Athens, Ann Arbor.

Leese, Michael (2022): Problems in the Long-Term Accumulation of Commercial and Financial Capital in Ancient Greece, in: Morley, Neville / Koedijk, Max (eds.), Capital in Classical Antiquity, Cham (Palgrave Studies in Ancient Economies), 19–46.

Meikle, Scott (1995): Aristotle's Economic Thought, Oxford.

Mikalson, Jon D. (2003): Herodotus and Religion in the Persian Wars, Chapel Hill.

Millett, Paul (1991): Lending and Borrowing in Ancient Athens, Cambridge.

Moreno, Alfonso (2007): Feeding the Democracy. The Athenian Grain Supply in the Fifth and Fourth Centuries BC, Oxford.

Ober, Josiah (2008): Democracy and Knowledge: Innovation and Learning in Classical Athens, Princeton.

Ober, Josiah (2016): The Rise and Fall of Classical Greece, Princeton.

Osborne, Robin (1991): Pride and Prejudice, Sense and Subsistence: Exchange and Society in the Greek City, in: Rich, John / Wallace-Hadrill, Andrew (eds.), City and Country in the Ancient World, London, 119–145.

Osborne, Robin / Rhodes, Peter J. (2017): Greek Historical Inscriptions, 478–404 BC, Oxford.

Peebles, Gustav (2009): Hoarding, Storing Value and the Credit Crunch: A Comment on Hart / Ortiz and Gudeman, in: Anthropology Today 25/2, 25.

Priddat, Birger P. (2012): Aristoteles über Markt und Geld, in: Günther, Sven (ed.), Ordnungsrahmen antiker Ökonomien: Ordnungskonzepte und Steuerungsmechanismen antiker Wirtschaftssysteme im Vergleich, Wiesbaden (Philippika 53), 5–21.

Pritchard, David M. (2014): The Public Payment of Magistrates in Fourth-Century Athens, in: Greek, Roman, and Byzantine Studies 54, 1–16.

Reger, Gary (1994): Regionalism and Change in the Economy of Independent Delos, 314–67 B.C., Berkeley.

Robertson, D.H. (1933): Saving and Hoarding, in: The Economic Journal 43/171, 399–413.

Robinson, Joan (1938): The Concept of Hoarding, in: The Economic Journal 48/190, 231–236.

Rohde, Dorothea (2019): Von der Deliberationsdemokratie zur Zustimmungsdemokratie. Die öffentlichen Finanzen Athens und die Ausbildung einer Kompetenzelite im 4. Jahrhundert v. Chr., Stuttgart (Schriften zur Alten Geschichte 1).

Schaps, David M. (2004): The Invention of Coinage and the Monetization of Ancient Greece, Ann Arbor.

Schönert-Geiss, Edith (1974): Die Geldzirkulation Attikas, in: Klio 56/2, 377–414.

Sharfman, Keith (2006): The Law and Economics of Hoarding, in: Loyola Consumer Law Review 19/2, 179–193.

Shipton, Kirsty (1997): The Private Banks in Fourth-Century B.C. Athens: A Reappraisal, in: Classical Quarterly N.S. 47, 396–422.

Shipton, Kirsty (2008): Bankers as Money Lenders: The Banks of Classical Athens, in: Verboven, Koenraad et al. (eds.), Pistoi dia tèn technèn: Bankers, Loans, and Archives in the Ancient World: Studies in Honour of Raymond Bogaert, Leuven (Studia Hellenistica 44), 93–114.

Szatmary, David P. (1980): Shays' Rebellion. The Making of an Agrarian Insurrection, Amherst.

Temin, Peter (2013): The Roman Market Economy, Princeton.

Thompson, Margaret et al. (1973): An Inventory of Greek Coin Hoards, New York.

Thompson, Wesley (1978): The Athenian Investor, in: Rivista di Studi Classici 36, 402–423.

Thompson, Wesley (1982): The Athenian Entrepreneur, in: L'Antiquité classique 51, 53–85.

Thomsen, Christian A. (2015): The Eranistai of Classical Athens, in: Greek, Roman, and Byzantine Studies 55/1, 154–175.

Thornton, Mary K. / Thornton, Robert L. (1990): The Financial Crisis of A.D. 33: A Keynesian Depression?, in: The Journal of Economic History 50/3, 655–662.

Thür, Gerhard (2014): Ownership and Secured Credit in Athens, in: Gagarin, Michael / Lanni, Adriaan (eds.), Symposion 2013. Papers on Greek and Hellenistic Legal History, Wien, 239–247.

Tod, M. Niebuhr (1933–1948): A Selection of Greek Historical Inscriptions, Oxford.

Tucker, Robert C. (ed.) ([2]1978): The Marx-Engels Reader, New York.

Verboven, Koenraad (2008): *Faeneratores, negotiatores* and Financial Intermediation in the Roman World (Late Republic and Early Empire), in: Verboven, Koenraad et al. (eds.), Pistoi dia tèn technèn: Bankers, Loans, and Archives in the Ancient World: Studies in Honour of Raymond Bogaert, Leuven (Studia Hellenistica 44), 211–230.

Von Reden, Sitta (2010): Money in Classical Antiquity, Cambridge.

Weber, Max (1976): The Agrarian Sociology of Ancient Civilizations, London.

Old Ideals and Adaptations to a New Reality

Columella's *De Re Rustica*, a Survival Handbook for an Elite?

José Remesal Rodríguez

Abstract: I begin by assuming that each individual is driven by his or her interests and that each individual creates a mental schema to justify his or her actions. This "rationalization" is a function of his position in the social fabric of the world in which he lives. Augustus' creation of his empire radically changed the political and economic structure of the society of republican Rome. Augustus concentrated in his person both the political power of the patriarchs and that of the *populus Romanus*. Rome was no longer the centre of Roman expansionism, but the centre which, as in all empires, was to attract to itself the resources of the vast territories conquered in the final phase of the Republic by both Caesar and Pompey. Columella was torn between the old ideals of the Roman elite and the effort to rationalise agricultural production within the new framework created by Augustan policy.

Keywords: Economy – Politics – Agriculture – Columella – Gades – Tarentum – Roman Empire

The life and work of L. Iunius Moderatus Columella has long been analysed from various perspectives. Here I would like to dwell on one aspect that, in my view, has not been sufficiently addressed yet. When we talk about the "rationality" of economic action, we have to take into account many other non-economic factors, such as, for example, the existence of food taboos that prevent certain economic developments, or certain economic actions that are not well regarded by the social framework in which the individual moves. Here I would like to focus on the study of the social and political environment in which Columella lived and show how his ideology was determined by the contrast between an ideal of status and the concrete position of the individual within this ideal status in which he was forced to act:[1]

> *... magnaque deum benignitate et modestia hiemis rebus extremis subventum. at hercule olim Italia legionibus longinquas in provincias commeatus portabat, nec nunc infecunditate laboratur, sed Africam potius et Aegyptum exercemus, navibusque et casibus vita populi Romani permissa est.*

1 Valencia Hernández 1991.

> ... and the crisis was relieved only by the especial grace of the gods and the mildness of the winter. And yet, Heaven knows, in the past, Italy exported supplies for the legions into remote provinces; nor is sterility the trouble now, but we cultivate Africa and Egypt by preference, and the life of the Roman nation has been staked upon cargo-boats and accidents. (Tac. *Ann.* 12.43.2; trans. taken from Loeb edition, 1937)

Tacitus states that once Rome and Italy were sufficient to supply the legions fighting in distant lands. Now Rome depended on ships from Egypt and Africa. Columella had already pointed out this fact:

> *Itaque in "hoc Latio et Saturnia terra," ubi di fructus agrorum progeniem suam docuerant, ibi nunc ad hastam locamus, ut nobis ex transmarinis provinciis advehatur frumentum, ne fame laboremus, et vindemias condimus ex insulis Cycladibus ac regionibus Baeticis Gallicisque. Nec mirum, cum sit publice concepta et confirmata iam vulgaris existimatio rem rusticam sordidum opus et id esse negotium quod nullius egeat magisterio praeceptove.*
>
> So, then, in "this Latium and Saturnian land," where the gods had taught their offspring of the fruits of the fields, we let contracts at auction for the importation of grain from our provinces beyond the sea, that we may not suffer hunger; and we lay up our stores of wine from the Cyclades Islands and from the districts of Baetica and Gaul. Nor is it to be wondered at, seeing that the common notion is now generally entertained and established that farming is a mean employment and a business which has no need of direction or of precept. (Colum. praef. 20; trans. taken from Loeb edition, 1941)

Yes, Rome, Italy, had supplied its legions as Rome expanded along the shores of the Mediterranean, but everything had changed: Caesar in the west and Pompey in the east had expanded Rome's controlled territory far beyond the shores of the Mediterranean. The long civil war had a clear winner, Octavian/Augustus, who had to reorganise such a vast territory and secure power in Rome, where he became both *princeps senatus* and in 23 BC, holder of the power of the plebeian tribune (*tribunicia potestas*). He dismissed much of the army that had led him to victory by granting them land in Italy or in the provinces; an army that now swore by the emperor and not by the Republic; an army on which Augustus imposed his conditions of life, pay and promotion.[2]

2 A current synthesis in Le Bohec 2018.

He allowed senators to continue to administer the old provinces on the shores of the Mediterranean, which he demilitarised, maintaining the fiction of senatorial government, and reserved direct control of most of the newly conquered territories, where he stationed his soldiers.

Pliny the Younger recalls, one hundred and fifty years later, that Pompey's most glorious act was to assume the *cura annonae* (Plin. *Pan.* 29.1).[3] Augustus understood that in order to maintain social peace in Rome and keep the plebs on his side, he had to provide Rome with food in general. A system Juvenal called *panem et circenses.* Hence, the first political action Augustus mentions in his *Res Gestae*, after listing his merits, was that in 22 BC he freed the whole city, *populum universum*, and at its own expense, *meis impensis*, from famine:

> *Non recusavi in summa frumenti penuria curationem annonae, quam ita administravi, ut intra paucos dies metu et periclo praesenti populum universum meis impensis liberarem.*
> I did not decline at a time of the greatest scarcity of grain the charge of the grain-supply, which I so administered that, within a few days, I freed the entire people, at my own expense, from the fear and danger in which they were. (*RGDA* 5.2; trans. taken from Loeb edition, 1924).

Contrary to general opinion, I have maintained that the function of the *praefectura annonae* was not only to ensure that sufficient grain reached Rome to meet the needs of the *frumentationes.*[4] More generally, the function of the *praefectura annonae* was to ensure that the market price of foodstuffs in Rome was not too high, and also to stockpile resources to supply the army. To this end, the emperor had at his disposal: firstly, the tribute paid in kind by the provinces; secondly, the produce of the extensive imperial possessions; and thirdly, if necessary, the imposition of *indictiones*, i.e., compulsory sales to the state at a price fixed by the administration.[5]

---

3 Kröss 2020.

4 The reference work on this view, in which the concept of *frumentationes* and *annona* are synonymous, is Pavis d'Escuracm 1976. A prosopographical update of the *praefecti annonae* can be found in Caldelli 2020.

5 I have discussed the subject in numerous works: Remesal Rodríguez 1986; 1990a/b; 1997; 1999; 2002a–c; 2008a; 2012. My views have promoted a wide discussion on the evolution of Roman administration, e.g., Wierschowski 2001, to which I replied in Remesal Rodríguez 2002c; or Eck 2006 and my reply in the same volume: Remesal Rodríguez 2006, 41 and in Remesal Rodríguez 2008b. Most recently Eck goes on to criticise my proposal, but without pointing out my arguments or his own against it: Eck 2018, 28.

Augustus soon realised that this system was detrimental to Roman agriculture and even thought of abolishing it:

> *... impetum se cepisse scribit frumentationes publicas in perpetuum abolendi, quod earum fiducia cultura agrorum cessaret; neque tamen perseverasse, quia certum haberet posse per ambitionem quandoque restitui. Atque ita posthac rem temperavit, ut non minorem aratorum ac negotiantium quam populi rationem deduceret.*
>
> "I was strongly inclined to do away forever with distributions of grain, because through dependence on them agriculture was neglected; but I did not carry out my purpose, feeling sure that they would one day be renewed through desire for popular favour." But from that time on he regulated the practice with no less regard for the interests of the farmers and grain-dealers than for those of the populace. (Suet. *Aug.* 42.3; trans. taken from Loeb edition, 1913)

In any case, Augustus tried to find a balance between the interests of the *populus Romanus*, the provincials and the merchants.[6]

Augustus entrusted the transport of all goods necessary for the state to private individuals, so that trade in other products could develop alongside the transport of *annona* resources, allowing merchants to transport and trade in other products freely. Only in this way can it be understood that a product exogenous to the diet of the Central European peoples, olive oil, could spread not only among the military, in whose diet it was included by the central administration, but also among the population of the Central European provinces.[7] In my opinion, the "*annona policy*" was one of the determining factors for the general development of Roman politics.[8]

Tiberius, in a year of scarcity, AD 19, subsidised those who brought wheat to Rome with two sesterces per modius, an interventionist measure, but a timely one (Tac. *Ann.* 2.87). Tacitus points to the year AD 23 as another time of shortage in Rome when the emperor tried to remedy the situation (Tac. *Ann.* 4.6.4). In AD 32 Tiberius complained about the treatment of the people at a time of famine, despite the fact that, in his time, he states in the words of Tacitus, more wheat came to Rome and from more places than in the time of Augustus (Tac. *Ann.* 6.13.1). Suetonius points

---

6 I translate "*aratores*" as "provincials", meaning all food producers anywhere in the empire, not exclusively in Italy.

7 As the Latin papyrus *P.Gen.Lat.* I recto, part I; Fink 1971, no. 68. The state retained two thirds of the soldier's salary as maintenance: Remesal Rodríguez 1990.

8 Remesal Rodríguez 1990b.

out (Suet. *Tib.* 32.2) that Tiberius did not want to increase the tribute to the provinces.[9]

However, in another time of scarcity, Claudius applied a much more profound interventionist policy. He granted social privileges to those who, depending on their social status, would put their ships at the service of the supply of Rome. The measure was in force at least until the middle of the second century AD:

> *... civi vacationem legis Papiae Poppaeae, Latino ius Quiritium, feminis ius IIII liberorum; quae constituta hodieque servantur.*
> ... to a citizen exemption from the lex Papia Poppaea; to a Latin the rights of Roman citizenship; to women the privileges allowed the mothers of four children. And all these provisions are in force to day. (Suet. *Claud.* 19; trans. taken from Loeb edition, 1914)[10]

Claudius had recognised the problem: Rome needed the support of the provinces to sustain itself, and it was natural that the city that created an empire should benefit from its conquests, and to facilitate this he built a port at Ostia.[11]

The social privileges granted by Claudius to individuals of various social strata, including women, created a new system, the survival of the empire depended on social stability in Rome, and social stability in Rome depended on the availability of food at a price acceptable to the *populus*, the plebs, in the broadest sense of these terms, for this mass of the inhabitants of Rome. The emperor, having the *potestas* of a *tribunus plebis*, was obliged to look after the plebs. Let us recall Vespasian's reaction when he was presented with a machine that could save labour:

> *... mechanico quoque quoque grandis columnas exigua impensa perducturum in Capitolium pollicenti praemium pro commento non mediocre optulit, operam remisit praefatus sineret se plebiculam pascere.*
> To a mechanical engineer, who promised to transport some heavy columns to the Capitol at small expense, he gave no mean reward for his invention, but refused to make use of it, saying: "You must let me feed my poor commons." (Suet. *Vesp.* 18; trans. taken from Loeb edition, 1914)

The emperor did not need new techniques to facilitate the great constructions in Rome, he only needed *plebiculam pascere*, to maintain the plebs.

---

9 On the years of calamity in Rome, see Virlouvet 1985; 2009.

10 Cf. Gai. *Inst.* 1.32c; Höbenreich 1997, 76–78; Kröss 2016.

11 Morelli / Marinucci / Arnoldus-Huyzendveld 2011.

We know little about the life of L. Iunius Moderatus Columella, from the personal data contained in his work it is assumed that he lived between AD 4 and 70, that he was from Gades in the Baetica, that he wrote his work between AD 61 and 65, that he must have lived not only his youth but also part of his maturity in the Baetica, given the knowledge he shows of Baetic agriculture, in which his uncle Marcus Columella, to whom he frequently refers, was his teacher.[12] In his work we also find references to notable figures of his time: the philosopher Seneca, his brother Iunius Gallio, Marcus Trebilius (Colum. 5.1.2). If we accept as authentic the inscription found in Tarentum: *L. Iunius L. F. Gal / Moderatus / Columellae / Trib. Mil. leg. VI Ferratae*,[13] we must assume that he aspired to a career in the service of the emperor, which he does not seem to have pursued. It is suggested that he held this office in AD 36 under his friend M. Trebellius, governor of Syria. This inscription is used to explain his knowledge of the eastern Mediterranean since Columella gives direct references to the cultivation of sesame which he claims to have seen in Syria and Cilicia (Colum. 2.10.18).

It is difficult to explain Columella's stay in Tarentum since in his work he only makes references to his possessions in Latium, Ardea, Carseoli and Alba (Colum. 3.9.2) and in Caere (Colum. 3.3.3), but not in southern Italy, although his stay in Tarentum could be later than the publication of his work, and therefore we lack references on it. Even if the Tarentum inscription were authentic, and I still have my doubts about its authenticity, it would have to be connected, in my opinion, with Nero's foundation of a colony in Tarentum in AD 60 (Tac. *Ann.* 14.27.2), Tacitus also states that the attempt failed precisely because it was composed of veterans of various legions, who were not accustomed to agricultural life, who eventually sold their land and returned to their home provinces or where they had served in the militia.

12 On Columella's biography and news about his work I refer, in general terms, to Olivares 2010. Cf. the introduction by Holgado Redondo 1988 and that of García Armendáriz 2004. These works contain the fundamental bibliography on the character and his work.

13 *CIL* IX 235 = *ILS* 2923. The inscription was already considered a forgery by Mommsen, although Grotefend considered it authentic. Recently Gallo 2019, 141–142 shows that the manuscript that transmits it, that of Merodio, a character always attentive to identifying the individuals he finds in the inscriptions, does not identify, in this case, the character of the inscription with the agronomist; proof, for her, of the authenticity of the inscription; for me it is rather proof of the opposite since, as A. Gallo points out, Merodio refers to the agronomist at another time. On ibid., 143 the author admits that Merodio also reproduces some forgeries. Cf. D'Angela 2000, who already points out that the inscription seemed false to Muratori. Certainly, the inscription is a "talking document" that is easily convincing because it is the only element, external to Columella's own work, to have any information about his life: Gasperini 1968, 389–390.

That this colonisation was a failure is shown by an inscription of AD 78/79 found near Taranto (Crispiano): *Imp(erator) Caesar / Vespasianus / Aug(ustus) co(n)s(ul) VIII / fines agror(um) / p(ublicorum) m(unicipii) T(arentini) ex forma / Gracchiana / restituit.*[14] Vespasian had to reorganise the territory in the old way.

Did Columella participate in the organisation of this colony as a "master farmer" to teach these soldiers how to turn iron swords into ploughshares? If so, he was unsuccessful in his endeavour. One would have to suppose that Columella received an official commission, of which we know nothing either, nor is it recorded in the inscription. A commission from the emperor? A commission promoted by his good friend Seneca, who was in leading position at the time? This is a suggestive idea that may help to raise other questions. But I must admit that it is only an idea, in my opinion, suggestive, but nothing more. Another idea, equally suggestive, provided we accept that the inscription is authentic, and perhaps more realistic, would be to suppose simply that Columella bought land from the holdings sold by the legionaries. He probably thought it prudent to move away from Rome after the fall of Seneca in AD 62.

Some considerations on the Tarentum inscription.[15] The earliest known information is that of Merodio, whose manuscript was licensed for printing in 1681,[16] but Merodio's manuscript was not published until recent times.[17] The earliest printed notice is that of Pacichelli,[18] who distributes the last two lines differently from Merodio and in his text gives the impression of having seen the inscription, but his commentary is palpably similar to Merodio's, and although at that time he does not quote Merodio, in the index of his work (*s.v.* Tarentum) he does quote Merodio's manuscript, indicating that it will be published in Lecce.

Muratori doubted the existence of this inscription (see above), as did Mommsen, but after Grotefend's defence of the authenticity of the inscription, no one else doubted the validity of the inscription, although it has never been clearly defined whether it is a funerary or honorary inscription. For some, therefore, Columella

14 Gallo 2020; in ead. 2021, the author relates this text to the more general Vespasian action of reorganisation of certain territories in southern Italy. In my opinion, this inscription should be placed in relation to the failure of the Neronian colonisation of the region of Taranto.

15 I thank Y. Le Bohec, A. Buenopane, M. Silvestrini, M. Mayer, and A. Gallo for patiently listening and answering my questions.

16 I am grateful to Annarosa Gallo for the information obtained on Merodio.

17 Merodio 2000.

18 Pacichelli 1685, 363. On Pacichelli, see Carrino 2014. Pacichelli arrived in Naples in 1679, and his work was published in 1685.

died in Taranto.[19] Cichorius in his biography of Columella devotes his efforts to linking the title of *tribunus militum* with the time when M. Trebellius Maximus *as legatus legionis* led a campaign against the Cieti, a Cilician people, in AD 36. Thus, he again explains Columella's knowledge of those regions (Colum. 2.10.8) and establishes the chronology of this knowledge and, furthermore, shows that Columella's friend Marcus Trebellius (Colum. 5.1.2) is none other than the aforementioned Trebellius Maximus.[20] In his article, Cichorius fixes another historical moment in Columella's life at AD 41, using a wide range of sources and showing that Columella was in Rome in that year. However, this additional fact has not been pointed out by those who have later dealt with Columella's life.[21]

It is certainly surprising that someone in the 17th century attributed to our character the title of *tribunus militum* of the legio VI Ferrata, but it is also surprising to see the eagerness with which later research has used this document: it is not necessary to think that Columella could only have been in Syria and Cilicia because he was holding a military post, he could have travelled for any other reason. Nor is it necessary that his friend, Marcus Trebellius, is the Trebellius Maximus mentioned by Tacitus. It is strange that, whether it is a funerary or honorary inscription, an equestrian office held many years before is indicated, knowing that Columella, as he points out in the preface to his work, showed no interest in holding public office (Colum. praef. 10).

There would be an explanation for the appearance of this title, if it is accepted that Columella had some role in the Neronian colonisation of Tarentum and that the office of *tribunus militum* is a function of his intervention in this colonization.[22] However, it is surprising that there is no reference in the inscription to this activity, the commissioning of which, if he had held it, would have been very significant for a personage who had not, as far as we know, had any other public activity.

In the light of these considerations, I would like to raise another question. At the request of Marcus Trebellius, Columella writes the fifth book on the measurement of fields:

19 Grotefend 1835, for whom the title of *tribunus militum* of the legio VI Ferrata already confirmed Columella's stay in Syria and Cilicia, based on Colum. 2.10.8.2; 10.8. Opinion followed by Dessau in *ILS* 2923.

20 On the character, see lately Camodeca 1983.

21 Cichorius 1922.

22 In imperial times we have evidence that those responsible for the reorganisation of territories held military posts: Hinrichs 1974, 92.

> *... ut proxime, cum de commetiendis agris rationem M. Trebellius noster requireret a me, vicinum adeo atque coniunctum esse censebat demonstranti, quemadmodum agrum pastinemus, praecipere etiam pastinatum quemadmodum metiri debeamus.*
> ... for example, only recently, when my friend Marcus Trebellius required from me a method of measuring land he expressed the opinion that it was a kindred and indeed closely connected task for one who was showing how we ought to trench land to give instructions also how we ought to measure the land thus trenched. (Colum. 5.1.2; trans. taken from Loeb edition, 1954)

If the friendly Trebellius is Marcus Trebellius Maximus, we know that in AD 61 he was commissioned to take the census in Gallia, together with Quintus Volusius Saturninus and Titus Sextius Africanus (Tac. *Ann.* 14.46). Since Columella states that he had "recently" been asked to do so by his friend, we can understand that Trebelius might have found this knowledge useful for his work in Gallia. In this case we would have to date the fifth book to this year, AD 61, or shortly thereafter. Columella ends up writing on the subject because Silvinus to whom Columella dedicates his work had also asked him to do so, but he begs to be excused if he makes mistakes because he is not a geometrician:

> *Verum quoniam familiariter a nobis tu quoque, Silvine, praecepta mensurarum desideras, obsequar voluntati tuae, cum eo, ne dubites id opus geometrarum magis esse quam rusticorum, desque veniam, si quid in eo fuerit erratum, cuius scientiam mihi non vindico.*
> But since, Silvinus, you also ask us in a friendly spirit for instructions about measurements, I will comply with your wish, on condition that you harbour no doubt that this is really the business of geometricians rather than of countrymen and make allowances for any errors that may be committed in a sphere where I do not claim to possess scientific knowledge. (Colum. 5.1.4; trans. taken from Loeb edition, 1954)

Columella never speaks of his father, but only of his paternal uncle, Marcus. It is thus assumed that he must have been orphaned in his childhood and raised by his uncle, who lived in the Baetica. In my opinion, there are a number of questions, certainly decisive ones, about which we have no information. Why did Columella go to Rome and when? Who was his protector there? Did he intend to make a career in the emperor's service? Was he an agent of his uncle to take charge of the sale of his products in Rome? If he intended to make a career in the emperor's service, he soon abandoned it, as is clear from the preface to his work, in which he renounces all the services he had to render in order to obtain any office (Colum. praef. 10; 1.19). As there was a long scholarly tradition in Gades, did he go to Rome just to learn?[23] Let us remember that the philosopher Moderatus of Gades has the same *nomen* and one of the *cognomina* of our character.[24]

Claudius, in the speech Tacitus gives in defence of the incorporation of provincials into the Senate, first cites Balbus of Cadiz as an example after the incorporation of the Gauls into the Senate (Tac. *Ann.* 11.24.3). Cornelius Balbus the Elder was the first consul of provincial origin. His nephew, Balbus the Younger, was the last to obtain the right to celebrate a triumph in Rome in the time of Augustus.[25] It is well known that in the Roman world, political power and economic power were closely linked, as the case of the Balbi, as well as that of the Annaei of Cordoba, demonstrates. Turranius Gracilis, a native of Gades (Cádiz), probably from the city of Mellaria, was the first *praefectus annonae*, who held office until the time of Claudius (AD 8–48), although Caligula tried unsuccessfully to remove him (Sen. *Brev. Vit.* 20.4). Turranius, along with the consuls, was among the first to show his submission to Tiberius after the death of Augustus (Tac. *Ann.* 1.7.2).[26] Turranius was undoubtedly the most economically influential man in Rome. Seneca, the philosopher, a friend of Columella, a certainly wealthy character, who on his return from exile in AD 49, married Pompeia Paulina, a woman who had been a member of the Roman family for many years. Seneca in his *De brevitate vitae* (18.5) says to his father-in-law: *cum ventre tibi humano negotium* est ("you have to deal with the belly of men"). This is a declaration of Seneca's interest as a great agricultural landowner.[27] Did Columella count on the help of Turranius? Unfortunately, we do not know since he does not quote him. It has been proposed that Lucius Iunius Gallio was of Baetican origin, given his friendship with Seneca senior, who allowed his eldest son, Lucius Annaeus Novatus, to be adopted by Gallio and given the name L. Iunius Annaeus Novatus.[28] Columella had the same *nomen* as Gallio, was there a kinship between the two?
The other great personality of Baetican origin at the time when Columella arrived in Rome was Sextus Marius, of whom we shall speak shortly.

I have referred to the personal conditions that may have surrounded Columella's arrival in Rome. It will be necessary to insist on the politico-economic situation: I have already referred to the creation of the *praefectura annonae* and its effective control during the Julio-Claudian dynasty by the Hispanics. I would like to point

23 Rodríguez Neila 1997; Almagro-Gorbea 2012.

24 Ramos Jurado 2003.

25 Rodríguez Neila 1996; 2011.

26 Pavis d'Escurac 1976, 317–319.

27 Remesal Rodríguez 2002b.

28 Castillo 1965, 105, n. 195.

out two other facts. When Sextus Marius, the great mine owner in Baetica, was condemned for incest, Tacitus states that his goods were not auctioned, but went directly into the hands of the emperor, and clarifies that his wealth was the real cause of his death (Tac. *Ann.* 6.19.1).

Another important event was the well-known economic crisis of AD 33. The numerous complaints following the fall of Sejanus had led to the auctioning of many agricultural goods. The *patricians,* in order to buy the auctioned land, had accepted loans at a higher interest rate than the legal rate, which in turn exposed them to the risk of being denounced. Tiberius' reaction was moderate: he granted a year and a half to rectify the situation: ... *secundum iussa legis rationes familiaris quisque componerent* (Tac. *Ann.* 6.16.3), i.e., to repay the loans contracted at excessive interest. But the money was in the hands of the emperor, the beneficiary of the proceeds of the auctions, or of the moneylenders. To protect its members, the Senate decided that it should be invested in the purchase of land in Italy for an amount equal to two-thirds of the capital owed. Finally, the debtors had to take out another loan, this time at a legal interest rate, to pay off their previous debts, or put their newly acquired land up for sale again to pay off the loans.

The lenders had to either lend money, this time at the interest rates allowed by the *lex Iulia de modo credenda possidendique intra Italiam* (Tac. *Ann.* 6.16.1), or buy the land from the debtors. However, the lenders preferred to withhold the money and hope that the oversupply would allow them to buy the land at a lower price, as the text clearly shows. Finally, Tiberius offered interest-free money for three years, provided that the debtor offered collateral in the form of property worth twice the money lent on these terms. This meant that many did not have to put their new property up for sale and, at the same time, received an interest-free loan for a period twice as long as that originally granted by the emperor himself (Tac. *Ann.* 6.16–17).

In my opinion, the crisis of AD 33 is not a systemic crisis. The fear of being denounced for breaking the *lex Iulia* could also put those members of the senatorial elite who had benefited from the confiscations in danger. A large part of the money supply was in the hands of the emperor or of speculators who wanted to benefit from the provisions established by the Senate itself. It was enough for the emperor to put part of the money he had hoarded into circulation for the crisis to be alleviated.[29]

The confiscations had filled the coffers of the empire, but they had changed the system of land ownership in Italy. According to Suetonius, when the Senate suggested to Tiberius that taxes be raised on the provinces to preserve the state,

29 Noè 2002, 73. Remesal Rodríguez 2012, 222–223; Schartmann 2012; Harris 2019, 175–177. Cf. also Leese in this volume, pp. 204–205.

Tiberius replied that a good shepherd shears the sheep, but does not skin them (Suet. *Tib.* 32.2). Tiberius found a way to fill his coffers: he skinned his rich political enemies and even his friends, such as Sextus Marius or Cornelius Lentulus, whom Tiberius, in order to inherit his property, incited to suicide (Suet. *Tib.* 49.1). The process of the concentration of property in Italy had already been going on for a long time,[30] but there is no doubt that the crisis of AD 33, with the disappearance of many notables, led to a significant increase in this concentration, especially in the hands of the emperor, not only in Italy but also in the provinces (Suet. *Tib.* 49.2). In this sense, it is necessary to re-read Pliny's text:

> *verumque confitentibus latifundia perdidere Italiam, iam vero et provincias – sex domini semissem Africae possidebant, cum interfecit eos Nero princeps.*
> And if the truth be confessed, large estates have been the ruin of Italy, and are now proving the ruin of the provinces too – half of Africa was owned by six landlords, when the Emperor Nero put them to death … . (Plin. *NH* 18.7.35; trans. taken from Loeb edition, 1950)

The six owners who possessed half of Africa became one: the emperor.

According to Suetonius (*Aug.* 42.1), when the plebs of Rome complained about the high price of wine and asked Augustus to intervene in the price of the product, he refused, saying that his son-in-law, Agrippa, had built aqueducts so that the people would not die of thirst. Some have seen this as a moralising stance on Augustus' part.[31] In my opinion, it is a desperate reaction. Augustus had emptied the Senate of political power, although he preserved the forms, but he knew that he should not touch the senators' pockets, so that wine, which was the business of the Roman elite in the final stages of the Republic, did not enter the *annona* cycle until the time of Aurelian (HA. *Aurel.* 48). Proof of this is that Columella recommends its cultivation as the most profitable, and that Seneca invested a large sum in the purchase of a famous vineyard, as implied by Pliny the Elder (*NH* 14.5.47–52) and also mentioned by Columella (Colum. 3.3.3). The price of wine depended on supply and demand and not on the intervention of the *praefectura annonae*, as was the case with grain and oil, products that came from the provinces, largely as a tax in kind, on the price of which the state could intervene. Columella carefully analyses the minimum profit from wine production, concluding that the profit was higher than six percent, the maximum profit that, according to the law, could be obtained by lending the money, which also indicates that if credit is obtained at that rate of interest it would be

30 Kuziscin 1984.

31 Tchernia 1986, 28.

beneficial to invest the money in the purchase of a vineyard.[32] It is interesting to note that the calculation developed by Columella also includes the cost of the time necessary for the development of production (Colum. 3.3.2–15). According to Columella's calculations two hundred *iugera* of vineyard would yield as much profit annually as a procurator of sexagenarian rank. Among the numerous properties, it must be assumed that an individual of senatorial rank would have more than two hundred *iugera* of vineyards, in addition to other profitable productions.[33]

I understand that the economic rationality of any actor is a function of the life context in which he or she lives. We need only recall the influence of food taboos on economic life. Columella lived between an ancient ideal, the *mos maiorum* just recreated by Augustus, remember that Virgil is frequently quoted by Columella; an economic reality, Italy was no longer the economic centre of the world, its great market, Rome, was supplied by the provinces, which Columella regrets; and a political reality, *Caesar omnia habet* (Sen. *Ben.* 7.6.3).[34]

Columella was a provincial who arrived in Rome, linked to a prestigious and influential social group integrated into the Roman elite, some acceded to the senatorial rank, and others, voluntarily, like Annaeus Mela (Tac. *Ann.* 16.17.3) remained in the equestrian rank, because by serving the emperor, they could enrich themselves and promote themselves socially. What were Columella's pretensions? Certainly, as I have pointed out, he does not seem to be interested in promoting himself in the political sphere, or perhaps he writes out of spite for not having achieved the promotion he had hoped for. Although his view of political life suggests that he was more interested in showing himself as an individual of senatorial pedigree than as a provincial newcomer.

He seems to be only interested in making a comfortable living from the activity he considers the noblest, agriculture, for which he certainly proposes a model of dedication and exploitation;[35] a model that proposes a rationalisation of production, but in which it seems that the farmer is only the producer of a series of products dedicated to a nearby market. The production of wine, in regions close to Rome, where his properties were located, allowed for a large market capable of absorbing

32 Carandini 1983; Tchernia 1986.

33 An overview of Columella's economic calculations of investments and overhead costs also for the production of other products in Martin 1971, 289–310 and in Noè 2002, 81–118.

34 Remesal Rodríguez 2001.

35 On Columella's agrarian ideas, reference works continue to be those of Martin 1971, 289–373; 1985. I refer here to the work of Noé 2002, which is a well-documented synthesis of all that is known about Columella's thought.

quality and cheaper wines. Basically, Columella proposes a rationalisation of agriculture, but, in my opinion, with a certain social perspective in mind: that of those well-to-do people in Rome who, living in the city, could personally take care of the exploitation of nearby estates. Columella subtly refers to the tension in which the elite of Rome lived (Colum. 1.1.19), on the one hand interested in obtaining office, on the other hand in need of an ethical justification, respect for the *mos maiorum*, an ideal of *Romanitas* which the provincials soon wanted to put on, and a need to survive economically by making use of an area, wine production, in which the emperor did not want to intervene. Certainly his ideal of rationalising agriculture could also be applied to the provinces, provided that the main condition laid down by Columella was met, namely, that the landowner could have effective control over production.

Moreover, dedication to agriculture, to the ideal of the *bonus agricola*, was also a way of demonstrating the *dignitas* necessary to dedicate oneself to political life, as can be understood from a reading of Pliny the Younger's letters.

Bibliography

Almagro-Gorbea, Martín (2012): El 'Círculo de Gadir' y el final de la literatura hispano-fenicia, in: Mora Serrano, Bartolomé / Cruz Andreotti, Gonzalo (eds.): La etapa neopúnica en Hispania y el Mediterráneo centro occidental: identidades compartidas, Cádiz, 75–112.

Caldelli, Maria Letizia (2020): I prefetti dell'annona da Augusto a Costantino, Rome.

Camodeca, Giuseppe (1983): I consoli des 55–56 e un nuovo collega di Seneca nel consolato: P. Cornelius Dolabella, in: Zeitschrift für Papyrologie und Epigraphik 63, 201–215.

Carandini, Andrea (1983): Columella's Vineyard and the Rationality of the Roman Economy, in: Opus 2, 177–204.

Carrino, Annastella (2014): s.v. Pacichelli, Giovanni Battista, in: Dizionario Biografico degli Italiani 80, URL: https://www.treccani.it/enciclopedia/giovanni-battista-pacichelli_%28Dizionario-Biografico%29, last accessed: 01.05.2023.

Castillo, Carmen (1965): Prosopographia Baetica, Pamplona.

Cichorius, Conrad (1922): Zur Biographie Columellas, in: Cichorius, Conrad, Römische Studien, Historisches, Epigraphisches, Literargeschichtliches aus vier Jahrhunderten Roms, Leipzig, 417–422.

D'Angela, Cosimo (2000), La ricerca epigrafica a Taranto nella prima metà del settecento: i falsi epigrafici di Giannagnolo de Ciocchis, in: Paci, Gianfranco (ed.), Epigrafai. Miscellanea epigrafica in onore di Lidio Gasperini. Vol. 1, Tivoli, 291–308.

Eck, Werner (2006): Der *praefectus annonae*: Ein Superminister im Imperium Romanum? Heeresversorgung und praefectura annonae: nicht eine Grossadministration, sondern zwei getrennte administrative Welten, in: Xantener Berichte 14, 49–57.

Eck, Werner (2018): Rom – Megalopolis und Zentrum der Reichsadministration, in: Wojciech, Katharina / Eich, Peter (eds.), Die Verwaltung der Stadt Rom in der Hohen Kaiserzeit. Formen der Kommunikation, Interaktion und Vernetzung, Leiden, 21–36.

Fink, Robert O. (1971): Roman Military Records on Papyrus, Princeton.

Gallo, Annarosa (2019): La tradizione manoscritta delle epigrafi latine di Tarentum, in: Calvelli, Lorenzo / Cresci Marrone, Giovannella / Buonopane, Alfredo (eds.), Altera pars laboris. Studi sulla tradizione manoscritta delle iscrizioni antiche, Venice (Antichistica 24 / Storia ed epigrafia 7), 131–150.

Gallo, Annarosa (2020): Ex forma Gracchiana: A New Boundary Stone about Vespasian's Land Survey of the ager Tarentinus, in: Zeitschrift für Papyrologie und Epigraphik 216, 311–314.

Gallo, Annarosa (2021): Una restitutio finium agrorum vespasianea, il municipio tarentino e la forma Gracchiana, in: Gallo, Luigi / Gallotta, Stefania (eds.), Administration, Politics, Culture and Society of the Ancient City, Rome (Ancient City 2), 67–90.

García Armendáriz, José Ignacio (2004): Columela. Libro de los árboles. La labranza, Madrid.

Gasperini, Lidio (1968), Su alcune epigrafi di Taranto romana, in: Gasperini, Lidio et al., Seconda Miscellanea Greca e Romana. Studi pubblicati dall'Istituto Italiano per la Storia Antica, Rome, 389–390.

Grotefend, Carl L. (1835): Beitrag zur Lebensgeschichte des Columella, in: Zeitschrift für Altertumswissenschaft 2, 179–180.

Kröss, Katja (2016): Die Datierung von Claudius' Maßnahmen zugunsten einer verlässlichen Getreideversorgung, Historia 65, 211–219.

Kröss, Katja (2020): Plebs und Politik in der späten Republik. Die Unruhen rund um Pompeius' *cura annonae* im September 57 v.Chr., in: Matijević, Krešimir (ed.): Wirtschaft und Gesellschaft in der späten Römischen Republik. Fachwissenschaftliche und fachdidaktische Aspekte, Ingelheim, 59–75.

Kuziscin, Vasilij I. (1984): La grande propietà agraria nell' Italia romana. II sec. B.C. – I sec. AD, Rome.

Harris, William V. (2019): Credit-Money in the Roman Economy, in: Klio 101/2, 158–189.

Höbenreich, Evelyn (1997): Annona. Juristische Aspekte der stadtrömischen Lebensmittelversorgung im Principat, Graz.

Holgado Redondo, Antonio (1988): De los trabajos del campo. Lucio Junio Moderato Columela, Madrid.

Hinrichs, Focke T. (1974): Die Geschichte der gromatischen Institutionen: Untersuchungen zu Landverteilung, Landvermessung, Bodenerwaltung und Bodenrecht im römischen Reich, Wiesbaden.

Le Bohec, Yann ([4]2018), L'armée romaine sous le Haut-Empire, Paris.

Martin, René (1971): Recherches sur les agronomes latins et leurs conceptions économiques et sociales, Paris.

Martin, René (1985): État présent des études sur Columelle, in: Aufstieg und Niedergang der Römischen Welt II.32.3, Berlin / New York, 1959–1979.

Merodio, Ambrogio (2000). Historia tarentina. A cura di Cosimo D. Fonseca, Taranto.

Morelli, Cinzia / Marinucci, Alfredo / Arnoldus-Huyzendveld, Antonia (2011): Il Porto di Claudio: nuove scoperte, in: Keay, Simon / Paroli, Lidia (eds.), Portus and its Hinterland, London (Archaeological Monographs of the British School at Rome 18), 47–65.

Noé, Eralda (2002): Il progetto di Columella. Profilo sociale, económico, culturale, Como.

Olivares, Juan Carlos (2010): s.v. Columela, in: Diccionario Biográfico Español 14, 299–304.

Pacichelli, Giovanni Battista (1685): Memorie de' viaggi per l'Europa christiana, scritte à diversi in occasione de' suoi ministeri dall'abate Pacichelli. Vol. 4/1, Naples.

Pavis d'Escurac, Henriette (1976), La préfecture de l'annone. Service administratif impérial d'Auguste à Constantin, Rome.

Ramos Jurado, Enrique A. (2003): Moderato de Gades: Estado de la cuestión cronológica y forma de vida, in: Habis 34, 149–160.

Remesal Rodríguez, José (1986): La annona militaris y la exportación de aceite bético a Germania, Madrid.

Remesal Rodríguez, José (1990a): Die procuratores Augusti und die Versorgung des römischen Heeres, in: Vetters, Hermann / Kandler, Manfred (ed.), Akten des 14. Internationalen Limeskongresses 1986 in Carnuntum, Wien, 55–65.

Remesal Rodríguez, José (1990b): El sistema annonario como base de la evolución económica del Imperio romano, in: Hackens, Tony / Miro, Marta (eds.), Le commerce maritime romain en Mediterranee occidentale: Colloque international tenu a Barcelone du 16 au 18 mai 1988, Strasbourg (PACT 27), 355–367.

Remesal Rodríguez, José (1997): Heeresversorgung und die wirtschaftlichen Beziehungen zwischen der Baetica und Germanien, Stuttgart.

Remesal Rodríguez, José (1999): Politica e regimi alimentari nel principato di Augusto, in: Vera, Domenico (ed.), Demografia, sistemi agrari, regimi alimentari nel Mondo Antico. Atti del Convegno Internazionale di Studi (Parma 17–19 ottobre 1997), Bari, 247–271.

Remesal Rodríguez, José (2001): Politik und Landwirtschaft im Imperium Romanum am Beispiel der Baetica, in: Herz, Peter / Waldherr, Gerhard (eds.): Landwirtschaft im Imperium Romanum, St. Katharinen, 235–255.

Remesal Rodríguez, José (2002a), Military Supply during Wartime, in: De Blois, Lukas / Rich, John (eds.), The Transformation of Economic Life under the Roman Empire, Amsterdam, 77–92.

Remesal Rodríguez, José (2002b): Providentia et annona. Cum ventri tibi humano negotium est, in: Marcos Simón, Francisco / Pina Polo, Francisco / Remesal Rodríguez, José (eds.), Religión y propaganda política en el mundo romano, Barcelona, 119–125.

Remesal Rodríguez, José (2002c): Heeresversorgung im frühen Principat. Eine Art, die antike Wirtschaft zu verstehen, in: Münstersche Beiträge zur Antiken Handelsgeschichte 21/1, 69–84.

Remesal Rodríguez, José (2006): Römische Amphoren aus Xanten. Epigraphische Aspekte, in: Xantener Berichte 14, 41–48.

Remesal Rodríguez, José (2008a): Provincial Interdependence in the Roman Empire: An Explanatory Model of Roman Economy, in: Funari, Pedro P. A. / Garraffoni, Renata S. / Letalien, Bethany (eds.), New Perspectives on the Ancient World. Modern Perceptions, Ancient Representations, Oxford (BAR International Series 1782), 155–159.

Remesal Rodríguez, José (2008b): Olearii, in: Caldelli, Maria Letizia / Gregori, Gian Luca / Orlando, Silvia (eds.), Epigrafia 2006. Atti della XIVe rencontre sur l'épigraphie in onore di Silvio Panciera con altri contributi di colleghi, allievi e collaboratori, Rome (Tituli 9), 349–374.

Remesal Rodríguez, José (2012), De emperador a depredador, in: Marcos Simón, Francisco / Pina Polo, Francisco / Remesal Rodríguez, José (eds.): ¡Vae Victis! Perdedores en el mundo antiguo, Barcelona, 217–227.

Rodríguez Neila, Juan Francisco (1996): Confidentes de César. Los Balbos de Cádiz, Madrid.

Rodríguez Neila, Juan Francisco (1997): Gades en tiempos de Columela, in: Maestre Maestre, José Maria / Charlo Brea, Luis / Serrano Cueto, Antonio (eds.): Estudios sobre Columela, Cádiz, 35–82.

Rodríguez Neila, Juan Francisco (2011): Los Cornelios Balbos: política y mecenazgo entre Gades y Roma, in: Bernal, Dario / Arévalo, Alicia (eds.): Theatrum Balbi de Gades: Actas del Seminario "El Teatro Romano de Gades, una Mirada al Futuro" (Cádiz, 18–19 November 2009), Cádiz, 307–333.

Schartmann, Günther (2012): Die Krise des Jahres 33 n.Chr, in: Günther, Sven (ed.), Ordnungsrahmen antiker Ökonomien. Ordnungskonzepte und Steuerungsmechanismen antiker Wirtschaftssysteme im Vergleich, Wiesbaden (Philippika 53), 145–164.

Tchernia, André (1986): Le vin de l'Italie romaine. Essai d'histoire économique d'après les amphores. Rome.

Valencia Hernández, Manuela (1991): Agricultura, comercio y ética. Ideología económica y economía en Roma (II a.e. – I d.e.), Zaragoza.

Virlouvet, Catherine (1985): Famines et émeutes à Rome des origines de la République à la mort de Néron, Rome.

Virlouvet, Catherine (2009): La plèbe frumentaire dans les témoignages épigraphiques. Essai d'histoire sociale et administrative du peuple de Rome Antique, Rome.

Wierschowski, Lothar (2001): Die römische Heeresversorgung in frühen Prinzipat, in: Münstersche Beiträge zur Antiken Handelsgeschichte 20/2, 37–61.

"The gold-possessing market where flags of the old town cast a shadow"

Some Remarks on Maritime Trade, Markets, and Money in the Early Cēra Panegyrics[1]

Roland Ferenczi

Abstract: This study discusses the ancient South Indian state of the Cēras together with its monarchical features, and its prominent position in the Indo-Roman trade. The paper draws on Early Old Tamil literary sources, particularly the royal panegyrics of the *Patiṟṟuppattu*, to reconstruct the economic history of the kingdom, touches upon the rational actor theory, and argues for the existence of an early monetized economy in ancient southwestern India and Koṅkunāṭu and the actions of rationally planning kings through it. The analysis will also suggest that the Cēra monarchy was a hybrid kingdom with Tamil literary culture, strong brāhmaṇical influences around the court, and perhaps Jaina and Buddhist merchant communities around the marketplaces.

Keywords: Cēra Kingdom – Caṅkam Literature – *Patiṟṟuppattu* – Indo-Roman Trade – South Indian Economic History

1. Introduction

Along with the Cōḻas and the Pāṇṭiyas, the Cēras' country was one of the most influential early states in southwestern India, expanded over the Malabar Coast and the regions of Koṅkunāṭu. Their rulers have been mentioned in Early Old Tamil literary works, in Tamil inscriptions, and in other non-Tamil sources, as, for instance, the edicts of Aśoka Maurya (II. Aśokan Rock Edict of Mānsehrā, II. Rock Edict of Girnār, II. Rock Edict of Kālsī, II. Rock Edict of Shāhbāzgaṛhī), the *Mahābhārata* (1.177.15.4; 2.28.48.1; 6.10.57.1; 8.8.15.1; 14.83.29.2), Pliny the Elder (*NH* 6.26.104), the *Periplus Maris Erythraei* (54), the geographical work of Ptolemy (*Geogr.* 7.1.86), perhaps Florus (*Epit.* 4.12.62 or with another numbering 2.34), and the *Matsyapurāṇa* (48.5.1;

1 This study is a revised subchapter of my doctoral dissertation 'History behind the praising words of the learned: An annotated translation of the *Patiṟṟuppattu* and the political geography of the early Cēra kingdom', which was defended on 2nd December 2022.

114.46.2).[2] The chronology of the early Cēra history is uncertain since the only useful sheet anchor for dating is the so-called Gajabāhu/Kayavāku synchronism of the early mediaeval *Cilappatikāram*, an epic work in Tamil, which would make Gajabāhu I., the Śrī Laṅkan ruler (latter half of the second century AD), and Ceṅkuṭṭuvaṉ, the Cēra king, contemporaries so that, with the help the *Patiṟṟuppattu*'s "epilogues", we can construe a chronology of Cēra history. Because of the shakiness of these dates, I do not refer to this chronology of the Cēras within this study, but talk about Cēra history as a *long durée* during the centuries of Indo-Roman trade (1st–4th centuries AD).

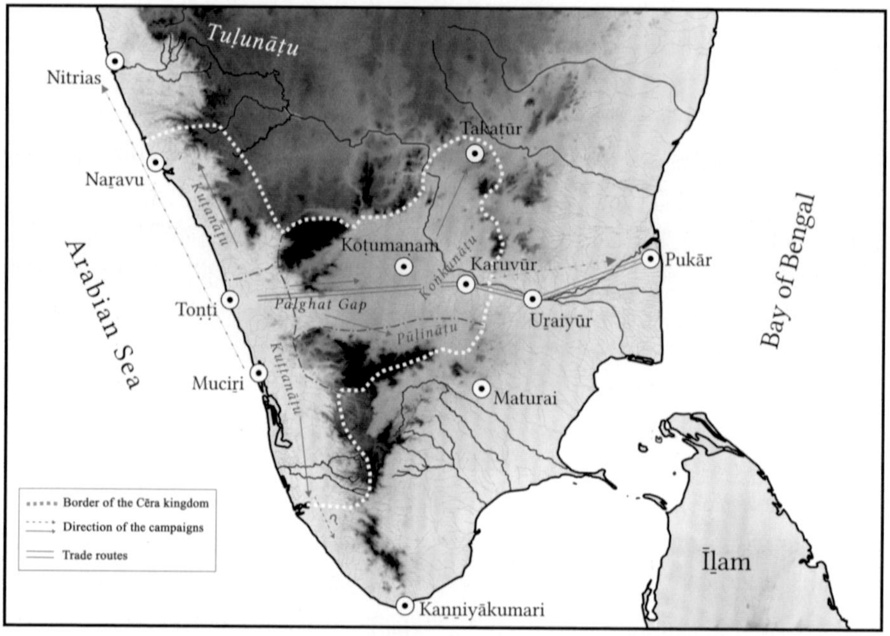

Fig. 1: A map on the political geography of the early Cēra kingdom (1st–3rd centuries AD). This map was made by Máté Rottár (Oriental Collection, LHAS) and Roland Ferenczi. Source of geographic data: Natural Earth.

2 Perhaps Florus is the last among the ancient authors who wrote about the Cēras; in that passage, which mentions *Seres* (a usual term for the "silk people", i.e., folks of ancient China) among Indians, which is still a matter of debate, but considering the context, the *Seres* in that special case could have been identical with the Cēras of South India, but that would also mean that Florus had an informant who was aware of the Tamil name of the kingdom (*Seres* < Cēra), which we could prove by the appearance of the 's' at the beginning of the word, instead of the names before derived from Kerala and Keralaputra.

Among the ancient South Indian monarchies, the Cēra kingdom was the foremost beneficiary of Indo-Roman trade (see Fig. 1).[3] In addition to the favorable geographical location of the kingdom, its priority depended on the ability to meet the needs of the Roman Empire and to promote/organize a well-functioning system of trade. At the same time it should be emphasized that the Cēras on the Malabar Coast were the original and main producers of black pepper which became one of the most popular import items of the Romans.[4] K. G. Sesha Aiyar in his famous monograph *Cēra kings of the Śangam Period* (1937) has already discussed the maritime trade of the Cēras, but did not carry out a comparative analysis of early economy.[5] From those times, we can observe a trend which lasted for an extended period that the authoritative studies on Tamil history were primarily based on the tangled mesh of early Tamil literary references, rarely if ever integrating secondary literature in contravention of modern historical methodology. N. Subrahmanian in his *Śangam Polity* (1966), which is an excellent introduction to the age of Caṅkam literature, devoted a long chapter to early Tamil economies.[6] The main problem with his monograph, however, is that he applied a broader concept of Caṅkam-literature analyzing the epics and post-Caṅkam texts together with the earliest anthologies without making critical remarks. V. I. Subramoniam in the *Culture of the Ancient Cheras* (1969) provides us a great catalogue of early literary references with a good sense of selection, but his primary goal seemed to be to outline a complex picture of the early Cēra country, and a detailed analysis of trade and economy was not carried out.[7] Ci. Pālacuppiramaṇiyaṉ in his *A Study of the Literature of the Cēra Kingdom* (1980) intended to focus on the literary sources of Cēra history, but in most of the cases he only paraphrases poems without further criticism. In the chapter called *The Generosity of the Cērās*,[8] preliminary statements are made on early economy, but the frequent lack of references makes the work somewhat unreliable.[9] A fresh voice has been brought

---

3 On the recent debate on terminology, see Gurukkal 2013, 181–206; 2016, 137–138; De Romanis 2020, 107–108.

4 The importance of pepper during the centuries of Indo-Roman trade caused much ink to flow. Two of the most recent research results are worth highlighting; the monograph of Federico De Romanis on Indo-Roman pepper trade (De Romanis 2020), and the article of Jean-Luc Chevillard on pepper in ancient Tamil literature (Chevillard 2022).

5 Aiyar 1937, 142–146.

6 Subrahmanian 1966, 219–244.

7 Subramoniam 1969, 247–275.

8 Balasubramanian 1980, 61–69.

9 To get an idea of the problematic parts, read the following: "The Patikams to Patiṟṟuppattu give us a clear idea of the charitableness of the Cērā monarchs. It is however held that the Patikams were a later interpolation to the text of the poems. But scholars are of

by the studies of R. Champakalakshmi[10] and Rajan Gurukkal.[11] Among their many ground-breaking results, which contributed to a better understanding of South Indian economic and social history, Gurukkal casts doubt on the monarchical nature of ancient Tamil polities,[12] and on the capability of ancient Tamil rulers to gain influence in pre-modern Indian Ocean trade, and to at least partially control/organize it.[13] Y. Subbarayalu[14] and recently Federico De Romanis have, I believe, correctly refuted these theories,[15] but their ideas still need to be supplemented. In the following pages, we turn our attention to the Early Old Tamil heroic literary sources, particularly to the royal panegyrics of the *Patiṟṟuppattu,*[16] in order to extract valuable data for the reconstruction of economic history. Thus, in the next Tamil-centric and literature-based study, I will examine the following: (1.) the political nature of the Cēra state at the time of the *Patiṟṟuppattu*; (2.) the maritime trade, the markets, the money, and the question of coinage in the Cēra panegyrics; and finally (3.) the economic activities of the Cēras from the point of view of the rational actor theory. I believe that archaeology and philology mutually complement each other in reconstructing ancient South Indian history, and as archaeologists excavate the forgotten past together with its material culture, the philologist-historian must attempt to discover the invisible depths and layers of the written sources. My study is an experiment in the latter, but due to the constraints of this study I am limited to make only some preliminary remarks, therefore a more extensive study is yet to come.

2. The political nature of the Cēra state at the time of the *Patiṟṟuppattu*

The primary task of my study is to determine whether the reign of the early Cēras can be defined as a tribal chiefdom or as a monarchy. To decide this question is the

---

the opinion that the information contained in the Patikams are trustworty. Anyhow, we shall explore the text of Patiṟṟuppattu." (Balasubramanian 1980, 61). Why those verses should be treated as interpolations, or who are those scholars with different opinion, we do not learn from the book.

10 Champakalakshmi 1997, 92–203.

11 Gurukkal 2010, 121–287.

12 Gurukkal 2013.

13 Gurukkal 2016, 277–289.

14 Subbarayalu 2014, 47–55.

15 De Romanis 2020, 107–120.

16 The *Patiṟṟuppattu* is an ancient anthology written exclusively for the early Cēra kings, which contains ten decades with hundred poems and summarizing eulogies at the end of each, from which decades the first and last are lost. The anthology was probably written around the 1st–4th centuries AD, and the summarizing eulogies were probably composed by an early editor in the early Middle Ages.

most important key to the reconstruction of early Cēra economy since a moderately strong chief, and a king in strong control of his vassals, would deal with economic concerns differently. Therefore, in the following pages a preliminary attempt is made to introduce the state of the Cēras, one among the Tamil dynasties.

Gurukkal outlined in many of his works that the ancient Tamil rulers were in fact tribal chieftains. The following crucial factors were identified by Gurukkal that would exclude the Tamil rulers from the circle of monarchs: (1.) the lack of government in a developed (North Indian) sense; (2.) the lack of the adequate stratified societal relations; (3.) the lack of proper territorial sense; (4.) the unsatisfying role of agriculture in the economy during continuous predatory warfare; (5.) the lack of any semblance of taxation; (6.) the lack of evidence that the chieftains had interest in the protection of trade and trade routes; (7.) the lack of the major role of trade in the economy, as chieftains mostly dealt with prestige goods.[17]

If we examine the early Cēra *state* (1.) in the *long durée* of the Indo-Roman trade when the *Patiṟṟuppattu* was possibly composed (around 1st–4th centuries AD), we can conclude that the Cēra state already seemed to possess a hybrid nature which meant both a distinctly Tamil literary life, culture, and identity alongside profound North Indian influences and dominant political theories from the North. At this point, it is important to emphasize that the Cēra ruler and his ancestors were familiar with the concept of the *wheel of virtues* (*aṟam teri tikiri*, Skt. *dharmacakra*) which was one of the most important attributes of a sovereign monarch in ancient India.[18] It is clear from the *Patiṟṟuppattu*'s encomia that early Cēra rulers used the *dharmacakra* as a royal symbol,[19] and they established the *aṟam*/*dharma*(?) across their country,[20] while following *śāstric* teachings in order to rule the country well.[21] It was believed that the

17 Gurukkal 2016, 270–289. Here I mainly followed the points listed by Subbarayalu 2014, 53.

18 Gonda 1957, 144–149.

19 *Patiṟṟuppattu* 22:1–4; 14:18–20; 69:17.

20 *Patiṟṟuppattu* 59:16; 85:9.

21 E.g., see *Patiṟṟuppattu* 21:1–4; 22:1–5. The enumeration in *Patiṟṟuppattu* 21:1 is very fascinating. Here we see a quasi-*specula principum* or *Fürstenspiegel*-like context, which conducts the king how to reign. It is possible to reconstruct one secular and at least one more religious list. The secular one could be: (1.) speech, (2.) fame, (3.) inspection, (4.) audience, (5.) intelligence/valour/conscience. The religious one could be: (1.) praises (cf. *col-mālai*), (2.) names (cf. *sahasranāma*), (3.) sight (cf. *darśana*), (4.) *śruti*/*kēḷvi*, (5.) mind/heart/meditation (cf. *vijñāna*). We can draw up another list of *vedāṅgas* following the old commentary of *Patiṟṟuppattu*: (1.) treatise on words (phonology), (2.) treatise on meanings (morphology), (3.) astrology/astronomy, (4.) Vedas, (5.) controlled heart/mind. However, all of these seem to be inspired by the śāstric *rājadharma*.

Goddess of Fortune, Tiru/Śrī resided on the chest of the Cēra rulers.[22] In the North Indian (and later South Indian) traditions, it is well known that there were close relations between kingship/dominion (*kṣatra*) and welfare/fortune (*śrī*). Śrī as a goddess is not just believed to select a mighty king as her husband, but also described as one who resides in the monarch and on the king's chest.[23] It is believed that the Cēras have gained superiority when they overcame seven kingdoms (*eḻu aracarai veṉṟu*) so that they also wore the seven crowns of those kings on their chests, though the obscure passage does not really explain what it could have meant in reality.[24] The Cēras also had a royal chaplain (*purōcu* < Skt. *purohita*) in the court, who conducted the main sacrifices for the favour of the king and served as an intimate advisor, which in fact shows another important northern influence.[25] The appearance of *purohitas* is not surprising since the Cēras are well-known about sheltering seers (*pārppār*) and gracious men (*antaṇar*) in their country, who both were brāhmaṇical groups in the *Patiṟṟuppattu*.[26] The Cēras, or at least one of their rulers, seem to have followed the ancient practice, well-attested in North Indian texts, that the old ruler goes to the forest together with his chaplain to resign from political duties; however, this story appears only in one of the probably later *patikams*.[27] In the Cēra country, we find established places of worship for Viṣṇu and for other deities. The Cēras ordered/conducted Vedic rituals (*pali* < Skt. *bali*; *āvuti* < Skt. *āhuti*; *cānti* < Skt. *śānti*)[28] and regularly made pilgrimages to their country's sacred places.[29] They also had fortified towns and courts with councils (*arac'-avai*) with learned

22 *Patiṟṟuppattu* 16:17; 31:7; 40:13.

23 Gonda 1956, 131.

24 See the old commentary on *Patiṟṟuppattu* 14:11. The possession of seven crowns seems to be a formulaic pattern, cf. *Patiṟṟuppattu* 40:3; and a quasi-formulaic usage in 45:6. Another hypothesis would be to understand those "crowns" as the seven "treasures" (*ratnāni*) of the king (chariot, elephant, horse, a jewel, [best] wife, [best] minister and [best] adviser) as a northern Indian borrowing. Gonda 1956, 145.

25 Their appearance is clear from the somewhat later *patikams*, the summarizing panegyrics of the decade poems, but we find at least one more reference in the decade poems (*Patiṟṟuppattu* 74:24), where the "old man with grey hair who helps to conduct" (*oḻukkum narai mūt' āḷaṉ*) was no doubt a chaplain, which was anyway the suggestion of the old commentary glossing *purōkitaṉ*.

26 For *pārppār*, see *Patiṟṟuppattu* VI.4; 63:1; for *antaṇar*, see *Patiṟṟuppattu* 24:8; 64:5.

27 *Patiṟṟuppattu* III.10. The ancient practice that a king resigned from politics around the end of his life and left for the forest to follow a reclusive lifestyle can be found, among others, in the *Mānavadharmaśāstra* 6.2. For more details, see Dezső 2022.

28 *Patiṟṟuppattu* 17:6; 21:7, 13; IX.15.

29 *Patiṟṟuppattu* III.8; 88:11, 90:19.

people around,[30] where the ruler held daily courts (*nāḷ makiḻ*) in order to meet his subjects.[31] Turning back to the question of regalia, we also see the royal drum, totemistic tree, flag, bow as dynastic symbol, garland, royal staff, chariot, elephant, horse, crown/chaplet, and parasol; these insignia show a complex system of symbols of royal power.[32] What is more, ancient Greek authors name the Cēra country a 'kingdom' (βασιλεία).[33] Thus we find a well-established monarchy of the Cēras in the centuries of Indo-Roman trade. This monarchy was characterized by Tamil culture and the embeddedness in the *brāhmaṇical/śāstric* religio-political context.[34]

Regarding the question of the *stratified society* (2.) with a hierarchy of clan relations, we know that there were three prominent groups, the *vēntaṉ/aracaṉ/kōṉ*, the *maṉṉaṉ*, and the *vēḷ* ruling over the different landscapes of Tamil countries (Tamiḻakam). From these ancient terms, *vēntaṉ/aracaṉ/kōṉ* represents the highest level of political power (usually translated as 'king', or 'crowned king'). We know only three Tamil dynasties of the category *vēntar*, the Cēras, the Cōḻas, and the Pāṇṭiyas. The term *maṉṉaṉ* can be considered as a synonym of *vēntaṉ*, but also meant a 'chief', 'chieftain', or 'ruler' (cf. *kuṟunila-maṉṉaṉ*). The term *vēḷ* signified de facto a 'chieftain' ruling over a chiefdom, but also a 'brave chief' where the term *vēḷ* served as a mere heroic title. While the *vēntaṉ* were traditionally the overlords of the Tamil South,[35] other chiefs were independent friends, disobedient rivals, or subjugated chiefs with a subordinate rulership. Even the grammarly (*ilakkaṇam*) sister-tradition of ancient literature (*ilakkiyam*), the *Tolkāppiyam* records differences between kings (*aracar*) and chiefs (*ēṉōr*), one of which was the possession of elephants (as discussed below), if we accept the interpretation of Pērāciriyar, the mediaeval commentator of that work.[36]

---

30 *Patiṟṟuppattu* 85:9.

31 *Patiṟṟuppattu* 38:9; 65:13; 85:8.

32 *Tolkāppiyam Poruḷatikāram Marapiyal* 72. cū. 616.

33 *PME* 54–55; Plin. *NH* 6.26.104–105; Ptol. *Geogr.* 7.1.86, 89.

34 Gurukkal recognized this (Gurukkal 2016, 275), though I do not think he attaches enough importance to it, while he confuses things that only the mediaeval commentator suggests but are not explicitly included in the ancient texts, e.g., "... the Cēras are praised as ... devotees of Korravai, the war goddess, and worshippers of Murukan (Karthikeya). However, unlike the case of the other two of the muventar, the poems equate the Cēras with the Vedic gods such as Sūrya, Agni, Marut, ...". Gurukkal 2016, 274.

35 The three kings appear as *mūvar/mūvir* in *Puṟanāṉūṟu* 35:4–5 and 110:1. Auvaiyār sang the 367th song for the Cēra, Cōḻa, and Pāṇṭiya kings. The *Patiṟṟuppattu*'s VIII.5 talks about the "allied state of the two great *vēntar*" (*iru perum vēntaraiyum uṭaṉ-nilai*), cf. *Patiṟṟuppattu* IX.4.

36 Vacek 2013, 331.

We have literary evidence that the early Cēras had a *sense of borders* (3.) in their kingdom. Such pieces of evidence are the poems which refer to a punitive naval expedition against the people of the totemistic *kaṭampu*-tree[37] living in the islands north from the Malabar Coast, who were either pirates, or the privateers of another chief/king, which shows a decisive action against the violation of the territory and of the Cēra economic interests.[38] We can extract evidence from the direction of Cēra military campaigns, and from their titles in which the conquered lands/populations appear, together with other titles that refer to their homeland: "The king of the westerners"; "Bull of the *kuṭṭuvar*"; "Fighter of the people in Marantai"; "King of the *koṅkar*"; "King of the *pūḻiyar*", etc.[39]

With regard to *agriculture* (4.), it should be emphasized that the early Cēra rulers were strongly committed to the growth and prosperity of their lands, and also to recreating harmony and fertility in their enemies' lands which had been destroyed to dust by them, as we read this in many of the royal hymns.[40] In the *Patiṟṟuppattu,* we see references to sluices and water-tanks;[41] agricultural workers sowing on the lowlands;[42] reapers with bending sickles;[43] ploughmen, fertile fields, and irrigated furrows,[44] etc. Thus, while the king marched against the land of the disobedient from time to time, the homeland of the Cēras appears to have been engaged in continuous agricultural production including the need to feed the army. It is indeed fascinating how Muciṟi/Muziris and the Cēra kingdom were able to make year by year thousands of tons of products, and, agreeing with De Romanis, this certainly would not have been possible without the existence of a "complex local economic system".[45] During the centuries of the Indo-Roman trade, it is likely that dozens of Roman merchant ships, which had cargo capacity between 75–500 tons, arrived to the shores of southwestern India every single year,[46] which was not just a magnificent attraction for the locals, but entailed a busy period when they only had a few months to fill the ships and carry out transactions. No doubt, it could not have

37 For a summary of the Tamil sources on *kaṭampu* tribe, read Marr 1985 [1958], 285–290.

38 *Akanāṉūṟu* 127:3–9; *Patiṟṟuppattu* 12:3; 17:5; 20:4; 88:6; IV.6.

39 For the enumerated titles, see *Patiṟṟuppattu* 55:9; V.2; 90:26; 90:28; 22:15–16; 88:19; 90:25; 21:23; 73:9; 84:6; 90:27.

40 For a beautiful example, see *Patiṟṟuppattu* 13:1–28.

41 *Patiṟṟuppattu* 13:8; 27:9; 30:17.

42 *Patiṟṟuppattu* 58:15.

43 *Patiṟṟuppattu* 19:22.

44 *Patiṟṟuppattu* 43:16; 58:17; 76:11.

45 De Romanis 2020, 115–116.

46 McLaughlin 2010, 36.

worked out without the active participation of the locals and their trading channels.

Taxation of the early Cēras (5.) is a problematic issue. Because of the scarcity of the primary sources, we are far from being able to reconstruct this early episode of economic history. From other texts of the Caṅkam corpus, we know that taxation (*vāri, iṟai*) existed at least around the last centuries when Caṅkam works were written.[47] What we see during the reign of the Cēras is that perhaps the army or a troop of soldiers had the duty to collect taxes (*vant' iṟai koṇṭaṉṟu tāṉai*).[48] The 'epilogue' of the V. *patikam*, which was possibly composed later by someone who edited the anthology, records the gifts given to the poet: "having sung, the [following] gifts had been obtained: that king gave Umpaṟkāṭu with [its incoming] taxes (*vāri*) and [also installed] his [own] son Kuṭṭuvaṉ Cēral [as an intendant]." Although we have only a few and uncertain references to taxation, the *Patiṟṟuppattu* contains several other passages where regular tributes (*tiṟai, koṇṭi*) are humbly given to the Cēra kings by other rulers.[49] We must conclude that even in the very formulaic Tamil heroic poetry, we can find an example of some level of organized taxation, but we do not have sufficient evidence in this area of research.

The last two questions to clarify are the *protection of trade* (6.) and the *role of trade in the economy* (7.). Regarding the *protection of trade*, I have stated above that the Cēras ensured to maintain their economic interests by punishing those who committed territorial violation or robbery against their ports. This, together with the fact that the royal capitals, the bigger towns, and the multicultural ports were often fortified and protected by warriors, as we shall see in the case of the fortified Muciṟi/Muziris, means that the Cēras sought to protect the people of their kingdom and thus also the merchants from the potential dangers. However, traders killed on dangerous roads of the wasteland (*pālai*) was a popular *topos* in Caṅkam literature, and at some time of South Indian history it was surely a cruel reality of everyday life. In the *Patiṟṟuppattu*, the king appears more than twenty times as the protector of the kingdom, of living beings, of his friends, and of poets, and their titles show that the Cēra kings intended to provide safety and maintain prosperity in those parts of the monarchy where peace had already become permanent. I agree with De Romanis, when he talks about the importance of the several hundreds of elephants of the Cēras, which enabled them to control the hinterland of ports and to harvest hundreds of

47 On taxes, *Puṟanāṉūṟu* 330:5; 75:4; on tax collectors, *Paṭṭiṉappālai* 116–125. For an informative introduction of the topic, see Subrahmanian 1966, 198–203.

48 I understand here *iṟai* (n.) as 'tax' derivable from *iṟu-ttal* 11. v. tr. 'to pay (as a tax, a debt)'. *Dravidian Etymological Dictionary* (= Burrow / Emeneau 1984, also in the following), 521; *Patiṟṟuppattu* 40:6.

49 *Patiṟṟuppattu* 17:3; 57:15; 59:12; 63:9; 80:10.

kilograms of ivory tusk fragments; to possess an elephant contingent, as the *Arthaśāstra* (2.2.13) states, was an effective means of victory.[50] However, for similar reasons, horses, which were sometimes imported via sea routes (*Paṭṭiṉappālai* 185), played a pivotal role in battles and also emphasized the authority of the kings/chieftains, but the possession of horses is perhaps less apt to distinguish a king from a tribal chief. Considering the question on the *role of trade in the economy*, I will answer it at length below.

I have tried to prove from the Early Old Tamil literary sources that it is untenable to interpret Cēra kings as chieftains and their state as tribal, since our available primary sources seem to suggest a different picture: the existence of a gradually growing 'early kingdom'[51] of the Cēras in southwestern India with all the necessary conditions to exploit the potential of trade. The rise of a ritually confirmed kingdom with royal insignia that connected it to the northern political tradition of India may have been part of a rational process that ensured the stable succession of the Cēra lineage, the acceptance of their dynasty among the people inside and outside their kingdom, and helped them to compete with the surrounding monarchies, e.g., in the field of economy and wealth. In the light of this, the study will subsequently reexamine the references of the *Patiṟṟuppattu* on maritime trade, markets, and money.

3. Maritime trade, markets, and money in the early Cēra panegyrics

In Caṅkam literature, both the love (*akam*) and the heroic (*puṟam*) poems include several songs that report directly or indirectly on early trade. Although we often read about merchants trading salt, paddy, gold, clothes, liquor, fragrance, flowers, etc., specific commercial terms such as 'market', 'shop', 'coin', 'money', 'warehouse' are not particularly frequent in the texts. These songs are either erotic compositions that proclaim love and the intricacies that come with it, or heroic poetry that glorifies the acts of heroes. Both obscure several aspects of real life, or do notattach much importance to them. Therefore, it is necessary to examine these textual references and, where it is worthwhile, take their attestations seriously. In the case of poems that deal with port towns, we have sometimes surprisingly informative descriptions of trade. For example, a very impressive picture of the early trade relations of the Cōḻas is found in the *Paṭṭiṉappālai*, in which we see:

> prancing, swift horses that arrived on water, bales of black pepper that arrived on legs (*kāl*)/by the winds (*kāl*), gold (*poṉ*) and sapphire (*maṇi*) that

50 De Romanis 2020, 119 and 221.

51 I believe that the kingdom of the Cēras meets the criteria of Kulke's 'early kingdoms': Kulke 1993.

> were produced by northern mountains, sandal- and eagle-wood (*akil*) that were produced by western mountains, pearls of the southern sea, corals of the eastern sea, exports (*vāri*) of the Kaṅkai (Gaṅgā), yields of the Kāviri, food from Īḻam (Śrī Laṅkā), and wealth from Kāḻakam (Burma).[52]

Regarding the Cēras, the beginning of the much quoted 343rd poem of the *Puṟanāṉūṟu* reads as follows:

> [With] heaping up paddy having sold fish, mound[-like]-boats (*ampi*) can be confused for houses. Due the bundles of black pepper (*kaṟi*) heaped in the houses, [the latter] are confused for shores with clamorous sound. The golden gift brought by vessels reaches the shores by boats (*tōṇi*) of the backwaters (*kaḻi*). Muciṟi where the sea roars like the *muḻavu*-drum, [the town of] Kuṭṭuvaṉ with a gold garland and toddy in streams, who gives the articles (*tāram*) of the seas and the articles of the mountains to those who gathered together and come [...][53]

In this extract, we see the early Cēra port called Muciṟi (Muziris) which was a fortified (*puricai*) town (*ūr*) with walls (*matil*),[54] where fish was sold, paddy was heaped on boats, warehouses (*maṉai*) were full of black pepper sacks, golden gifts (*poṉ paricam*) were brought to the shore by the boats/canoes of the backwaters, and Kuṭṭuvaṉ, the king gave rare articles (*tāram*) of the mountains and of the seas to his visitors (*varunar*).

In his monograph on the Muziris papyrus,[55] De Romanis understood that the king is the one "who offers toddy as if it were water to those who come to pour there the goods from the mountains and those from the sea", however, the word order suggests that the king has two attributes: he is the one with a *golden garland* (*polan tār*), and with *stream-like toddy* (*puṉal am kaḷ*); he is also the one who "gives liberally"

52 *Paṭṭiṉappālai* 185–191: *Nīriṉ vanta nimir parippuraviyum / kāliṉ vanta karuṅkaṟi mūṭaiyum / vaṭamalaippiṟanta maṇiyum poṉṉum / kuṭamalaippiṟanta āramum akilum / teṉkaṭal muttum kuṇakaṭal tukirum / kaṅkai vāriyum kāvirippayaṉum / īḻatt' uṇavum kāḻakatt' ākkamum.*

53 *Puṟanāṉūṟu* 343:1–10: *Mīṉ noṭuttu nel kuvaii / micai ampiyiṉ maṉai maṟukkuntu / maṉaik kuvaiiya kaṟi mūṭaiyāl / kalic cummaiya karai kalakkuṟuntu / kalam tanta poṉ paricam / kaḻit tōṇiyāl karai cērkkuntu / malait tāramum kaṭal tāramum / talaip peytu varunarkku īyum / puṉal am kaḷḷiṉ polan tārk kuṭṭuvaṉ / muḻaṅku kaṭal muḻaviṉ muciṟi [...].*

54 *Puṟanāṉūṟu* 343:16–17.

55 The Muziris Papyrus (*P.Vindob.* G 40822) is a Greek papyrus from the 2nd century AD, which records a contract between a merchant and a financier and also the cargo of the ship called Hermapollon (Ἑρμαπόλλων). For a recent edition and interpretation of the text, see De Romanis 2020, here 118.

(*īyum*) the articles of seas and mountains, in which case *talaippeytu* is an absolutive used as an adverb that is related (1.) either to the imperfective *peyareccam* '*īyum*', or (2.) to '*varunar*', 'those who come'. Here, the meaning of *talaippeytu* is obscure. The interpretation chosen by V. I. Subramoniam as "having mixed"[56] derived from the compound verb *talaippey-tal*[57] does not seem to be attested in the old corpus.[58] Considering our oldest attestations, there are different ways to interpret this passage. The word *peytu* could be understood as 'having showered', and *talai* as an intensifier of the verb ("having intensely showered"). In this case the *articles* (*tāram*) which have been given by the king are the only possible subjects of the sequence, otherwise, if the *articles* would be showered by the *visitors* themselves, *īyum* as a transitive verb would remain without subject. Nevertheless, the best way seems to be to choose the other old meaning of *talaippeytu* as 'having joined' or 'having gathered' (a contracted form of *talaippeyar-tal*),[59] and to connect it as an adverb to *varunar*, so that we translate "the ones who come having joined/gathered". De Romanis in his translation mistakenly connects *maṟukkuntu* (Line 2), *kalakkuṟuntu* (Line 4), and *cērkkuntu* (Line 6) as the acts of the *visitors*. Since these are all main predicates (3rd person neuter singular)[60] of three separate sentences (or *muṟṟeccam*s connected to Muciṟi), the first six lines serve as a description of the port.

Regarding the Tamil syntax, we do not see the 'golden gifts' in the hands of the king's visitors anymore, at least not in the hands of those who received 'the articles of seas and mountains', so we cannot even talk about *direct* exchange of gifts in this poem. When McLaughlin cites the above-mentioned passage of the poem, he concludes "it seems the Tamil elites regarded their contacts with the Roman traders as a form of gift exchange rather than straightforward commercial dealings".[61] In contrast, the appearance of gift-giving is a result of the milieu of early Tamil literature, when the ability to liberally "shower" gifts to the gift-seekers (*paricilar*) and suppliants (*iravalar*) was one of the most important features to define a hero.[62] Therefore, in these cases it is very difficult to extract data for the reconstruction of early economy since there are dozens of poems where chiefs and kings give away gifts in order

56 *Index of Puranaanuuru* (= Subramoniam 1962, as in the following) 328.

57 *Tamil Lexicon* (= Pillai et al. 1924–1938, as in the following) 1782.

58 The old meanings of *talaippey-tal* are: (1.) to pour on the head, (2.) to shower intensely, (3.) to join/gather. Cf. *Kalittokai* 95:27; *Akanāṉūṟu* 256:20; *Patiṟṟuppattu* II.9; *Aiṅkuṟunūṟu* 86:4.

59 *Tamiḻ Ilakkiyap Pērakarāti* 99; *Tamil Lexicon* 1782; cf. *Aiṅkuṟunūṟu* 86:4.

60 Rajam 1992, 605.

61 McLaughlin 2010, 49.

62 On gift-giving, see Subbiah 1991, 133–158.

to meet the criteria of ancient Tamil heroism. For instance, the chief called Pāri gifted a chariot to a creeper (*Puṟanāṉūṟu* 201:3), while another one, Pēkaṉ, gifted a garment (*paṭam*) to a peacock (*Puṟanāṉūṟu* 141:11), etc. These are definitely not cases of economically rational 'gift-exchange'. I agree with Subbiah that in these early centuries gift-exchange could have a "magical-cum-religious function" and "operated as a major mode of circulation of wealth, and as a process for legitimizing or reinforcing social and moral ties between individuals and/or groups of peoples".[63] The exchange of prestigious gifts in the Roman trade between Roman traders and Tamil rulers was a side-product rather to strengthen relations, and I believe it had little to do with actual trade. As economically rational actors, the Roman traders certainly knew that with prestigious gifts they could facilitate favourable deals with the Indians and a safe stay as important guests of the Cēra kingdom surrounded with envious enemies. As such, the personal interests (safety and making profit) of the actual traders were certainly more important than those of the Empire, and the Cēra king knew that with eye-catching presents, he could ensure that his economic partner would sail to him year after year with tons of products and with an insatiable desire for the goods available in his country, which resulted in a trade boosting the prosperity of his kingdom and strengthening his power and popularity. Thus, in the case of prestigious gifts, we are most probably talking about a mere economic calculation, and only in the case of the wandering bards, their families, and the poor, can we talk about gifts as a redistribution of wealth that ensured someone's livelihood. Otherwise, gift-giving was a mere liberal act and a manifestation of grace of the kings and heroes that happened around the court by chance, or regularly, for the sake of stabilizing relations. Additionally, we have evidence for those who tried to trade in the gifts given by the king. Peruñcittiraṉār said in frustration: "I am not a gift-seeker for business" (*yāṉ ōr vāṇikapparicilaṉ allēṉ*),[64] since he humiliatingly received a gift without the king meeting him in person. Thus, although it is possible to point out the local fish- and pepper-trade, the gift-giving tradition of kings, and the existence of 'golden gifts' brought by boats in the 343rd poem of the *Puṟanāṉūṟu*, it is not possible to prove that the visitors of the king were either "Greeks" (*yavaṉar*), or the ones who actually brought there the golden articles. The people who came to the king (*varunar*) could rather be identified as *paricilar* or the traditional 'gift-seekers' who quite frequently appear in the poems, which, however, does not exclude the possibility that we could have found "Greeks" among them.

In the *Akanāṉūṟu* 149, we see the Pāṇṭiya siege of the fortified Muciṟi where *yavaṉas* arrived on their ships (*kalam*):

---

63 Subbiah 1991, 134.

64 *Puṟanāṉūṟu* 208:6–7.

> He, Ceḻiyaṉ with a tall and good elephant murderous in war seized a statue (*paṭimam*), after he had overcome in a difficult battle, after he had surrounded [the town], so that clamour arose [in] the prosperous Muciṟi [where] gloriously crafted, *yavaṉar*-driven (*tanta*) good vessels came with gold (*poṉ*) and returned with pepper (*kaṟi*), while they stirred up the white foam of Cuḷḷi, the big river (*pēriyāṟu*) of the Cēralar.[65]

In these lines, we read about 'Greeks' who imported gold to Muciṟi and exported black pepper from the port. Regarding the misunderstandings around this poem, the name of the river was certainly Cuḷḷi[66] and not the anyway anachronistic *pēriyāṟu*, 'big river'. In fact, we do not have evidence to prove that a river called 'Pēriyāṟu' existed in the Cēra kingdom in these early centuries.[67] Later and even today, the biggest river of Kerala is called Periyār, but regarding the Caṅkam texts, in all the cases when the compound *pēriyāṟu* 'big river' appears, except the one that has been just mentioned, we cannot surely identify the river. The second possible misinterpretation is that the Muziris trade was an actual gold-pepper exchange. During the Indo-Roman trade pepper and gold changed hands in huge amounts, but it is unclear what happened in the port towns of the Malabar Coast when the 'Greeks' arrived and stayed for a few months every year. It might seem like a nuance, but we cannot confidently call the Muziris trade a goods-for-goods 'exchange' (in the end, maybe it is or looks like)[68] since, as we shall see, markets with gold as a measure of value and at least partial monetization existed in the early Cēra kingdom, which must have played some role during the transactions.

---

65 *Akanāṉūṟu* 149:7–11: ... *cēralar / cuḷḷiyam pēriyāṟṟu veṇ nurai kalaṅka / yavaṉar tanta viṉai māṇ naṉkalam / poṉṉoṭu vantu kaṟiyoṭu peyarum / vaḷam keḻu muciṟi ārpp' eḻa vaḷaii.*

66 *Pre-Pallavan Tamil Index* (= Subrahmanian 1990, as in the following) 375.

67 Regarding the other attestations, not even the old commentator of the *Patiṟṟuppattu*, nor Turaicāmi Piḷḷai or U. Vē. Cāminātaiyar talk about other than a 'big river' of the Cēras. See *Patiṟṟuppattu* 28:10; 43:15; 88:25. The famous port, Muciṟi laid at the mouth of the river called Pseudostomos or Cuḷḷi (today's Periyār), so that the cargoes had to be conveyed in boats for loading or discharging, taking into account the great distance between the coast and the riverside port. The Greek name seems to be surprisingly far from the earliest and later names of the river, however, Malayalam speaking scholars figured out that the word *aḻimukhaṃ*, which means 'estuary' in Malayalam, can be translated as 'false mouth'. The problem is that *aḻimukhaṃ* is a clear derivation from Old Tamil *kaḻimukam* 'the mouth of the backwaters', 'estuary', and neither *kaḻi* in Old Tamil, nor *aḻi* in Malayalam means 'falsity'.

68 De Romanis 2020, 39.

The 57th poem of the *Akanāṉūṟu* describes again the Pāṇṭiya siege of Muciṟi/Muziris, when "Ceḻiyaṉ [whose] chariot [has] flags and horses with trimmed manes, besieged Muciṟi, the harbour at the sea".[69] These passages underline the fact that Muciṟi/Muziris was an important town and a busy harbour that was threatened by both the neighbouring kings and the pirates or privateers roaming around the port.[70] Although the Cēra kings do not seem to have been seafarers and probably did not reach the shores of the western Asian harbours on their own, Neṭuñcēralātaṉ (around the second half of the 2nd century AD) and Ceṅkuṭṭuvaṉ built a maritime fleet, with or without the help of the 'Greeks', and sailed against the *kaṭampu* tribe, defeating them on an island north of the Malabar Coast.[71] Nevertheless, aside from this, we do not know much about the seafaring of the Cēras.

Turning back to trade, we also see the Cēra king as a ruler of the big harbour(s), where storehouses were standing on the shores:

> O fighter of the good country with gardens at the cool sea [around] the big harbour which have fragrant *tāḻai*-groves at the sleeping storehouses (*pantar*), [and] wealth of the good vessels[72] of the ocean where sweetly melodious waves resound![73]

Here the existence of storehouses or arbors (*pantar*)[74] at the old harbours (cf. *Puṟanāṉūṟu* 343) shows the rational planning of the South Indian merchant communities

---

69 *Akanāṉūṟu* 57:14–15: *koy cuval puravik koṭit tēr ceḻiyaṉ / mutunīr muṉṟuṟai muciṟi muṟṟi.*

70 For the pirates of the Malabar Coast, see Plin. *NH* 6.26.101; *PME* 53; Ptol. *Geogr.* 7.1.7 as well as the *Tabula Peutingeriana*'s scroll (XII) on India.

71 *Akanāṉūṟu* 127:6–8; *Patiṟṟuppattu* 12:3; 11:12; 17:4–5; 20:2–4; *Cilappatikāram* 3.25:1; 3.25:185–187.

72 *Tamil Lexicon*, 778: *kalam*: 'jewel', 'vessel', 'ship'.

73 *Patiṟṟuppattu* 55:3–6: *iṉ icaip puṇari iraṅkum pauvattu / nal kalam veṟukkai tuñcum pantark / kamaḻum tāḻaik kāṉalam perum tuṟait / taṇ kaṭal paṭappai nal nāṭṭup poruna.*

74 Although the word *pantar* is either an harbour (*Patiṟṟuppattu* 51:16), or the proper name of a Cēra town/harbour (*Patiṟṟuppattu* 67:2; 74:6), it seems that the word itself meant also "storehouses" (*paṇṭacālaikaḷ*) at least at the time when the old commentary had been composed. The Persian origin of the word (Selvakumar 2008, 26) still seems to be anachronistic and cannot even be proved, nor the attestation of the word *bandar* as a 'port of trade' earlier than the second millennium AD. *Encyclopedia of Islam* (= Gibb et al. 1960), 1013. The question arises whether the word *pantar* had rather an Indo-Aryan origin. In fact, we already see the words *bhāṇḍhāra* and *bhāṇḍāgāra* attested in the *Mahābhārata*, which meant 'treasury' or 'storehouse'. *A Sanskrit-English Dictionary* 752. This word found its place in the Old Tamil language as *paṇṭāram* 'treasury' (*Paripāṭal* 11:123). The old commentator of the *Patiṟṟuppattu*, as I mentioned before, once glosses the word *pantar* with a word meaning "storehouses" (*paṇṭacālaikaḷ*). In this case, I think the mediaeval

to ensure the accumulation and the preservation of articles in the desired quantity. Hence, either the kings also encouraged the development of the port infrastructure, or the merchants were interested in the trade relations leading up to the royal court or to its loyal officials.

In the previous pages, I introduced fragments of the love and the heroic poetry of ancient Tamils that contained valuable information on the trade of the Cēras. What we see in the *Patiṟṟuppattu*, the heroic anthology written exclusively for the Cēras, is that this text (1.) rarely mentions trade; (2.) mentions the 'Greeks' only once in a later composed *panegyricus* (II. *patikam* in which sinful *yavaṉas* were punished while their properties were confiscated); (3.) mostly deals with the wealth of those countries that were destroyed by the Cēras. Nevertheless, there are poems which show the prosperity of the Cēra kings and the fertility of their country, which are interesting in terms of trade. The 22nd poem, for example, talks about the ancestors of the Cēra king, who "helped with the many profits of the forests and the seas", which refers to the distribution of resources to those in need.[75] We also have poems in the *Patiṟṟuppattu* that sing about the fertility and the excellent yields of the lands.[76]

The 76th poem of the *Patiṟṟuppattu* talks about the king who "healed the wounds [of the elephants] like a merchant of stores (*paṇṇiya-vilaiñar*)[77] who strengthen the wood[78] that swam on the great sea, after [he] went to the difficult[-to-approach] haven".[79] Thus we have arrived at the question of the markets. Regarding the 'merchants of stores', the Tamil compound *paṇṇiya-vilaiñar* (lit. "the ones with the price of the articles of trade") contains the loanword *paṇṇiyam* < Skt. *paṇya* 'article of trade', and the Tamil word *vilai* 'price' from which the word for 'merchants' (*vilaiñar*)

---

commentator certainly thought of *bhāṇḍaśālā* ("hall with boxes/commodities", "storehouse") while glossing *pantar*, so one might wonder where the retroflex consonants disappeared? The word *pantar* appears as of Dravidian origin in the *Dravidian Etymological Dictionary*, which means 'shed of leaves', 'arbour', or 'pavillon' in the Dravidian languages, but means 'storehouse' only in Tamil. *Dravidian Etymological Dictionary*, 3922.

75 *Patiṟṟuppattu* 22:6.

76 *Patiṟṟuppattu* 60:8; 69:12–17; 78:7; 89:6.

77 *Tamil Lexicon*, 2453: *paṇṇiya-vilañar*: dealers in stores and provisions. Here *paṇṇiyam* is certainly a Sanskrit loanword from *paṇya* 'article of trade', 'ware'.

78 The old commentator of the *Patiṟṟuppattu*, tends to understand '*kaṭal nīntiya maram*' as *marakkalam*. I would suggest to translate literally since *marakkalam* usually meant a boat or larger ship in later texts, however, here *maram* might mean only a seafaring raft (an *ampi*?).

79 *Patiṟṟuppattu* 76:3–5.

derived. The Sanskrit word *paṇya* 'ware', 'commodity'[80] is a derivation of *paṇa* 'a weight of copper', 'coin', 'commodity'[81] from which another Sanskrit term, the *āpaṇa* was derived, a word for 'marketplace' or 'shop', which we find in Early Old Tamil texts as *āvaṇam*.[82] In fact, the word *āvaṇam* appears only six times in the whole Caṅkam corpus. The 77th poem of the *Akanāṉūṟu* suggests that the people of the marketplace (*āvaṇamākkaḷ*) were literate people who destroyed the seal of a rope-bound pot (as a quasi-envelope?) in which palm-leaves (*ōlai*) were stored.[83] In the 122nd poem, we see the wealthy marketplace together with streets "fall asleep", which means at least that these South Indian markets were busy places surrounded with streets that emptied at night when they were closed.[84] In the 227th poem, we read about the noisy marketplace of Maruṅkūrpaṭṭiṉam that emits lustre, which was either a poetic image to emphasize its wealth, or the markets were indeed illuminated places shining afar.[85] In the *Paṭṭiṉappālai*, we read about continuous festivals (*viḻavu*) in the wide marketplaces (*viyal āvaṇattu*), inferring that the markets must have also been places where festivals of the kingdoms were held.[86] In the *Neṭunalvāṭai*, women worship with folded palms in the prosperous evening-market.[87] It is, of course, not surprising to see a monarch or an elite organising festivals in market towns or capitals, to foster market activities among other things.[88] We can find just in the *Patiṟṟuppattu* eleven references to festivals,[89] when people played music, recited hymns, danced, attended feasts, received gifts, and met the king personally, which highlight the cultural and economic importance of festivals around the Cēra court. However, their real economic functions cannot be sufficiently explained from those laconic passages. Thus, we have seen the festivals of the Cēras, but we have not yet found references to Cēra markets. For that, let us read the following passage of the *Patiṟṟuppattu*'s 68th song:

---

80 *A Sanskrit-English Dictionary* (= Monier-Williams / Leumann / Cappeller 1899, as in the following), 580.

81 *A Sanskrit-English Dictionary*, 580.

82 *Tamil Lexicon*, 249.

83 *Patiṟṟuppattu* 77:7–8.

84 *Patiṟṟuppattu* 122:3: *mallal āvaṇam maṟukuṭaṉ maṭiyiṉ*.

85 *Akanāṉūṟu* 227:19–20.

86 *Paṭṭiṉappālai* 158.

87 *Neṭunalvāṭai* 44.

88 For the 'Festbetrieb' in the Mediterranean antiquity, see Joerdens 2019.

89 Festival mentioned as *viḻavu*, see *Patiṟṟuppattu* 15:18, 38; 22:20; 29:7; 30:15, 20; 48:14; 56:1; 61:18; mentioned as *cāṟu*; see *Patiṟṟuppattu* 72:13; 81:20.

> [...] after the price of the precious/rare toddy (*kaḷ*) was paid out as soon as [the Cēra warriors] entered the market (*āvaṇam*), [where] flags of the toddy[-selling places] swayed, after [they] brought [there] the white tusks of the elephant that a king rode on [...][90]

Here the precious/rare toddy/wine with a remarkably high price could refer to the expensive Mediterranean (Campanian or Laodicean) wine that arrived at South India in amphorae during the centuries of Indo-Roman trade. It is also possible that the wine mentioned here was only a sort of refined, aged palm-wine, in which case the 'tusk-for-toddy' transaction was conducted by local intermediaries. We see the same thing happen in the 30th poem of the *Patiṟṟuppattu*:

> [On] the areas of low lands which are densely surrounded by hills, the hunters (*vēṭṭuvar*), [who have] murderous bows and *kāntaḷ*-chaplets,[91] give the price of wine (*piḻi*) in the gold-possessing[92] markets (*niyamam*), [after they] brought the white tusks of rutting forest-elephants together with the meat of wild cows (*āmāṉ*) with red horns.[93]

What is certain after reading these passages in terms of Indo-Roman trade is that (1.) there was a kind of rare/precious and expensive toddy/wine available in the Cēra markets; (2.) there were expensive elephant tusks (as one of the favourite imports of the Romans) collected by hunters or warriors in the battle, which had been exchanged directly or indirectly for Indian or non-Indian toddy/wine; and (3.) there were 'markets' which possessed (*uṭai*) gold. Here we find another Indo-Aryan word for 'market', *niyamam* < Skt. *nigama*, which, taking into account the possible meanings in Sanskrit[94] and the other eight attestations in Early Old Tamil literature,[95] rather denotes a 'market town' or a 'market street'.[96]

---

90 *Patiṟṟuppattu*, 68:9–11: *vēnt' ūr yāṉai veḷ kōṭu koṇṭu / kaḷ koṭi nuṭaṅkum āvaṇam pukk' uṭaṉ / arum kaḷ noṭaimai tīrnta piṉ* [...] .

91 *kāntaḷ*: Malabar glory lily (*Gloriosa superba*), a fiery colour flower of the high mountains. *Dravidian Etymological Dictionary*, 1451.

92 *poṉ uṭai niyamam*: "the gold-possessing market", "the golden market". Here I would rather see a reference to the actual gold (coins, bars, jewels, treasures, etc.) that the market possessed.

93 *Patiṟṟuppattu* 30:9–12: *kāntaḷ am kaṇṇik kolai vil vēṭṭuvar / cem kōṭṭ' ā māṉ ūṉoṭu kāṭṭa / mataṉ uṭai vēḻattu veḷ kōṭu koṇṭu / poṉ uṭai niyamattup piḻi noṭai koṭukkum.*

94 *A Sanskrit-English Dictionary*, 545.

95 See *niyama* in *Akanāṉūṟu* 83:7; *Naṟṟiṇai* 45:4; *niyamattu* (obl. case) in *Tirumurukāṟṟuppaṭai* 70; *Patiṟṟuppatu* 15:19; 30:12; 75:10; *Maturaikkāñci* 365; *Malaipaṭukaṭām* 480; *niyamam* in *Akanāṉūṟu* 90:12.

96 According to the *Tamiḻ Ilakkiyap Pērakarāti* (p. 1366), the word *niyamam* means "bazaar/

> O [you], the wealth of the gift-seekers! O [you], the king of strong men, [who possess] the *muracam*-drum[97] that sounds in [your] excellent court[98] [that is surrounded by] the gold-possessing market street (*niyamam*), [where] the flags of [your] old town cast a shadow, [where] the *muḻavu*-drum sounds and the festivals (*viḻavu*) do not know the end; [the old town] of the good country with vast areas, [where] many goods enter from the seas, mountains, rivers, and other [places]![99]

It is remarkable that, according to this passage, the marketplaces were close enough to the royal town so that it cast a shadow over the shops, which might be a covert reference to state influence and state control over early trade. We have also seen the many goods entering from the seas, mountains, rivers, and other regions, which made the Cēra king wealthy and the bustling markets profitable.[100] Moreover, an *ostrakon* found at Koṭumaṇal also shows that markets (*nikama*) de facto existed in the Cēra kingdom.[101]

So far that is all that is preserved on Cēra markets in the Caṅkam texts. Even if it seems limited, these remarks should not be dismissed. For instance, from their names of Indo-Aryan origins, we can conclude that (1.) the markets were, at least

---

market street" (*kaṭai teru*) in the old literature, which has a clear Indo-Aryan origin (< *nigama*). Cf. *Naṟṟiṇai* 45:4–5. Its meaning as a "temple" is a later development that might be reflected first in the *Cilappatikāram* 2.14:8. I think that the temples referred as *niyamam* were perhaps temple-economies uniting the two functions, the ritual and the economic. There is one more word connected to the question of markets, *aṅkāṭi* 'bazaar', see *Akanāṉūṟu* 93:10; *Naṟṟiṇai* 258:7; *Paripāṭal* 2:9; however, these passages do not contribute much to our research.

97 The royal drum called *muracu* / *muraicu* / *muracam* is one and (might be the most important) among the regalia of the sovereign monarch in ancient South India: Dubyanskiy 2013, 310, 313–314.

98 According to the *Tamil Lexicon*, 783, the *kalimakiḻ* as a lexicalized compound can be interpreted as 'public audience', or 'royal court'. Occasionally, we can consider the literal meaning as 'bustling mirth' although it clearly refers here to the daily court of the Cēra king.

99 *Patiṟṟuppattu* 15:16–21: *kaṭalavum kallavum āṟṟavum piṟavum / vaḷam pala nikaḻtarum naṉam talai nal nāṭṭu / viḻav' aṟup' aṟiyā muḻav' imiḻ mūt' ūrk / koṭi niḻal paṭṭa poṉ uṭai niyamattu / cīr peṟu kali makiḻ iyampum muraciṉ / vayavar vēntē paricilar veṟukkai.*

100 We still have one more reference on *niyamam* in the *Patiṟṟuppattu*, but that reports only on the country of one of their enemies mentioning the "bright price that is given in the market street/town that possess toddy" / *kaḷ uṭai niyamatt' oḷ vilai koṭukkum* (*Patiṟṟuppattu* 75:10).

101 Mahadevan 2003, 141.

initially, in the hands of speakers of Indo-Aryan languages, perhaps Jaina or Buddhist merchants; and (2.) the kingdom was not just influenced by northern Indian groups in terms of religion and policy as we have seen before, but we can also suspect "northern" influences on the institutions of trade. We should emphasize that when Pliny the Elder, the author of the *Periplus Maris Erythraei*, and Ptolemy reported on the Cēra kingdom, they were still aware only of the external, Indo-Aryan name of the dynasty, the Cēraputra (Caelobothras, Κηπρόβοτος, Κηροβόθρος), "the son of the Cēras", which seems to be an 'official name' of the state also known from the Aśoka inscriptions (Kelalapute / Keralaputo / Keraḍaputro). The fact that in the 1st–2nd centuries AD this name is still in use suggests that either the kingdom proudly promoted its hybrid identity (Tamil cultural life with *brāhmaṇical* influences around the court), or/and the traders as intermediaries between westerners and the locals were not Dravidian, but Indo-Aryan speakers. Even if the Caṅkam texts are silent, we know well from epigraphical remains that Jainas and Buddhists were living in the Tamil kingdoms, even around Muciṟi/Muziris[102] and the Karuvūr, the Cēra capital (modern Karūr, Tamil Nadu), and some of them were surely involved in trade which was connected to the functioning markets.[103] Mahadevan states that at Veḷḷaṟai (modern Vellarippatti) a "merchant guild" (*nikamatu*) was functioning in ancient times since the name of Antai Assutaṉ, the superintendant of pearls (*kāḻatika*) and the *kāviti* (an honorary rank and title) of the 'guild', and the name of Nantasiri Kuvaṉ, the learned one (*kaṇi*), can be found in the 3rd Māṅkuḷam inscription (2nd century BC); moreover, the "members of the merchant guild" (*nikamatōr*) appears in the 6th Māṅkuḷam inscription.[104] It is perhaps better to translate *nikamatu* of the 3rd inscription as 'market(-street)' of Veḷḷaṟai, and *nikamatōr* of the 6th inscription as the 'men of the market(-street)', while we leave open the possibility that here *nikamam* meant a 'merchant guild' or something else, since this specific meaning of *niyamam*/*nikamam* cannot be satisfactorily proved from the contemporary Tamil sources. Interestingly, Ptolemy in the 2nd century AD also mentions a "capital city" (*μητρόπολις*) called Nigama (Νίγαμα) in the Tamil South, which could have been a market-place whose name reflected the Sanskrit term (*nigama*) for 'market'.[105]

Thus, we have arrived at the last topic that needs to be examined: gold and money. The complaints of Pliny the Elder that a huge amount of coins happened to

102 A recent discovery reveals the presence of Jaina traders around Muziris, URL: https://www.thehindu.com/news/national/Tamil-Brahmi-script-found-at-Pattanam-in-Kerala/article14947188.ece, last accessed: 17.12.2021.

103 Champakalakshmi 2011, 259–360; Mahadevan 2003, 315–319, 405–409.

104 Mahadevan 2003, 141, 319, 323.

105 Ptol. *Geogr.* 7.1.12.

be absorbed by the eastern trade year by year,[106] together with the record of the *Periplus* which talks about large amount of money (χρήματα πλεῖστα) imported into southern India,[107] give us the preconception that the Cēra kingdom must have been full of "money" from the West. As a general statement, we should point out that the Caṅkam literature abounds in gold-related passages; we see golden treasures, ornaments, and jewellery everywhere. This also means that the Tamils from the earliest times had to have other sources of gold than the Roman Empire, including Indian mines. On the other hand, the Romans may have been the first ones in South Indian history who paid with gold in large quantities on a regular basis at the coasts of South India. While formerly a significant portion of the gold stocks had been obtained by the Tamils in the battles against other Indian chiefs and monarchs, now trade was a peaceful and secure way to acquire treasures and necessary articles at the same time, by which the kingdoms could embark on the path of prosperity. For the period of the 1st–4th centuries AD, when the poems of the *Patiṟṟuppattu* were composed, the Cēra tribal supremacy had already crossed the threshold of becoming an early kingdom, changes behind which trade must have been the engine of the economic stability. In the literature, predatory warfare still existed to punish those who challenged the superiority of the Cēras. However, if we consider the direction of the Cēra expansions (not speaking of the legendary march to the Himālayas), we can assume that the intrusion into Koṇku Nāṭu through the river valleys, where hoards of Mediterranean coins were found, which in fact seem to trace an important trade route in these centuries,[108] and the further conquests to the eastern shores of Pukār

106 Plin. *NH* 6.26.101; 12.41.84.

107 *PME* 56. See Meyer 2007, 61.

108 For the maps with the locations where the coins were found, see MacDowall 1995. We know that important trade routes (*peruvaḻi*) passed through mediaeval Koṅkunāṭu, such as the*koṅkapperuvaḻi*, the *vīranārāyaṇaṉperuvaḻi*, the *nāṭṭupperuvaḻi*, the *rājakēśaripperuvaḻi*, the *ayiraipperuvaḻi*, the *makadēsaṉ-peruvaḻi*, the *atiyaṉmāṉ-peruvaḻi*, the *pēraṟrupperuvaḻi*, the *cōḻamādēvipperuvaḻi*, the *pālapperuvaḻi*, and the *kāraitturaipperuvaḻi*. Among these, two have particular importance for us: the *koṅkapperuvaḻi*, an ancient east-west route that connected the Kāviri delta with Koṅkunāṭu, which route might have passed Uṟaiyūr, Kuḻittalai, and Karūr, and the *rājakēśaripperuvaḻi* that connected Koṅkunāṭu with Malaimaṇṭalam of Kerala: Rajan 2015, 1. Selvakumar in his excellent paper analyzes the routes of early historic Tamil Nadu in detail. According to his research, we find an important highway that starts at Karuvūr, the Cēra capital and goes on the southern bank of the Kāviri to Uṟaiyūṟ, the Cōḻa capital. There was another important highway that connected Karuvūr with northern settlements and the Mysore Plateau of Karnataka. This route linked Pukaḻūr, Araccalūr, Erettimalai; deviated west from Peruntuṟai, and through Avināci, Kōpiccеṭṭippāḷaiyam, and Cattiyamaṅkalam reached the Mysore Plateau via the

(e.g., see the vocative *pukāar celva* in *Patiṟṟuppattu* 73:9) were aimed at stabilizing inland trade via Palghat Gap and making efforts to reach the east coast to get their hands on the trade of both the Malabar and the Coromandel Coast.

Gold, no doubt, played an important role in early trade; however, the evidence extracted from the poems is again very scarce. We have already seen the references in the *Patiṟṟuppattu* to markets which possess gold. From the phrasing, which appears only in this particular text in this way and which very much focuses on gold, we assume that in these early markets gold could have been a medium of exchange, a store of value, and perhaps a standard of payment. Unfortunately, we do not know how these transactions were executed and who the actors were, but from the Indo-Aryan terms of these early markets (*āvaṇam* and *niyamam*) we can assume that Jaina or Buddhist traders might have been involved to a greater or lesser extent. We saw that people could bring their valuable articles (such as elephant tusks) to the markets, while the poets also emphasize in the Cēra texts that after they brought rare and valuable things there, they had to pay a 'bright price' for the articles they wanted (such as wine/toddy). It is possible that we see a tusk-for-wine 'direct' exchange without being articulated in the texts, but since these markets were trading places where gold was stored, we might already find monetized markets in the Cēra kingdom where people obtained gold (either bars or coins) in exchange for their goods, and they could spend this 'money' on their needs, or spare and exchange at another marketplace. In any case, this system of market-trade would make it easier to collect and sort the articles which changed hands in huge quantities during the transactions with the Romans; however, it also makes easier for the local elite or for the king himself to collect taxes and tolls from trade. The 'bright price' is again not a frequent phrase in the Caṅkam texts. 'Price' (*vilai* and *noṭai/noṭaimai*) as 'bright' (*oḷ*) appears only in the *Patiṟṟuppattu*, and the combinations of these words with the verb *koṭu-ttal* 'to give' and with *tīr-tal* 'to leave' are also attested only in this text. Is the 'bright price' a 'high/expensive' price, or is it 'bright' because of the standard of payment, i.e., gold was de facto 'bright'? We should also emphasize that in the available passages in which the words *noṭai* and *vilai* are attested (twenty-eight in number), we find references to 'bride-price,' 'barter-price,' 'flower-selling women,' 'price for toddy or salt,' 'rare price for jewel,' but we have only a few passages in which prices are connected to markets.[109]

Timpam Ghat. Karuvūr was the junction of the most important routes of the age. It was connected to the Cēra homeland across the Pālakkāṭ Gap through the sites of Koṭumuṭi, Nattakkāṭaiyūr, Koṭumanal, Cūlūr, Veḷḷalūr, Pērūr on the banks of the Noyyal river to the settlements and ports of Kuṭanāṭu and Kuṭṭanāṭu: Selvakumar 2016, 295–297.

109 Lehmann / Malten 2007, 282 and 410.

Several passages on the traditional open barter between the different eco-regions (*tiṇai*) point out the presence of barter in these early societies. However, to examine the possibility to find monetized markets in these kingdoms is not so easy from the sources. The *Patiṟṟuppattu* connected to the Cēras has a special importance in this case since we find a few sequences which talk about gold-possessing markets and large-value transactions there, which appear only in this text of the Caṅkam corpus. Regarding the question of money, in the 81st poem of the *Patiṟṟuppattu* we see "lustre-emitting bars which were completed by the work of flames, became solid in the moulds".[110] The text certainly talks about cast gold bars which bears a great economic historical significance, because these bars served to accumulate wealth, as we also see in the *Perumpāṇāṟṟuppaṭai*:

> [...] the cattle-herder-woman, having fed [her] relatives with the food [from] the price of buttermilk, does not take pure gold (*pacum poṉ*) in bars (*kaṭṭi*)[111] [from] the price of ghī (*ney*), [but] obtains black calves (*nāku*) [of] the good cow of the buffalo (*erumai*) [...][112]

Adding to these, we have evidence for gold bars not only from literary sources, but Tamil Brāhmī inscribed gold bars have already been found by archaeologists in recent years at Thenur near Madurai.[113]

While gold bars were used primarily in the accumulation of wealth, gold and other coins were in circulation, which could be used for marketplace-transactions not only by the merchants and the elite, but by all the people who in some way received such money. I agree with De Romanis who points out that local coins found at Muziris "suggest the strong presence of local people with a monetized economy of their own".[114] In fact, as Mahadevan says, enormous quatities of Cēra coins have been found in the Amarāvati riverbed; among them hundreds of square-shaped copper coins with the Cēra insignia of the bow and the arrow.[115] The earliest Cēra coins without inscriptions have to be dated back to the 2nd century BC, whilst the inscribed

110 *Patiṟṟuppattu* 81:16–17: *aḻal viṉai amainta niḻal viṭu kaṭṭi kaṭṭaḷai valippa.*

111 Another reading is to understand *kaṭṭi* as an absolutive from the verb *kaṭṭu-tal* 5. tr. (*Tamil Lexicon*, 651): "does not take pure gold having fixed/tied the price of the ghī". Still, pure gold here meant accumulated wealth from which the relatives cannot be fed.

112 *Perumpāṇāṟṟuppaṭai* 162–165: *[...] āymakaḷ / aḷai vilai uṇaviṉ kiḷai uṭaṉ arutti / ney vilai kaṭṭi pacum poṉ koḷḷāḷ / erumai nal āṉ karu nāku peṟūum.*

113 URL: https://timesofindia.indiatimes.com/city/madurai/thenur-gold-treasure-found-four-years-ago-is-2300-years-old-recent-study-reveals/articleshow/23754735.cms, last accessed: 17.12.2021.

114 De Romanis 2020, 115.

115 Mahadevan 2003, 153.

silver ones with portraits of the Cēras are most probably from the 3rd century AD.[116] Majumdar adds to this that the Koṅku region came within the Cēra political orbit around the middle of the 2nd century BC.[117] No doubt, the numismatic evidence points in this direction. However, the early silver punch-marked coins of the Cēras, according to Majumdar, imitate the Series IV coins of the Mauryans, and they were probably Mauryan coins and the reverse symbol of the Cēras (bow) was added later as a checking mark or a mark of appropriation.[118] Majumdar mentions that it is also possible that the coins were mere imitations in order to mint their own coinage, or these coins were minted with the permission of the Mauryan state, if the rules of minting recorded in the *Arthaśāstra* (2.22.25) were still valid around this region,[119] under which a significant penalty (25 *paṇa*) had to be paid for those who manufactured coins elsewhere than the Mauryan Empire.

Does that show the tribal period of the Cēra history, when the homeland was Koṅkunāṭu, which was lost during their expansion to the west and reconquered after Neṭuñcēralātaṉ? Focusing on the inscribed coins of the Cēras from the ca. 3rd century AD, we find legends like *mākkōtai* 'The Great Kōtai', *kuṭṭuva-kōtai* 'Kuṭṭuvaṉ Kōtai', *kol-i-p-puṟai* 'Poṟai of Kolli', and *kol-irumpuṟai-y* 'Irumpoṟai of Kolli', which already shows the importance of Karūr region in the Irumpoṟai period of Cēra history. Kolli or Kollikkuṭavarai was an important mountain range in the Cēra kingdom (supported by dozens of Caṅkam poems, but even the later 9th-century *Tivākaram* mentions the Cēraṉ as Kolliccilampaṉ). The Kolli Hills were once ruled by the chief called Ōri, and they were perhaps an important place of worship where the goddess Kollippāvai found her abode.[120] The Kolli Hills still bear the same name in Tamil Nadu north of Karūr. I assume that the variant that calls it Kuṭavarai ("The Western Mountain") comes from those who lived on the eastern parts of South India, or weirdly referred to the Cēras (*kuṭamalai=*kuṭavar-malai?*). Even if numismatics cannot answer all our questions – as these coins do not necessarily appear where they were used, e.g., in the case of hoards, while others have disappeared without a trace due to being melted down or lost to the modern antiquities trade – it still points out the presence of the Cēras in Karūr. What epigraphy can tell us is no less important: the Pukaḷūr inscription no. 9 mentions the seat of Natti, the gold merchant (*poṉ vaṇikaṉ*) of Karuūr,[121] who had perhaps become connected to the local Jaina

116 Ibid., 153.

117 Majumdar 2008, 404.

118 Ibid.

119 Ibid., 404–405.

120 *Pre-Pallavan Tamil Index*, 327.

121 Mahadevan 2003, 417.

community. Even his rare name is telling since we know another Natti from the early inscriptions (4th of the Māṅkuḷam inscriptions), who was a senior Jaina monk.[122] The Pukaḷūr inscription no. 10 talks about an oil merchant called Veṉṉi Ātaṉ (*eṇṇai vāṇṇikaṉ veni ātaṉ*); others like nos. 1–2 mention a Jaina monk namely Mutā Amaṇṇaṉ Yāṟṟūr Ceṅkāyapaṉ and Cēra rulers such as Iḷankaṭuṅkō, Peruṅkaṭuṅkō, and Ātaṉ Cellirumpoṟai.[123] In short, metalsmithing and local minting were well-established in the early kingdom of the Cēras in the centuries of the Indo-Roman trade.

Beside hoards of local coins, the presence of Roman gold and silver coins discovered in South India is a well-researched topic.[124] More than six thousand Roman silver and gold coins have been found in the Indian peninsula, from which the largest quantity derive from the Tamil South. The chronological distribution of the silver *denarii* found in India shows a dominance of coinage from the times of Octavian/Augustus (31 BC – AD 14) and Tiberius (AD 14–37), while we have almost no findings after the currency reform introduced by Nero (AD 54–68) in AD 64, debasing the silver with about 7 % copper alloy. Regarding the gold *aurei*, most of the findings are from the reign of Tiberius, Claudius (AD 41–54) and Nero (AD 54–68), while *aurei* after the reform of Nero which reduced the weight while preserving the purity, are rare. Later, from the 2nd century AD, we have only coins from the times of Antoninus Pius (AD 138–161) and Septimius Severus (AD 193–211), but less in quantity than from the 1st century AD. 3rd century Roman coins seem to be absent in India, whereas we have gold *solidi* coins from the 4th century AD found in India and Sri Lanka. Large quantities of Roman copper from the 4th and 5th centuries AD were found in India and Sri Lanka, the last gold coins coming from the age of Heraclius' reign (AD 610–641).[125]

In terms of the silver *denarii*, since the older coins found in Indian hoards are usually much more worn than later ones but still have a high silver purity, this likely means that the coins, after they had circulated for some time in the Roman Empire,[126] were carefully selected for export to India, which happened long after they had been issued, probably around the end of the 1st century AD.[127] Analyzing the findings, Meyer arrived at the conclusion that Indian traders had a good knowledge of silver purity and Roman coinage, and that they preferred to receive coins from

122 Ibid., 321.

123 Ibid., 405–421.

124 See Turner 1989; MacDowall-Jha 2003; Meyer 2007; Ruffing 2009, etc.

125 This summary was based on Meyer 2007, 59.

126 Ibid., 60.

127 Seland 2010, 65.

the time before the reform of Nero.[128] What made this conclusion necessary is the fact that most of the places where Roman hoards have been found in South India lie in Koṅkunāṭu with Karuvūr, the Cēra capital as their centre, where more than a thousand Roman coins have been discovered.[129] The unearthed coins of Koṅkunāṭu constitute ca. 70% silver coins and 90% coins from the 1st century AD.[130] We should also emphasize that most of the coins were found in hoards, e.g., the Pūtinattam (Budinathan) hoard near Uṭumalpēṭ, Koṅkunāṭu contained 1,398 silver coins.[131] A coin die bearing a Roman device has been found at Karūr, which suggests that Roman coins were also manufactured here.[132] What is more, over five thousand late Roman coins in copper or bronze have been found at Karūr, and Roman coins do not stop arriving to Karūr until the 5th century AD.[133] All these prove that Roman coins arrived in large numbers in the Cēra kingdom, and since they were forged, coins were probably sought after not only as precious metal, but also as actual money.

Turning back to the *Patiṟṟuppattu*, we see that there are several poems that talk about coins and money, but their value as historical sources concerning the circulation of coins are uncertain, as they must be identified as later compositions. These special comments are epilogues in prose that appear at the end of the "summary poems" (*patikam*) of each decade (*pattu*) of the *Patiṟṟuppattu*. Reading these poems, one has the impression that these were composed by an editor in the early Middle Ages, perhaps the one(s) who collected the poems into a chronologically ordered anthology. The author must have been the editor since the language and the verse form are uniform, and the author clearly seemed to already know the whole anthology when he added the "summary poems" to each decade. I speculate that the author of these epilogues might have been the same as the author of the *patikams*, and the differences in word usage can be explained by the fact that the *patikams* were still written in an archaic form befitting the poems, while the epilogues were mere appendices that helped the recipient/scholar to contextualize the poems and their backgrounds.

We find coins exclusively in those lines when the author speaks about the gifts that were received by the poets. In the VI. *patikam*, we read that the king gave hundred-thousand *kāṇam*-coins (an ancient weight; an ancient gold coin; gold; *Tamil Lexicon*, 859) and nine *kā*-measure (a standard weight, hundred *palam*; *Tamil Lexicon*,

---

128 Meyer 2007, 60.

129 Nagaswamy 1974, 397.

130 Meyer 2007, 61.

131 Ibid., 62.

132 Majumdar 2008, 405.

133 Ibid., 413.

840) of gold to the poetess. In the VII. *patikam*, we read that the king gave to the poet hundred-thousand *kāṇam*-coins as a little gift (*ciṟu-puṟam*). In the VIII. *patikam*, we read that the king gave to the poet nine-times-hundred-thousand *kāṇam*-coins and the royal throne or bed. In the IX. *patikam*, the king gave to the poet thirty-two-thousand *kāṇam*-coins. However, too many conclusions cannot be drawn from this because of the uncertain date of these passages. Two interpretations can however be outlined: (1.) the author of these epilogues had a certain knowledge of the ages he wrote about, and indeed a large amount of money changed hands as gifts in exchange of these ancient poems; or (2.) the author projects the monetized economy of his own early mediaeval age (probably around the 5th–6th centuries AD) into the past and records imaginary quantities when he speaks of gifts given to the poets. Even so, we have seen the ancient literary evidence of monetized markets in the early Cēra kingdom, the archaeological evidence, and we have seen those who speak probably a few centuries later of these ages with coins and gold in circulation in large quantities.

The accumulation of coins, treasures, taxes, tributes, booty, and royal income required an institutionalized treasury. The reconstruction of such in the Cēra kingdom might be possible from the *Akanāṉūṟu*:

> [...] having heaped in one place the *āmpal* measure rows of diamonds (*vayiram*), female-statues (*pāvai*) made from gold, and good vessels worthy to praise, which had been given as humble tributes by the disobedient, at the court of Māntai, the good town [of Cēralātaṉ] [...][134]

This could mean that in the Cēra residency at Māntai a designated place or room existed where the tributes had been accumulated. We see another ruler, Naṉṉaṉ Utiyaṉ who had well-protected golden treasures in his town, "at Pāḻi with a difficult defence, where the gold was put [down] by the very ancient chiefs (*vēḷir*) for the sake of protection."[135] This again underlines the fact that the early Cēra kings were very much interested in accumulating wealth in order to provide a stable foundation for the economy, since they also certainly knew what Kauṭilya had said wisely in the *Arthaśāstra* that "all undertakings presuppose the treasury";[136] but also, all undertakings assume rational planning.

134 *Akanāṉūṟu* 127:6–9: *nal nakar māntai muṟṟatt' oṉṉār paṇi tiṟai tanta pāṭu cāl nal kalam poṉ cey pāvai vayiramoṭu āmpal oṉṟuvāy niṟaiyak kuvaii.*

135 *Akanāṉūṟu* 258:1–3: *naṉṉaṉ utiyaṉ aruṅkaṭip pāḻit toṉ mutir vēḷir ōmpiṉar vaitta poṉṉiṉum ....*

136 *Arthaśāstra* 2.8.1: *kośa pūrvāḥ sarvārambhāḥ*. Trans. by Olivelle 2013, 40.

4. Conclusion

I have introduced the literary evidence on maritime trade, markets, and money found in Early Old Tamil texts written about the ancient Cēra kings. Despite the fact that the often flattering Tamil literature ordered by kings and chiefs is rather laconic about certain themes, the main results of this study are that (1.) the monarchical character of the early state formation of the Cēras has been introduced, (2.) the suggestion that Cēra kings would have thought of Indo-Roman trade only as gift-exchange has been refuted, and (3.) a Tamil literature-based study has been carried out that has argued for the existence of an early money economy in ancient southwestern India. From the available textual sources and the related archaeological findings I create the following model of the early Cēra economy: (1.) a traditional barter-exchange between the different eco-regions as the most mentioned mode of trade in the Caṅkam corpus; (2.) a monetized system of marketplaces where wealthy people, local elite, and merchants carried out monetized transactions, and (3.) a system of gift-exchange as a distribution of one's wealth in order to establish or stabilize political, economic, and ritual relations. As Selvakumar also suggests, below the level of open barter there must be at least another one: the gift/credit/debt-based reciprocal micro-economies between relatives and fellow villagers.[137] Thus, the closed communities or micro-economies, which were out of the scope of this paper, would be based on trust, sympathy, and caring for each other; the open barter took place between "strangers" of the eco-zones and "people who are familiar with the use of money, but for one reason or another, don't have a lot of it around",[138] and the monetized world of markets would be available only for those who have gained wealth measurable in some kind of money which was recognized by the local ruler and accepted by the merchant community. I think we are far from being able to fully understand what the function of the local coins and the Roman coins in this economy was, but I assume that they could have been in use and circulated not just as treasure but as actual money to pay with, withdrawn from circulation in the Mediterranean.

On the level of economic actors, we can determine economically rational acts of the Cēra kings in order to create a predictable economy with great promise, such as the fortification of port towns where warehouses were built in order to accumulate and preserve the articles; the military campaigns in which Cēra kings sought to get access to trading routes and occupy ports of the Coromandel Coast; the fact that kings allowed to establish gold-possessing markets and managed to mint local coins

137 Graeber 2011, 29.

138 Ibid., 37.

in order to show off their authority and perhaps to establish a monetized trading system beyond barter, and the possibility to exchange one's wealth to gold bars as *commodity money*. 'Light houses,' as quite a modern infrastructure, were built at the ports of Tamil kings.[139] Although these are not attested in the Cēra texts, we can still assume that these buildings were in use also at the Malabar Coast, which shows the intention of ports to facilitate long-distance maritime navigation. Broadly speaking we are still in the early stages of state development; however, our sources show that in the case of the Cēras, we have to deal with an early kingdom of a hybrid nature which has Tamil literary life and culture but strong *brāhmaṇical* influences around the court; a partly monetized economy with perhaps Jaina and Buddhist merchant communities in the background; a well-organised hinterland which was able to serve the Indian Ocean trade and to make vast stocks of goods regularly and reliably available, a fascinating example of which is the Muziris Papyrus. The transport of tons of goods from inland to the shores, even if it is somewhat invisible in the Caṅkam corpus, required rigorous supervision by the state which could not base the service of merchant ships that arrived on a regular basis on chance. Through the lens of the rational actor theory, I have considered common goals, opportunities, and constraints of both the Romans and the Cēras. Regarding the goals, both the Romans and the Cēras were interested to maintain trading relations, to gain high profit, and to acquire necessary goods; regarding the opportunities, both of them intended to organise and protect the trade. Regarding the constraints, both of them were facing with rivals, fraudsters, robbers, and pirates, and also with cultural difficulties such as the language. The Romans have set the goals to boost Roman economy (traders, of course, for an actual living), and the Cēras did it for the same reason but also in order to strengthen the royal power. They both struggled with rivals, enemies, and pirates to maximize their profits from the trade, and while the Roman traders certainly got a foothold in India and occasionally provided military assistance to the Tamil rulers,[140] the Cēra kings extended their influence on the markets and the merchant communities in order to be starring in a large-scale business.

Maritime trade has thus boosted the Cēra country's economy and at the same time made it vulnerable to the Mediterranean, the center of the Indo-Roman trading system. Thus, when the kingdom of the Cēras declines probably around the same century when the decline of the Roman Empire takes place, only the Cēra kings and their stakeholders, who have not survived the loss of regular incomes and a change in maritime trade paradigm, failed, but everyday life continued on a lower level

139 *Akanāṉūṟu* 255:5–6; *Perumpāṇāṟruppaṭai* 346–351.

140 *Mullaippāṭṭu* 45–49, 59–63, 63–66; *Cilappatikāram* 2.14:66–67.

during the early medieval transition period preparing for the political-economic rebirth under the mediaeval Hindu kingdom of the Perumāḷs.

Bibliography

[Anonymous] (2013): Thenur Gold Treasure Found Four Years ago is 2300 Years Old, Recent Study Reveals, URL: https://timesofindia.indiatimes.com/city/madurai/thenur-gold-treasure-found-four-years-ago-is-2300-years-old-recent-study-reveals/articleshow/23754735.cms, last accessed: 17.12.2021.

Balasubramanian, C. (1980): A Study of the Literature of the Cēra Kingdom, Madras.

Burrow, Thomas / Emeneau, Murray T. ([2]1984): A Dravidian Etymological Dictionary, New York.

Champakalakshmi, R. (1997): Trade, Ideology, and Urbanization. South India 300 BC to AD 1300, Delhi / New York.

Champakalakshmi, R. (2011): Religion, Tradition, and Ideology: Pre-colonial South India, New Delhi.

Chevillard, Jean-Luc (2022): The Riches Coming from the Mountain. "Pepper", as kaṟi and miḷaku in Ancient Tamil Literature. In: Trinquier, Jean / Schneider, Pierre (eds.), Le poivre, fragments d'histoire globale. Circulations et consommations, de l'Antiquité à l'époque moderne, Paris, 105–139.

Dezső, Csaba (2022): Vṛddhekṣvākuvratam. The Commentators' Interpretations of the Passages Describing the Renunciation of Kings in the Raghuvaṃśa. In: Asiatische Studien – Études Asiatiques, ahead of print, URL: https://doi.org/10.1515/asia-2021-0021, last accessed: 01.05.2023.

De Romanis, Federico (2020): The Indo-Roman Pepper Trade and the Muziris Papyrus, New York.

Dubyanskiy, Alexander (2013): Royal Attributes as Reflected in "Caṅkam" Poetry, in: Cracow Indological Studies 15, 307–324.

Gibb, Hamilton A. R. et al. (1960): Encyclopedia of Islam. New Edition. Vol. 1, Leiden.

Gonda, Jan (1957): Ancient Indian Kingship from the Religious Point of View, in: Numen 4/1, 24–58.

Graeber, David (2011): Debt. The First 5,000 Years, New York.

Gurukkal, Rajan (2010): Social Formations of Early South India, New Delhi.

Gurukkal, Rajan (2013): Classical Indo-Roman Trade. A Historiographical Reconsideration, in: Indian Historical Review 40/2, 181–206.

Gurukkal, Rajan (2016): Rethinking Classical Indo-Roman Trade. Political Economy of Eastern Mediterranean Exchange Relations, New Delhi.

Jördens, Andrea (2018): Festbetrieb als Wirtschaftsfaktor, in: Marburger Beiträge zur antiken Handels-, Wirtschafts- und Sozialgeschichte 36, 217–247.

Krishnamurty, R. (1997): Sangam Age Tamil Coins, Chennai.

Kulke, Hermann (1993): State Formation and Legitimation in India and Southeast Asia, Delhi.

Lehmann, Thomas / Malten, Thomas (2007): A Word Index for Caṅkam Literature, Madras.

MacDowall, David W. (1995): The Evidence of the Gazetteer of Roman Artefacts in India, in: Ray, Himanshu Prabha / Salles, Jean-François (eds.), Tradition and Archaeology. Early Maritime Contacts in the Indian Ocean, New Delhi.

MacDowall, David W. / Jha, Amiteshwar (2003): Foreign Coins Found in the Indian Sub-Continent, New Delhi.

Mahadevan, Iravatham (2003): Early Tamil Epigraphy. From the Earliest Times to the Sixth Century C.E., Cambridge.

Majumdar, Susmita Basu (2008): Money Matters: Indigenous and Foreign Coins in the Malabar Coast (Second Century BCE – Second Century CE). In: Mathew, Kuzhippalli S. (ed.), Imperial Rome, Indian Ocean Regions and Muziris: New Perspectives on Maritime Trade, London / New York, 395–423.

Marr, John Ralston (1985=[1958]): The Eight Anthologies. A Study in Early Tamil Literature, Madras.

McLaughlin, Raoul (2010): Rome and the Distant East. Trade Routes to the Ancient Lands of Arabia, India and China, London / New York.

Meyer, Jørgen C. (2007): Roman Coins as a Source for Roman Trading Activities in the Indian Ocean, in: Seland, Eivind H. (ed.), The Indian Ocean in the Ancient Period. Definite Places, Translocal Exchange, Oxford (BAR International Series 1593), 58–67.

Monier-Williams, Monier / Leumann, Ernst / Cappeller, Carl (1899): A Sanskrit-English Dictionary Etymologically and Philologically Arranged with Special Reference to Cognate Indo-European Languages, Oxford.

Nagaswamy, R. (1974): Karuvūr Vañji: The Capital of the Sangam Cēras, in: Journal of Kerala Studies 1/4, 395–402.

Olivelle, Patrick (2013): King, Governance, and Law in Ancient India. Kauṭilya's *Arthaśāstra*, New York.

Pillai, Vaiyapuri et al. (1924–1938): Madras Tamil Lexicon. Published in 7 vols. under the Authority of the University of Madras, Madras.

Rajan, K. (2015): Early Writing System: A Journey from Graffiti to Brāhmī, Madurai.

Rajam, S. et al. (2002): Varalāṟṟu muṟait tamiḻ ilakkiyap pērakarāti, Ceṉṉai.

Rajam, V. S. (1992): A Reference Grammar of Classical Tamil Poetry. 150 B.C. – Pre-fifth/Sixth Century A.D., Philadelphia.

Ruffing, Kai (2009): Römisches Geld in Indien?, in: Geldgeschichte im Geldmuseum 2009, Frankfurt, 57–75.

Seland, Eivind Heldaas (2010): Ports and Political Power in the Periplus: Complex Societies and Maritime Trade on the Indian Ocean in the First Century AD, Oxford (Society for Arabian Studies Monographs 9 / BAR International Series 2102).

Selvakumar, V. (2016): The Routes of Early Historic Tamil Nadu, South India. In: Boussac, Marie-Francoise / Salles, Jean-Francois / Yon, Jean-Baptiste (eds.), Ports of the Indian Ocean, New Delhi, 289–321.

Sesha Aiyar, K. G. (1937): Cēra Kings of the Śangam Period, London.

Subbarayalu, Yellava (2014): Early Tamil Polity, in: Karashima, Noboru (ed.), A Concise History of South India. Issues and Interpretations, New Delhi, 47–55.

Subbiah, Ganapathy (1991): The Roots of Tamil Religious Thoughts, Pondicherry.

Subrahmanian, N. (1966): Śaṅgam Polity. The Administration and Social Life of the Śaṅgam Tamils, Madurai.

Subrahmanian, N. (1990): Pre-Pallavan Tamil Index. Index of Historical Material in Pre-Pallavan Tamil Literature, Madras.

Subramanian, T. S. (2011): Tamil-Brahmi Script Found at Pattanam in Kerala, URL: https://www.thehindu.com/news/national/Tamil-Brahmi-script-found-at-Pattanam-in-Kerala/article14947188.ece, last accessed: 17.12.2021.

Subramoniam, V. I. (1962): Index of Puranaanuuru, Trivandrum.

Subramoniam, V. I. (1969): Culture of the Ancient Cheras. A Study in Cultural Reconstruction, Kovilpatti.

Turner, Paula J. (1989): Roman Coins from India, London.

Vacek, Jaroslav (2013): Old Tamil Kings and Chieftains as Described in Sangam Literature, in: Cracow Indological Studies 15, 325–354.

Are the Moderns Rational? The View from Qin*

Jason Hagler

Abstract: Enlightenment thinkers were not the first to conceive of humans as motivated by rational self-interest. From the Warring States Period to the Western Han, policymakers and political philosophers discussed and implemented policies that leveraged human self-interest. The body of theory and practice around this discourse made different assumptions than Classical Economists did about the bounds of human rationality, the stability of the market, and the impacts of market friction. By considering actual Qin-Han policies in terms of their intellectual background through texts such as *The Book of Lord Shang* and *Guanzi* in the framework of New Institutional Economics (NIE), we gain several insights. Most immediately, in the question of the applicability of Rational Actor Theory to the ancient world, we see that while rationality as we know it does still operate, the assumptions about things like human nature and the behavior of markets substantiatively impact policy. By examining the outcomes of areas integrated into the Empire vis-a-vis the application of what we might call "Warring States" rational actor driven policy, we can also observe the key role that the bureaucracy and the institutions that it actuated and made possible such as taxation, corvee, public works, and opportunities for social advancement produced unity and consensus through communication and rational policy in a diverse and fragmented Empire, allowing us to bring Early Imperial China into discussions of more recent history by scholars such as Douglass C. North.

Keywords: Rational Actor Theory – Book of Lord Shang – Early Imperial China – Qin – New Institutional Economics (NIE) – Warring States – Western Han

1. Introduction

The topic for this volume is the question of the applicability of Rational Actor Theory to the ancient world, which is, in turn, part of the Formalist-Substantivist debate and its afterlife.[1] Rational Actor Theory is a core assumption of Classical and Neo-Classical Economics, which states that humans will tend to maximize their self-

---

* Translations of selections from *Mozi*, *Han Feizi*, and *Xunzi* can be found in Watson 1964; translation of selections from Mencius can be found in Van Norden 2008.

1 See Barry Isaac's unfortunately premature 1993-paper "Retrospective on the Formalist-Substantivist Debate".

interest, according to their preferences, in a logically optimal way. While the applicability of this assumption and models deriving from it to actual human population has been criticized from a number of angles (below), the Formalist-Substantivist debate stems from Polyani's 1944 *The Great Transformation*, where he argued that the idea of and behavior associated with Rational Actor Theory was a product of markets and their capitalist ideology. He suggested that rationality is culturally embedded in the (also culturally embedded) capitalist market, the substantivist position; his angle was that market rationality was not natural as (Neo-)Classical Economists since Adam Smith had suggested, but rather, was a cultural imposition. In the substantivist position, the context matters. The counter-position, formalism, is that these patterns do indeed apply across human behavior because humans really are driven by some sort of rational core.

There are at least two factors preventing the issue from being settled. Firstly, the approach to human behavior, methods, and forms of evidence in economics differ from those in many other humanities disciplines. For example, in their 2007 overview of Economic Anthropology, *Economies and Cultures*, Wilk and Cligget suggest part of the problem is that the methods and disciplinary assumptions, but also that the assessments of human nature are different, outlining three dominant paradigms in Anthropology, which are also applicable to history and other fields. Self-Interest, the tradition of Rational Actor Theory, focuses on individuals maximizing their own benefit. This is the default economic approach. Social approaches posit that social groups like culture, class, and ethnicity; and group identity are the driving forces, group selection/rationality. Durkheim is a classic example. Moral or cultural approaches posit that cultural mores (morality) are the primary driver as people internalize social values. Here, something like Weber's *Protestant Work Ethic and the Spirit of Capitalism* is a classic example, with a more recent one being Lakoff's more empirically driven application of conceptual metaphors and embodied psychology to political behavior in *Moral Politics*. The Self-Interest approach focuses on the individual actor while in the other two, larger scale structures are the rational "agents", with these larger entities generating irrational activity on the local level that, nonetheless, produces a net social benefit. In effect, market thinking would be rationality at the individual level. Assuming that humans are only motivated by either groups or internalized mores leads to issues in explaining when humans fail to show class consciousness or act in immoral ways. However, in the Humanities, fields usually blend these approaches, while economics tends strongly towards the rational actor paradigm investigated in the "rational" manner. While more traditional humanistic approaches are used in the latter two approaches, economic ones are favored with the former, where mathematical models are employed to explain human behavior. The catch is that disagreements over the weighting of factors and coefficients lead to drastically different models.[2] This approach has also been increasingly criticized from within the field of Economics since the 2008 financial crisis, there has been concern over the approach economic modeling has taken. For example, Spiegler's methodological critique of economic modeling argues that there is an overreliance on mathematical models that have no clear relationship with actual behavior. While models can be useful, economics is all too often a rational pursuit, rather than an empirical one.[3]

Secondly, the meaning of rational action is not an entirely settled matter. Most contemporary economists recognize that human behavior is not rational, and while "mainstream" economists accept it as a satisfactory model, the expression of this rationality has changed over time and the significance of contextual factors is still debated. Bounded rationality, which takes uncertainty and limited information into account in its assessment of rational behavior, is now part of economic assessments of human behavior, but the inclusion of things such as institutional (i.e., social level) are fairly recent such as the focus on institutions in the works of North. "Institutions are the rules of the game";[4] the human-devised formal (laws) and informal (custom) constraints that structure interaction.[5] Further outside the mainstream is behavioral economics, which is derived from experiments on human decision making and has found that factors such as how options are presented, while the actual information is the same, framing makes a substantial difference in decision making such that humans are predictably irrational.[6] With the recent methodological reflection since 2008, new approaches are being increasingly more integrated into mainstream economics, but what this all means for us is that the terms of the debate have not remained the same.

The case of Early Imperial China (here c. 360–100 BC) gives us a somewhat different approach to the question. Enlightenment and Post-Enlightenment thought is

2 See, e.g., Basle's argument that economists have historically underestimated the resources available during a recession and overestimated limitations to resources, causing misinterpretation of events such as the 1873–1879 depression; cf. Basle 2017. Similarly, De Vroey's *History of Macroeconomics* (2015) is presented in terms of a divide between Marshall and Walras, whose approaches differed by their assumptions. Finally, Heijdra's 2009-textbook *Foundations of Modern Macroeconomics*' introduction to different schools of economic thought on pp. 3–28 discusses the differences between their preferred model for the labor market, expectation formation, and money demand.

3 Spiegler 2015; Hodgson 1999, 1–17 makes much the same complaint.

4 North 2015, 62.

5 North 1991, 97.

6 See, e.g., Tomer 2017.

not the only time in human history such a model of human behavior has been advanced. By the 5th century BC, a model of self-interested humans seeking to maximize their own interests arose in China.[7] By the time of the beginning of the composition of the *Book of Lord Shang 商君書 Shangjun Shu* in the 4th century, this human self-interest is understood as both agent of, but also solution to, social disorder. This text and the broader discourse of which it was part was hugely influential and seems to have impacted policy in the state of Qin 秦 during its rise to power during the Warring States 戰國 period between 360 and 221 BC and the period of Imperial rule (221–206 BC), whose policies were carried over into the Western Han 西漢 period[8] (202 BC – AD 9). I will refer to this as Early Imperial China and will focus on policy and thought primarily from the roughly 300 year period from about 360 to 60 BC.[9] Because the Qin Empire was built on its Warring States policies, when I talk about Qin policy, I am actually talking about more than a century of policy, and it is this longer tradition that the Western Han continues. There is change during this time, but we do not seem to be dealing with sudden breaks.[10]

To be clear, this was not the only model of human behavior (for example, Confucian traditions), nor was it the only force behind policy-making (for example, various esoteric specialists).[11] However, with *Lord Shang* and other Early Chinese texts such as the *Guanzi 管子*, we can observe discourse around self-interest in human nature as well as about markets.[12] In addition to *Lord Shang*, we also have excavated documents, including working documents from the tombs of officials, giving us insight into the application of policy. By observing their discourse and practice, we can arrive at an assessment not simply of the results of the application of rational incentives to a premodern population, but also the assumptions and evaluations that likely went into those policies. In seeing how similar starting points in human motivation can lead to different conclusions and the way that these differences compare to objections and modifications to Rational Actor Theory in contemporary

7 The *Mozi*, in "Universal Love 偏愛上 (Pianai Shang)", for example, asserts that social disorder is because of people prioritizing self-interest at all costs and by any means. For a translation, see Watson 1964, 39–49.

8 The Han Dynasty is divided into two periods: Western Han (202 BC – AD 9) and Eastern Han (AD 25–220), split by Wang Mang's Xin Dynasty. In Chinese, they are usually referred to as the Two Hans; their structures differed greatly.

9 The reason is the documentation, historiography, and changes in late Western Han institutions, see below.

10 See further discussion below.

11 See, e.g., the so-called Huang Lao school of thought or texts such as the Huainanzi.

12 Traditionally, texts espousing this understanding of human behavior have been grouped as "Legalist." I do not use the term because it is anachronistic, see below for more.

scholarship, we can observe ways in which Rational Actor Theory itself is socially conditioned. This is not to say that everything is socially constructed, rather, in line with NIE, I am suggesting that the institutions shape the outcomes. Looking at Qin-Han "Rational Actor Theory," I suggest that we find a model of human behavior that tallies with approaches such as NIE. This Qin-Han rational actor approach does not endorse free markets, not because they could not imagine them, but because concerns about human decision making in real conditions with imperfect knowledge. Most notably, is the central role that institutions in the NIE sense play in the thought of this period. While human nature is invariantly self-interested, the way that this manifests and the well-suited policy set is dependent upon the existing set of social institutions. The contextual limitations of these institutions in the face of existing complexity drives the need for the creation of new institutions.

Furthermore, we find that the assumptions and conclusions at odds with orthodox classical and neoclassical economics often have parallels in more recent challenges to the conventional approach to rationality. In other words, the difference is not that these Early Chinese models are more primitive or rationally deficient, but rather there are certain idiosyncrasies in modern economics and its history just as there are in these Early Chinese models. Without empirical data and context sensitivity, we cannot figure out what unwarranted assumptions are built into modern economic theories. Finally, Qin-Han policy and its implementation actually provides us with an interesting glimpse into the efficacy of a successfully implemented rational policy set for producing social cohesion.

This paper will thus first lay out thought on rational self interest in Early China to use as a basis for considering its influence on policies. We will also consider how this impacted thinking on markets and prices, before considering whether or not these policies performed in accordance with the theory.

2. Historical context

Before we can proceed to the texts and policies, some historical context is required. The period of the texts and policies we will consider is the Warring States (c. 475–221 BC), Qin (221–206 BC), and Western Han (202 BC – AD 9) periods.[13] This is because there is strong institutional continuity. I will introduce the grounds for this statement at the end of this section. The Warring States period was a time of intense interstate competition to attempt to take the mantle of the Zhou 周 King as world

13 For more information on economic trends in this period, see Leese-Messing 2020a/b; for a more general historical overview of the Warring States, Qin, Western Han, and Eastern Han, see their respective chapters in Goldin 2018, and, for an in depth work on Qin and the Two Hans, see Lewis 2007.

ruler. Previously, the Kings of Zhou had held a hegemony over a community of subordinate rulers. As their authority waned, starting in the 9th century, but particularly in the 7th century,[14] the resulting power vacuum attracts elites first to rule in the name of, and then replace, the Zhou royal house. Some of these contenders are long-term members of this world, such as Jin 晉, while others are newcomers, such as powerful Chu. The lords of Jin were a cadet branch of the Zhou royal family. Chu 楚, along the middle Yangzi (Yangtze), on the other hand, were understood as cultural others.

Competition intensified as population increased; underpopulation was the persistent plague of the state planner for most of Chinese history and the diffusion of new agricultural technologies allowed for vastly increased production. As the resources available increase, so too does need for management, resulting in stresses on the existing system. Mercantile and industrial activity had always been important – recent excavation from the Anyang (Late Shang) Period (1250–1050 BC) has spurred a reanalysis of the Shang economy; the new analysis is that production was decentralized and trade was a significant part of the economy, even at the lower levels of society.[15] While there had been this mode of production and the long-term use of currency,[16] the intensification of these processes in the Spring and Autumn period (8th–5th centuries) leads to a new era in society. As early as the 5th century, rulers attempted to track and manage every household in their jurisdiction in written form at Houma, in the state of Jin 晉. Jin's partition by three powerful noble houses hung heavily in the minds of Warring States and Han commentators. In several stages over the course of the 5th century, these three clans partitioned the state amongst themselves, resulting in 3 distinct polities, Hann 韓,[17] Zhao 趙, and Wei 魏. The lesson was that independent power-bases and ties to a specific locality would endanger the state.

Newly independent Wei needed to build its administrative corps quickly, thus Lord Wen (r. 446–396 BC) began accepting advisors from all social backgrounds and countries. This quickly paid off and was borrowed across the states.[18] Furthermore,

---

14 For more on the Western Zhou system, see Li 2006.

15 Campbell et al. 2018.

16 Thierry 2018.

17 In modern Mandarin, 韓 Hán **[g]ˤar* is pronounced similarly to 漢 Hàn, Old Chinese **n̥ˤar-s*. Particularly before the ability to easily print accents, the writing Hann, an older romanization, serves to distinguish the Warring States period country from the Han Dynasty. For simplicity's sake, I follow the older convention. All Old Chinese reconstructions are from Baxter / Sagart 2014.

18 Pines 2017, 8.

the need for scribes at all levels of the hierarchy was already resulting in massively increased recruitment from all backgrounds, creating a new class of literate administrators known as the *shi* 士.[19] Even before Lord Wen's policy, we see good evidence for even lower class individuals having the chance to learn and a chance at a career in the bureaucracy of a state during the lifetime of Confucius (551–479 BC) in texts such as the *Analects*. We also see the changes in material culture and management capacity come together in the form of peasant levee armies armed with mass produced weapons such as crossbows as conscription, and taxes become part of daily life.

This increase in the reach of the state, the resources it had access to, and the issues of practical administration lead to a flurry of intellectual activity, including philosophers such as Mencius 孟子, Xunzi 荀子, and Han Feizi.[20] A common thread in this discourse is the awareness that past societies had been smaller and less complex,[21] triggering debate on what lessons, if any, could be drawn from history. While the Confucians asserted the techniques of the sages of the past could be employed in the present, texts such as *Laozi* posited eternal, if esoteric principles could be of use, the fiercely iconoclastic *Book of Lord Shang* declared that only consideration of the present conditions and an understanding of human behavior was productive. The text itself was the result of a growing corpus of essays first by Lord Shang himself and later by his intellectual circle and descendants. As we shall see, this text is an interesting starting point for us because it takes as its starting point the assumption that humans are driven by a self-interested cost-benefit analysis, using this for its program of social reforms aimed at maximizing military strength.

The man who would become Lord Shang, born Gongsun Yang 公孫鞅, was a scion of a branch of the royal family of Wey 衛.[22] With little hope for advancement at home, Gongsun Yang went to Wei before ultimately heading to Qin 秦 to serve Lord Xiao between 361 and 359 BC, bringing with him ideas about law and administration from Wei. Qin is in the far west of the Warring States world and was often regarded as backwards by its rivals. There Shang rose to a position of authority, and archeology corroborates texts in suggesting that policies similar to those he

19 Ibid., 12–13.

20 As we shall see there is dramatic social change during this time and the philosophers are responding to questions of their moment. For an excellent introduction to these philosophers, see Goldin's 2020 *The Art of Chinese Philosophy*.

21 For more on the topic, see below.

22 In modern Mandarin, 衛 *Wèi*, Old Chinese **ɢʷat-s* is pronounced identically to its more powerful rival, Wei 魏, Old Chinese **N-qʰuj-s*. The older romanization, Wey, is often used to avoid confusion.

suggested about reforming landholding and administration were implemented. Specifically it appears that, in accordance with advice in the *Book of Lord Shang*, the maximum size of households was reduced by imposing penalties on having more than five adults cohabitating. This forced the population to spread out and cultivate more land. Roads were then constructed for this new field organization system and administration was reorganized into standardized units, rather than the old convention-driven fiefdoms. In tandem with this, the hereditary aristocracy was abolished and replaced with a set of semi-inheritable ranks to be handed out based on merit while the penal code was reorganized so as to optimize the use of penal labor.

In 340 BC, Gongsun Yang led a Qin army against his former employer, Wei, and defeated them. For his achievements, he was awarded fifteen settlements in Shang 商 and Yu 於 near the Chu and Wei border, thus gaining the title Lord [of] Shang, *shangjun* 商君. Unfortunately for Lord Shang, his successes seem to have caused resentment at court and Lord Xiao's successor, Huiwen (337–311 BC) had him executed.[23] However, the policies he initiated were continued and his intellectual circle continued working and writing up until the 230s, producing the texts found in *The Book of Lord Shang*.[24]

Over the chronological span of the text, there is an increased tendency to prioritize incentives as "the book's authors as well as Qin policy makers in general gradually learned that coercive means are insufficient for agricultural advancement and that lenient policies may be more expedient in the long term."[25] At the same time, the text is largely silent on the specifics of agromanagerial policy, perhaps because the text was intended to be "a polemical treatise rather than as a comprehensive blueprint for social and political development"[26] and the specific implementation was a distinct task. When the chapter, "Calculating the Land" was written ca. 350–330 BC underpopulation persisted, means of incentivizing new farmers came into greater focus, including ways of attracting immigrants. Still later, likely in the 250s BC, the "Attracting the People" chapter, seeing a chronic need to increase cultivation after Qin expansion and hydraulic projects across their domain, specifically advises exempting immigrants from taxes and military service for three generations and granting them unfettered access to wastelands for their first ten years in Qin. Archeology suggests that some policies along these lines were implemented, resulting in a massive influx.[27] In terms of systematic bureaucracy and a

23 Pines 2017, 1–24.

24 Ibid., 36–54.

25 Ibid., 77–78.

26 Ibid., 79.

27 Ibid., 199–200.

rational incentive structure, Qin policy (and the Han policies that followed) not only took much of what is seen in *Lord Shang*, but, in light of excavated texts, substantially expanded upon it. We find the Qin system lent draft animals, gave tax incentives to settle new land, distributed iron tools, and deployed convicts and corvee laborers to aid in the development of infrastructure projects.[28]

Expanding through a mix of annexation, subject domains, and puppets in the form of independent kings whose prime ministers were sent by Qin to encourage them to support Qin interests, Qin expansion slowed in the 320s BC, as Qin expansion now drew enough attention that coalitions formed against it much as they later did with Napoleon. Lacking the manpower to campaign under such conditions, Qin opted to mollify the coalition by returning some of the territory it had conquered and instead direct its attention south, towards the distant Sichuan basin. Because Qin is hemmed in by increasingly dry land to the north and mountains everywhere else, the fertile but less organized Sichuan basin would provide a sizable boost to the war effort. Launching the conquest in 316 BC, Qin then initiated policies to attract immigrants to cultivate new land even as it began massive flood control and irrigation projects. With its agricultural base secure, Qin defeated all rivals by 221 BC. Its ruler, King Zheng, invented a new title and renamed himself Qin Shi Huangdi 秦始皇帝, literally "First Qin Emperor", and is usually called Qin Shihuang. Eliminating competitors was sufficient cause to declare "reunification" complete, but the task of conquest did not end with the rivals; the Empire envisaged by Qin had no boundaries and armies marched in all directions. Qin Shihuang died suddenly in 210 BC and was succeeded by Qin Ershi, who seems to have been incompetent at best. The Qin soon collapsed amid mass uprisings and rebelling generals.

The question was not whether someone would continue the Qin's empire, but rather who. That person was Liu Bang 劉邦, a peasant from Chu and former Qin official. He had had a promising career until, while escorting a corvee labor column, some of his charges escaped, and, knowing the penalty was death, decided it would be better to die fighting. This is a repeated theme. While it may be literary flourish, it does seem many people, from high officials down to the average laborer, knowing the penalties that awaited them for events beyond their control performed a quick and rational cost-benefit analysis.[29] Thus, Liu Bang, like many others, was not a rebel of conscience against the Qin system, but rather was exemplifying the tendencies that *Lord Shang* had identified. His initial domain as an independent ruler was the region along the Han River, from whence his dynasty derived its name. It is worth noting at this point that most political names in Chinese history are toponyms. Qin

28 Ibid., 78.

29 Sage 1992, 158–161.

refers to a "fief"[30] in Western Shanxi, as does Zhou, and Han is ultimately derived from the Han River, which rises in southern Shaanxi and flows into the Yangzi in Hubei. Han 漢, in this paper, refers specifically to the Western Han, Xin, and Eastern Han Dynasties. While the Qin and Han ruling houses were from different regions and had their own traditions, the ruling elite was the same; a coalition of figures from across the territory of said Empire.

While the resulting struggle for dominance resulted in mass destruction as Liu Bang defeated his primary rival, Xiang Yu, most of the Qin apparatus was left in place. Liu Bang himself was not in nearly as secure a place as Qin Shihuang had been and had to grant greater leeway to his powerful supporters. These took the form of semi-independent kingdoms, resulting in a sort of hybrid system where the territory directly administered by the Emperor's bureaucracy was riddled with independent kings or princes. Some of these kingdoms were at the "margins" of the Empire, but others were in territory that had long been part of the "Chinese" world. For example, Shandong was home to a number of kingdoms between 195 and 110 BC, while Liu Bang's home territory in Jiangsu was also often a kingdom; the motive was administrative and political, rather than granting "unassimilated territories" a degree of autonomy. Some of these kings were Imperial scions.[31] While these kingdoms existed at the pleasure of the Emperor and could, in theory, be revoked at any time, but some, such as Nanyue, were de facto independent realms only notionally in the Han Empire. Liu Bang's legitimacy ultimately rested on his ability to share power and link incentives.[32] While the Han appeal to legitimacy came to rest on not being the Qin, and, only much later, on Confucianism,[33] the Han actually continued the legal and administrative practices of the Qin. The Qin are ultimately remade as a mirror to what the writer wants the Han to be.[34] To be sure, the Qin, like the Han, engaged in bloody warfare, spent lives in massive construction projects, and even engaged in the occasional text control program. However, they do not seem to have suppressed Confucianism, engaged in mass text destruction, levied harsher taxes, or imposed crueler punishments than their contemporaries and successor.[35] It is also important to note that the Qin did not have a comprehensive state ideology.

30 Technically the pre-Imperial system was not feudal. For a discussion, see Li 2006. However, the term "fief", in its non-technical sense, is close enough for our purposes that I will use it throughout the paper.

31 Leung 2018.

32 Wang 2001.

33 Cai 2014.

34 For a discussion of the historiographic issues around the Qin Dynasty, see Sanft 2018.

35 Kim / Lai 2018.

Qin display texts show that Qin Shihuang himself employed normative virtues commonly associated with Confucian thought and antithetical to *Lord Shang*.

Since Hulsewé's pessimistic dictum in 1955 that little could be known for certain about Early Imperial Law,[36] decades of excavated texts, both properly excavated and looted, have transformed our understanding of Early Imperial Law.[37] The body of text is too large for me to deal with in this text; instead, I am working off of Sanft; Barbieri-Low and Yates; and Kim and Lai.

Barbieri-Low and Yates' study of the Zhangjiashan Tomb 247 texts examine them in terms of the continuity between earlier Qin texts and later Han texts. This particular tomb, sealed in 186 BC, contained two legal texts, *The Second Year Ordinances* (*Ernian lüling* 二年律令) and *Book of Submitted Doubtful Cases* (*Zouyan shu* 奏讞書).

Barbieri-Low and Yates consider 11 other corpora from Warring States to Han. Tomb 50 at Haojiaping, in Suchuan, sealed 309 BC, has a copy of a royal mandate cites from what we recognize as an ancestor to the Statutes on Agriculture.[38] Shuihudi, Tomb 11 (late warring states) provides us with legal and administrative material. The Yuelu Academy texts (which were looted, rather than being properly excavated) contain 7 cases from the reign of King Zheng (better known as Qin Shihuang) spanning 225–215 BC. The Liye Cache, from Hunan (222–209 BC), mostly unpublished in 2015 is from a town in Chu conquered by Qin. The cache is a set of working documents dumped in a well at the end of that administration, giving us rich insight into Qin legal and bureaucratic procedure.[39] Longgang, Tomb 6 in Hubei, with material dating from 221–207 BC has post 221 copies of pre-221 BC statutes; elements of vocabulary have been changed to fit the new realities. Shortly postdating Tomb 247 is Zhangjiashan Tomb 336, sealed 173 BC, and we have a number of other Han legal material:

- Songbai Tomb 1 in Hubei, sealed 133 BC
- Juyuan Gansu, mostly 102 BC – AD 31
- Dunhuang, Gansu, 98 BC – AD 137
- Xuquan Postal Relay Station near Dunhuang, in Gansu, which spans the Western Han to the Western Jin was mostly unpublished as of 2015.
- Yinwan Tomb 6 in Jiangsu dated to 13–10 BC
- Gurenti in Hunan, AD 89–104

36 Hulsewé 1955, 4 (*non vidi*).

37 Kim / Lai 2018, 386.

38 Barbieri-Low / Yates 2015, 41.

39 Ibid., 45–46.

Ancient legal scholars and commentators tell us Statutes, 律 *Lü* are time-honored legal principles, with broad or general application, the fundamental laws of the state. Ordinances, 令 *Ling* are created for exigent conditions, like Gaozu's ordinance of May–June 202 BC, offering amnesty to refugees and debt slaves. However in legal caches such as Zhangjiashan we see that the distinction is not so clear cut. What we see across these documents is that laws and procedures largely remain in place. Laws are changed, added, or suspended on occasion, but the texts show a great deal of continuity between 309, 221, 186 BC, and beyond. [40] For example, the Statutes at Zhangjiashan tomb 247 are dated partly on the size of the coins involved, namely the banliang issued by Empress Lü in 186 BC, as well as reviving older Qin laws banning private casting of coins in an attempt to secure a government monopoly on minting. Said law was promptly abrogated by Emperor Wen in 174 BC.[41]

The catch is that according to the received tradition in the *Shiji* and *Hanshu*. In those traditions, Liu Bang, upon capturing the Qin capital Xianyang in 207 BC, made a contract with the local elders, discarding all Qin law save for three simple rules on murder, assault, and robbery. According to the "suspiciously more detailed" account in the much later *Hanshu*, these three laws proved insufficient, and so he ordered Chancellor of State, Xiao He to prepare a collection statutes based on the laws of Qin, selecting those that were appropriate and discarding the rest.[42] If such a document ever existed, it does not survive and, indeed, Barbieri-Low and Yates find that it is impossible for Xiao He to have created a code in nine sections from scratch on the orders of Emperor Gaozu:[43]

> The Zhangjiashan legal texts do not represent an isolated early-Han expression of legal principles or legislation but reside in a continuous stream in the development of traditional Chinese law. They demonstrate a nearly comprehensive continuation of Qin legal norms and procedures into the Early Han, with only minor modifications and innovations.[44]

In other words, the Han continued the institutions of the Qin, and the difference between the two regimes would have been non-existent to the average peasant. Interestingly, law could be created top down or bottom up, with lower ranking offices being able to submit a proposal for a law (and paying a large processing fee) either

40 Ibid., 80–82.

41 Ibid., 63.

42 Ibid., 78–79.

43 Ibid., 65.

44 Ibid., 220.

way, the Emperor had final say.[45] The legal code just kept growing and it was left until 230 BC, under the Wei, to promulgate an entire new code.[46]

Much of how the Han and Qin operated must be left to reconstruction and there is the risk of historiographic bias, particularly when dealing with texts like *Shiji*, *Hanshu*, or *Debate on Salt and Iron*, but with these texts, we have periodic windows into not simply laws, but bureaucratic caches of working documents across the period.

Where Hulsewé in 1981 declared that the Qin legal rules for regulating the minutae were absurdities that were unimportant, Barbieri-Low and Yates strongly disagree. This was how the Qin hoped to win the "hearts and minds"; managing the flow of information and personnel through the empire was essential to binding it together as in these texts we see the Empire in action.[47]

Thus, policy and thought flows smoothly across these historiographic boundaries, with a real institutional turning point coming late in the Western Han, which had never fully solved the problem of controlling the elite. Furthermore, legalism, the putative school of Lord Shang, Guanzi, and Han Feizi 韓非子, is anachronistic.[48] There was no self-identified legalist school of thought in the Warring States period nor does it meaningfully delineate a particular intellectual current. The law *fa* 法 in legalism *fajia* 法家, has a somewhat different semantic sphere than the English "law". Long division, a cake recipe, the collating order of a file system, and the tax code are all *fa*, i.e., methods. The word for penal law is *xing* 刑, and statutes more broadly are *lü* 律, so a better translation of *fa* would be "method," but unfortunately, we cannot speak of Ancient Chinese Methodists.

In terms of policy, the Western Han administration was characterized by the need to compromise, a legacy of its foundation. There was a constant tension between the central bureaucracy and the nobility. Early in the dynasty, these were more typically larger kingdoms, but under Han Wudi (r. 141–87 BC), they were more typically smaller marquisates.[49] Regardless of their scope and name, Western Han rulers regularly conferred such feudal titles to supporters, only for them to have to be revoked by successors.[50] The pivotal moment in the Western Han seems to have been the reign of Emperor Wudi (r. 104–87 BC), who managed to largely reign in the

---

45 Ibid., 82–83.

46 Ibid., 88.

47 Ibid., 212.

48 For a thorough discussion of the problems with the idea of Legalism and the translation as Legalism, see Goldin 2011.

49 Leung 2018, 170.

50 Ibid., *passim*.

nobility as the Qin had before him. However, Wudi's balancing act was unstable and his expansionist policies against the Xiongnu created financial problems that plagued his successors. It is also during his reign that a coup attempt seems to have resulted in purges of various forms of ritual specialists, leading to a play for power from the Confucians. This would eventually bear fruit for them under Emperor Xuan (r. 74–48 BC), but until then, the Confucians held very little political power. [51] The result of Wudi's reign was a civil bureaucracy attempting to do more with less. Even as raising revenues from the peasantry became crucial, changes in land ownership patterns lead to the rise of large landowners, who continued to grow in power even after the usurper Wang Mang's (r. AD 9–23) attempts to redistribute land.[52] Thus, with the refounding of the Empire following his death and the increasing antiquarian rhetoric used to justify the restoration of the Imperial House, the Eastern Han was very different in terms of its administrative structure.[53] What all of this means for us is that we will consider policy from the Warring States into the Western Han together.

Finally, it is important to be aware of the diversity in this world. Despite the modern narrative of the unification of China, a push for unity in the Warring States period, and the creation of a historiographic sequence beginning with the legendary *Xia* 夏 and an identity that took Xia as its name, we simultaneously see an increasingly strong awareness of regional difference.[54] This is not simply in the form of a nascent Chinese self and cultural others, but also and particularly in terms of difference between "Chinese" states. At the same time, cultural others are major and legitimate players in the competition to succeed the Zhou, and despite the differences in language and material culture, the strategy tends to be one of incorporation. While some elite forms are privileged, the self-other boundary is quite fluid.[55] The goal of this competition is not to rule over the Xia, but rather to rule over the world, *tianxia* 天下. China is not the thing to be unified, but rather the result of the unified Empire.[56] In sum, when we look at policy and philosophy from the Warring States to Western Han, we are seeing the reflection of people living in an increasingly complex society looking to unite and rule a diverse realm. Despite historiographic boundaries, these systems flow into each other, and the Qin and Western Han are very similar.

---

51 Cai 2014, Chapter 5.

52 Leung 2018, 176–177.

53 For an introduction to Eastern Han, see Tse 2018.

54 Goldin 2015.

55 See, e.g., Poo 2005.

56 Pines 2009.

3. *The Book of Lord Shang*'s Rational Actor Theory

The Book of Lord Shang is a practical text, not a systematic one. Its focus is on harnessing human self-interest to build a state strong enough not only to survive, but conquer the world. This requires the focusing of society on warfare, which in turn, requires a focus on agriculture in order to supply a massive army.

Three key ideas are:

- Humans are motivated by rational self-interest, i.e., a key tenet of Rational Actor Theory.
- Institutions modulate how that rational self-interest manifests. As in NIE, institutions are formal and informal, but here, their origins are attributed to sages.
- Dissemination of knowledge of the incentive structure and its impartial implementation suffices to achieve compliance.

Given the intensifying warfare of the Warring States Period, the starting premise that a strong army is needed for the survival of the state, much less the goal of reunification, is quite understandable. Survival requires a strong army and a strong economic base. An efficiently organized state, it suggests, will be able to take up the Zhou mantle and rule the world. All other concerns, such as morality, can wait until after unification has been achieved. Towards this end, proper use and motivation of human resources is needed. According to the text,

> 民[57]之性，度而取長，稱而取重，權而索利
> The nature of the people is such that when measuring, they take what is longer; when weighing, they take what is heavier; when using scales, they seek profits.[58]

This is then put in the context of the state's interests, seeing as the state requires soldiers and farmers. However:

> 夫農民之所苦；而戰，民之所危也。犯其所苦，行其所危者，計也。故民生則計利，死則慮名。名利之所出，不可不審也。利出於地，則民盡力；名出於戰，則民致死。
> Farming is what the people consider bitter; war is what the people consider dangerous. Yet they brave what they consider bitter and perform what they consider dangerous because of calculation [of name and benefit]. *Thus, in [ordinary] life, the people calculate benefits; [facing] death, they think of name*

57 I am aware of Gassmann's suggestion that the *min* and *ren* are different groups, but in all of the texts used here, I do not believe there is grounds to suspect that they are anything but synonymous. For a response to Gassmann 2006, see Crone 2017.

58 All translations of *Book of Lord Shang* are from Pines 2017, here ibid., 6.8.

> *(repute).*[59] One cannot but investigate whence name and benefit come. When benefits come from land, the people fully utilize their strength; when name comes from war, the people are ready to die.[60]

As we can see, the means to motivate people are based on taking advantage of their calculation of name and benefit. These are forms of self-interest:

> 夫治國者能盡地力而致民死者，名與利交至。民之生，饑而求食，勞而求佚，苦則索樂，辱則求榮，此民之情也。民之求利，失禮之法；求名，失性之常。奚以論其然也？今夫盜賊上犯君上之所禁，下失臣子之禮，故名辱而身危，猶不止者，利也。其上世之士，衣不煖膚，食不滿腸，苦其志意，勞其四肢，傷其五臟，而益裕廣耳，非性之常，而為之者，名也。故曰名利之所湊，則民道之。
>
> The ability of the well-governed state to fully utilize its land resources and to cause the people to die [for its sake] is due to the name (repute) and benefit that it brings [to the people]. The nature of the people is to seek food when they are hungry, to seek respite when they are belabored, to seek joy when they are embittered, to seek glory when they are humiliated: this is the people's disposition. In seeking benefit, the people lose the standard of ritual; in seeking name (repute), they lose the constant of their nature. How can I demonstrate this? Now, criminals above violate the prohibitions of rulers and superiors and below lose the ritual of subjects and sons; hence, their name is dishonored and their body endangered, but they still do not stop: this is because of benefit. In the generations of old, there were men-of-service (*shi*) who did not have enough clothes to warm their skin or enough food to fill their bowels; they exerted their four limbs and injured their five internal organs above, but they behaved ever more broad-heartedly: this is because of name (repute). Hence, it is said: wherever name and benefit meet, the people will go in this direction.[61]

There are a few significant things to take note of here. Firstly, full utilization of resources in production and warfare is based on the use of self-interest. Benefit is material; as we can see with the criminals. Nature is similarly straightforward, being, as we saw above, self-interested fulfillment of preferences. Name (repute) and ritual require a bit more explanation. Name is reputation and contains much in terms of one's social standing, but also has more tangible benefits. In the system *Lord Shang* proposes, the noble titles one can earn for compliance with policy are a part of this

59 Emphasis mine.

60 Pines 2017, 6.5.

61 Ibid., 6.4.

idea of name. Leveraging name requires specific social institutions, as we shall see in a moment. Ritual is a set of behaviors that structure human social relationships, with prototypical examples being rulers and ministers, parents and children, and spouses. One who loses their sense of ritual will have no problem harming others for their goals, while one who seeks name will act in accordance with behaviors prized by their society. One might be left wondering why *Lord Shang* does not simply propose instituting a cult of self-sacrifice on behalf of the state or nation and thus avoid the radical reforms of abolishing the nobility and instituting a complex administrative bureaucracy, instead using more traditional appeals to masculinity or patriotism to motivate people to do the "right" thing. The answer here is complicated and gets to the heart of Lord Shang's assessment of human behavior and social structure.

Most simply, *Lord Shang* does not believe that it is feasible to use ritual to guide people with virtue under the present circumstances. However, there are a few other reasons tied into human behavior. *Lord Shang* sees human behavior as fundamentally self-interested such that virtue is not "foolproof" and also has a deep distrust of rhetoric. We will begin with the former as a way of looking at *Lord Shang*'s ideas of social institutions and later return to the topic of rhetoric. To begin with, the search for social recognition is still a form of self-interest and thus the complement to the quest for material benefits in 7.2:

> 親親者，以私為道也，而中正者使私無行也。此三者，非事相反也，民道弊而所重易也世事變而行道異也。
>
> Thus, in the early ages, [the people] were attached to relatives and were devoted to themselves; in the middle ages, they elevated the worthy and rejoiced in benevolence; in the recent age, they esteem nobility and respect officials. When they elevated the worthy, they used the Way to overcome each other; but the establishment of the ruler caused the worthies to become useless. Being attached to relatives, they considered selfishness as the Way; but the establishment of impartiality and propriety caused selfishness no longer to be practiced. In these three cases, it is not that their affairs are opposite; it is that the Way of the people is base and what they value changes. When the affairs of the world change, one should implement a different Way.

So here, we can see that while the surface behavior is different, the underlying motivations are the same. This means that in *Lord Shang*, institutions play a crucial role in structuring behavior. This becomes clearer as we see the model of social development operant in *Lord Shang*.

Institutions are the key factor in structuring the outcomes of rational behavior down to the most basic units of society. As we shall see, the text believes that social institutions are instituted to facilitate cooperation as society grows more complex. Even kinship is not a socially unmediated scale for cooperation as we see in 7.1:

> 天地設，而民生之。當此之時也，民知其母而不知其父，其道親親而愛私 When Heaven and Earth were formed, the people were born.[62] At that time, the people knew their mothers but not their fathers; their way was one of attachment to relatives and of selfishness.

Primeval kinship structure the text imagines was drastically different from what was common in *Lord Shang*'s time.[63] Similarly, in another description of primeval social development, we are told that (18.1):

> 昔者昊英之世，以伐木殺獸，人民少而木獸多。人帝[64]之世，不麛不卵，官無供備之民，死不得用槨。事不同，皆王者，時異也。神農之世，男耕而食，婦織而衣，刑政不用而治，甲兵不起而王。神農既沒，以強勝弱，以眾暴寡。故黃帝作為君臣上下之義，父子兄弟之禮，夫婦妃匹之合
>
> Formerly, in the age of Hao Ying, the people cut trees and slaughtered animals [for food]; the people were few, whereas trees and animals plenty. In the age of the Human Thearch the people consumed neither fawns nor eggs; officials had no servants to support them, and at death they could not obtain outer coffins. Undertakings [of Hao Ying and the Human Thearch] were not the same, but they all were Monarchs: this is because the times were different. In the age of Shennong, men plowed to obtain food, women wove to obtain clothing; he used neither punishments nor regulations, yet there was order; armor and weapons were not set up, but [Shennong] became a Monarch. After Shennong, the strong overpowered the weak, the many lorded over the few. Hence, the Yellow Thearch created the duties of rulers and ministers and of superiors and inferiors, rituals of fathers and

62 Pines translation here is odd since the 之 does not permit a passive, but in the context, no other meaning makes sense. Presumably the 之 is serving as a deictic, "there".

63 The text may have one of a few things in mind here; a society of such low complexity that there is no tracking of paternity, or some form of matriarchal society. Uxorilocal structures are traditional in parts of Southern China, so it is possible something like this is envisaged.

64 Many recensions have *Huangdi* 黃帝, the Yellow Thearch here, but there is considerable reason to understand this as a mistake for *Rendi* 人帝, the Human Thearch. For a discussion, see Pines 2017, 297.

> sons and of elder and younger brothers, and harmony between husband and wife and between spouses.

Here, the text imagines rulers as preceding agriculture. As social complexity and population grow, further organizational measures are required. It is the Yellow Thearch who teaches proper kinship behavior, arising after population increase forces agriculture and division of labor under Shennong, whose name literally means Divine Farmer. These kinship behaviors accompany behaviors for other forms of social hierarchy. Notice that officials existed at least since the age of the Human Thearch, but codification is not required until later.

This idea that kinship, like other forms of social organization, does not come naturally is seen in Confucian texts as well. For example, in "Da Xue", we are told that family is to be used as the paradigm not because it is easy, but rather because it is so difficult to do right.[65] Family units are the focus of so much of this discourse because they are the context in which people live and thus the practical locus of action, not because they are idealized a sort of primal base-case. Kin norms are introduced as part of a larger structure of social organization. In 18.1 we see Sages innovate new structures of organization, when families are introduced as a level of organization, it is alongside other forms of social organization. This is part of a process of specialization and the development of institutions.

This developmental model is picked up by Lord Shang's intellectual opponents, most notably Xunzi and his intellectual heir, Lu Jia.[66] For *Xunzi*, as with *Lord Shang* and *Lu Jia*, social institutions are well considered, deliberate responses on the part of Sages. *Xunzi* is interesting because, unlike *Lord Shang*, we are given a clear explanation of how human reasoning works; while *Xunzi* has great faith that the former sages got things right, they are not fundamentally different from the rest of humanity and work through what we would recognize as an empirical method of abductive reasoning.

---

65 人之其所親愛而辟焉... 故好而知其惡，惡而知其美者，天下鮮矣... 此謂身不修不可以齊其家 / "People are partial to that which they love ... there are few in the world who recognize the bad qualities in what they love and the merits of that which they hate. Thus, it is said that if a person is not cultivated, they cannot manage their family." *Liji* 2000, "Daxue 大學", 187.

66 Xunzi lived at the end of the Warring States period and Lu Jia in the Early Western Han. See Pines / Shelach 2005 for the legacy and antecedents of Lord Shang's model of state formation.

Firstly, human language is a construct:

> 名無固宜，約之以命，約定俗成謂之宜，異於約則謂之不宜。名無固實，約之以命實，約定俗成，謂之實名。名有固善，徑易而不拂，謂之善名。
> Names are without intrinsic suitability. It is agreed upon and declared [appropriate], the consensus becomes custom and thus it is called appropriate. If it differs from the agreed [upon meaning], then it is called inappropriate. Names have no intrinsic reality. It is agreed upon and declared real. The consensus becomes custom and thus it is called a real name. Names have an intrinsic goodness: If they are direct, easy, and not at odds with the object, then that is a good name.[67]

Thus we depend on sensory perception:

> 心有**徵**知。**徵**知，則**緣**耳而知聲可也，**緣**目而知形可也。
> The mind has a discriminating perception. Discriminating perception works because the evidence of the ears allows the perception of sounds, the evidence of the eyes allows the perception of forms.[68]

The critical verb here is *zhi* 知, which covers perception, recognition, and knowledge. The senses provide data, which then allow for the identification of various sounds and objects:

> 然而**徵**知必將待天官之當簿其類，然後可也。五官簿之而不知，心**徵**知而無說，則人莫不然謂之不知。此所緣而以同異也
> This discriminating knowledge must wait for the sense organs to be impressed by its type [of sensory data], and only after that can [recognition occur]. If the five senses experience something, but it is not recognized, or the mind perceives it discriminatingly, but can offer no explanation, then among people, nobody will not call it not knowing. This testimony [of the senses] is [how we] make sameness and difference.[69]

In other words, the process of understanding relies on building up a model based on the data one has collected. This is thus the process by which social institutions were generated in any given case. However, the actual development of institutions is best seen in the work of Xunzi's intellectual descendant, Lu Jia.

In his essay "道基 Daoji" "Foundation of the Way", narrating the formation of the natural world, Lu Jia gives the narrative of human history as a sequence of

67 *Xunzi*, "Zhengming 正名", 707–740.

68 *Xunzi*, "Zhengming 正名", 707–740.

69 *Xunzi*, "Zhengming 正名", 707–740.

historical moments that necessitate a responses. Note that these innovations are based on an examination of the situation that lead to a solution to a problem and that for Lu Jia, this is an ongoing process requiring human intervention at specific moments, typically when increases in social complexity have rendered old structures inviable. I have selected a few of the episodes:[70]

> 民人食肉飲血，衣皮毛；至於神農，以為行蟲走獸，難以養民，乃求可食之物，嘗百草之實，察酸苦之味，教人食五穀。
> The populace ate flesh and drank blood; was clothed with skin and fur. Then Shennong, saw the bugs and beasts could not feed the populace, and sought edible things, prized the hundred grass' seeds, investigated sour and bitter flavors, and taught the people to eat the 5 grains ...
>
> 川谷交錯，風化未通，九州絕隔，未有舟車之用，以濟深致遠；於是奚仲乃橈曲為輪，因直為轅，駕馬服牛，浮舟杖楫，以代人力。
> The rivers and valleys were muddled and the customs had not spread, the nine territories were divided, but there were no boats and carts in use to cross the deeps and reach the far. At this, Xi Zhong bent the wood to make wheels, made straight axles, bridled horses and domesticated the ox, and floated boats and made oars to row and punt so as to replace human labor ...
>
> 鑠金、鏤木、分苞、燒埴以備器械，於是民知輕重，好利惡難，避勞就逸；於是皋陶乃立獄制罪，懸賞設罰，異是非，明好惡，檢奸邪，消佚亂。
> Xi Zhong smelt metal, inlaid wood, divided rushes, heated pots so as to make tools, at this people understood Qing Zhong[71]. They liked profit and disliked difficulty, avoided labor and fled. At this, Gaoyao then established prisons to control felons, hung rewards and established punishments, distinguished correct and incorrect, illuminated good and bad, investigated crime and wickedness, and diminished excess and chaos ...
>
> 民知畏法，而無禮義；於是中聖乃設辟雍庠序之教，以正上下之儀，明父子之禮、君臣之義，使強不凌弱、眾不暴寡，棄貪鄙之心，興清潔之行。
> The people recognized and feared law, but were without ritual and goodness. At this, the middle sages [King Wen and the Duke of Zhou] then built palace and village schools to teach protocol; with correcting the high and low's virtue, illuminate father and son's ritual, minister and ruler's benevolence, set the strong to not oppress the weak, made the many not abuse

70 Lu Jia 2020, 21–34.

71 This is the economic principle of value, see below.

> the few, rejected greedy and low minds, and implemented clear and placid conduct …

Notice the logical sequence in these innovations. Equally significant is that these sages appear throughout history. Sagehood is something people can and do achieve, but of equal import is that a single primeval sage like Shennong does not invent everything. Why? Beside the existence of a larger set of traditions about these figures that places them in different times, it would make no sense. There was no social need for carts and barges before the invention of agriculture. Morality was not of critical import before agriculture demanded that people collaborate. Inventions are socially conditioned and behavioral codes are one of those innovations.

By the time of the composition of the *Hanshu* in the Eastern Han, this is so much of a given that in the section on "Laws" 刑法志 *Xingfa Zhi*, the introduction tells us that humans, lacking claws and fangs, fur and feathers, simply could not survive in nature without cooperation. To ensure that there would be enough, the first sages created behavioral codes and instantiated morality. The purpose of law is to codify moral customs. The purpose of moral customs is to allow for cooperation, which in turn allow increased output. Morality, statecraft, and technologies are innovations conditioned by social moments. This process of social fine-tuning is ongoing. At the same time, these developments are in response to the underlying constancies and cycles.

When then, is the difference between *Lord Shang* and Confucians? While *Mencius* argued that moral sentiments built into human nature were sufficient to provide the basis for moral behavior, this text did not form the basis of the mainstream until late in the Eastern Han. Instead, arguing specifically against *Mencius*, *Xunzi* fully admits that laws, rewards, and punishments do work for the exact reasons that *Lord Shang* says they do. However, after this point, Xunzi diverges, arguing that ritual is transformative.[72] Crucial is the method by which ritual operates; it works through emotive cognition. It communicates on an emotional level, but also it gives ways of sublimating and dealing with emotions.[73] The rites habituate proper human relationships, but *Xunzi* takes emotions seriously not just as a source of human rationality, but as a mode of cognition. Pure rationality may be prioritized and understood as being able to override emotive cognition, but *Xunzi* sees it as something that can be constructively utilized. Thus *Xunzi*'s theory of ritual is predicated on complexity

72 This is more or less the critique of Qin he levels in the essays "Ruxiao 儒效" and "Qiangguo 彊國," where Qin has everything except the transformative approach to virtue that a Confucian would provide.

73 Goldin 2020, 174–182.

in human motivation and cognition. Here then, we see that *Lord Shang*'s emphasis on the law is distinctive and derives from a theory of human motivation that understands humans as beings whose emotional lives are ultimately reducible to and overruled by rationality and thus can be neglected on the grand scale. At the same time, the self-interested nature of humans requires an administrative structure to coordinate them.

With this model in mind, then, we are equipped to understand the way *Lord Shang* envisages feedback between the ruler and the population. In *Lord Shang*, while sweeping social reforms are proposed so as to orient the entire society around warfare and agriculture, people are understood not to be perfectly elastic, they need to be communicated to through existing social/cultural structures (6.9):

> 故聖人之為國也，觀俗立法則治，察國事本則宜。不觀時俗，不察國本，則其法立而民亂，事劇而功寡，此臣之所謂過也。
> Hence, in ruling the state, the sage establishes laws after observing customs and then attains orderly rule; he inspects the roots of the state's affairs and then acts appropriately. Without the observation of current customs and without the inspection of the roots of the state, laws can be established, but the people will be in turmoil; undertakings will be numerous, but achievements few. This is what I, your minister, call "to err."

In other words, the laws need to make sense to the people in order for them to be followed. In addition to this, because institutions are coordinating spontaneous behavior already occurring across society, it is better to work in tandem with and simply direct productive behavior people are already engaged in:

> 上令而民知所以應，器成於家而行於官，則事斷於家。故王者刑賞斷於民心，器用斷於家。...治則家斷，亂則君斷.治國貴下斷...家斷則有餘
> When superiors issue orders and the people know how to respond,[74] when utensils take shape in the household and are utilized by officials, then affairs are determined by a household. Hence, [in the state of] the True Monarch, punishments and rewards are determined by the people's hearts; the use of the utensils is determined at the household level ... When there is orderly rule, decisions are made by a household; when there is turmoil, they are made by the ruler. The well-ordered state values decisions made below ... When decisions are made by the household, one has extra [time][75]

74 Pines has "know to respond", but the 所以應 means something closer to "how to respond", which fits the point better.

75 Pines 2017, 5.9.

Local affairs can be handled at the local level; there is no need to mandate every aspect of society. In fact, we see this enshrined in actual Qin and Han legal procedures, where protocol exists for local offices to submit proposals for new laws up the chain to their superiors.[76]

Instead, the government's task is to structure incentives to guide people's natural behavior. There are two things to take from this. Firstly, people are understood to have some degree of attachment to existing institutions, a limitation to rationality. Secondly, behavior across society on the local level is understood to naturally produce patterns of exchange. We will return to both of these topics below, but before that, we must return to the matter of rhetoric and ideology in motivation by considering the attitudes towards law/method and rhetoric in the text.

Firstly, because people are understood as rational actors, the text's emphasis on harsh punishment is based on a notion that "clear punishments eliminate executions" because people are expected to do a cost-benefit analysis.[77] Again, contrary to traditional historiography that claims that the Qin code was particularly brutal, excavated legal texts show us that it was not significantly different from those around it and continued to be used in the Han. This said, to our eyes, it seems very cruel. Penal mutilation is common, but the core of the system is penal labor. *Lord Shang* makes crime and punishment into an economic transaction. Convicts are to be used as part of the corvee labor system, working on various government projects. All this said, repeated statements such as the promise that merciless punishments will eventually restore "the utmost virtue" in the world (7.5), (4.8), (17.3), etc. indicate a more optimistic note. The idea is that when it becomes practical, moral rule can and must be restored. Pines argues that it is best to understand the text as placing itself at a transitional stage, wherein the extreme measures it advocates will be able to secure a better future.[78]

Rewards and punishments only work when universally known and understood (26.6):

> 故聖人立[79]天下而無刑死者，非不刑殺也，法令明白易知，為置法官吏為之師以道之知。萬民皆知所避就；避禍就福，而皆以自治也。
> Hence, when the sages are established in All-under-Heaven, and nobody suffers capital punishment, it is not because they have abolished capital punishment. Rather, the laws are clear and easily understandable, and law

76 Barbieri-Low / Yates 2015, 82–83.

77 Pines 2017, 7.3.

78 Ibid., 98–99.

79 Here, either a preposition is elided or the sages are establishing those in All-Under-Heaven. Either way, Pines' translation suffices.

> officials and clerks are established as teachers to direct [the people] to understand [the law]. The myriad people all understand what should be avoided and what should be pursued. They should avoid disaster and pursue good fortune: all will thereby govern themselves.

The idea is that people will internalize the law code and, in seeking benefit, will do what the state desires. Awareness of this law code is also the best check on the greatest threat to the state, official malfeasance.[80] But what form is this "teaching"? Why law and not ritual?

This brings us back to the topic of rhetoric, ideology, and indoctrination. Quite simply, *Lord Shang* thinks that universal awareness of the law is the only standardization of information required to produce the desired ends. The text has an intense dislike for rhetoric and virtue appeals, seeing them as a plague upon a country. Experts in the rites spend their time arguing about the minutiae of things like the tuning of the bells required for ritual music instead of focused on maximizing agricultural output.[81] Ideology is also inimical to the ruthless pragmatism that *Lord Shang* advises.

Finally, as they say, talk is cheap. To an extent, *Lord Shang* advocates controlling the information the general population can access. By keeping the people "ignorant", they also will be easier to motivate. However, the "learning" here, a term central in Confucian discourse, is here associated with rhetoric. In passages such as 3.10, we see the concern that if the peasantry begins "learning", they will begin acting like the hordes of "persuaders" who use "grand words" to befuddle rulers and take advantage of them. The concern is not about the content of this "learning", but rather that it will distract the populace from the essential matters as they begin to seek social advancement through rhetoric instead of tangible benefit.

Pines points out that the text does talk of *jiao* 教 "teaching" or "indoctrinating" the populace, but he argues that this is not ideological, but rather "the people should understand where their benefit lies and whence the danger comes, as a result of which they will comply with the state's demands out of sheer self-interest".[82] While he hesitates to attribute irony to a text as humorless as *Lord Shang*, Shang's usage of "teaching", together with the treatment of knowledge and learning as empty rhetoric does seem like an attack on schools such as Confucianism or even

---

80 Pines 2017, 82–83. For a translation, see Watson 1964, 56–78.

81 A good example of what Lord Shang has in mind here can be seen in the "Debating Warfare" chapter of *Xunzi*, where Xunzi argues that, rather than investing in the army, the better option is to focus on proper ritual because that will obviate the need for fighting.

82 Pines 2017, 93.

Mohists, whose adherents would have been trained in the classics, the arts of persuasion, and looked to virtue for solutions to their problems. While a Confucian sees education as a constant process to mold the population into one capable of behaving humanely on their own, *Lord Shang* is content to take the more immediate solution and thus a proper education consists of knowing the rules.[83]

In the case of *Lord Shang*, all of this energy is to be directed towards warfare and here Pines makes another point that is significant enough that I will simply cite it in full:

> It is important to notice here that, fundamentally, the *Book of Lord Shang* does not envision any more sophisticated military indoctrination. Any person knowledgeable of the history of mass armies in the Western Hemisphere may be perplexed: Why did the authors not promote any positive means of encouraging the people's commitment to war? Why do we never encounter in this text (or any other) the adoration of the martial spirit akin, for example, to the Romans' maxim '*Dulce et decorum est pro patria mori*' (It is sweet and glorious to die for the fatherland); the dehumanization of the enemy; the identification of martiality with masculinity; the presentation of war as the only way to ensure the people's security; or any other device employed worldwide to encourage men to fight? The answer perhaps has to do with the authors' fundamental mistrust of any education and indoctrination. Rather than being brainwashed to sacrifice themselves for the state out of some abstract commitment, the people should be directed to do so according to their intrinsic and immutable selfishness. Fighting to the death in order to attain rank or just to avoid the inevitable punishment inflicted on deserters and their kin is preferable to fighting for the sake of some chimera. Instead of cheating the people with hollow ideological constructs, the authors prefer to clarify substantial gains and losses from engagement in war or evading it, respectively, and then let the people's basic 'disposition' direct them to the ends desired by the state.[84]

In the final reckoning, *The Book of Lord Shang* does not propose an ideological superstructure that should bind the people together or that should somehow influence their actions. Indoctrination is envisioned primarily as a negative action, which should prevent the corrosive impact of moralizing discourse from distracting the people from agriculture and warfare. The authors, however, do not put forward any alternative set of messages to replace this discourse. Similarly, whenever they talk

83 Ibid., 92–94.

84 Ibid., 94–95.

of 'teaching' or of 'transforming' (*hua* 化) and unifying the people's customs, they do not imply any active dissemination of ideas or ideals among the populace. A perfect state should manipulate its subjects exclusively through the combination of rewards and punishments: clearly outlined rules that explicate personal gains and losses for compliance or transgression. Any ideological incentives then become redundant.[85]

Furthermore, while the state does not and cannot practically have a monopoly on thought,[86] according to *Lord Shang*, it can and should have a monopoly on paths to social advancement and material benefit. With the backing of the state, ideology has nothing to offer but ideals, whereas compliance with policy has tangible benefits. Since *Lord Shang* understands compliance with ideology as part of the search for self-interest, it is redundant alongside the tangible incentives the state can offer and should the state invest in virtue-based appeals, it becomes susceptible to fouling by self-interested rhetoricians.

In fact, not only did the Qin and Han, in contrast to some later dynasties, take pains to ensure their legal codes were available and understood by the broader population,[87] texts such as the *Hanshu* contain a number of instances where the common people sought redress; reactions from the government characters suggest that the people were well within their rights to assemble, complain, and protest.[88] Sanft argues that Qin policy was designed to communicate the new social reality, not simply through monuments such as inscriptions, but by making the bureaucracy a part of life.[89] As we saw above, it was not simply for collecting taxes, but also source of support, providing not just agricultural equipment but loans. In fact, excavated texts suggest that the bureaucracy even provided forms of welfare, granting clothes in return for labor.[90]

In summary, *Lord Shang*'s approach to human motivation certainly falls within the bounds of the contemporary variations in Rational Actor Theory. People are taken as selfish beings who optimize towards fulfilling utility. At the same time, similar to NIE, the social institutions around them condition the manifestation of this selfishness. *Lord Shang* sees the system of incentives and the structuring institutions as the path to producing cohesion and advocates the structuring of institutions to

85 Ibid., 95–96.

86 While it can restrict the flow of information, Lord Shang advocates neither book burning nor propaganda.

87 Sanft 2014, 141–143.

88 Ibid., 142.

89 Ibid., 33–56.

90 Sou 2013, 192–193.

maximize the impact of these incentives. While making use of local initiative is ideal, it is worth noting that this does not lead to the ideal of a free market. We will examine Early Imperial thought on markets in the next section.

4. Classical thought and markets

With all this in mind, then, we can turn to thinking about markets in these texts. Because there is no concept of "The Market" as it does in modern economics, we will look at ideas about prices, exchange, and the role of merchants. As we have seen, Early Chinese texts agree that exchange encourages and is necessitated by specialization, without which, human society cannot exist. *Lord Shang* is the only pre-Han text that is anti-mercantile, contrary to the common misconception that Early Chinese thought was generally anti-mercantile.[91] *Lord Shang's* theoretical objections to a free market are largely occluded by the practical objections arising from the need for control and maximized output, such as in Chapter 2, "Orders to Cultivate Wastelands", predictably enough is a set of suggested measures to encourage cultivation of new land. It includes measures such as abolishing inns for travelers (2.8), banning the use of hired labor so that noble lineages will not be able to engage in their own construction projects (2.7), and a number of measures to harm merchants.

However, looking at contemporaries and interlocutors, we do have some options for what someone who espoused *Lord Shang*'s theory of human motivation would have thought of the idea of a self-regulating market, and thus, by extension, the way that Rational Actor Theory operates as the basis for the idea of a free market. Outside of Sinology, the most famous Han economic text may be the *Debate on Salt and Iron*, which has, at times, been read as a pro-free market text. A piece of Eastern Han literature about a Western Han policy debate where the Confucian literati oppose a program of monopolies on salt and iron for the purpose of raising money to fund campaigns into Central Asia. The Confucians argue that the state should not interfere with the economy and that such monopolies should not be implemented.

As Goldin has pointed out, the Confucians' logic in the *Debate*, however, is not about price-setting, but rather about virtue.[92] In this regard, they are consonant with the broader tradition. Confucians are looking at price setting in terms of something that moral conditioning will be able to deal with. Mencius talks about markets like they are a given and sees them as a way of facilitating specialization – human society cannot exist without exchange:

---

91 Sterckx 2015.

92 Goldin 2022.

> 子不通功易事，以羨補不足，則農有餘粟，女有餘布
> If you do not interchange goods and exchange services so that surplus can supply deficiency, then the farmer will have an excess of grain and women will have an excess of cloth.[93]

However, the text does not get into market regulation much beyond the assessment that taxation was begun as a way of preventing any one player from dominating the market, similarly, social institutions come into being as a means of structuring these interactions to prevent people from getting taken advantage of 3A4, when Mencius debates with someone who espouses an undifferentiated society. With the interlocutor envisioning self-sufficient individuals, Mencius asks where they get their metal agricultural tools, forcing them to admit that they cannot make them themselves and thus must trade for them. Therefore differentiation is required. But this differentiation also requires coordination. Because specialization is required, a means to regulate and ensure fairness in the exchange between different people with different specialties and needs is also required. In fact, Mencius is against over-governing, chiding a king for moving the population around, instead advocating providing the structure for people to tend to their own agriculture and support themselves. While this is largely hands-off, it still includes dispersing grain from central granaries in times of famine. Mencius sees moral development as strongly influenced by a conducive environment, which includes good material conditions and a moral state structure. This is what will produce a harmonious society that has moral exchange. Xunzi's view is similar, where in a well-run state, the government will need levy no taxes or tariffs.[94] Implicitly, price will be set through habituated ethical behavior where buyer and seller agree upon a price that will be mutually beneficial.

For them, social order will naturally arise, should the rites actually be instituted. While trade is taken for granted as part of people's daily lives, price is not directly dealt with because in the ideal state, while the market will set its own prices, these prices will be set by virtue, not by self-interest. As such, advice is less about regulating the market than establishing the conditions so that virtuous practice can regulate the market. Thus, while the Confucians in the *Debate on Salt and Iron* may advocate less government intervention, the reasoning is not that natural competition will generate fair prices, but rather that a moral government will cause people to be benevolent enough that they can harmonize prices themselves through cooperation.

93 *Mencius* 3B4, *Mengzi* 2000, 198.

94 *Xunzi*, "Wangzhi 王制", 209–262.

If we only had *Lord Shang* and the Confucians, we would be at a dead end. However, other texts have more to say. The two most developed accounts are in the *Guanzi* 管子 and the *Yuejueshu* 越絕書,[95] both of which are heterogenous texts assembled during the Han Dynasty. In the case of the Guanzi, the dating of the Qingzhong and other economic chapters is uncertain – there is debate as to whether they are Warring States or Han (with some conservative Chinese sources attributing them to Guanzi himself in the 7th century). The *Yuejueshu*'s chapters "Boy Reckoner" and "[Kept] Inside the Pillow" are probably Warring States period.[96]

Part of "Boy Reckoner" focuses on the impact of the 12-year Jupiter cycle on harvests to suggest a practice of contrarian investing (G 49–53), while the "[Kept] Inside the Pillow" focuses on shorter price cycles based on alternations of the elements and Yin and Yang. (G53-4). "Boy Reckoner" goes on to argue that price fluctuations harm participants in the economy and therefore prices should be stabilized so that despite the fluctuations in price, neither consumers nor producers are harmed, noting that if the cost of grain is too low (20 cash per picul), then the farmers will be harmed, while if it is too high (90 cash per picul), the rest of the economy will be harmed. The ideal cost of grain is somewhere between those two extremes (between 80 and 30 cash per picul).[97] In other words, these texts implicitly see price as set by supply and demand, and since prices fluctuate due to long term cycles as well as shorter things like droughts, they suggest the state should act to stabilize prices because extremes in either direction will disrupt the network of exchange. While currency is discussed, the emphasis is on grain because that is understood to be the commodity whose price drives the rest, much as how fluctuations in the oil market have repercussions for prices in different sectors of the economy.

The *Guanzi*'s Qingzhong chapters continue this discussion. While the terminology is new, the core understanding of the economy is not.[98] This should hardly be surprising as, in addition to the two aforementioned chapters, *Lord Shang* also understands that prices fluctuate and advises using variable pricing of noble titles, rewards, and fines to float with the market so that they remain relevant. At the same time, the *Guanzi* texts go further than either *Lord Shang* or the texts in the *Yuejueshu*.

---

95 The meaning of the title is debated, and thus I have elected to leave it in romanization.

96 The compilation of the *Yuejueshu* is fascinating because it appears to have been assembled from texts with primarily local circulation about the history of Yue. The fact that there is such material hints at what must have been lost over the centuries. For a full discussion of the *Yuejueshu*'s compilation and a translation, see Milburn's 2010 translation.

97 Goldin 2022, 55.

98 Ibid., 59.

They further elaborate on supply and demand and its interaction with currency value, though they are still grain focused for the same reasons as the *Yuejueshu* texts.[99]

Their assessment of price cycles is also similar, but here, we see the suggestion that the state stabilize prices through a buffer stock scheme. Something similar to the one described here was actually implemented during the Han and similar ones seem to have existed as far back as the early 4th century.[100] As with the *Yuejueshu* texts, the *Guanzi* values merchants and sees ways that the price is a function of supply and demand. These texts also understand people as rationally self-interested. In that case, why cannot the market regulate itself? The answer seems to be a mix between the negative impact of price fluctuations and market friction/asymmetry preventing natural stabilization of good prices. In fact, the *Guanzi* states directly that prices cannot be fixed. The Duke of Qi asks Guanzi whether there is a way to fix prices. The answer is that balancing the economy requires prices to vary due to fluctuations in supply and demand. Were prices to be arbitrarily set, then exchange would break down.[101]

Price cycles are driven by things beyond the scale of the individual. While the causes of most of these cycles are natural, it is understood that the prices of goods move with the prices of other goods. At several points, the text even details the use of controlled buying and selling of grain, and the extension and recalling of loans to control the value of currency.[102] The use of contract laborers is also encouraged because the form that their payment takes – grain or currency – is also a means of regulating the exchange value.[103] Thus the text seems to imagine both grain and currency as media of exchange, with currency being the more convenient one, but grain being the commodity whose price is central to the entire economy. Lending and government expenditures are means of influencing the value of currency and the price of grain. What all of this means is that while agriculture is understood as the core and basis of this economy, and thus natural cycles are given primary focus, as Goldin notes, the patterns invoked in these explanations are not irrational, but part of the theoretical models of the time. In the absence of econometric data, there is not all that much separating their understanding from Minsky Moments, which, even now, is something we are working to understand.[104] Since the fluctuations of

---

99 Ibid., 61.

100 Ibid., 57.

101 Rickett 1998, 478–479.

102 Ibid., 412–414 and 390, respectively.

103 Ibid., 391.

104 Goldin 2022, 52–53.

the prices of goods harm and benefit different sectors differentially, these market cycles preclude ideal prices from lasting under natural conditions. It is worth noting that here, cycles are intrinsic to the market, and while some, notably Minsky, have argued that such fluctuations are intrinsic to the complex, chaotic system that is the market, the intrinsicness of market instability and even the existence of cycles has long been debated in modern economics.[105]

In addition to inherent instability, markets can be used to send bad signals. In the Qingzhong chapters of *Guanzi*, there are several humorous stories of clever rulers who manipulated the prices of goods by creating artificial demand to bankrupt opponents or cleverly tax the rich. On the surface level, this would simply seem to be that the authors of the *Guanzi* are thinking on the level of the economy, not the firm in their planning, however, the logic of the various ploys is inevitably that by generating demand or the illusion of demand, you can manipulate the value of commodities and thus drive imprudent behavior, such as abandoning agriculture to capture live deer.[106] In other words, the markets themselves can transmit bad information, which means that a clever operator can manipulate it. The text also advises what we might recognize as "nudges" from behavioral economics to generate desired behaviors such as a ploy to reduce the cost of fabric by removing branches from trees providing shade along the roads with the "logic" that the lack of shade prevented people from gathering and talking, thus forcing them to get back to work.[107]

This ties into concerns over asymmetrical information and practical pressures. Because human nature and capability is universal, it is not that the peasants getting swindled are irrational, it is that they are not as good at it as the merchants who negotiate for a living. It is what they are good at and have the ability to travel widely and find good deals. A farmer, not so much. A farmer also has few choices because of practical concerns like transporting their harvest to market. This asymmetry means that the farmer is easily taken advantage of.[108] The state intervention by buying and selling grain thus stabilizes the prices not by fixing a price, but rather by using market processes. With grain prices available from the government granaries, merchants are forced to offer comparable deals.

Given that government intervention seems a fixture in Early Chinese economic thought even when market processes are employed, one might be inclined to ask

105 E.g., Austrian School Economists see market cycles as the result of the intervention of central banking.

106 Rickett 1998, 505.

107 Ibid., 492–493.

108 Goldin 2022, 59.

whether the idea that free competition could drive down prices was ever seen in Early China and, in fact, it is in *Han Feizi*.[109] *Han Feizi* is a set of essays probably written by the eponymous author at the end of the Warring States period. Despite the conventional assessment that he was the ideological architect of the Qin Dynasty, there is no evidence that he ever had much power. Similarly, despite his claims that he was the intellectual heir of Lord Shang, Han Feizi is rather different and is more a management consultant than a state theorist. What he does retain is the idea that humans are self-interested, which he applies to the problem of ruler-minister relationships. The crucial issue here is that in the states of his era, the king is a highly replaceable source of power for ambitious people around them, be they princes, spouses, or ministers. At best the king is a puppet, at worst an obstacle. Most of the essays are advice to the ruler on how to avoid getting killed. While the King is average, the ministers are far more talented because they had to compete to get their positions. Thus the King relies on clear methods for survival. *Han Feizi* is a political realist and has little to say about the ideal state.

Because the king cannot rule alone – the state is too large and complex for that – and the King cannot trust his self-interested ministers, *Han Feizi* suggests open bidding for contracts as a means for getting the "real" price of the project. *Han Feizi*, advising the King about how to deal with his subordinates, suggests that the King simply sit back and allow the ministers to come forward with their proposals. Then, once an undertaking has been laid out, he should allow his ministers to make bids and select the lowest.[110] The competition to be selected will cause the ministers to compete against each other, intrinsically useful for preventing a coup, but also generating a good price for the task.[111] In other words, in this situation, we have a system of actors with opposed interests where competition between rival producers yields benefits to the consumer.

So is *Han Feizi* a free market advocate? Could it work for the entire economy? Not really. It only works in the situation where the King has a monopoly on power, gives out minimal information, can keep track of the promises and the actual outcomes, and can punish deviations from the contract.[112] While the King is no more intellectually capable than the average peasant, after all, the King's only credential is their heritage, for an average peasant to do what the King is suggested to do here, they would need perfect information, including competing bids from merchants, as well as a low cost system for enforcement of contracts with harsh penalties for fraud,

109 For a good introduction to Han Feizi, see Goldin 2020.

110 Watson 1964, 90–93.

111 Ibid., 92.

112 This being Han Feizi, consistent punishment is very important.

a consumer-allied legal system. The King also has a fundamental advantage the peasant can never have: the King's desires can (and must) remain a mystery.[113] This is very important for Han Feizi, because if the King gives hints as to what they want or, worse, need, it gives the ministers ways to scheme. In the peasant's case, the merchant knows exactly what the peasant needs: someone to buy their harvest. Worse still, they know the peasant has a limited window of opportunity and, while there are many peasants, there is only one king meaning that the merchant has the leverage in this negotiation.

So in both cases, the issue is that the information and pressure is asymmetrical and it is in the merchant's interests to keep it that way. It is not that the merchants are useless; even *Lord Shang* softens its view of them over time, it is that given the incentives, human nature, and the practical limitations in information and negotiation, i.e., market friction, these authors do not seem to consider the sorts of communication required for the market to set its own prices possible, unless there is some sort of intervention.[114]

What is interesting here is that when we look at the policies that Qin and Han actually implement, while they do not directly reference any of this (or any other theory, for that matter), we see policies in line with these suggestions to actually promote a stable market price. Firstly, buffer stock schemes are reported as early as the time of Li Kui's tenure as advisor to Marquis Wen of Jin in the late 5th century in the *Hanshu*. His policies inspired Lord Shang, who brought with him a copy of Li Kui's writings.[115] On the other end of our time period, inasmuch as the *Debate on Salt and Iron* is faithful, it shows the Western Han period pro-monopoly bureaucrat using the economic terminology we observe in Guanzi; and indeed, we see both monopoly policies and buffer stock granary policies during the Western Han.[116] But beyond these direct policies, Qin policies focus on construction of infrastructure, including roads and marketplaces. Weights, measures, and currencies are standardized across the empire and this information is publicly available. The laws are designed to be

---

113 Watson 1964, 16–17.

114 Of course, in actuality, markets that most would consider quite free have some degree of regulation. In other words, it is quite possible that a Guanzi influenced bureaucrat would see the fixing of lending rates by central banks as something in the spirit of their proposals.

115 While there is a text that exists purporting to be just that, it is likely a medieval forgery. Quite what form Li Kui's writings would have taken is unclear; given the period and the texts we have recovered archeologically, I would suggest that a legal code, a chrestomathy of sayings, or a set of short anecdotes is far more likely than a set of essays.

116 See Lesse-Messing 2020b.

clear and known to the entire population and the bureaucracy is deployed towards that end. Not only do proclamations of these economic policies say that they are to promote fairness in the marketplace,[117] they are exactly the three factors that North identifies as crucial to improving economic performance.[118]

While individual peasants are not supposed to travel, the resulting system of freeholding peasants whose subsistence was secured on a stabilized price for essential commodities would present a uniform market for a merchant – they would have a harder time taking advantage of someone and the prices they would get for exotic goods would be keyed to the difficulty of transportation, i.e., the amount of labor required according to the economic thinking of the time; for example, *Lord Shang*'s concern that value is being extracted in the process of grain transportation in 2.19. Here we can also come back to the government monopolies on key goods. As Goldin notes, the idea that people might catch on to the fact that the government is extracting taxes through these goods is never raised, and while limited price information may have something to do with it, we also have observed a preference to harness things that people are going to do anyway, with a tax being considered an extra imposition, while simply being the merchant for a good is less "obtrusive". It is also possible that some of the reasoning here was a sort of income tax: *Guanzi* advocates the use of fees as a way of preferentially extracting revenue from the rich while leaving the poor alone,[119] though this would be less effective with a universally required commodity like salt, which is selected for the express reason that it is universally required.

Regardless, understanding the Qin-Han policies through the economic thought we have examined above certainly makes a great deal of sense and would allow most sectors of the market to set their own prices. While this aspect of price model is conjecture, it fits with the way that these texts want to allow autonomy at lower levels (if only to reduce administrative burden) as well as the way that the *Guanzi* and *Yuejueshu* texts focus on stabilizing the prices of grain, allowing the rest of the prices to set themselves in relation to that. These texts and policy makers are thinking about markets and thinking about rational actors in those markets, it is just that they have a different assessment of what is feasible in reality than a Neo-Classical Economist. At the same time, the factors these thinkers would have been likely to raise as objections to a free market are exactly ones that have been raised as critiques of Neo-Classical Economics while their opponents would have reasoning entirely incompatible with Rational Actor Theory. In sum, this would suggest that, at

117 E.g., Qin Shihuang's 20th Year Inscription.

118 North 2005, 159.

119 Rickett 1998, 395.

least in certain corners of Early Imperial China, we do, in fact, see Rational Actor Theory of a sort which advocates for government intervention in the economy for the purpose of stabilizing prices. Both supporters of non-intervention and intervention believe that social institutions will do a better job of setting prices than competition in the market because of limitations in the market institution itself.

5. Bureaucracy and unity in the early imperial period

With all this in mind, we can then turn to the matter of Early Imperial unity. As we have seen, the philosophical texts focus on the bureaucracy as the key institution here. Excavated texts outlining proper behavior for bureaucrats both in terms of official proclamations and independent texts also focus on even application of laws over individual virtue as the best means of securing the loyalty of the public.[120] Steps were taken to ensure that the law was accessible to the general population; Officials were to read official documents aloud to those unable to read them themselves[121] and Han proclamations state that they must be posted in public places.[122] Barbieri-Low and Yates also note a number of occasions when people attempted to use their knowledge of the law to defend themselves, indicating that there was general knowledge of the law.[123]

The control structure was not monodirectional. In addition to the fact that lower level offices, down to the lowest levels of the bureaucracy could suggest laws,[124] in texts such as the *Hanshu*, in a number of incidents, the reactions from the government characters suggest that the people were well within their rights to assemble, complain, and protest.[125]An's advisor Wu Pi is depicted in sources as recommending creating ill will amongst the peasants through arbitrary exercise of political power. Successful revolt is not simply a matter of gathering some soldiers, but rather lies in disordering the entire system from the ground up by fouling the order-giving structure. An's advisor Wu Pi is depicted in sources as recommending creating ill will amongst the peasants through arbitrary exercise of political power. Successful revolt is not simply a matter of gathering some soldiers, but rather lies in disordering the entire system from the ground up by fouling the order-giving structure.[126]

120 Sou 2013.

121 Sanft 2014, 91.

122 Ibid., 144.

123 Barbieri-Low / Yates 2015, 218.

124 Ibid., 82–83.

125 Sanft 2014, 142.

126 Ibid., 138.

Excavated texts suggest that these incentives and contacts were ubiquitous. In addition to granting plots of land and farm equipment, Qin bureaus also lent clothes and food, repayable by labor in the event that the recipient did not have means to repay through other means. Thus the state was a place not simply for social advancement, but also social support. Han policymakers continued to tweak the system, for example, implementing the *Lord Shang*-esque rewards for farmers who exceeded their quotas in 191 BC.[127] With incentives, grants, and taxes, the peasants under such an administration would have quickly come to see the Empire as a constant, and often beneficial part of daily life. By structuring information to make compliance rational and thus direct mass human activity, indeed, the very approach *Lord Shang* suggests in its focus on public knowledge of rewards and punishments, the bureaucracy made the Empire real, not just in territorial extent and in ledgers, but in the minds of the population.

This is unsurprising from multiple recent perspectives. NIE understands institutions as playing a key role in structuring human behavior because they are the system that structures the incentive structure.[128] This tallies with anthropologically driven studies on how cooperation happens, where, for example, Blanton and Fargher's 2016 study of cooperation, which argues that social institutions play a large role in structuring human cooperation. This is not culture as conventionally conceived, but rather includes things like market structure. Cooperation is collective action, best understood, not by considering people in isolation, but rather examining them in their contexts. Cooperation is mutualism, but also requires structure. Humans cannot build a cooperative network from scratch, arguing that Chinese policy under Mao, relying on the expectation of spontaneous human cooperation in Marxist theory, expected a new system to appear the moment the old market system had been destroyed and consequently failed to provide any structure.[129] In this observation that cooperation requires coordination at multiple levels and, while it is grounded in innate human capacity, it also requires habituation, one cannot help but be reminded of the Warring States theorists. Meanwhile, Skyrms' *Stag Hunt* reaches similar conclusions through an entirely theoretical, game theory driven study of optimal strategies in different games. Skyrms finds that while cooperation is suboptimal in a population of generalists, cooperation becomes increasingly beneficial in tandem with specialization, which also requires communication. These

127 Sterckx 2018, 312.

128 North 1991, 97.

129 Blanton 2016, 286.

factors are coeval.[130] At the same time, the import of these ideas has not been fully appreciated.

Accounts of state formation have tended to focus on competition and coercion. Indeed, Sanft's work on Qin is notable because of how iconoclastic it is. Studies of Early China tend to focus on conflict and difference, with power imagined to radiate outwards from the center and irresistibly forcing compliance. As we have seen, this image is not consonant with the ideas in the texts and Sanft argues that it is also not consonant with the practice. Even when Foucault is brought into the picture, pointing out in Western Theory what is already obvious in the Early Chinese texts, i.e., that power is negotiated, Foucauldian analyses ultimately leave people's actual compliance as an open and unnatural matter, an internal fascism that is a disease of power, like a society-wide Stockholm syndrome.[131] For example, Scott's 2017 work on state formation, *Against the Grain*, while innovative in understanding state phenomena, not simply as a continuum, but also as the marked state of affairs in human experience, focuses on coercion as the mechanism of early state formation (which, for him, includes the Qin), and never mentions cooperation. He is arguing against a sort of Whiggist vision of the progress of civilization, but the resulting account misses the intrinsic incentives to cooperation.

In a similar vein, Blanton and Fargher note a number of limitations in the standard "biomathematic" model of cooperation that has emerged over the past several decades, which has mostly focused on small, homogenous groups in the modern West. It treats cooperation as mostly instinctive and keyed to kin and "group", i.e., social or ethnic group. They also tend to overlook the possibility that social acts that benefit others may also benefit the actor, treating cooperation as a dilemma. Finally, there is a tendency to dismiss the role of institutions, preferring "bottom-up" to "top-down" cooperation, focusing on individual actors.[132] We see exactly this at play in Wilson's *Sociobiology* that defines altruism as something that "increases the fitness of another at the expense of his own fitness".[133] It is explained in terms of kin-selection and altruism and selfishness are still fundamentally opposed.[134] Indeed, Skyrms' aforementioned approach is notable precisely because it argues for a mathematical justification for institutions; as he notes, unless one takes the unorthodox step of accounting for dynamic interaction structures (communication practices,

130 Skyrms 2004.

131 Sanft 2014, 30–31.

132 Blanton 2016, 12–23 and 39–40.

133 Wilson 2000, 117.

134 Ibid., 120–129.

etc.), cooperation appears suboptimal.[135] Without considering the structure of interactions and the signaling involved, i.e. looking solely at the actors without considering the system, our models will be unable to arrive at the correct answer.

Considering Shelach and Pines' 2006 account of Qin identity displays here is enlightening because it provides us with an example of an issue in the opposite direction, over-specifying the structure of signaling.[136] While the assumption that there is, what are we seeing in various tombs is,[137] in fact, Qin identity, has issues, Shelach and Pines note that what I suggest we call Qin identities are not fixed.[138] While during the Spring and Autumn period, Qin elite burials had attempted to display prestige items associated with the international Zhou ritual, there is a sudden spike in diversity in the 4th century BC, coincident with Lord Shang's reforms and the expansion of Qin.[139] Even as this happens, Qin begins to be referred to as cultural other and while Qin maintains certain forms of archaism, Qin rhetoric suggests a self-differentiation from the *Xia*.[140] Shelach and Pines attribute this, in part, to upward mobility on of commoners thanks to bureaucratic reform, but also consider Qin through the lens of an emergent Qin ethnic or nationalism,[141] seeing it in terms of the emergence of a popular culture wherein the elite adopted elements of the local culture rather than an enforcement of the high culture.[142] In turn, this raises a problem; if Qin does have an emergent sense of national identity, why is it abandoned upon imperial unification?[143] And it is at this point that the problems in this interpretation show. The suggestion that the Warring States were a unified job market for thinkers diminished incentives to rigidly support one's homeland doubtlessly has merit,[144] however, Sanft argues that while Pines and Shelach are quite right that the ideal of unity existed long before unification occurred, it was restricted to the elite and had to be communicated to the population by the Qin (and Han)

135 Skyrms 2004, 1–14 and 105.

136 To be clear, both authors have written a great deal since then, but they have not revised their discussion of Qin unity. I do not believe either author would agree with their 2006 model anymore, but it gives us a good starting point and is noteworthy because they are also questioning conventional models of identity and social cohesion in suggesting a more dynamic structure, albeit one still primarily within an identity driven paradigm.

137 In their sample, primarily upper class, cf. Shelach / Pines 2006, 206.

138 Ibid., 205.

139 Ibid., 216–217.

140 Ibid., 218.

141 Ibid., 219.

142 Ibid., 221.

143 Ibid., 222.

144 Ibid., 223.

governments after the fact.[145] At the popular level, Qin does indeed borrow aspects of various cultures, but more than that, we see a proliferation of local traits, not simply from the core Qin domain, but also in freshly conquered territories. Shelach and Pines suggest that elevation of local identities would have served as an effective buffer against defection,[146] but this seems incompatible with the sort of exclusivity that Shelach and Pines seem to have in their assessment of Qin identity. Here, they have in mind an exclusive sense of belonging in Qin based on both place of birth and descent.[147] While this may have been true in certain early periods of the Qin polity, more recent excavations have indicated that what mattered in Qin law was not birth, but registration. A good way to see this is in the usage of the term *qinren* 秦人, literally Qin person.

The legal definition of a Qin person was entirely jurisdictional. In manuscripts we see that direct administration is the thing that decides whether or not someone is a "Qin person". For example, where officials are uncertain what bounty to award a "bounty hunter" who has caught bandits from Jingzhou in the state of Chu because between the time the bandits left Chu, originally intending to register themselves with Qin officials, and the time they committed crimes and were caught, Qin conquered Jingzhou. The question is thus whether they count as Qin people (*qinren*) or foreign. The answer is that because they were registered in Jingzhou, which is now under direct Qin administration, they are people of Qin.[148] Here we see the thing that makes someone a Qin person is entirely a matter of whose population census they are in. Furthermore, while there are subordinate domains *chenbang* 臣邦 and the law treats people registered to one of those subordinate domains differently from Qin people, the distinction is not ethnic given that Qin *chenbang*s would seem to include the heartland of "Xia" culture along the Yellow River and areas directly adjacent to the capital as we observed with Lord Rang, etc. The status of people in Qin records does not reflect ethnic distinctions, but rather administrative structure.

Furthermore, archeologically, the Qin do not homogenize material culture of conquered areas, instead, regional diversity persists.[149] In conquered Chu territory, Chao's recent study finds complex local agency in negotiating elements of new goods and influences while displaying local identities in the Qin and Han periods.[150] Shelach and Pines even note that the Qin polity adopts aspects from across the

145 Sanft 2004, 75.

146 Shelach / Pines 2006, 222.

147 Ibid., 220.

148 Lau / Staack 2015, Case 1.5, 167–173.

149 Shi Dangshe 2017.

150 Chao 2017.

realm as part of a dialogue.[151] To be sure, there are mass population movements, but these occur across the entire empire as the Qin bureaucracy relocated people, assigned reward plots, and enticed immigrants. In any given region, opened for cultivation, be it near the Qin capital or in remote Sichuan, it was an influx of more Qin people in the administrative (Qin) sense, and not the cultural (our) sense. Settlers came from all corners of the ecumene even as they also flocked to the newly irrigated land around the Qin capital, too. It was not simply the locals, but everyone who was suddenly surrounded by strangers and difference.[152]

Sage's 1992 *Ancient Sichuan and the Unification of China* characterizes this and what follows as Sinicization by a totalitarian Qin regime, but it is important to observe what he means by that and what actually happened, given the way that the term Sinicization is linked with nationalist historiographies of modern China. Even working before reappraisals of Qin totalitarianism and invested in the classic image of the brutal Qin, Sage notes that annexing Sichuan required "flexibility, patience, and compromise" and Sinicization here is "an adaptive cultural process ancillary to the political unification of a region with China" and makes the population Chinese.[153] The question then, is what it meant to be Chinese. According to Sage, Chinese-ness is what arises from the Qin conquests and reforms.[154] As Pines later argued, what matters is not culture or ethnicity, but rather that one is ruled by the same Empire. China is what emerges from the experience of this Empire.[155] The goal is homogenization in terms of administration, not culture and the development of a shared cultural identity (and the loss of diversity) was a side effect. To be sure, the Qin and the Han did take pains to promulgate a centralized Imperial cult and made provisions for local rituals, but as we shall see the massive variance in grave goods, burial practices, and even promotion of local cultic practice suggest that the goal was less to homogenize the population, but rather to monopolize this domain of power signaling as they did all others.[156]

151 Shelach / Pines 2006, 222.

152 Sage 1992, 154.

153 Ibid., 119.

154 Ibid., 119 and 121.

155 Pines 2009.

156 See Barbieri-Low / Yates 2015, 212–213 for a discussion of the laws, but the characterization of standardized ritual amongst the people is entirely at odds with recent studies of the material record such as Chao 2017. Instead, I think the intention behind these laws and the role that their implementation played. The threat is not local ritual, it is ritual that exalts an alternate locus of authority, a very real possibility in a world of ancestor veneration, where a fallen king could serve as a local patron.

Instead, if we think about the question Shelach and Pines raise about a nascent Warring States Qin identity that was ultimately dropped in favor of imperial ideology with the idea suggested by our sources, namely that the institution of the bureaucracy, through providing a rational incentive structure, will provide unity, we are able to simply and quickly solve the quandary. Cultural identity need not be standardized and local identity presents no problem if the way that groups are incorporated into the whole is through a system of incentives that structure perception of cooperation with the single Imperial administration. This actually fits quite well with studies on means of reducing intergroup tensions and promoting intergroup cooperation. For example, Gaetner and Dovidio's 2000 work on reducing intergroup bias notes that practices treating groups homogeneously through the use of things like integrated seating arrangements, similar clothing, and common group names have been shown to erode group boundaries in contemporary experiments.[157] Producing a sense of interdependence through interaction and the support of authorities generates a sense of a new shared group identity,[158] as do shared experiences.[159] The experimenters express reticence about the durability of these benefits without a structure to facilitate them.[160] These structures are precisely the sort that would have been produced by Qin administrative practices, particularly corvee labor, where, at least with infrastructure projects, the benefits to society would have been quite clear. Beyond this, however, Gaetner and Dovidio find that, while harder to construct and maintain, a system that allows for multiple identities (in their case multicultural models) promotes group cohesion better than an assimilationist one. This works by allowing multiple smaller identities (in their case, ethnic ones) to associate with a superordinate group (a school, or the Qin Empire) and works because it reduces social costs for participation in the shared community. Gaetner and Dovidio note that the success of such a system is contingent on the institution acting in such a way as to be conducive to facilitating trust across groups.[161] They have majority-minority scenarios in mind for this, but in the case of the Qin, where it might be better to speak of different sorts of pluralities, it seems as if this is more or less what happened.

Under the Qin and Han systems, one would have a local identity rooted in the place of one's birth or ancestral home, but would understand this as part of a larger, diverse system because the bureaucratic institutions placed focus on the whole.

157 Gaetner / Dovidio 2000, Chapter 4.

158 Ibid., Chapter 5.

159 Ibid., Chapter 6.

160 Ibid., 162.

161 Ibid., 163–168.

Things like loans to peasants from centrally appointed bureaucrats under standard imperial policy, the common experiences of corvee, the omnipresence of imperial infrastructure, and the universal standards of rewards and punishments would have communicated this superordinate identity to the populace. At the more elite level, the bureaucracy seems to have focused incentives towards the center, with officials above a given rank being forbidden from serving in their home province.[162] Advancement lay not in local power bases, but rather in networks in the capital. It should hardly be surprising, then, that we see officials prioritize connections made in education and the bureaucracy over ties to their ancestral region with regional identity ceasing to matter within two generations and classmates and students being selected over kin for cultural capital.[163] Furthermore, merchant families often intermarried with officials and while this presented certain challenges in terms of accumulation of resources, the arrangement also linked the economic elite to the political one.[164]

The best example of the crucial role of the bureaucracy in providing stability for the new structure may be the differential outcomes between Sichuan and Lingnan (roughly modern Guangxi, Guangdong, and the Red River Valley in Vietnam). Briefly, Sichuan became firmly incorporated into the Empire in a way that took much longer in Lingnan or not at all.[165] The reason, I suggest, is that Sichuan was incorporated into the administration in a way that Lingnan was not. As we have seen, Qin conquest did not mean the end of local diversity and, as with regions across the empire in the Han period, local diversity continued in both Sichuan[166] and Lingnan.[167]

Both Sichuan and Lingnan were dramatically different from the Warring States world. There is no Chinese writing from pre-Qin Sichuan, home to settled, agricultural Shu 蜀 on the plains and the less organized Ba 巴 in the Eastern Highlands, nor is there any in Lingnan. Shu and Ba material culture shows evidence of strong commonalities with Highland Southeast Asia and the Dong Son culture, whose typical bronzes are found from Yunnan to Vietnam, as well as interaction down the Yangzi

162 Leese-Messing 2020a, 151–157.

163 Cai 2019 studies the careers and social networks of men from the Donghai region (parts of modern Shandong and Jiangsu) due to the availability of data for them. Given the standard structure of the bureaucracy, the results would seem to be generalizable.

164 See, for example, the life of Sima Xiangru; cf. Sage 1992.

165 To this day, the Guangxi province is home to myriad non-Sinitic languages.

166 Sage 1992, 135–136.

167 Allard 2006, 241.

River.[168] Lingnan, which includes the heartland of the Dong Son culture, is similarly distinct. While there was a great deal of diversity in the Chinese writing world, even setting aside the culturally other Chu, Wu, and Yue and just focusing on Zhou successor states such as Qi and Wei, Shu, Ba, and the amorphous realm of the southern Yue in which Lingnan was located were on another level of difference.

Sichuan was conquered by Qin in 316 BC as a means of increasing agricultural land, with Qin leaders correctly supposing that the less organized Shu polity and Ba groups would be easier than facing a coalition of other states along the Yellow River, and that, owing to lower population density and less developed infrastructure, investment in the region would yield great dividends. Meanwhile, Lingnan was the end of the Qin march south, coming under Qin control in 214 BC.[169] After the Qin fell in , one of the generals, Zhao Tuo, declared himself King of Nanyue in 204 BC and ruled it with ostensible recognition from the Han Emperors until 111 BC. In contrast, Shu and Ba were part of the domain Liu Bang was granted as King of Han[170] by Xiang Yu, who briefly lead the coalition of rulers in the wake of the fall of the Qin, and formed his power base from which he was able to defeat Xiang Yu and declare himself Emperor. Thus, for the first century of the Han Dynasty, while Nanyue was functionally independent, Shu and Ba were core parts of the Imperial domain. So crucial is this area that some have gone so far as to suggest that the Western Han was functionally the domination of the arc from Sichuan up to the old Qin heartland over the rest of the Empire.[171]

Allard notes that the limited success of the Han Empire in Lingnan as observed by limited mixing of funerary goods was due to a lack of effective economic and cultural integration of the local population and suggests that part of Zhao Tuo's dynasty's success in the area was due to selective integration of local custom albeit in a way that prioritized northern traditions.[172] However, in light of the material trends in the Shu commandery over the same period, where native boat shaped burials, themselves brought to Shu from Dian[173] and Ba alongside bronze drums during the Spring and Autumn Period, continue for more than a century, allow us to identify indigenous Shu graves, where we find material signs that they had access to

168 Yao 2016.

169 Allard 2006, 135–138.

170 This is the Han for which the Dynasty was named.

171 Lewis 2007, 16–20.

172 Allard 2006, 250–251.

173 In modern Yunnan.

prosperity and social mobility, with many elites becoming merchants.[174] This would suggest better integration of the locals into the economic and administrative structure in Shu as opposed to what would seem to be a firmer separation in Lingnan.

It seems equally likely that Zhao Tuo's local administration promoted better economic integration, particularly since, as Allard notes, the area is very diverse, culturally.[175] It is remarkable that when the Han Dynasty ultimately annexed the region in 111 BC, it had limited success in registering and interacting with the population despite a century of what Allard identifies as Chinese rule.[176] In fact, both Shu and Lingnan had seen substantial influxes of outsiders during Qin rule. The numbers of settlers are not clear in either case; early texts are not always clear and texts that do provide numbers are centuries later. Sage, in his work on Sichuan, estimates between tens of thousands to hundreds of thousands of forced and voluntary immigrants to Sichuan during the century of Qin rule.[177] In the case of Lingnan, while Allard estimates there were few willing immigrants in the Han period, he does not consider involuntary relocations common during the Qin period.[178] Working from a variety of textual sources, Barbieri-Low found reference to not simply the initial invasion force, but three waves of settlers, including one of 500,000 people as well as the movement of native Yue to the north in the decade between Qin unification and the first Emperor's death in 221 BC.[179] While there is certainly scope for exaggeration, he finds numerous examples of relocations referenced in primary material about the Qin, including relocation or expulsion of conquered groups (regardless of whether or not they were "Chinese"),[180] estimating that Qin Shihuang may have relocated between 10 and 25 % of the population of the Empire in all directions. Since settlers were from across the Empire, loyalty would hardly be a given, but

---

174 Sage 1992, 135–136. Note that using burial style and assemblage as a proxy for ethnicity has methodological issues, it is common in Chinese archeology, and in this particular case, the burial style is so distinct as to strongly imply the difference.

175 Allard 2006, 250.

176 Ibid., 235–238.

177 Sage 1992, 134.

178 Allard 2006, 237.

179 Barbieri-Low 2021, 198.

180 Though the fact that the Qin did sometimes displace local populations from conquered territory is important to note because while not the typical behavior, it would suggest that at certain times, some administrators seem to have preferred to use already loyal populations rather than going through the trouble of integrating conquered ones (as opposed to mutual relocation). Further research is required to determine the factors involved, however it seems that it was sufficiently rare as not to impact the present discussion greatly.

rather, this would be a means of dissolving old identities.[181] Such policies would have been more drastic than those taken in Sichuan in terms of speed and comparable in scale.

While Allard, understandably working within a conventional historiographic frame, focuses on the failure of (quite novel) policies of deliberate assimilation through education in the Eastern Han,[182] comparison with Qin Sichuan and, indeed, the rest of the empire during the Western Han, prompts us to question whether the explanation may not be backwards: the region was poorly integrated culturally because it was poorly integrated administratively, not the other way around. Lingnan ca. 210 BC would have been on a broadly similar (or more extreme) trajectory than Shu a century earlier. There is even evidence of canal and road construction to facilitate access to the south during the Qin period,[183] which is parallel to the initial moves that Qin made in its consolidation of Sichuan. However, even if the Zhaos had run their domains in the Qin fashion, provided services to the lower strata and limited the authority of local leaders, such conditions would have been reversed during the late Western Han. Han policy in Lingnan seems to have been largely motivated by controlling trade points rather than the more comprehensive approach the Qin took during the Warring States. This meant that control was exercised through local elites, and while this had benefits for opening trade routes,[184] it also limited contact of the inhabitants, particularly in areas away from the cities and main roads, with the bureaucracy and its incentive structure.

Here, geography was also doubtlessly a contributing factor. Where Shu was located in the Sichuan plains and thus easy to get around in once the surrounding mountains had been crossed, the Lingnan region was far more mountainous, with settlements (and administrators) clustered in river valleys, particularly port cities along the southern coast from near modern Guangzhou and Hongkong, with nearly two thirds of the population reported in a AD 2 census in the fertile Red River Delta (where modern Hanoi). This meant that logistically, administration was difficult.[185]

Where the Qin government was able to immediately begin a number of irrigation and flood control programs and subject the population to the same incentives and punishments as elsewhere in the Empire, the last century of the Western Han faced a number of administrative crises and the Eastern Han did not even try to

181 Barbieri-Low 2021, 201–202.

182 Allard 2006, 236 and 251–252.

183 Demandt 2020.

184 Ibid.

185 Ibid.

establish the sort of efficient administration we had seen previously.[186] This meant that while both administrations were capable of putting down a revolt, only the Qin were able to follow up with positive incentives to the population. In effect, in late Western Han and Eastern Han Lingnan, there was little incentive to cooperate for anyone and, as local power became entrenched across the empire, the entire system came apart. The breakup of the Eastern Han and loss of territory on the periphery of the Empire occurred as a new nobility with firmly entrenched hereditary power bases began to fight over who would be primus inter pares.

The drastic difference in outcomes in Sichuan and Lingnan would suggest that the administrative structures' interaction with the population played a key role in building shared institutions. The bureaucracy created order. Measures like not simply the standardization of the script, but also of reporting forms used in offices, the universal experiences of taxation, corvee, and conscription, as well as the weights and measures used at markets across the Empire as crucial as the irrigation, agricultural loans, and the bridges and roads that allowed for increases in mobility for trade and transport. These institutions facilitated and actuated by the bureaucracy were the key to the creation of a sense of a shared Empire and the integrating dynamic. Thus, not only incentives and infrastructure but also administrative framework that delivered them to the population played an important role in the establishment of a transnational community. The bureaucracy was the system by which the institutions were communicated to the population and incentives were extended, which is worth considering in reference to North's discussion of sources of order and disorder in society in a 2005 work on NIE. He compares the USA's process of independence and subsequent growth to that of Latin America.[187]

In his narration, the pervasive French threat prior to the 7 Years War, bound the colonies to the crown through the imperial federal system. Following this war, radicals within the colonies began to fear a weakening commitment to colonial autonomy. Later British policy appeared to confirm these fears, leading to a shift in popular sentiment. Following the revolution, the inherited framework and institutions produced the cohesion that allowed for economic growth. In contrast, North argues that there was nothing holding the Latin American colonies together, highlighting the lack of a consensus about the role of the government and while there was a shared set of beliefs around personal exchange, the institutions of impersonal exchange clashed with this. "The absence of agreement about basic political structure combined with an absence of a shared belief system resulted in an absence of

---

186 Allard 2006, 237.

187 North 2005, 103–114.

credible commitment by the new states and in inherent political instability."[188] Using Mexico as an example, the problem was that the ruling coalition ended up being strongly selective in its protection of property rights wherein corruption was crucial to the stability of the state. He acknowledges that the colonial legacy also impacted Latin American development, but what is interesting for our purposes is that the Qin and Han example provides us with a refinement on the notion of sources of cohesion. Firstly, we can observe that a shared belief system need not stray much into the realm of culture, but instead, revolve around a belief that the government can and will uniformly implement its policies. What matters more are shared assumptions about the nature of governance. Secondly, in the form of local collaboration with the new Qin rulers and in the assembly of the Han coalition, we see that self-interest was again crucial, with the incentive being not an external foe, but rather the desire to obtain a piece of the profits that come with power. In effect, the issue at the end of the Qin system may well have been that the elite did not believe that the Qin ruler was best suited to rule. The transition was not institutional, but rather a shift in the ruling coalition. The crucial difference between North's model of Mexico and the Qin-Han case is that keeping the peasants happy (or at least docile) was a priority and that this had to be achieved not through coercion, but rather through the less costly means of benefits; peasants have less overhead than slaves, after all. In other words, the Qin-Han example leads us to suppose that had one of the colonies belonged not to the British, but to a hypothetical British ally ethnically, or culturally distinct from the others, but with an economy at least as well integrated into the rest as those of the Carolinas and sharing the ideals of Enlightenment government, American cohesion would not have been adversely affected. Indeed, the role of economic institutions in the American Civil War shows us what institutional differences can do regardless of shared culture. It may even be that the current cohesion troubles the United States faces are due, in no small part, to a lack of consistent and coherent social services.

This would also tend to rule out accounts of Chinese imperial unity that focus on Confucian ideology such as Zhao's account of Han bureaucracy. Zhao focuses on Confucian ideology as the key institution of the Western Han,[189] noting that it came into vogue under Emperor Wu.[190] While Zhao likely overestimates Wu's commitment to Confucian thought,[191] this gives us the problem of explaining the empire in

188 Ibid., 113.

189 Zhao 2015, 75.

190 Ibid., 77.

191 Cf. Cai 2015 suggesting that it was really after Wu that Confucian thought became a major force in the state.

the first place, seeing as the first century of Western Han bureaucracy is not Confucian. Furthermore, it does nothing to explain the century of Qin expansion. Zhao does not devote much space to the Warring States period, understandably focusing on the Han as part of the Han-Rome comparison, and treating it as a result of militarized society.[192] However, the empire already existed at the beginning of the Western Han, and while there was local dissatisfaction with the Qin, it was about who should rule, not about the nature of that rule. This would suggest that they had already been effective in generating a sense of a single empire. Here, as elsewhere, it would seem that the structure of the bureaucratic institutions themselves were the agents of unity.

In sum, then, it seems likely that regular contact with the bureaucracy served to communicate the rational incentive structure that unified expectations around rule and generated a shared identities of subjects of the Empire. Later, particularly in times of crisis when the incentives could not be distributed by the administration, subject of the Empire came to take on elements of an ethnic or national identity, but Early Imperial China was bound not by common historical narrative or sense of kinship, but by application of Rational Actor Theory to the question of human cooperation.

6. Conclusion

As we have seen, philosophical texts, excavated documents, and actual policy suggest that there was a group of administrators in Early Imperial China who understood human behavior as being driven by rational self-interest. They sought to employ this through economic incentives. They also envisaged prices as being conditioned by supply and demand. However, unlike Classical and Neo-Classical Economics, they saw human rationality as operating under constraints. Between this, inherent instability of the market, and asymmetries in the information and abilities of the participants, they did not believe that the market could set good prices on its own. Meanwhile, Confucians tended to oppose the rational actor assumption, not on the grounds that people were not rationally self-interested, but that they were not solely rational and that by making use of emotive cognition, the state could and should have further reaching social goals to transform the behavior of its population, giving them the tools to be moral agents in their own right, rather than obedient tools. A moral society would have no need of state economic intervention because prices would determine themselves, not by competition, but by moral cooperation. While we are inclined to see this as overly idealistic, the core objection to Rational Actor Theory is one that has also been raised in our own time.

192 Zhao 2015, 63.

In both cases, human behavioral norms are understood as being modulated by the social institutions. These institutions include practices of production, social norms, and technologies and are intentional solutions to proximal problems; products of virtuoso feats of human rationality. Rational policies, clearly explicated and evenly instituted rather than an external foe or ideology seem to have been a major source of the unity that bound the diverse empire together.

In short, I think it is fair to call the stream of thought observed in texts such as *The Book of Lord Shang* and *Guanzi* a something close to the NIE instantiation of "Rational Actor Theory" as the differences in the conclusions they come to vis-a-vis Neo-Classical Economics are due to the weighting of factors, with the most significant theoretical difference being the inclusion of institutions as a crucial component to human behavior. Furthermore, while we may observe limitations to the rationality of humans in practice, the outcomes of Early Imperial policy also suggest that people who are not in an ideologically capitalist market do respond to rational incentives. Thus, both the substantivist and formalist positions in the debate of the applicability to premodern societies have a point. Market behavior is not reducible to individual rationality, but neither are institutions all determining; the differences in this early imperial Rational Actor Theory are actually comprehensible to us and while we might disagree with the effects of Jupiter on crop yields, the difference is less in method and more in the content of our empirical models.

In this regard, the critiques of mainstream economics from within mainstream economics are quite interesting, with many observing an overreliance on rationality illustrated by mathematical proofs rather than empirical testing.[193] In this respect, modern Rational Actor Theory may well be being irrationally applied. This need not surprise us; western Rational Actor Theory emerged in a specific time and place and is path dependent. Just as institutions inform what courses of action appear rational, they also inform our beliefs and assumptions about what is rational. This is not relativist, but rather something more Bayesian (or Xunzian). Since our models are built up by our observations and weighting of these variables, two intelligent people can look at the same data and come to different interpretations. Across time and space, such models are unsurprisingly entangled with knowledge networks and systems of praxis, but equally unsurprisingly, it is not a matter of totally different cultural narratives with no connection to anything material, but rather the structures of institutions of thought nudging us towards this or that interpretation. In other words, the apparent irrationality of classical Rational Actor Theory is a good example of bounded rationality in the context of institutions.

193 Spiegler 2015; Hodgson 1999.

Bibliography

Allard, Francis (2006): Frontiers and Boundaries: The Han Empire from its Southern Periphery, in: Stark, Miriam (ed.), Archeology of Asia, Hoboken, 233–254.

Barbieri-Lo, Anthony (2011): Craftsman's Literacy: Uses of Writing by Male and Female Artisans in Qin and Han China, in: Li, Feng / Branner, David (eds.), Writing and Literacy in Early China: Studies from the Columbia Early China Seminar, Seattle / London, 370–400.

Barbieri-Lo, Anthony (2021): Coerced Migration and Resettlement in the Qin Imperial Expansion, in: Journal of Chinese History 5/2, 181–202.

Baslé, Maurice (2017): Mistaking a Phase of Endogenous Growth with a New Role for the State for a "Great Depression": The Recent Financial Crisis Compared to that of 1873–1879, in: Alcouffe, Alain / Poettinger, Monika / Schefold, Bertram (eds.), Business Cycles in Economic Thought. A History, London, 14–27.

Baxter, William and Sagart, Laurent (2014): Old Chinese Reconstructions, version 1.1, URL: https://ocbaxtersagart.lsait.lsa.umich.edu/BaxterSagartOCbyMandarinMC2014-09-20.pdf, last accessed 01.05.2023.

Blanton, Richard with Fargher, Lane (2016): How Humans Cooperate, Boulder.

Cai, Liang (2014): Witchcraft and the Rise of the First Confucian Empire, Albany.

Cai, Liang (2019): Ru Scholars, Social Networks, and Bureaucracy: Donghai Men and Models for Success in Western Han China (206 B.C.E. – 9 C.E.), in: Early China 42, 237–271.

Campbell, Roderick et al. (2018): The Guandimiao Bone Assemblage (and What it Says about the Shang Economy), in: Asian Perspectives 57, 2.

Chao, Glenda (2017): Culture Change and Imperial Incorporation in Early China: An Archeological Study of the Middle Han River Valley (ca. 8th century BCE – 1st century CE), PhD-thesis, Columbia University.

Crone, Thomas (2017): The Semantic Change of the Word *min* 民 in Texts of the Eastern Zhou Period (771–221 BC), in: Asiatische Studien – Etudes Asiatiques 70/3, 675–699.

De Vroey, Michel (2015): A History of Macroeconomics from Keynes to Lucas and Beyond, Cambridge.

Demandt, Michele (2020): Reaching "the Southern Wilderness": Expansion and the Formation of the Lingnan Transportation Network during the Qin and Han Dynasties, in: Journal of the Economic and Social History of the Orient 63/1–2, 157–194.

Gaetner, Samuel L. / Bovidio, John F. (2000): Reducing Intergroup Bias: The Common Identity Model, Essays in Social Psychology, Philadelphia.

Goldin, Paul R. (2011): Persistent Misconceptions about Chinese Legalism, Journal of Chinese Philosophy 38/1, 88–104.

Goldin, Paul R. (2015): Representations of Regional Diversity during the Eastern Zhou Dynasty, in: Pines, Yuri / Goldin, Paul / Kern, Martin (2015): Ideology of Power and Power of Ideology in Early China, Leiden (Sinica Leidensia 124), 31–48.

Goldin, Paul R. (ed.) (2018): Routledge Handbook of Early Chinese History, London / New York.

Goldin, Paul R. (2020): The Art of Chinese Philosophy: Eight Classical Texts and How to Read Them, Princeton / Oxford.

Goldin, Paul R. (2022): Economic Cycles and Price Theory in Early Chinese Texts, in: Sabattini, Elisa / Schwermann, Christian (eds.), Between Command and Market. Economic Thought and Practice in Early China, Leiden (Sinica Leidensia 154), 43–77.

Heijdra, Ben J. (2009): Foundations of Modern Macroeconomics, Oxford.

Hodgson, Geoffrey (1999): Evolution and Institutions, Cheltenham.

Hulsewé, Anthony F. P. (1955): Remnants of Han Law. Vol. I: Introductory Studies and Annotated Translation of Chapter 22 and 23 of the History of the Former Han Dynasty, Leiden.

Isaac, Barry L. (1993): Retrospective on the Formalist-Substantivist Debate, in: Research in Economic Anthropology 14, 213–233.

Kim, Kyong-ho and Lai, Ming-chiu (2018): An Overview of the Qin-Han Legal System from the Perspective of Recently Unearthed Documents, in: Goldin, Paul R. (ed.), Routledge Handbook of Early Chinese History, London / New York, 386–404.

Kong, Yingda et al. (eds.) (2000): Mengzi. Shi San Jing Zhu Shu (zheng Li Ben), vol. 25, Beijing.

Kong, Yingda, et al. eds. (2000): Liji. Shi San Jing Zhu Shu (zheng Li Ben). Vol 15, Beijing.

Lau, Ulrich / Staack, Thies (2015): Legal Practice in the Formative Stages of the Chinese Empire, Leiden / Boston (Sinica Leidensia 130).

Leese-Messing, Kathrin (2020): The Qin and Han Empires, in: von Reden, Sitta (ed.), Handbook of Ancient Afro-Eurasian Economies. Vol. 1: Contexts, Berlin, 129–204.

Leese-Messing, Kathrin (2020): Qin and Han Evidence, in: von Reden, Sitta (ed.), Handbook of Ancient Afro-Eurasian Economies. Vol. 1: Contexts, Berlin, 497–528.

Leung, Vincent (2018) The Former Han, in: Goldin, Paul R. (ed.), Routledge Handbook of Early Chinese History. London / New York, 160–179.

Li, Feng (2006): Landscape and Power in Early China: The Crisis and Fall of the Western Zhou, 1045–771 B.C., Cambridge.

Lu, Jia (auth.) / Goldin, Paul (trans.) / Sabattini, Elisa (trans.) (2020): Lu Jia's New Discourses: A Political Manifesto from the Early Han Dynasty, Leiden.

North, Douglass C. (1991): Institutions, in: Journal of Economic Perspectives 5/1, 97–112.

North, Douglass C. (2005): Understanding the Process of Economic Change, Princeton.

Pines, Yuri / Shelach, Gideon (2005): 'Using the Past to Serve the Present': Comparative Perspectives on Chinese and Western Theories of the Origins of the State, in: Shaked, Shaul (ed.), Genesis and Regeneration: Essays on Conceptions of Origins, Jerusalem, 127–163.

Pines, Yuri (2009): Envisioning Eternal Empire: Chinese Political Thought of the Warring States Era, Honolulu.

Pines, Yuri / Goldin, Paul / Kern, Martin (2015): Ideology of Power and Power of Ideology in Early China, Leiden (Sinica Leidensia 124).

Pines, Yuri (trans.) (2017): The Book of Lord Shang: Apologetics of State Power in Early China, New York.

Pines, Yuri (2021): Limits of All-under-Heaven: Ideology and Praxis of 'Great Unity' in Early Chinese Empire. In: Pines, Yuri (ed.), The Limits of Universal Rule: Eurasian Empires Compared, Cambridge, 79–110.

Poo, Mu-chou (2005): Enemies of Civilization: Attitudes towards Foreigners in Ancient Mesopotamia, Egypt, and China, Albany.

Rickett, W. Allyn (1998): Guanzi. Vol. 2, Princeton.

Sage, Steven F. (1992): Ancient Sichuan and the Unification of China, Albany.

Sanft, Charles (2014): Communication and Cooperation in Early Imperial China: Publicizing the Qin Dynasty, Albany.

Sanft, Charles (2018): The Qin Dynasty, in: Goldin, Paul R. (ed.), Routledge Handbook of Early Chinese History, London / New York, 146–159.

Shelach, Gideon / Pines, Yuri (2006): Secondary State Formation and the Development of Local Identity: Change and Continuity in the State of Qin (770–221 B.C.), in: Stark, Miriam (ed.), Archeology of Asia, Hoboken, 202–230.

Shi Dangshe (2017): Cong muzangzhongde 'yilie' kan qin wenhua de chuanbo, in: Qinling qintong yanjiu dongtai 5/3, 28–35.

Skyrms, Brian (2004): The Stag Hunt and the Evolution of Social Structure, Cambridge.

Sou, Daniel (2013): In the Government's Service: A Study of the Role and Practice of Early China's Officials Based on Excavated Manuscripts, Phd-thesis, University of Pennsylvania.

Spiegler, Peter (2015): Behind the Model, Cambridge.

Stark, Miriam (ed.) (2005): Archeology of Asia, Hoboken.

Sterckx, Roel (2015): Ideologies of the Peasant and Merchant in Warring States China, in: Pines, Yuri / Goldin, Paul / Kern, Martin (eds.), Ideology of Power and Power of Ideology in Early China, Leiden (Sinica Leidensia 124), 211–248.

Sterckx, Roel (2018): Food and Agriculture, in: Goldin, Paul R. (ed.), Routledge Handbook of Early Chinese History, London / New York, 300–318.

Sterckx, Roel (2020). Agrarian and Mercantile Ideologies in Western Han, in: Journal of the Economic and Social History of the Orient 63/4, 465–504.

Thierry, François (2018): Currency, in: Goldin, Paul R. (ed.), Routledge Handbook of Early Chinese History, London / New York, 336–366.

Tomer, John F. (2017): Advanced Introduction to Behavioral Economics, Chettenham.

Tse, Wicky (2018): The Latter Han Empire and The End of Antiquity, in: Goldin, Paul R. (ed.), Routledge Handbook of Early Chinese History, London / New York, 189–196.

Van Norden, Bryan (trans.) (2008): Mengzi: with Selections from Traditional Commentaries, Indianapolis.

Von Reden, Sitta (ed.) (2020): Handbook of Ancient Afro-Eurasian Economies. Vol. 1: Contexts, Berlin.

Wang, Aihe (2001): Creators of an Emperor: The Political Group behind the Founding of the Han Empire, in: Asia Major 14/1, 19–50.

Watson, Burton (trans.) (1964): Basic Writings of Mo Tzu, Hsün Tzu, and Han Fei Tzu, New York.

Wilson, Edward O. (2000): Sociobiology, Cambridge.

Xunzi / Knoblock, John / Zhang, Jue (1999): Xunzi. Da Zhonghua Wenku, Changsha.

Zhao, Dingxin (2015): The Han Bureaucracy, in: Scheidel, Walter (ed.), State Power in Ancient China and Rome, Oxford, 56–89.

Zhou, Caizhu et al. (eds.) (2006): Mozi, Changsha.

Land and Credit in the History of Economic Thought

Traditional China and Premodern Europe: *Dian* and "*pactum antichriseos*[1]"

Bertram Schefold[2]

Abstract: The paper compares land lease in Germany with China. Kaspar Klock, 1651, speaks of a contract for mutual use: a landowner leases land to a farmer who gets the annual harvest for a specified period and is obliged to pay at the beginning, the land remaining the property of the owner. In the eyes of Klock, the landowner thus gets a credit from the farmer, for which he pays by means of allowing the farmer to harvest. Klock asks whether the contract is usurious, but is unable to calculate the implicit rate of interest and whether it exceeds the legal rate. The same arrangement would in China be a purchase, distinguishing between the "bone" and the "skin" of the land: the farmer would have "bought" the skin, but not the bone. Paradoxically, the "irrationality" of the prohibition of usury contributed, via the analysis of "licit" reasons to take interest and via the mathematical analysis of compound interest to intellectual progress, while the Chinese (who looked down on merchants, but had no misgivings about interest) saw no need to develop their juridical categories in this area.

Keywords: Usury – Rationality – Land Tenure – Premodern Europe – Premodern China – Kaspar Klock – Gottfried Wilhelm Leibniz – Carl Chassot de Florencourt

1. Introduction

If asked which element of traditional economic thinking was most obviously irrational and had yet most tenaciously been maintained over many centuries, from the dawn of written history down to the 19th century, most Western economists would probably respond: usury and the usury laws. A prohibition of usury seems irrational from the point of modern economic theory, except in very special circumstances,

---

1 This term is rather unusual and reflects Klock's education in Ancient Greek. Since all other sources refer to the antichretic contract as "*pactum antichreticum*", we shall use this term hereafter.

2 I should like to thank Johanna Kleensang for her great contribution in composing this paper.

and historians of economic thought might add that the desire to eradicate usury had much to do with passions, social conditions, and – perhaps above all – religion, and what is more opposed to rationality than insistence on beliefs? "Rationality" of course here means economic rationality – I do not want to deny that theology, within its system of beliefs, may be rational, reasonable, and intellectually sophisticated.

The concept of rationality has been given different meanings in economics. There is the basic distinction between the pursuit of one's own interest as opposed to acting according to notions of fairness and traditional norms; there is the question what rationality means, if actions may lead into inconsistencies, for instance, because an option may lead to addiction ("I hate my desire to smoke"); and rationality also involves the question whether the actor is at all able to see through the situation with its uncertainties and possesses the knowledge which is necessary to calculate the consequences, in particular the monetary gain, for instance, the chances of making a profit by an investment. Irrational are therefore not only actions motivated by magic, belief, and tradition, but also actions based on simplistic assessments, ignorance, and miscalculation. Some degree of irrationality cannot be avoided in complex and uncertain situations. It was Max Weber's great theme that rationality evolves in the historical process, which is ambivalent. It might seem that it would be rational to overcome capitalism with its vagaries and to replace it by a system of rational planning, but if planning is not feasible, the result was foreseen by Weber to be worse. The process of rationalisation may appear as a cultural achievement, but it is accompanied by a loss of other human faculties.[3] Usury is an excellent example of irrationality since it involves all the dimensions, which we have mentioned, in particular solidarity vs. egotism, and changing beliefs vs. progress in mathematics.

As is well known, the prohibition of usury is common to the Abrahamitic religions and has an early root in tribal solidarity:[4] the Jews were allowed to take interest from foreigners, but not from their tribal companions (cf. the paper of Højgaard in this volume). There is another root in Greek and Roman tradition, plausibly originally motivated by similar feelings. The necessity to use credit arises in archaic societies, first where help from neighbours is expected, if in barter the desired objects are not at hand and must be promised for another day, or, more importantly, if some calamity arises and one needs support. Entrepreneurial activity, extended by means of credit, comes later. To demand interest and expect punctual repayment, where generosity is expected, subverts the spirit of the community as long as society is not

3 Weber 1976, 35–37, 44–45, 55.

4 Nelson 1962.

yet used to the rules of commercial market exchange and the separation of the sphere of the family and personal relationships from the market society. In this transition, Aristotle saw the sole function of money in its potential to serve as a medium of exchange, and hence he provided a logical argument to exclude interest-taking: it involved a misuse of money in that money was used to generate more money.[5]

Credit could also be seen as an institution for mutual benefit, and so it appears in Roman law. If a service is promised to be exchanged for another service, the underlying credit relationship is usually not even perceived. One form, which we shall encounter, is the *antichresis*, which existed also in Greece. Person A provides capital to person B and can use B's services or a good belonging to B, such as land, in exchange. The Roman institution of *pactum antichreticum* was of this type. The persons could interpret this contract as a lease of land from B to A and the capital paid from A to B as an advance payment of the rent, but they could also see it as a lending from A to B and with an amortisation of the loan in the form of the opportunity offered from B to A to exploit B's land. If there existed a maximum legal rate of interest, the value of the services obtained by A from B could exceed the value of the capital lent plus interest, and *this* would then represent usury, when the credit system had developed. So the problem of usury would shift from the disdain for interest-taking in general to the violation of the rules regarding interest rates governing a mercantile society in which credit was common. Misgivings because of abuses, because crises endangered the edifice of credit relationships or because contracts such as the *pactum antichreticum* were not transparent could resuscitate old prejudices against usury and let lenders be perceived as usurers at any time.

The story of how prohibition of usury was rationalised in subsequent periods, notably by the Scholastic authors, has often been told.[6] It was accompanied by the endeavour to create institutions that would function without usury and yet provide the advantages of a credit economy. Islamic banking is the latest outgrowth of the attempt to reconcile the view that sharing the profit of enterprise is licit, while demanding interest for mere lending is not.

I have argued elsewhere[7] that the usury debate in the West had an ambiguous effect on European development. On the one hand, the restriction on credit – which only rarely consisted in a total prohibition of interest-taking not only by the church, but also by the state – was an obstacle to growth, because the free intercourse of merchants and producers was hindered and because it became difficult to create

5 *Politics* 1.3.23, in particular 1258a39–b8.

6 Schumpeter 1954, Roover 1955, Nelson 1962, Amelung / Schefold 2021.

7 Schefold 2018.

lasting sources of income for the old in retirement, for widows and orphans. The damnation of usury was inconvenient even for the church itself, for it was rich, but actually not a market producer and therefore dependent on unearned income flowing from its wealth. At the same time, the reasons why there was opposition against interest-taking remained visible: there were countless poor borrowers not able to pay up, there were draconic measures to enforce payment, repeated conflict between rich and poor, and the tendency to denounce moneylenders by pushing them to the margin of society and creating ghettos.

But there was also a positive side to the usury debate. It forced the antagonists to think about interest as an institution that could not be eradicated, from the beginnings of its prohibition. One tried to distinguish between legitimate forms of taking interest and illegitimate usury. In recognition of the fact that the instruments of credit and interest were useful, merchants, lawyers, and theologians had to argue, when and where the instruments of credit helped development, and this became one of the origins of modern economic theorising.[8] One of the most troubling questions was whether interest-taking was licit because the lender could have used the money for his own profit, for instance, by trading himself at a fair to which a borrower went, equipped with the money of the lender. This was called the argument of *lucrum cessans*. The churchmen knew that it was not licit to use this argument in the form: if you borrow money from me, you have to pay 5 %, because your colleague would be ready to pay as much, for such a statement would be circular in so far as monetary interest would be rationalised by means of monetary interest. One could invoke *lucrum cessans* only if one had a proven alternative for the use of the money in the form of some real investment, but opinions were divided and changed over time as to how severely this criterion was to be used. Eventually, the pursuit of this question led to the problem of where the profit came from – which was the true source for the payment of interest – and thus political economy was born.

It is a curious fact that China reached a relatively high level of development in premodern times without either profiting or suffering from the advantages or disadvantages of a usury debate since interest was accepted at all levels without questioning it in principle. There was private credit in the city and in the countryside. There was credit provided by the state (the state was a lender rather than a borrower), and monasteries used and provided credit. The interest rates seemed high to the Western observer.[9] The farmer, who had run out of grain, needed seeds and typically took a loan from the beginning of the period of production to the harvest at the end. If the contract was made for this time span, if it lasted 6 months and the

8 Ibid.

9 Davis 1836.

rate of interest was 30 %, the annual interest rate was about 15 %, and this seems bearable. Credit contracts of this kind were frequent and were entered voluntarily.

This paper shall extend comparisons between China and the West[10] regarding the status of merchants and the treatment of credit institutions in particular through the role which land can play in this context. We will examine concepts involving land lease that developed in Europe concerning the circumvention of usury and compare them to similar concepts in China. Paradoxically, the ideological discussions about interest-taking and usury led to theoretical progress via mathematical analyses of licit reasons to take interest, as we shall show by means of the examples of Leibniz and Florencourt.

Institutional regulations of land lease have varied greatly throughout history. We here compare concepts about land holding in China and in Germany during the 17th and 18th century. In traditional China, the average farm size was rather small, as primogeniture did not exist, and the land was therefore divided between all sons of a family. One could expect that this led to a strong aversion against forms of land tenure that implied interest-taking because of the precarious position of smallholders as debtors. In fact, there were some concerns about interest. Instead of forbidding compound interest, the total accumulation of interest debt was restricted by a ceiling: total interest outstanding could not exceed the principal,[11] and this was regulated not by civil, but by criminal law and custom. However, a heavy ideological opposition against interest-taking as in Europe did not develop in China. There were no significant attempts to denounce interest on systematic theoretical grounds. Hence, there was no need to develop a theory in order to justify interest against such opposition either. Interest was a fact of life, not a paradoxical phenomenon requiring an explanation of its origin.

2. Kaspar Klock, the *pactum antichreticum*, and the "calculating jurists"

Kaspar Klock (1583–1655) was a German jurist, cameralist, and specialist for taxation and public finance in the first half of the 17th century. We use his example as a starting point for the analysis of European thought on the connection between credit and land tenure, and we begin with an introduction to his main work since he was regarded as an authority in his time but is little known today. Against the backdrop of the Thirty Years War, he published his extensive work *De Aerario* (*On the Treasury*). The first book contains a detailed overview of the different states and their economic and political systems, centred on the finances of princes and republics. In the

10 Amelung and Schefold 2021.

11 Davis 1836, 396.

second book, Klock deals with the question of just taxation. He also reflects on agriculture, manufacture, money, prices, usury, and monopolies.

In the first book, one chapter is dedicated to China. Klock admires China as being exceptionally peaceful: "*ideo hic floret Justitia, quietis mater*"; "*haec regni lex est, ut ad nihil aliud, quam ad pacem & conservationem Rei publicae colliment*".[12] Indeed, in China, the 16th century was followed by a long period of domestic peace and stability that lasted until the crises-ridden 19th century.[13] He analyses the role of the Chinese emperor whom he says to have accumulated incredible treasures (his annual revenues would be as much as the Roman emperor Vespasian received during his lifetime). These treasures of the Chinese emperor would circulate back to the people as expenditures of the palace. He uses this observation as an opportunity to elaborate on his cameralist conviction: "*si enim extra Regnum expenderet, angariae dupliciter consumerent populum: Nam ex ejus manibus elaberentur pecuniae, facultatesque, neque spes superesset emolumenti, aut fructus alicujus*".[14] According to Klock and the cameralists, imports would cause a decline of expenditure for domestic products. Moreover, the inhabitants would have less command over international currency, and the diminution of silver would reduce what now is called the monetary base. Therefore, a positive trade balance was to be achieved. The Chinese emperor, if he forgoes luxury imports, thus becomes a model for Europe. Klock also values the Chinese inventive spirit, yet he still criticizes their pride: "*in inventionibus suis videntur sibi omnium mortalium esse ingeniosissimi, multumque & crebris industriam suam iactant sermonibus, dicentes: Chinenses solos habere duos oculos, Europaeos unum, alios caecos esse*".[15]

Klock's work exhibits his attachment to humanism as well as a profound knowledge of ancient literature: his concepts of just taxation draw on Aristotle, and he gives a precise definition of geometric and arithmetic proportion, applied to questions of taxation. He refers to Cicero's *De Officiis* when he mentions the useful and the honourable,[16] he cites Petronius and Horace, and in chapter 145 of the second book, he translates and comments on the Pseudo-Aristotelian *Oikonomika*.

Although he is progressive when it comes to taxation, Klock – influenced by scholasticism – is rather conservative regarding usury: he sees it as an evil ("*malum*") that has to be contained. One might be surprised since Klock was a Protestant

12 Klock 2009 (1651), book I, XIX, 3; the sources for his subsequent description of the country and for his estimates of taxes paid to the emperor – Jesuit missionaries? traders? Giovanni Botero? – are not known.

13 Von Glahn 2016, 345.

14 Klock 2009 (1651), book I, XIX, 18.

15 Klock 2009 (1651), book I, XIX, 26.

16 Cic. *Off.* 1.1.13–14.

(a Lutheran) and yet follows the long tradition to denounce usury (dating from antiquity). He draws upon the Catholic tradition by referring to the scholastics and the authors of the School of Salamanca. He quotes Cato, who compared interest taking to homicide,[17] and refers to the famous biblical "*mutuum date nihil inde sperantes*".[18] Besides the traditional arguments to denounce usury, Klock also invokes a sociological one: the usurer is seen as inertly and maliciously waiting at home ("*segnis & exitiabilis est vita usurarii*"[19]) until the disasters befall others and he can lend out his money. Klock knows the arguments debated by the School of Salamanca to justify interest: *periculum sortis* (risk of the loss of capital), *damnum emergens* (recovery of damages), and *lucrum cessans* (opportunity cost), but he remains sceptical since they could justify payments that exceed the legal rate of interest ("*annuas pensiones legitimum usurarum modum excedentes*"[20]). When it comes to taxation, he follows the School of Salamanca more closely.[21] Klock furthermore complains that new techniques ("*artes novas*") to circumvent usury have developed repeatedly. These new techniques involve, for example, the "*locationes fructuum*" (a merchant buys the fruit prior to the harvest) and the "*venditiones cum pacto de retrovendendo*": the debtor receives a loan by selling something to the creditor who immediately asserts that he would resell the good to the debtor later, but at a higher price which reflects interest. This apparently usurious transaction (receiving a loan and paying interest) is disguised as a simple sale of a pledge with the promise to buy it back. We will refer to this type of circumvention of usury again when we compare it to the Chinese "live sale".

Klock also elaborates on a specific form of land tenure: the old Roman *pactum antichreticum* which he views as another technique to circumvent usury. The borrower of a loan would give the creditor a piece of fruit-bearing land (or something similar, for example, cattle) which the creditor would then be allowed to use until the debtor settled the debt. The usage of the land would replace any interest claims of the creditor. The usage could also suffice to amortise the debt – wholly or in part – in the latter case, the debtor could take the land or cattle back and pay for the difference. This operation does not require any explicit calculations of interest, and the usurious nature therefore seems to be concealed as the transaction appears as a simple swap. Interestingly, Roedenbeck has stressed that the *pactum antichreticum* does not necessarily imply a pawnage and that its juridical form is a barter

17 Klock 2009 (1651), book II, XIX, 14.
18 Klock 2009 (1651), book II, XIX, 49–51.
19 Klock 2009 (1651), book II, XIX, 19.
20 Klock 2009 (1651), book II, XIX, 66.
21 Schefold 2011.

agreement (the usage of the money is bartered for the usage of the land) rather than a pledge agreement.[22] The barter agreement would, in contrast to the pledge agreement, not imply a legal relationship between the parties.[23] The literal translation of "*antichresis*" is also noteworthy: mutual usage. Wigmore sees the *antichresis* as a "reciprocal loan" and states that "the transaction is not primarily a pledge at all; the lessee of the house or farm has merely a subsidiary lien on it for the return of its money; and the whole transaction plays practically no part in the history of pledge-law".[24] Matic emphasises differences between *antichresis* and *pactum antichreticum*.[25] The latter would contain the explicit permission for the lender to use the pledge provided by the borrower, while this would not be allowed in the former case. Matic quotes from Gaius: "*si pignore creditor utatur, furti tenetur*".[26] The problem still ghosts in modern civil law. § 1372 ABGB of Austrian civil law states: "Der Nebenvertrag, daß dem Gläubiger die Fruchtnießung der verpfändeten Sache zustehen solle, ist ohne rechtliche Wirkung", and the comment says (my translation): "§ 1372 prohibts to the creditor to demand the usus fructus of the pledge; this is the old pactum antichreticum, because there arises the danger of usury."[27]

Clearly, Klock assumes the use of the pledge. He now asks whether the profit, which the creditor obtains from the usage of the pawn, is licit even if it exceeds the legal rate of interest (which was set by the worldly authority and was typically quoted as at around 4 % or 5 % by several authors of the School of Salamanca). He draws the conclusion that this is a nice question ("*pulchrae indaginis quaestio est*"[28]). He is, however, unable to calculate the rate of interest that the transaction implies. Hence, he is unable to decide whether the *pactum antichreticum* is usurious at all – for lack of ability to rationally calculate it.

This conundrum could only later be solved on the basis of the achievements by Leibniz and the "calculating jurists", such as Florencourt.[29] They overcame the simple denouncement of interest-taking. The legal interest rate was accepted, but the problem remained that compound interest was forbidden. The idea behind the prohibition of compound interest was to protect the debtor from an overbearing accumulation of debt. In China, the idea of restricting the amount of debt also existed,

22 Roedenbeck 1874, 4.

23 Ibid., 6.

24 Wigmore 1897, 35.

25 Matic 2016.

26 Gai. Dig. 47.2.55pr.

27 Online Lehrbuch Zivilrecht 2022.

28 Klock 2009 (1651), book II, XIX, 41.

29 For an extensive analysis on this, see Schefold 2021a and 2021b.

but, instead of denouncing compound interest, the quantity of debt was limited. Leibniz, still using the theological terminology, mathematically calculates the *interusurium* in his work "Meditatio juridico-mathematica de interusurio simplice".[30] The *interusurium* is a rebate – meaning that the debtor, who has to settle a debt a year from now, can demand a rebate from the creditor by paying today. Leibniz sees that there is a mutual compensation between the debtor and the creditor. Via the calculus of a geometric series, he obtains the formula for the present value of the loan.

As an intermediate author, let us quote Johann Philipp Colonius, who explains our problem in a textbook of arithmetic as follows: "Cajus leihet Titio 100 Rthlr. und lässt sich von seinem Debitore etliche Acker Landes verschreiben zum Unterpfande sub pacto antichreseos, so daß er an Statt derer Zinsen, die Fructus von der Hypothec einhebet."[31] The creditor lends 100 for 5 years. The debtor lends land for the use of the creditor, which could be rented at 10 %, but the legal interest rate is 5 %. The debtor will have to pay back the capital at the end, but may deduct what the creditor has earned in excess of interest. Colonius calculates this laboriously from year to year. The result is, of course, that interest of 5 % for five years on 100 may be deducted from 100; the debt reduces to "72 Rthlr. 8Gr." and some pennies.

Carl Chassot de Florencourt (1756–1790), professor of philosophy in Göttingen and counsellor for finance and mining in Germany, refers to Leibniz' calculation of the *interusurium*. On this basis, Florencourt analyses the antichretic contract. He is able to make the *pactum antichreticum* transparent by calculating the amount that is transferred between borrower and lender. It seems to be a matter of course for Florencourt that the *pactum antichreticum* makes no sense if the time period over which it is to run is not made explicit. The main calculation is short and clear:

> Antichretischer Vertrag: Er ist dann vorhanden, wenn der Schuldner dem Gläubiger, eine nutzbare Sache, auf eine gewisse Zeit übergiebt, sie gehörig zu nutzen, damit der Gläubiger, wegen des Verlustes am Nutzen seines Capitals, den der Schuldner zieht, entschädigt werde. Trägt sie mehr ein, als der Gläubiger für seinen Verlust fordern darf, so muß er den Ueberschuß vom Capitale abziehen. [...] Das verliehene Capital sey = C; der jährliche Ertrag der nutzbaren Sache = S; die Zeit, welche sie der Gläubiger nützet = n; [...] Der Gläubiger zieht also am Ende jedes Jahres S; folglich ist der Werth aller dieser S, mit dem Nutzen davon, nach n Jahren = $\frac{(1+i)^n-1}{i}$ S; [for the creditor obtains S in each of n years, and the value of these payments at the end is $(1+i)^{n-1}$ S + $(1+i)^{n-2}$ S + ... + (1 + i) S + S = $\frac{(1+i)^n-1}{i}$, i being the rate

30 Leibniz 1962 (1863, 1683).

31 Colonius 1748, 482.

> of interest – B.S.] Das verliehene Capital C ist in der Zeit gestiegen, auf $(1+i)^n$C. Folglich ist das, was einer von dem anderen heraus bekömmt $= (1+i)^n C - \frac{(1+i)^n - 1}{i} S = M$ (Florencourt 1781, 35).

Florencourt is able to calculate the balance, because he takes the rate of interest as given and, at least in his textbook, this must be the legal rate of interest. He clearly reckons with compound interest and excuses this practice with the assertion that there is here no question of real anatocism.[32] He probably meant that debtor and creditor were of equal standing so that there was no danger of crushing the debtor by the accumulation of debt; the "nutzbare Sache" would be returned in the end. It is clear that land is only one example of a useful object that could be taken as the object of exchange in the antichretic contract. Another example would be a machine, where amortisation would be paid annually by the borrower of the machine to its lender. The calculation is therefore the first step towards a correct calculation of the amortisation of machines. Hence, the irrational denouncement of usury has led, via considerations on licit reasons to take interest and the mathematical reflections upon compound interest, to theoretical advances in economics and to general intellectual progress – here to the economic application of the calculation of the geometric series, and these applications inspired Leibniz also to extend the mathematical theory itself.[33]

3. Land tenure in traditional China

We shall now compare these forms of land tenure to similar concepts in China. Long Denggao and Chi Xiang emphasize – using neoclassical terminology – that there existed an elaborate transaction system for property rights in land, which could be traded.[34] According to Long and Chi, this land transaction system improved economic efficiency and enabled landowners to "make choices according to market prices".[35] This suggests rational decision-making concerning land transactions. The tenant who borrows money in order to rent more land and hire more workers is for Long and Chi not an impoverished farmer dependent on the favours of a rich gentry, but an entrepreneur who, like modern managers, combines factors of production and extends his business by means of credit. Reality, however, was more complex. Chapter 3.2 will show an example of a form of land tenure in traditional China that was very common even though it was not economically efficient and not strictly

32 Florencourt 1781, 4.

33 Schefold 2021b.

34 Long / Chi 2021, 2.

35 Ibid., 7.

rational, but where the seller instead accepted an amount of money for his property that deviated significantly from the market price for sociological reasons.

Sino-Marxism took an entirely different view in Maoist times. Compare the approach adopted by Fu Zhufu at the end of that period.[36] He sees China's land system as heavily influenced by feudalistic structures that opposed market transactions regarding land rights. He also stresses that in China there was never a free and autonomous city that could have led to a prosperity of commerce, but instead, feudal structures also prevailed in the cities.[37] He emphasizes that the lack of guilds in China did on the one hand free merchants from rigid restrictions but, on the other hand, it also inhibited the development of capitalism as innovations could only individually be protected by the family. This inhibited the growth of an innovative industrial development.[38] In such an environment, credit relationships in the countryside led to personal dependence. The debtor in difficulties offers all sorts of services to the creditor in order to postpone payment and to avoid bankruptcy. Hence, Marx's writings on usury in *Das Kapital*, inspired by observations of debt bondage made in occidental societies, were applied to the interpretation of Chinese history.

These two examples show that there are contrasting approaches to Chinese economic history: we shall show that traditional Chinese forms of land tenure had rational elements connected to the existence of land markets but were still strongly embedded in a sociological environment, which caused deviations from the neoclassical model.

3.1 The dian *land right*

There exists a legal institution in China that bears similarities to the antichretic contract: the *dian* land right. It was known since the Tang Dynasty, further developed in Song times,[39] and exists until today. It is constituted as follows: a creditor obtains a piece of land from the debtor by giving a certain amount of money as a loan. Later, the debtor can redeem his land by settling the debt. The *dian* buyer (the creditor) may either farm the land himself or lease it, which he would often do, even to the original landowner, the *dian* seller (the debtor).[40] As with the antichretic contract, the usage of the land replaces any interest that the creditor might have expected for his loan. In contrast to the *dian*, however, the antichretic contract seems to have a much stronger moral implication: in fact, if we follow Klock, the *pactum*

36 Fu 1981.

37 Ibid., 20.

38 Ibid., 25.

39 Glück 1999, 17.

40 Long / Chi 2021, 3.

antichreticum is constructed to circumvent usury and is therefore directly based on the long tradition of denouncing interest-taking. As opposed to this, the *dian* is merely a specific form of land transaction without implying a strong moral aspect that denounces interest. In China, land is perceived as being composed of the top-soil (*tianmian*) and the sub-soil (*tiandi*), which could be owned by different people, and the creditor could therefore simply hold the top-soil of the land (the right to the surface) while the sub-soil was still owned by the debtor.[41] Parallels can be drawn to medieval German legal terminology ("geteiltes Eigentum" – "divided property", my translation). Medieval jurists derived from Roman law the terms "*dominium directum*" and "*dominium utile*" to characterise the relations of possession in the Middle Ages.[42] The "*dominium utile*" is similar to the top-soil land right in that the owner had the right to use the land and extract yields from it. His property right was somewhat restricted as he was not the original owner, but he still owned the land. Both the system of top- and sub-soil ownership and the "*dominium directum*" – "*dominium utile*" system are proof that two people could have legitimate claims to one piece of land.

The time frame for redemption in the *dian* was originally unlimited.[43] One can easily imagine that this led to difficulties. Later, the timeframe was specified in the contract. Glück points out that redemption of the pawn in the *dian* was a right, not an obligation, and that the creditor had no right to demand a refund of the money he had given to the debtor.[44] As opposed to the other forms of land tenure that are examined here, the *dian* also regulated the earliest date at which the property could be redeemed: prior to this date, the debtor had no right to redeem the property. This was instituted in order to protect the creditor's right to use the land.[45] It is obvious that agricultural fields bring cyclical returns: in some months, the yields are much higher than in others. Therefore, only after a number of time periods will the creditor have had a fairly sure chance to benefit from the transaction at all. Florencourt sees the problem of volatile yields in his calculation of the returns in the antichretic contract: he suggests overcoming the problem by taking arithmetical averages. The implications for legal institutions remain unclear in his case, but – as stated above – he calculates the transfer that renders the swap licit at the legal interest rate and therefore makes the transaction transparent. The application of the model of the *pactum antichreticum* to land is straightforward, because it is assumed

41 Glück 1999, 44–45.

42 Schwab 1975, 70–71.

43 Glück 1999, 43.

44 Ibid., 91.

45 Ibid.

that the land is returned in the end so that it is not necessary to make the land price explicit in the calculation. *Dian* is insofar a more complicated and general construction. The perspective adopted with the *pactum antichreticum* renders it paradoxical: the owner of the land "lends" land and borrows money, the tenant borrows land and lends money and touches the annual interest – and perhaps the full amortisation – in the form of the net revenue of the harvest, instead of paying an annual rent, as ordinary tenants do. The Chinese perspective on the arrangement is different, of course, insofar as the tenant *buys* the surface of the land temporarily. Because of this terminology, one can lose sight of the fact that the "purchase" reflects a credit relationship.

If measured against Florencourt's calculation, transaction of the *dian* lacks transparency. In practice, it had to be based on estimates that somehow had to reckon with the influence of the rate of interest on the subjective value of the transaction for each part. This lack of rationality helps to explain why the *dian* was not free from moral conceptions. In fact, the *dian* constituted that family members and neighbours had a pre-emptive right.[46] In imperial China, land was more often held by families than by individuals,[47] and it is easily imagined that, in traditional times, when agriculture and farming played an important role in sustaining a family, it was seen as unethical to give away land. In fact, sources seem to indicate that during the Western Zhou period, the sale of land was prohibited altogether.[48] The distinction between a property right to the sub-soil or the top-soil of the land seems to be also beneficial to the family as this way it might have been easier to permanently hold on to the land even if financial distress occurred.

In modern times, only immobile objects (such as farmland or houses) can serve as a pawn in the *dian*, but it is unclear whether this was already the case in traditional times and whether a distinction between mobile and immobile objects was practiced at all in traditional China.[49] Interestingly, Klock does not distinguish between mobile and immobile goods, for he thinks that taxes must be gathered "*de omnibus bonis tam mobilibus quam immobilibus quae fructificant*".[50] Evidence suggests that, at least in early times, people (both slaves and free people as a form of debt bondage) could serve as a *dian* security, and this suggests that mobile objects could serve as a pawn in the *dian* at least in early times.[51]

46 Ibid., 66–67.

47 Pomeranz 2008, 113.

48 Glück 1999, 66.

49 Ibid., 44–46.

50 Klock 2009 (1651), XIX.

51 Glück 1999, 62.

3.2 Live sales: a rational form of land tenure?

A legal institution in traditional China that is very similar to the *dian* are "live sales" or "conditional sales" (*huomai*) which sometimes seem to be put on a level with the *dian*.[52] A "live sale" is a sale in which the seller could rebuy his property after a certain time (the timeframe was often only vaguely specified). The seller had to forego part of the profit from selling for the privilege of having the option to rebuy: he would often merely get 60 to 80 % of the market value. It was furthermore common for this transaction that the buyer paid "additional payments" to finalise the sale and deprive the seller from all claims to regain his property.[53] Pomeranz has shown that "live sales" were ultimately rather unprofitable for the seller: even if he received additional payments, selling land in a "live sale" was still by far not as profitable as selling it in a "permanent sale".[54] The seller's decision for a "live sale" therefore cannot simply be explained by the financial aspect and, as "live sales" were quite common, there has to be a strong other reason that prompted the seller to choose this form of sale. As Pomeranz analyses: "sellers [...] were actually purchasing an expensive form of insurance [...] to avoid as long as possible the social embarrassment of having lost land they had inherited".[55] Land served not only to sustain a family but was also irreplaceable for ancestral worship: not merely as a place to exert the worship, but also because the yield of the land was used to make sacrifices to the ancestors – Böhling points out that customary law stipulated that sacrifices to the ancestors had to be extracted from the family's own land.[56] This might be another reason for the very strong attachment to land.

Glück translates "live sales" (*huomai*) as "Verkauf unter Wiederkaufsvorbehalt"[57] ("sale with the possibility to rebuy", my translation), and the term seems almost identical to Klock's *venditiones cum pacto de retrovendendo.* Both transactions imply forms of irrationality. For the seller, the entire transaction of a "live sale" seems irrational as he obtains much less profit than he would, had he sold his land outright on the market. As mentioned above, he chooses this transaction form to secure the family and to escape the embarrassment of losing the land which he had inherited. The latter is an irrational argument, at least from the strict economic point of view. By wanting to secure the land for his family, however, the seller

52 For an analysis on the state of research regarding the connection and difference between *dian* and "live sales", see Glück 1999, 42 and Long / Chi 2021, 3.

53 Pomeranz 2008, 124.

54 Ibid., 127.

55 Ibid., 128.

56 Böhling 1934, 13–14.

57 Glück 1999, 42.

protects the inheritance of his sons and ultimately assures his own well-being. Klock's *venditiones cum pacto de retrovendendo* also mean that a piece of land is sold with the option to redeem it later (as does the Ancient Greek πρᾶσις ἐπὶ λύσει which will be discussed below). But, in contrast to "live sales", the *venditiones cum pacto de retrovendendo* are not a proper form of land transaction, but a means to disguise a usurious transaction, as Klock views it, as a simple land lease. While this shows that Chinese forms of land tenure were not free from irrationality (there are furthermore early examples of heavily irrational concepts influencing land tenure: one might think for example about the well-field system), the moral connotation that accompanies European land rights in the 17th century seems to have been very different from those in China: family and the heavenly order modify economic behaviour in the East; solidarity in tribal times, preserved by religion and transformed in philosophical, logical, and ethical discourses in the West. Austrian economists, especially von Mises,[58] have argued against such a Weberian rationality that the economist should regard the institutions as given and rate archaic belief as superstition: The seller in a *huomai* transaction then simply errs by not claiming the highest price or is rational, given an immutable rule. I am inclined to regard the adoption of this perspective as an analytical trick, which helps to create the appearance of a coherent general theory at the expense of historical and sociological understanding.

4. The ancient Greek "πρᾶσις ἐπὶ λύσει"

The idea of holding land for a certain period of time and then redeeming it existed in Europe already in antiquity. The ancient Greek legal institution "πρᾶσις ἐπὶ λύσει" ("sale on condition of release" – Finley's translation) was constituted as follows: the debtor sold a piece of land to the creditor but had the opportunity to regain it, if he settled the debt within a certain period of time. If he failed, his right to redeem the property would expire. One might get the impression that a limited set of legal institutions exists which – going by different names – reappear over time. But they are not identical, and be it only because of the endless variations in the contexts.

The πρᾶσις ἐπὶ λύσει is mainly documented on ὅροι: boundary stones that should indicate to the public that a piece of land was mortgaged. Finley has pointed out that, as the ὅροι often omitted further information on the transaction, such as the names of debtor and creditor or the date of repayment, they must have been useless as evidence in litigation.[59] Their main purpose was to serve as a public notice of the land tenure: both the state and private citizens had an interest in public

58 Von Mises 1933, 78–82.

59 Finley 1951, 21.

knowledge of land tenure. The state for fiscal reasons, the private citizens as they were concerned with the equitable collection of taxes or liturgies.[60] And as official public records about land tenure did not exist, "the poor alternative of *horoi* came upon us".[61] Written contracts that accompanied the public notion of the ὅροι existed, but were rather scarce[62] and it can be imaged that land transactions were mostly based on informal agreements.

Demosthenes' 37th speech *Nikobulos against Pantainetos* gives an example of this form of land transaction.[63] Here, we will only give a broad outline of the transaction, which is very complex: a sale with option of release where the land serves as a security to multiple creditors. Pantainetos wants to buy a mine from Telemachos together with the slaves working on it.[64] Being in financial distress, he takes up a loan from Mnesikles. The land serves as a security for the loan and is directly conveyed by Telemachos to Mnesikles, the creditor of Pantainetos. The latter, who is unable to settle the debt he now owes to Mnesikles, takes up another loan, this time from Nikobulos and Euergos and again, the land serves as a security. From the speech, however, we also learn that Mnesikles sells the land to Nikobulos and Euergos. This seems paradoxical at first, because, if Mnesikles sold the land to Nikobulos and Euergos, Pantainetos could no longer use it as a security. But, as Harris remarks,[65] it is common for these transactions that the creditors viewed themselves as the owners of the property that was pledged to them. Nikobulos and Euergos receive the land as a consequence of cashing out Mnesikles. The claim against Pantainetos is thereby conveyed from Mnesikles to Nikobulos and Euergos. Then, the latter agree to lease the land to Pantainetos at 12 percent rent. As mentioned above, leasing the property that serves as the pawn to the original owner, was common in *dian* and "live sales" as well and it also makes sense here, when we recall that the creditors viewed themselves as the owners of the property. Furthermore, Pantainetos had the right to redeem the land "ἒν τινι ῥητῷ χρόνῳ". A vague timeframe in which the property could be redeemed seems to be common for this type of land lease and shows the importance of customary law. Pantainetos' failure of paying the rent led to seizure

60 Ibid., 13.

61 Ibid.

62 Ibid., 23.

63 For a detailed account of the complex transaction, as well as an analysis of silver mines in Ancient Greece, see Kennedy's introduction to Demosthenes: 1889, vol. IV, 219–224.

64 In contrast to the *dian*, slaves are here considered as inventory of the land and therefore as immobile objects. It seems to be unclear, whether mobile objects could be part of the πρᾶσις ἐπὶ λύσει.

65 Harris 1988, 371.

of the property by Euergos. As new creditors of Pantainetos appear (Fine points out that they could have been fictitious and that Pantainetos might have invented them as a threat to Nikobulos and Euergos),[66] Nikobulos wants to evade the complicated situation. Both he and Euergos arrange to sell the property in Pantainetos' name, and they regain exactly the amount which they had lent to him. Nikobulos furthermore demands from Pantainetos a release from all claims. The new creditors granted Pantainetos to finally sell the land. He sold it for 20,600 drachmas: considerably more than the 10,500 drachmas he had owed to Nikobulos and Euergos, and the transaction therefore seems to be quite beneficial for Pantainetos.

Fine points out that the 12 % rent, which Pantainetos pays, are not calculated on the value of the property, but on the amount of the loan, and is therefore to be seen as interest paid for the loan rather than rent[67] – a fact that has already been pointed out by Libanios of Antiochia.[68] But a moral connotation to disguise interest (as with Klock's antichretic contract or the *venditiones cum pacto de retrovendendo*) does not seem to be implied. In fact, in the case of the πρᾶσις ἐπὶ λύσει the price of the land *was* the amount of the loan. As Kennedy points out: "The reader will not fail to see, that this transaction, which was ostensibly a purchase, was really a loan of money, secured by the conveyance of the mine and slaves".[69] Finley emphasizes that the πρᾶσις ἐπὶ λύσει is neither a "fictitious sale" (as are Klock's *venditiones cum pacto de retrovendendo*) nor a "genuine, complete sale" and that it rather was a "security in the form of conditional sale".[70]

5. Conclusion

The comparison between *dian* and *pactum antichreticum* was an attempt to capture the evolution of different forms of rationality in the East and the West, as based on institutional arrangements, legal frameworks and traditions of economic thought. The institutions which underly the *dian* transactions can be traced back directly to the Tang Dynasty, indirectly over thousands of years to the Han Dynasty and even earlier times, as can the tradition of the usury critique, which goes back to the ancient Near East, last traces of which still exist. A rational response can be found in Florencourt. His calculation is neat because he assumes a fixed framework. The land is to be returned after a given number of years, the rate of interest is the legal rate, and hence it follows who owes what to whom in the end. But the original *pactum*

66 Fine 1951, 149.

67 Ibid., 143–144.

68 Finley 1951, 33.

69 Kennedy 1889, 222–223.

70 Finley 1951, 35.

antichreticum was more flexible or could be combined with other arrangements, such as the *venditiones cum pacto de retrovendendo*. The complexity of the situation limits the possibilities for a rational calculation. The interpretation of the *pactum antichreticum* as a credit relationship by Klock increased the difficulty of a rational assessment because it now had to be asked whether usury was involved. Klock indulges in these arguments perhaps because they offer an escape from what was the real task at hand: to develop a method of calculation to determine whether a contract was just. Lack of transparency causes distrust and litigation. In the end, elements of power had evolved and possibly cheating. These ambiguities explain why so different perspectives on the history of land tenure could evolve in the case of China. Where Long and Chi see a near perfect market, the functioning of which can be explained in terms of neoclassical theory, the Maoists believed to identify inequality and exploitation. Florencourt admits only a small remnant of sociological considerations. He countered the argument that anatocism might be involved in his calculations with the admission that the receiver of annual amortisation payments might be tempted to consume these annual incomes instead of using them for accumulation. But the *pactum antichreticum* as such seemed to him just and such that each party could be of equal standing.

Men and women have at all times tried to arrange for their daily survival with practical and reasonable arrangements. In this limited sense, they have always been rational. On the other hand, we are never able to comprehend the economic relationships and our interaction with nature fully. Hence, the perennial strife: on the one hand, the attempts to expand the realm of rational calculation, on the other the distrust of the limits of rational thought and the desire to be able to rely on reasonable rules and tradition. In this, our future will not be different from our past.

Bibliography

Amelung, Iwo / Schefold, Bertram (eds.) (2021): European and Chinese Histories of Economic Thought. Theories and Images of Good Governance, London.

Böhling, Horst (1934): Chinesisches Sachenrecht. Nach dem modernen Zivilgesetzbuch und Bodengesetz mit europäischen Rechten verglichen unter Berücksichtigung des alten chinesischen Rechts, Diss. Universität Jena.

Colonius, Johann Philipp (1748): Systema Arithmeticum Speciosum: Das ist: Ein auf die neueste Art wohleingerichtetes vollkommenes Rechen-Buch ..., Franckfurt am Mayn. URL: https://www.deutsche-digitale-bibliothek.de/item/FHPNNE64RIDAQA34B6N2CFYSZOZRSWAU, last accessed: 26.04.2023.

Davis, John Francis (1836): A General Description of the Empire of China and its Inhabitants. Vol. 2, New York.

Fine, John V. A. (1951): Horoi. Studies in Mortgage, Real Security, and Land Tenure in Ancient Athens, Athens (Hesperia Supplements 9).

Finley, Moses I. (1951): Studies in Land and Credit in Ancient Athens. 500–200 BC. The Horos-Inscriptions, New Brunswick.

Florencourt Chassot de, Carl (1781): Abhandlungen aus der juristischen und politischen Rechenkunst, Altenburg.

Fu, Zhufu (1981): The Economic History of China. Some Special Problems, in: Modern China 7/1, 3–30.

Glahn, Richard von (2016): The Economic History of China. From Antiquity to the Nineteenth Century, Cambridge.

Glück, Ulrike (1999): Das Dian. Ein traditionelles chinesisches Rechtsinstitut in Gegenwart und Vergangenheit, Berlin (Freiburger rechtsgeschichtliche Abhandlungen 34).

Harris, Edward M. (1988): When is a Sale not a Sale? The Riddle of Athenian Terminology for Real Security Revisited, in: Classical Quarterly 38, 351–381.

Kennedy, Charles Rann (1889): The Orations of Demosthenes against Timocrates, Aristogiton, Aphobus, Onetor, Zenothemis, Apaturius, Phormio, Lacritus, Pantaenetus, Nausimachus, Boeotus, Spudius, Phoenippus and for Phormio, London.

Klock, Kaspar (2009 [1651]): Tractatus juridico-politico-polemico-historicus De Aerario, sive censu per honesta media absque divexatione populi licite conficiendo, libri duo. Edited and with an Introduction by Bertram Schefold, Hildesheim.

Leibniz, Gottfried Wilhelm (1962 [1863, 1683]): Meditatio juridico – mathematica de interusurio simplice, in: Gerhardt, Carl Immanuel (ed.), Gottfried Wilhelm Leibniz: Mathematische Schriften. Vol. VII, Hildesheim, 125–132.

Long, Denggao / Chi, Xiang (2021): Outline of the Institutions for Land Transactions in Traditional China, in: Amelung, Iwo / Schefold, Bertram (eds.), European and Chinese Histories of Economic Thought. Theories and Images of Good Governance, London, 49–55.

Matić, Ines (2016): Pactum antichreticum in Roman and Modern Civil Law. Rijeka Doctoral Conference. Rijeka 2016, URL: https://www.bib.irb.hr/847702, last accessed: 26.04.2023.

Mises, Ludwig von (1933): Grundprobleme der Nationalökonomie. Untersuchungen über Verfahren, Aufgaben und Inhalt der Wirtschafts- und Gesellschaftslehre, Jena.

Nelson, Benjamin ([2]1969): The Idea of Usury. From Tribal Brotherhood to Universal Otherhood, Chicago.

Online Lehrbuch Zivilrecht (2022), URL: https://www.uibk.ac.at/zivilrecht/buch/kap15_0.xml?section-view=true;section=2, last accessed: 26.04.2023.

Pomeranz, Kenneth (2008): Land Markets in Late Imperial and Republican China, in: Continuity and Change 23/1, 101–150.

Roedenbeck, Siegfried (1874): Die Antichresis, Diss. Halle-Wittenberg.

Roover, Raymond de (1955): Scholastic Economics: Survival and Lasting Influence from the Sixteenth Century to Adam Smith, in: The Quarterly Journal of Economics 69, 161–190.

Schefold, Bertram (2011): Cameralism as an Intermediary between Mediterranean Scholastic Economic Thought and Classical Economics, in: Kurz, Heinz D. / Nishizawa, Tamotsu / Tribe, Keith (eds.), The Dissemination of Economic Ideas, Cheltenham / Northampton, 13–40.

Schefold, Bertram (2018): Die Bedeutung des ökonomischen Wissens für Wohlfahrt und wirtschaftliches Wachstum in der Geschichte, Stuttgart (Sitzungsberichte der Wissenschaftlichen Gesellschaft an der Johann Wolfgang Goethe-Universität Frankfurt am Main, Band LV, Nr. 2).

Schefold, Bertram (2021a): From Kaspar Klock's "De aerario" (1651) and Leibniz's "Meditatio de interusurio simplice" to Florencourt's "Abhandlungen aus der juristischen und der politischen Rechenkunst" (1781): How Calculus Led from the Logic of a Device for Circumventing the Prohibition of Usury to a Modern Theory of Depreciation, in: Amelung, Iwo / Schefold, Betram (eds.), European and Chinese Histories of Economic Thought. Theories and Images of Good Governance, London, 119–132.

Schefold, Bertram (2021b): Wie Gottfried Leibniz trotz Zinseszinsverbot die Barwertformel begründete, in: Dutzi, Andreas / Gros, Marius / Nowak, Karsten / Roese, Bernd (eds.), Corporate Governance, Rechenschaft und Abschlussprüfung. Festschrift für Hans-Joachim Böcking zum 65. Geburtstag, München, 801–810.

Schumpeter, Joseph Alois (1954): History of Economic Analysis, London.

Schwab, Dieter (1975): Eigentum, in: Brunner, Otto / Conze, Werner / Koselleck, Reinhart (eds.), Geschichtliche Grundbegriffe. Historisches Lexikon zur politisch-sozialen Sprache in Deutschland. Vol. 2, Stuttgart, 65–115.

Weber, Max ([5]1976): Wirtschaft und Gesellschaft. Grundriss der verstehenden Soziologie. 5. rev. Aufl., bes. v. Johannes Winckelmann, Tübingen.

Wigmore, John H. (1897): The Pledge-Idea. A Study in Comparative Legal Ideas, in: Harvard Law Review 11/1, 18–39.

Index of Sources

The abbreviations follow the conventions in the respective disciplines. In addition, the following abbreviations are used:

De Graef 2018 = De Graef, Katrien (2018): "Kîma napišti māti eqlum ma ul tîdê?" Field Work in Old Babylonian Sippar, in: Garcia-Ventura, Agnès (ed.), What's in a Name? Terminology Related to the Work Force and Job Categories in the Ancient Near East, Münster (Alter Orient und Altes Testament 440), 189–241.

Fink, Robert O. (1971): Roman Military Records on Papyrus, Princeton.

Gallo, Annarosa (2020): Ex forma Gracchiana: A New Boundary Stone about Vespasian's Land Survey of the ager Tarentinus, in: Zeitschrift für Papyrologie und Epigraphik 216, 311–314.

Krebernik 2001 = Krebernik, Manfred (2001): Tall Bi'a/Tuttul II: Die Altorientalischen Schriftfunde, Saarbrücken.

Michel 2020 = Michel, Cécile (2020): Women of Assur and Kanesh: Texts from the Archives of Assyrian Merchants, Atlanta.

Ancient Near Eastern Sources

AbB
6, 178 • 19–20, n. 32
7, 53 (= CT 52) • 32
9, 240 • 19–20 with n. 32; 27; 29
12, 173 • 68–69, n. 33

Akkadian Counsels of Wisdom • 36 with ns. 116–117

BDHP
15 • 67

BM
16764 • 77
16970 (= CT 43, 39) • 27
81810 • 44 with n. 149

CT
2, 50 • 67, n. 25
4, 25c • 66
6, 40c • 66
8, 10c • 70
8, 21b • 70
8, 30c • 67, n. 25
33, 41 • 66, n. 23
43, 39 (= BM 16970) • 27
52 (= AbB 7, 53) • 32

De Graef 2018
no. 9 • 66

Debate between Sheep and Grain • 36–37 with n. 119

Debate between Silver and Copper
Segment D, 38–51 • 75 with n. 63
Segment D, 52–59 • 76 with n. 65

Debate between Summer and Winter • 27, n. 57

Di
1848 • 66, n. 23
1954 • 69, n. 34
1966 • 66, n. 23

Edict of Ammiṣaduqa
16 • 30–31
17 • 30–31

Instructions of Shurrupak • 34, n. 106

Krebernik 2001
no. 22 • 27 with n. 59

Laws of Eshnunna
15 • 28–29 with n. 68
41 • 39–40 with n. 132; 44; 45

Laws of Hammurabi
108 • paper Kelley, *passim*
108–111 • 28
110 • 28, n. 67; 29
111 • 28; 40–41; 44
143 • 37 with n. 123; 45
155 • 45
209 • 26
211 • 26

Marriage of Martu • 23 with n. 45

MHET
2/2, 283 • 66, n. 23
2/4, 549 • 67, n. 25

Michel 2020
no. 206 • 27 with n. 60

Old Babylonian Gilgamesh • 23; 31; 48

RIM
E.4.2.9.2 • 36 with n. 115

Rositani RSO 82 Sup. 1
116 • 67, n. 25

Shamash Hymn • 33–34; 43, n. 143

Sumerian Counsels of Wisdom • 17 with n. 17

Sumerian King List • 31

Sumerian Proverbs
Collection 1 • 24
Collection 17 • 33 with n. 99

Šu-suen A • 31

Shulgi of Ur to Ishbi-Erra 1 • 40 with ns. 133–134

Šurpu • 33; 43, n. 143

TCL
1, 68/69 • 66
1, 113 • 68–69, n. 33
1, 188 • 75, n. 74

Two Women B • 37 with n. 121

VS
9, 83 • 68–69, n. 33
29, 183/184 • 68–69, n. 33

UET
5, 160 • 78, n. 77

YOS
12, 451 • 66, n. 23
13, 12 • 67
13, 374 • 69, n. 34

Biblical Sources

Gen
17:8 • 98
23:18 • 103
26:3 • 98
28:13 • 98

Exod
19:13 • 92, n. 7
20:22–23:33 • 93
21–22 • 103

Lev
17–26 • 93
17:3 • 104
25 • 92, n. 7
25:1–7 • 93–94
25:2 • 104
25:9 • 92, n. 7
25:14 • 103; 104
25:14–17 • 96
25:23 • 103
25:25–28 • 96–97
25:29–30 • 98
25:32–34 • 98, n. 30
25:35 • 103
25:35–38 • 97
25:36 • 100, n. 38
25:36–37 • 103
25:38 • 104
25:39 • 103
25:39–55 • 97
25:41 • 103
25:42 • 104
25:43 • 97, n. 26
25:46 • 97, n. 26
25:47 • 95
25:48–49 • 95
25:49 • 103
25:53 • 97
25:55 • 104
26:4 • 92, n. 7

Num
26:52–56 • 98

Deut
12–26 • 93
17 • 103
17:5 • 103
21:19 • 103
25:7 • 103

Josh
6:4 • 92, n. 7
6:5 • 92, n. 7
6:6 • 92, n. 7
6:13 • 92, n. 7
20:4 • 103

1 Sam
2:8 • 92, n. 7

2 Kings
17:24 • 63, n. 7
17:31 • 63, n. 7
18:34 • 63, n. 7
19:13 • 63, n. 7

Isa
30:25 • 92, n. 7
37:13 • 63, n. 7
61 • 92, n. 6

Jer
34:8–10 • 92

Ezek
46:17 • 92, n. 6

Ruth
4:1 • 103

Neh
5 • 92

Chinese Sources

Book of Lord Shang (Shangjun Shu 商君書)
2.7 • 290
2.8 • 290
4.8 • 286
5.9 • 285, n. 75
6.4 • 278 with n. 61
6.5 • 278 with n. 60
6.8 • 277 with n. 58
6.9 • 285
7.1 • 280
7.2 • 279
7.5 • 286
17.3 • 286
18.1 • 280–281
26.6 • 286–287

Book of Submitted Doubtful Cases (Zouyan shu 奏讞書)
1.5 • 302, n. 148

Guanzi
"Qingzhong IV" • 292; 294

Han Feizi
"The Way of the Ruler" • 294–295

Mencius
3A4 • 291
3B4 • 291 with n. 93

Mozi
"Universal Love 偏愛上 (Pianai Shang)" • 266, n. 7

Liji
"Daxue 大學" • 281 with n. 65

Lu Jia
"Daoji 道基" • 282–283 with n. 70

Yuejueshu
"Boy Reckoner" • 292; 297

Xunzi
"Wangzhi 王制" • 291 with n. 94

"Zhengming 正名" • 282 with ns. 67–69

Early-Modern Authors/Works

Johann Philipp Colonius
Systema Arithmeticum Speciosum (1748)
p. 482 • 325 with n. 31

Carl Chassot de Florencourt
Abhandlungen aus der juristischen und politischen Rechenkunst (1781)
p. 4 • 325–326 with n. 32
p. 35 • 325–326

Kaspar Klock
De Aerario (On the Treasury) (1651)
book I, XIX, 3 • 322 with n. 12
book I, XIX, 18 • 322 with n. 14
book I, XIX, 26 • 322 with n. 15
book II, XIX, 14 • 323 with n. 17
book II, XIX, 19 • 323 with n. 19
book II, XIX, 41 • 324 with n. 28
book II, XIX, 49–51 • 323 with n. 18
book II, XIX, 66 • 323 with n. 20
book II, XIX, 145 • 322

Bernhard de Mandeville
Fable of the Bees (1732)
pp. 23–24 • 157

Adam Smith
History of Astronomy (1795)
3.2 • 167 with n. 81

The Theory of Moral Sentiments (1759)
1.1.5.7 • 153
2.2.2.1 • 168–169
3.2.31–33 • 158–159
3.3.11 • 160; 161, n. 70
4.1.10 • 163; 166
6.2.1.1 • 162
7.2.1.15 • 162
7.2.1.35 • 165
7.2.1.42 • 154
7.2.1.44 • 157–158
7.2.1.46 • 164

The Wealth of Nations (1776)
1.2.2 • 154; 162; 163
1.2.3.4 • 164
1.8.36 • 154, n. 52
1.11.c.7 • 153
2.2.2.1 • 162–163
3.3.11 • 160; 161, n. 70
4.1–8 • 167, n. 84
4.2.9 • 155; 166
4.2.10 • 155–156
4.9.51 • 156–157; 161, n. 70; 168

Greek & Roman Sources

Literary Sources

Aesch.
Pers.
194–199 • 152

Anonymus Iamblichi
fr. 7.1–8 • 196–197 with n. 71

Aristoph.
Eccl.
813–822 • 204, n. 104

Ran.
718–737 • 204, n. 104
725 (schol.) • 204, n. 104

Aristot. / [Aristot.]
Eth. Eud.
1231b28–1233b15 • 188, n. 36

Eth. Nic.
1102b13–18 • 152–153
1107b • 188, n. 36
1119b22–1125b9 • 188, n. 36
1133a–b • 187, n. 30
1133b • 123–124 with n. 47; 204 with n. 107

Oec.
1344b28–29 • 187
1345b21–23 • 204 with n. 108
1348b–1349a • 204, n. 106
1349b • 196, n. 68
1350a • 204, n. 105
1353b • 200, n. 84

Pol.
1252a31–b12 • 153
1253b14–1255b15 • 153
1253b14–1255b40 • 153
1254a13–17 • 153
1256b • 122
1256b–1258a • 123, n. 43
1257a • 118–199 with n. 26; 123
1257a–b • 187, n. 30
1259b17–1260b7 • 153
1291a • 114

Virt. et Vit.
passim • 188, n. 36

Cic.
Fin.
3.16 (= *SVF* 3.182) • 163
3.16–18 (= *SVF* 3.182) • 162, n. 74
3.20–21 (= *SVF* 3.186–189) • 162, n. 74
3.23 (= *SVF* 3.186–189) • 162, n. 74

Off.
1.1.13–14 • 322 with n. 16
3.42 (= *SVF* 3.689) • 169

Colum.
praef. 10 • 220; 221–222
praef. 20 • 214
1.1.19 • 226
1.19 • 221–222
2.10.8 • 220
3.3.2–15 • 225
3.3.3 • 218; 224
3.9.2 • 218
5.1.2 • 218; 220; 221
5.1.4 • 221

Dem.
21.144 • 203, n. 100
27–28 • 189–190; 201, n. 89
37 • 332–333 with n. 64
42 • 196, n. 67
49.68 • 198, n. 77

Dig.
47.2.55pr (Gaius) • 324 with n. 26

Diod.
16.56 • 202, n. 94
16.56.6 • 200, n. 83
16.56.6–7 • 202 with n. 97
17.66.1–2 • 203
17.71.2 • 203
17.80.3 • 203

Diog. Laert.
7.85 (= *SVF* 3.178) • 162, n. 74

Epict.
1.19.11–15 • 164–165
1.22.13 • 165
2.22.15–16 • 162, n. 73; 165
3.7.31–33 • 153

Flor.
Epit.
4.12.62 (= 2.34) • 231–232

Gai.
Inst.
1.32c • 217, n. 10

HA
Aurel.
48 • 224

Hellanicus *FGrH* 323a
F26 • 200, n. 82

Hom.
Od.
20.17–24 • 158–159

Is.
8.35 • 192, n. 49
11.42–43 • 192, n. 48

Lys.
12.11 • 190 with n. 43
12.19 • 116, n. 16
32 • 191–192
32.4–15 • 191 with n. 46

M. Ant.
3.16.3 • 159
9.29.5 • 153

Periplus Maris Erythraei (PME)
53 • 245, n. 70
54 • 231
54–55 • 237, n. 33
56 • 251 with n. 107

Philochorus *FGrH* 328
F144 • 200, n. 82
F169A & B • 203, n. 99

Pl.
Ap.
22c • 127

Chrm.
167a • 118, n. 22

Grg.
517b–c • 151, n. 40

Hipparch.
225a • 127
231a–c • 117, n. 21

Leg.
341c • 112, n. 4
693b4 • 150
693c2–3 • 150
701d • 150
704b–705c • 147
711c4 • 151, n. 40
718b3 • 151, n. 40
735b–736a • 146
735d–e • 146
735e–736a • 147
741e1–742a5 • 148
742a • 188, n. 35
742a7–c2 • 148

743d2–4 • 148
777b4–c1 • 152
846d • 147
847b • 147
850a–b • 147
909a8–c6 • 147
915b • 147
918a–c • 141
918b • 120, n. 33
918c9–d8 • 142–143
918d • 123, n. 44
918d6–8 • 143, n. 16; 144
918d8–919b4 • 143–144
919b2–4 • 146
919d • 147
920a • 147
920b • 146
920c • 147
921a1–d3 • 149

Phdr.
253e–254e • 152

Plt.
293d5 • 146
304d4 • 151, n. 40

Resp.
327c • 115
331b • 122
331c–d • 122
332a • 122
332b • 122
332d • 125
333b • 120, n. 35; 121
333e–334b • 127
342d • 125
343d • 121
345a • 116
346c–d • 121
346d • 125
349e • 126
350a–b • 126
354a • 116
359c • 125; 126; 142
359c1 • 146
359c–360b • 143
360c • 121
360d • 121
362a–b • 121
364a–c • 116, n. 17
365a • 116
365c • 116; 121
367a • 116
369b • 117
369b–c • 114
369b–372e • 111
369b–374a • 141
369c • 117; 125–126
369d • 115
369e–370a • 117–118
370c • 118; 125–126
370c–372d • 114
370e–371a • 128
371a • 128
371b • 119; 120, n. 33; 129, n. 57
371c–d • 127; 149
371e • 120
372a • 120
372a–b • 114
372b • 119
372c • 120
372d8–373a4 • 144
372e • 111–112; 119; 145
372e6–8 • 145
373d–e • 116–117; 123

374a–c • 125–126
397e • 125–126
399e4–5 • 145–146
399e7 • 145–146
414b–415c • 151, n. 41
416e4–417a5 • 147
419a • 115 – 115–116
419a–420a • 115
421d–e • 129, n. 61
425c10–e2 • 152
426e3–7 • 152
428b–c • 126–127
428b–d • 150
428b–429a • 150
428b1–429a3 • 151–152
430e • 130
431d • 130–131
432a • 130, n. 66; 131
432d • 130
433a • 117–118 with n. 22; 124; 125–126
433a–b • 157
434d–435a • 113
441c4–6 • 151
443c • 125–126
443c4–8 • 151–152
449a • 115, n. 8
449d • 115, n. 12
452a • 113
472e • 113
473c11–d6 • 151–152
474c1–3 • 151–152
501a • 146
514a–517a • 150–151
516e4 • 151
517a3 • 151
517a4–6 • 151
519e4 • 151, n. 40
540d–541a • 146
545a–591d • 188 with n. 37
548a–b • 188, n. 38
548d • 117, n. 20
550d • 188, n. 38
550e • 131
551e–552e • 116, n. 19
554a • 188, n. 38
554a–b • 130
557b4–6 • 146
562b–569c • 146
580d2–4 • 151
588b10–e3 • 151
590c–d • 152

Plin. (maior)
NH
6.26.101 • 245, n. 70; 250–251 with n. 106
6.26.104 • 231
6.26.104–105 • 237, n. 33
12.41.84 • 250–251 with n. 106
14.5.47–52 • 224
18.7.35 • 224

Plin. (min.)
Pan.
29.1 • 215

Plut.
Lyc.
9.3 • 188 with n. 34

Pol.
2.67 • 202, n. 95

Ptol.

Geogr.

7.1.7 • 245, n. 70

7.1.86 • 231; 237, n. 33

7.1.89 • 237, n. 33

Sen.

Ben.

7.6.3 • 225

Brev. Vit.

18.5 • 222

20.4 • 222

Ep.

7.11 • 159, n. 60

47.1 • 153

Vit. Beat.

21–28 • 163

Sol.

fr. 13 • 123 with n. 43

Strab.

Geogr.

8.6.20 • 202, n. 98

Suet.

Aug.

42.1 • 224

42.3 • 216

Tib.

32.2 • 217

49.1 • 224

49.2 • 224

Claud.

19 • 217

Vesp.

18 • 217

SVF

3.178–189 • 162; 163

3.178 (= Diog. Laert. 7.85) • 162, n. 74

3.182 (= Cic. *Fin.* 3.16–18) • 162, n. 74; 163

3.186–189 (= Cic. *Fin.* 3.186–189) • 162, n. 74

3.689 (= Cic. *Off.* 3.42) • 169

Tac.

Ann.

1.7.2 • 222

2.87 • 216

4.6.4 • 216

6.13.1 • 216–217

6.16.1 • 223

6.16.3 • 223

6.16–17 • 223

6.17.3 • 225

6.19.1 • 223

11.24.3 • 222

12.43.2 • 213–214

14.27.2 • 218

14.46 • 221

16.17.3 • 225

Thuc.

1.121.3 • 200, n. 81

Xen.

Vect.

1.1 • 7

3.3–6 • 4
3.6–11 • 4–5 with n. 15
3.7–8 • 5–6
3.9 • 6
3.9–10 • 6
3.10 • 6
4.7 • 185
5.1–13 • 7–8

Inscriptions

CIL
IX 235 (= *ILS* 2923) • 218 with n. 13; 219

Gallo 2020 • 219

IG
I^2 377 • 201 with n. 90
I^3 248 • 201 with n. 88
II^2 1635 • 201 with n. 91

ILS
2923 (= *CIL* IX 235) • 218 with n. 13; 219–220

RGDA
5.2 • 215

SIG^3
958, l. 31 • 191 with n. 45

Papyri

Fink 1971, no. 68 (= *P.Gen.Lat.* I recto, part I) • 216, n. 7

P.Gen.Lat.
I recto, part I (= Fink 1971, no. 68) • 216, n. 7

P.Oxy.
13.1606 • 191, n. 44

Indian Sources

Literary Sources

Aiṉkuṟunūṟu
86:4 • 242, ns. 58–59

Akanāṉūṟu
57:14–15 • 245 with n. 69
83:7 • 248, n. 95
90:12 • 248, n. 95
93:10 • 248–249, n. 96
127:3–9 • 238, n. 38
127:6–8 • 245, n. 71
127:6–9 • 257 with n. 134
149:7–11 • 243–244 with n. 65
227:19–20 • 247 with n. 85
255:5–6 • 259, n. 139
256:20 • 242, n. 58
258:1–3 • 257 with n. 135

Arthaśāstra
2.2.13 • 239–240
2.8.1 • 257 with n. 136
2.22.25 • 254

Cilappatikāram
2.14:8 • 248–249, n. 96
2.14:66–67 • 259, n. 140
3.25:1 • 245, n. 71
3.25:185–187 • 245, n. 71

Kalittokai
95:27 • 242, n. 58

Mahābhārata
1.177.15.4 • 231

2.28.48.1 • 231
6.10.57.1 • 231
8.8.15.1 • 231
14.83.29.2 • 231

Mānavadharmaśāstra
6.2 • 236, n. 27

Matsyapurāṇa
48.5.1 • 231
114.46.2 • 232

Mullaippāṭṭu
45–49 • 259, n. 140
59–63 • 259, n. 140
63–66 • 259, n. 140

Paripāṭal
2:9 • 248–249, n. 96
11:123 • 245, n. 74

Patiṟṟuppattu
11:12 • 245, n. 71
12:3 • 238, n. 38; 245, n. 71
13:1–28 • 238, n. 40
13:8 • 238, n. 41
14:11 • 236, n. 24
14:18–20 • 235, n. 19
15:16–21 • 249 with n. 99
15:18 • 247, n. 89
15:38 • 247, n. 89
16:17 • 236, n. 22
17:3 • 239, n. 49
17:4–5 • 245, n. 71
17:6 • 236, n. 28
19:22 • 238, n. 43
20:2–4 • 245, n. 71
20:4 • 238, n. 38
21:1 • 235, n .21
21:1–4 • 235, n. 21
21:7 • 236, n. 28
21:13 • 236, n. 28
21:23 • 238, n. 39
22:1–4 • 235, n. 19
22:1–5 • 235, n. 21
22:6 • 246 with n. 75
22:15–16 • 238, n. 39
22:20 • 247, n. 89
24:8 • 236, n. 26
27:9 • 238, n. 41
28:10 • 244, n. 67
29:7 • 247, n. 89
30:9–12 • 248 with ns. 91–93
30:15 • 247, n. 89
30:17 • 238, n. 41
30:20 • 247, n. 89
31:7 • 235–236, n. 22
38:9 • 237, n. 31
40:3 • 236, n. 24
40:6 • 239, n. 48
40:13 • 235–236, n. 22
43:15 • 244, n. 67
43:16 • 238, n. 44
48:14 • 247, n. 89
51:16 • 245, n. 74
55:3–6 • 245 with n. 73
55:9 • 238, n. 39
56:1 • 247, n. 89
57:14–15 • 245 with n. 69
57:15 • 239, n. 49
58:15 • 238, n. 42
58:17 • 238, n. 44
59:12 • 239, n. 49
59:16 • 235, n. 20
60:8 • 246 with n. 76
61:18 • 247, n. 89

63:1 • 236, n. 26
63:9 • 239, n. 49
64:5 • 236, n. 26
65:13 • 237, n. 31
67:2 • 245, n. 74
68:9–11 • 247–248 with n. 90
69:12–17 • 246 with n. 76
69: 17 • 235, n. 19
72:13 • 247, n. 89
73:9 • 238, n. 39; 251–252
74:6 • 245, n. 72
74:24 • 236, n. 25
75:10 • 248, n. 95
76:3–5 • 246 with n. 79
76:11 • 238, n. 44
77:7–8 • 247 with n. 83
78:7 • 246 with n. 76
80:10 • 239, n. 49
81:16–17 • 253 with n. 110
81:20 • 247, n. 89
84:6 • 238, n. 39
85:8 • 237, n. 31
85:9 • 235, n. 20; 236–237, n. 30
88:6 • 238, n. 38
88:11 • 236, n. 29
88:19 • 238, n. 39
88:25 • 244, n. 67
89:6 • 246 with n. 76
90:19 • 236, n. 29
90:25 • 238, n. 39
90:26 • 238, n. 39
90:27 • 238, n. 39
90:28 • 238, n. 39
122:3 • 247 with n. 84
II.9 • 242, n. 58
III.8 • 236, n. 29
III.10 • 236 with n. 27
IV.6 • 238, n. 38
V.2 • 238, n. 39
VI.4 • 236, n. 26
VIII.5 • 237, n. 35
IX.4 • 237, n. 35
IX.15 • 236, n. 28

Paṭṭiṉappālai
116–125 • 239, n. 47
158 • 247 with n. 86
185 • 240
185–191 • 240–241 with n. 52

Perumpāṇāṟṟuppaṭai
162–165 • 253 with n. 112
346–351 • 259, n. 139

Puṟanāṉūṟu
35:4–5 • 237, n. 35
75:4 • 239, n. 47
110:1 • 237, n. 35
141:11 • 243
201:3 • 243
208:6–7 • 243 with n. 64
330:5 • 239, n. 47
343: • 241; 243; 245–246
343:1–10 • 241 with n. 53
343:16–17 • 241, n. 54

Tolkāppiyam Poruḷatikāram Marapiyal
72. cū. 616 • 237, . 32

Inscriptions
Aśoka inscriptions • 250

II. Rock Edict of Mānsehrā • 231

II. Rock Edict of Girnār • 231

II. Rock Edict of Kālsī • 231

II. Rock Edict of Shāhbāzgaṛhī • 231

Māṅkuḷam inscriptions
no. 3 • 250
no. 4 • 255
no. 6 • 250

Pukaḷūr inscriptions
no. 1 • 255
no. 2 • 255
no. 9 • 254–255
no. 10 • 255